THE MERCANTILE LAW OF SCOTLAND

THE
MERCANTILE LAW
OF SCOTLAND

BY

ALLAN M'NEIL, M.A., S.S.C.

LECTURER ON BANKING IN THE UNIVERSITY OF EDINBURGH
AUTHOR OF "BANKING LAW," ETC.

AND

J. A. LILLIE, M.A., LL.B.

ADVOCATE, AND OF THE MIDDLE TEMPLE, BARRISTER-AT-LAW

SECOND EDITION

EDINBURGH

W. GREEN AND SON, LIMITED

LAW PUBLISHERS

1929

Printed in Great Britain by
NEILL & CO., LTD., EDINBURGH.

PREFACE TO SECOND EDITION

In presenting this edition the authors have taken the opportunity of bringing each chapter up to date in respect of statutory legislation and case law, and also have widened the scope of the book by the inclusion of a new chapter on Rights in Security over Moveables. The chapter on the Law of Joint Stock Companies has been entirely rewritten in view of the Companies Act, 1929, which comes into force on 1st November 1929.

Acknowledgment is due for assistance to Mr J. F. G. Thomson, Advocate, Mr W. Boyd Berry, Advocate, and Mr T. Menzies M'Neil, W.S.

A. M'N.
J. A. L.

EDINBURGH, 20th July 1929.

PREFACE TO FIRST EDITION

THE aim of this volume is to supply an acknowledged deficiency, and to provide students preparing for the many examinations where Mercantile Law is now a compulsory subject with a comprehensive and systematic exposition of this branch of law divested as far as possible of technicalities of expression. To the student a comprehension of the systematic or scientific scheme of the law is of the utmost importance if his study of it is not to amount to little more than the memorising of a mass of undigested details. On the other hand, a real advance will have been made by the student who has appreciated the uniformity which the law seeks to achieve by the application of suitable principles to the diversity of circumstance. In treating of the application of these principles in detail, selection has had, necessarily, to be resorted to, and has been dictated by a regard to those matters which best illustrate the working out of principle and are most common in practice.

The citation of authority is not full, and has been more or less confined to the noting of leading cases and the latest decisions. The citation is intended not merely for the purpose of vouching the statements in the text, but also for the use of those who desire further examples or to improve their study by an examination of the reasoning which underlies the decisions.

It is believed that the book, as containing a concise statement of principles and a collection of leading cases, may be of use to practitioners for preliminary reference before consulting detailed treatises on particular branches of the subject.

Each chapter is the separate work of either Mr M'Neil or Mr Lillie, and the work of each has been revised by the other.

Acknowledgment is due to Mr C. de B. Murray, Advocate, for assistance in checking references to authorities.

EDINBURGH, 16*th March* 1923.

CONTENTS

TABLE OF CASES CITED

MERCANTILE LAW

CHAPTER I

THE LAW OF CONTRACT

1. What is a Contract ?—A contract has been defined as an agreement which creates, or is intended to create, a legal obligation between the parties to it.[1]

A contract accordingly is a particular kind of agreement. It necessarily involves at least two parties to it. Whether in the first place there is in any particular case an agreement is a question of the interpretation of, or inference from, the words or acts of the parties to it whereby each conveys to the other the expression of his intention. When the minds of the parties meet in agreement there is said to be *consensus in idem*.

Whether in the second place an agreement is one which creates, or is intended to create, a legal obligation between the parties to it depends in the first place on whether the parties so intended. Their intention may be indicated by the words they use or by the nature of the agreement itself. For instance, an agreement to dine with a friend plainly is not intended to create any legal obligation to do so. In the second place, the creation of a legal obligation depends on whether the Court will treat the agreement as binding the parties and will enforce it by compelling either party to observe it. Thus, for instance, a bet or wager is not a contract because the relations involved are held, in the law of Scotland, not to be among those subjects for which Courts of Justice were instituted.[2] The same applies to a social engagement, such as the agreement to dine instanced above.[3] Some patrimonial interest, *i.e.* some material gain or loss,

---

[1] Jenks, Digest of English Civil Law, bk. ii. tit. i.
[2] Gloag on Contract, 2nd ed., p. 8.
[3] And *vide* Illegal and Immoral Contracts, *infra* p. 27.

must be involved.[1] To sum up, to constitute a binding contract the parties must have intended and agreed to bind each other, and the agreement must be one of a nature which the Courts will enforce.

2. How Contract Constituted.—Formation.—To create a legal

obligation there is required the expression by the party undertaking the obligation of willingness to be bound. In all cases the obligation requires for its constitution expression in words or acts. Whatever may have been the real intention of a party the Court, in a question of legal obligation, gathers his intention to bind himself from such expression. Such an expression may consist of a promise made by one party only, a unilateral obligation. To amount to a contract binding on both parties, it must be followed by an acceptance. No one can be forced to accept a gift. But it is irrevocable unless refused, and can be enforced if fulfilment be demanded within a reasonable time, acceptance being sufficiently indicated by a demand for fulfilment.[2] If both parties undertake obligations to each other, the legal obligations are created by offer by the one party and acceptance by the other. The offer is not binding, however, unless and until clinched by words or acts indicating acceptance. An undertaking to keep an offer open for a time is an example of an offer combined with a promise.

Offer.—What constitutes an offer ? A mere expression of intention may not have obligatory force. Thus where a shareholder of a company said he was willing to take up an issue of new shares and did not apply for them, he was held not bound to take up shares allotted to him.[3] A request for tenders, unless providing that the lowest will be accepted, is not binding as an offer. Again, a mere proposal to do business may or may not, according to circumstances, amount to an offer. Thus where a merchant who dealt in a particular commodity wrote to other merchants dealing in the same commodity quoting prices he was held bound by an acceptance, an example of an " order in trade." [4] Again, a common carrier, who is bound to exercise his vocation on demand, is bound by the list of fares he publishes as an offer to carry for these fares. An offer of reward for lost property is binding if the property is restored by a person in knowledge of the offer.[5] A general offer to the public, if accepted by a particular person, is good. For example, an advertisement of goods for sale,

---

[1] Anderson v. Manson, 1909 S.C. 838.
[2] Wallace v. Gibson, 1895, 22 R. (H.L.) 56.
[3] Mason v. Benhar Coal Co., 1882, 9 R. 883.
[4] Philp v. Knoblauch, 1907 S.C. 994.
[5] Petrie v. Earl of Airlie, 1834, 13 S. 68.

on the inducement that they will produce certain results, is an offer, as where the Carbolic Smoke Ball Co. offered a reward to users of their smoke ball if they took influenza.[1]

Acceptance.—What constitutes a valid acceptance ? (1) Acceptance may be made by words or acts, and in either case must be communicated to the offerer. Thus if goods ordered are supplied, the act of supplying them constitutes an acceptance. Failure to refuse an offer may amount to acceptance, as in orders in trade, or where there is a previous course of dealing between the parties, or by custom of trade or when acceptance is waived by the offerer. (2) An acceptance, to bind the offerer, must be unqualified. Where the parties negotiate in a correspondence, each conditional acceptance amounts to a new offer or counter-offer. (3) The acceptance must meet the offer. But it need not recapitulate it.[2] Slight variations may not matter, and if acted on cannot be afterwards repudiated.

When is a Contract completed by Acceptance ?—Acceptance by Post.—A very usual method of forming a contract is by letter through the post or telegram. The contract is completed when the acceptance is despatched, *i.e.* posted or telegraphed. Unless otherwise stipulated or shown to be intended it is presumed the offerer intended reply to be by post or telegram. The post office is supposed to be the agent of the offerer, hence delivery of the letter to the post office is delivery to the offerer. If the offer gives a definite time for acceptance it is accepted if despatched though not received within the time.[3] It is undecided what the effect is if the acceptance though despatched never arrives.[4] In England posting is held sufficient to complete the contract.[5] If the offerer is made aware of the fact of acceptance that is of course enough.[6]

Timeous Acceptance.—As a general rule an offer remains open until accepted or recalled. When no time for acceptance is fixed it must be made within a reasonable time. An undertaking to keep an offer open for a certain time or until the happening of a certain event is binding. Also, as a general rule, an acceptance posted in the

---

[1] Carlill *v.* Carbolic Smoke Ball Co., [1893] 1 Q.B. 256 ; *cf.* Hunter *v.* General Accident, etc., Corporation, 1909 S.C. 344 ; affd. 1909 S.C. (H.L.) 30.

[2] Philp *v.* Knoblauch, *supra.*

[3] Jacobsen *v.* Underwood, 1894, 21 R. 654.

[4] Mason *v.* Benhar Coal Co., 1882, 9 R. 883, per Lord Shand at p. 890 ; Higgins *v.* Wilson & Co., 1847, 9 D. 1407, per Lord Fullerton at p. 1414 ; affd. 1848, 6 Bell's App. 195.

[5] Household Fire Insurance Co. *v.* Grant, (1879) 4 Ex. D. 216.

[6] Chapman *v.* Sulphite Paper Pulp Co., 1892, 19 R. 837.

ordinary course of business is timeous, even though there be delay in delivery.[1] If the offerer indicates a particular method of despatch, the risk of loss or delay in transmission falls on the accepter if he does not follow the method indicated, and the offerer is not otherwise made aware of the fact of acceptance.

Recall of Offer.—An offer may be recalled at any time before it has been validly accepted. There is said to be *locus pœnitentiæ*. In addition, it falls by the death of either party, by the insanity of the offerer,[2] or his bankruptcy before acceptance, by refusal of the offer or by failure to accept within the time stated or a reasonable time when no time for acceptance is fixed.[3] What is a reasonable time depends on the circumstances. Thus in mercantile offers to sell or buy particular goods acceptance should be by return of post, otherwise it may be ignored.[4]

Recall of Acceptance.—Whether an acceptance once despatched can be recalled by bringing the recall to the notice of the offerer before receipt of the acceptance has not been definitely decided in Scotland.[5]

3. Proof of the Constitution of Contracts.—(*a*) **Mutual Contracts.**—The method of proof of the constitution of a contract depends to a large extent on the way in which it has been or may be constituted. Broadly speaking, a contract may be constituted by writing or without.

　　(i.) **Verbal Contracts.**—In the absence of any writing the ordinary rule is that verbal agreement is sufficient to bind the parties,[6] and this may be proved by parole evidence, *i.e.* the oral evidence of witnesses. Some contracts, however, while they may be constituted verbally, may not be proved by parole evidence, but only by the writ or the oath of the party. In this case writing is not necessary to the formation of the contract, but merely as a rule of evidence—*in modum probationis*, as it is called. The writ or the oath of the party denying the contract is required here in the absence of admission of an agreement. Contrast this case with that

---

[1] Higgins *v.* Dunlop, 1847, 9 D. 1407 ; affd. 1848, 6 Bell's App. 195.

[2] Loudon *v.* Elder's Trs., 1923, S.L.T. 226.

[3] Thomson *v.* James, 1855, 18 D. 1.

[4] Wylie & Lochhead *v.* M'Elroy, 1873, 1 R. 41, per Lord President Inglis.

[5] *Vide* Countess of Dunmore *v.* Alexander, 1830, 9 S. 190 ; Thomson *v.* James, 1855, 18 D. 1 ; Curtice *v.* London City and Midland Bank, [1908] 1 K.B. 293 ; Gloag on Contract, p. 56.

[6] Stair Instit., iv. 434 ; Erskine Instit., iii. 2, 1.

about to be mentioned where writing is a solemnity—that is, essential to the formation of the contract. Where the solemnity is wanting an admission of agreement would not bind a party, as without the solemnity there is no completed contract.

The following contracts require proof, though not constitution, by writ or oath, viz.—gratuitous obligations [1]; loan,[2] but not a loan not exceeding £100 Scots (£8, 6s. 8d.); trust [3]; obligations of relief [4]; innominate and unusual contracts, *i.e.* a contract not one of those usually known by a distinctive name, for example a contract expressed in sale notes and intended as a contract of agency [5]; and a prescribed debt.[6]

(ii.) **Contracts in Writing.**—Some contracts, however, at common law or by statute require to be entered into in writing, and mere verbal agreement is not sufficient to bind the parties. Such obligations are known as *obligationes literis*. Here writing is, as it is called, a solemnity and necessary to the constitution, not merely to the proof, of the contract. This requirement ensures deliberation on the part of those who enter into certain contracts of importance. These contracts are: (1) Contracts for the sale of heritage and for the lease of heritage for not less than a year; (2) contracts for service for more than a year; (3) contracts for the assignation of incorporeal rights; (4) contracts of insurance; (5) cautionary obligations; (6) contracts of mandate.

It must, however, be kept in mind that, where writing has been resorted to though not necessary to constitute or prove the contract, it is incompetent to introduce parole evidence to contradict the writing. This rule is subject to certain reservations to be afterwards noticed.[7]

It should also be noted that, there being a contract in form validly constituted, where the question is raised whether there ever was that *consensus in idem* which is necessary to its validity, such a question may be the subject of parole or other proof. Thus it is competent by parole evidence to prove that one party never gave any assent or that his assent was obtained by misrepresentation, fraud, or other

---

[1] Dickson on Evidence, § 598. [2] *Ibid.*, § 594.
[3] Act 1696, c. 25. [4] *Cf.* Gloag on Contract, 2nd ed., p. 195.
[5] Müller & Co. *v.* Weber & Schaer, 1901, 3 F. 401.
[6] See Prescription, *infra*, p. 56 *et seq.*
[7] *Vide* Interpretation of Contracts, *infra*, p. 27.

improper means,[1] or that the contract was entered into in circumstances or with objects which would make it void or reducible as a
pactum illicitum or illegal agreement.[2]

(*b*) **Unilateral Writings.—Delivery.**—When a mutual contract, that
is one involving obligations on both sides, is reduced to writing, it is
complete and becomes binding on both parties when duly executed,
and it is immaterial in whose custody the actual document may be.
The obligations on both sides are created by the signatures, and there
is no necessity for delivery.[3] Where, on the other hand, the deed of
writing is unilateral, *i.e.* involving obligations on the granter only,
its delivery by the granter to the grantee, or some equivalent for
delivery, is necessary to bind the granter. Until delivery the deed
is merely deliberative, not obligatory. There are, however, exceptions, namely, where the granter of a unilateral deed was under a
prior obligation to execute it, for then the grantee is entitled to it,
and where a creditor is granter of an assignation of a debt due him,
followed by intimation to the debtor. That is enough without
delivery to complete the transfer.

The question whether a deed has been delivered is always one of
fact. That question is whether the granter has consented to place
the deed absolutely beyond his own control.[4] There are certain
presumptions. Thus a deed in the hands of the granter is presumably not delivered. And a deed in the hands of the grantee
presumably is. But where the deed is in the hands of a third party
it depends on the capacity in which he holds the deed which way the
presumption lies. The agent of either party is presumed to hold for
his client. A neutral depository is presumed to hold for the granter
if the deed is gratuitous, but for the grantee if it is granted for onerous
considerations.[5] Again, in certain circumstances there may be a
strong presumption that a deed undelivered was intended by the
granter to be binding, as where it has been recorded by him in the
Books of Council and Session for preservation or preservation and
execution,[6] and registration of a disposition of land in the Register
of Sasines may be equivalent to delivery.[7]

[1] Duran *v.* Duran, 1904, 7 F. 87.

[2] *Vide* Validity of Contracts, *infra*, p. 27 *et seq.*

[3] Robertson's Trs. *v.* Lindsay, 1873, 1 R. 323, per Lord President Inglis.

[4] Cameron's Trs. *v.* Cameron, 1907 S.C. 407.   [5] Ersk. Instit., iii. 2, 43.

[6] Obers *v.* Paton's Trs., 1897, 24 R. 719 ; Carmichael *v.* Carmichael's Exrx.,
1920 S.C. (H.L.) 195, per Lord Dunedin at p. 201.

[7] Cameron's Trs. *v.* Cameron, *supra*, per Lord President Dunedin ; Carmichael
v. Carmichael's Exrx., *supra*.

Sometimes a deed contains a clause dispensing with delivery. That does not give it any contractual effect so long as it is undelivered and the granter is alive and so able to revoke it. If he dies without revoking the effect is testamentary, not contractual.

A deed is presumed to be delivered from its date if it be in the hands of the grantee or of someone holding for him.[1]

(c) **Formalities of Written Contracts.**—The sufficiency of various kinds of writings to constitute or to prove the constitution of various kinds of contracts may now be shortly considered.

Writings for this purpose may be conveniently classified, according to the considerations which govern their value as proof, as probative, *i.e.* tested or holograph, writings *in re mercatoria* and other "privileged" writings, and improbative or informal writings.

Probative Writings.—A probative document is one which, in consequence of its being tested or holograph, does not require to be proved genuine by extrinsic evidence. That is to say, the formality of attestation or the fact of its being written by the granter himself is taken as proof of its genuineness. Such a document may be set aside if it can be proved to have been granted because of fraud or essential error,[2] but these are different questions, and do not touch the question of the genuineness of the document as being truly the document of the person by whom it bears to have been granted.

All deeds relating to heritable title, and obligations of importance, *i.e.* with regard to sums over £100 Scots (£8, 6s. 8d.), except writings *in re mercatoria*, and several others of a non-mercantile character,[3] must in order to be probative be either holograph or tested.

Formalities of Attestation.—An attested writing to be probative should be signed by the granter on each page and by two witnesses on the last page. But the Memorandum of Association and the Articles of Association of a company registered under the Companies Acts and a bill of sale of a ship require the signature of one witness only. A witness must be at least fourteen years of age. The designations of the witnesses should be appended to their signatures or set forth in a testing clause at the end of the deed. These designations when appended to their signatures may be added at any time before the deed is recorded in any register for preservation or founded on in any court, and need not be written by the witnesses themselves.[4] Witnesses must either see the party sign or hear him acknowledge

---

[1] Bell's Prin., § 23.
[2] See Validity of Contracts, *infra*, p. 27 *et seq.*
[3] See *infra*, p. 9.
[4] Conveyancing Act, 1874, § 38.

his signature and have credible information as to the party's identity.[1] A witness who sees the granter sign or hears him acknowledge his signature should also sign there and then. The signing of the granter and then the witnesses should be a continuous transaction.[2] The date of signing, though not essential, being in most cases very important should be stated in the testing clause.

The testing clause is added at the end of the deed after it is executed above the signatures. It sets forth the details regarding the execution in the following manner :—" In witness whereof these presents are subscribed by me at Glasgow on the 1st day of June 1929, before these witnesses, John Smith [*designation*] and Alexander Anderson [*designation*]." All alterations in the body of the document should be authenticated by the initials of the granter, and declared in the testing clause. No deed, subscribed by the granter and bearing to be attested by two witnesses subscribing, is, however, to be deemed invalid or denied effect according to its legal import because of any informality of execution, but the burden of proving that such deed so attested was subscribed by the granter and by the witnesses by whom such deed bears to be attested lies upon the party using or upholding the same.[3] If, however, the execution was *ex facie* correct, the burden of proving the want of a solemnity, such as that the witness did not see the granter sign or hear him acknowledge his signature, would be on the party challenging the validity of the execution.[4]

If the granter of a deed is, from any cause permanent or temporary, blind or unable to write, a law agent, notary public, or justice of the peace may sign the document for him. The deed must first be read over to the granter in the presence of two witnesses who must hear or see authority given to sign the deed. The law agent, notary, or justice must sign the deed in the presence of the granter and the witnesses. A docquet is then written on the deed by the law agent, notary, or justice in his own hand and subscribed by him and the witnesses.[5] The following is the statutory docquet [6] :—

" Read over to and signed by me for and by authority of the above-named A. B. [*without designation*], who declares that he is blind

---

[1] Brock *v.* Brock, 1908 S.C. 964.
[2] Walker *v.* Whitwell, 1916 S.C. (H.L.) 75.
[3] Conveyancing Act, 1874, § 39 ; Walker *v.* Whitwell, 1916 S.C. (H.L.) 75.
[4] Walker *v.* Whitwell, *supra.*
[5] Conveyancing Act, 1924, § 18.
[6] *Ibid.*, Schedule I.

(*or* is unable to write), all in his presence and in the presence of the witnesses hereto subscribing.

> C. D., Law Agent (*or* Notary Public), Edinburgh (*or as the case may be*),
>   *or* E. F., Justice of the Peace for the County of   .
> M. N., *witness.*
> P. Q., *witness.*

Any deed to which a company is a party is validly executed in Scotland on behalf of the company if it is sealed with the common seal of the company and subscribed on behalf of the company by two of the directors and the secretary, whether attested by witnesses or not.[1] A contract requiring to be in writing may be made on behalf of the company in writing, signed by any person acting under its authority, express or implied.[2] It is usual in Scotland for a company to execute deeds by sealing, and with witnesses. When with witnesses the benefits of the Conveyancing (Scotland) Act, 1874, § 39, whereby informalities in execution are not to invalidate a deed " bearing to be attested by two witnesses," would appear to be available.

Holograph Writings.—Holograph deeds are probative when they declare that they have been wholly, or at least in their essential parts, written by the granter. The fact that the deed is holograph, if not stated but disputed,[3] must be proved by extrinsic evidence. Alterations should be initialed by the granter, but holograph additions need not be signed. In some cases the document need not be signed if it bears the granter's name *in gremio, i.e.* in the body of the document, or if it be of a kind not usually signed, as an entry in an account book or a postscript to a letter. A letter signed by one of several partners on behalf of a firm is holograph of the firm.[4]

Writings in re mercatoria.—The international character of trade relations and the necessity for rapid despatch in business furnish the ground for dispensing, in the case of mercantile writings, with the ordinary rules as to authentication and date.[5] Such writings and some others are therefore called " privileged " writings. For, while not probative in the sense of being tested or holograph, they are accorded a probative quality out of consideration for the practical

---

[1] Companies (Consolidation) Act, 1908, § 76 (3).
[2] *Ibid.*
[3] M'Intyre *v.* National Bank of Scotland, 1910 S.C. 150 (bill).
[4] Nisbet *v.* Neil's Tr., 1869, 7 M. 1097.
[5] 1 Bell's Comm. 325.

convenience of trade so long as their authenticity is not challenged. Accordingly, such documents are valid to prove the constitution of the contract they embody if merely subscribed. If their authenticity is challenged it may be proved by parole evidence. Subscription may be by initials or by cross or mark, but in these cases the subscription must be proved to be genuine, and to be the form ordinarily employed by the subscriber.[1] It is proper but not essential it be adhibited before witnesses.

Under this privilege are held to be comprehended bills, notes and cheques on bankers ; orders for goods, mandates, and procurations ; guarantees (but it is a question whether it extends to a guarantee granted to a bank for future advances),[2] offers and acceptances to sell or to buy wares or merchandise or to transport them from place to place, and, in general, all the variety of engagements, or mandates, or acknowledgments which the infinite occasions of trade may require.[3]

A writ *in re mercatoria* proves its own date only in a question which relates to the ordinary mercantile purposes for which such a document is granted.[4]

Other Privileged Writings.—The most important writings of a non-mercantile character to which are extended the same privileges as writings *in re mercatoria* are discharges for rent, feu-duties, wages, and, on the ground of mercantile usage, other termly payments, such as interest and premiums of insurance, also awards of judicial referees or of counsel to whom parties have agreed to submit their case.[5] Accounts relating to business transactions, though not *in re mercatoria*, if docqueted by the debtor admitting them to be correct are also privileged.

Improbative Writings.—Where the law does not require the constitution of a contract in probative writing the proof of it is as a rule unlimited, and therefore an informal writing may be of value along with other evidence to that end.

Where, on the other hand, probative writing is essential to the constitution of a contract, if the writing be improbative it is not

---

[1] 1 Bell's Comm. 325.

[2] National Bank of Scotland *v.* Campbell, 1892, 19 R. 885, per Lord Kyllachy and Lord M'Laren.

[3] 1 Bell's Comm. 325 ; U.K. Advertising Co. *v.* Glasgow Bagwash Laundry, 1926 S.C. 303.

[4] Dickson on Evidence, § 794 ; Maxwell Witham *v.* Teenan's Tr., 1884, 11 R. 776.

[5] Fraser *v.* Lovat, 1850, 7 Bell's App. 171.

necessarily null. Thus, where a deed is signed by the granter and two witnesses but is lacking in some other formality it may be enforced on proof that the signatures are genuine.[1] Where the want of formality is more deep-seated the improbative document, even if admittedly genuine, is inept, unless (1) it has been followed by *rei interventus*, that is, actings by one party known to the other on the faith of the informal contract so that he would be prejudiced if the other were allowed to repudiate the contract on the ground of the informality of the writing, or (2) validated by homologation, that is, by the act of the granter himself in treating it as if valid. Where *rei interventus* or homologation is alleged the informal writ is admissible in evidence and if impugned may be proved by parole evidence, as may also the *rei interventus*. These exceptions, *rei interventus* and homologation, are applications of the doctrine of personal bar. A party to an incomplete contract has *locus pœnitentiœ*, *i.e.* right to withdraw up to the time the contract is complete. In the case of a contract incomplete for the want of a fully probative writing, the granter of the improbative writing is personally barred from exercising his right to resile if he has permitted *rei interventus* to take place or has himself homologated the document.

Rei Interventus.—*Rei interventus* is " inferred from any proceedings not unimportant on the part of the obligee, known to and permitted by the obligor to take place on the faith of the contract as if it were perfect, and productive of alteration of circumstances, loss, or inconvenience, though not irretrievable." [2] Thus where the tenant of an hotel maintained a formally incomplete contract of lease until it was too late for the landlord to apply for a licence, he was held barred from founding upon the incompleteness to get rid of the lease.[3]

The averment of *rei interventus* must be specific. It is not enough to aver generally that the parties acted on the faith of the agreement.[4]

The actings relied on as setting up *rei interventus* must have been known to and permitted by the granter of the obligation. Actual knowledge is not necessary if the actings were those which would normally and almost necessarily take place if he relied on the improbative agreement. Thus an improbative guarantee was held

---

[1] Conveyancing (Scotland) Act, 1874, § 39, and *vide supra*, p. 8.
[2] Bell's Prin., § 26.
[3] Station Hotel, Nairn *v.* Macpherson, 1905, 13 S.L.T. 456.
[4] Van Laun *v.* Neilson, Reid & Co., 1904, 6 F. 644, per Lord Kinnear at p. 653.

established by advances made to the principal debtor although it was not proved the guarantor was aware the advances were made.[1]

The acts constituting *rei interventus* must be unequivocally referable to the contract. (Acts done before it are necessarily excluded.) Thus where a tenant negotiated for the purchase of his farm, but certain conditions had not been finally arranged, and he proceeded to make considerable alterations on the subjects, acquiesced in by the seller, these actings were held to be ascribable to purchase, not to contract of lease.[2]

The personal bar affects not only the party who has allowed the other to act on it, but also the party who so acts.[3]

Homologation.—Homologation is present where the granter of a deed, unenforceable because improbative, himself supplies by his actings the defect. Rules of authentication being for the benefit of the granter of a deed cannot deprive him of the power of remedying the defects himself. He may recognise the binding character of the writ by treating it as binding upon him, *e.g.* by paying interest on an improbative bond. There is not apparently any rule that the homologator of an improbative deed must have known of its improbative character at the time he homologated it.

Adoption.—Where the contract is itself void, as where the granter being under age is incapable of contracting, there is no room for homologation. But the writ may afterwards be adopted by the granter should he acquire the power to contract. Adoption as a general rule makes the contract binding only as from the date of the adoption unless the person adopting by his words or acts otherwise undertakes.

(*d*) **Stamping of Documents.**—In connection with the subject of proof the question may arise whether a fact can be proved by means of an unstamped document which the law requires to be stamped and declares null if unstamped. If the document is probative it cannot receive effect as a probative document. Unstamped documents have, however, been admitted when supported by other evidence, in proof of obligations which by themselves they are not admissible to prove.[4] A judge or arbiter must take notice of any omission or insufficiency of the stamp on a document.[5]

[1] Johnston *v.* Grant, 1844, 6 D. 875 ; National Bank of Scotland *v.* Campbell, 1892, 19 R. 885.　　　　[2] Colquhoun *v.* Wilson's Trs., 1860, 22 D. 1035.

[3] Different in England—Caton *v.* Caton, (1866) L.R. 1 Ch. 137.

[4] Bannatyne *v.* Wilson, 13th Dec. 1855, 18 D. 230 ; Matheson *v.* Ross, 1849, 6 Bell's App. 374 ; Fraser *v.* Bruce, 25th Nov. 1857, 20 D. 115.

[5] Stamp Act, 1891, § 14 (1).

The law requiring stamping is entirely statutory. The principal Act is the Stamp Act, 1891. Stamps may be adhesive, where permitted, but not over 2s. 6d.,[1] or impressed. Where the stamp is adhesive the instrument is not deemed duly stamped unless (a) the person required by law to cancel it does so by writing on or across the stamp his name or initials together with the date of so doing, or otherwise effectively cancels the stamp and renders it incapable of being used for any other instrument or for postal purposes ; or (b) it is otherwise proved that the stamp appearing on the instrument was affixed thereto at the proper time.[2] In certain cases special adhesive stamps are required to be used, called " appropriated adhesive stamps." These are required on bills of exchange or promissory notes drawn or made out of the United Kingdom and on contract notes liable to the duty of one shilling. Adhesive or impressed stamps may be used in the case of agreements liable to the fixed duty of 6d., bills of exchange (including cheques) payable on demand, charter-parties, contract notes liable to the duty of one penny, delivery orders, policies of insurance other than sea or life insurance, protests of bills or notes, receipts, and warrants for goods, and others.

An unstamped or insufficiently stamped instrument may, as a rule, be stamped after the execution thereof on payment of the unpaid duty and a penalty of £10, or, if the duty is over £10, with in addition interest on the duty from the time when first executed.[3]

4. Matters affecting the Validity of Contracts.—There are some contracts which confer no rights or are at least unenforceable by one or both of the parties even though they are formally complete. This may be due to the incapacity of the parties to bind themselves, or the contract may have been entered into in error or obtained by improper means such as misrepresentation, fraud, force, or undue influence, or be prohibited by law. A contract which is open to any of these objections may be void and null, may be voidable and reducible, or may be merely unenforceable. The difference in effect between a void and a voidable contract is that in the former case no third party can acquire rights under the contract whatever, whereas in the latter a third party can do so before it is challenged and reduced.

(a) **Capacity to Contract.**—Incapacity to contract on the part of one or both parties to the contract has the same effect as if no contract had been entered into, i.e. the contract is void

---

[1] Stamp Act, 1891, § 7.   [2] Ibid., § 8 (1).
[3] Ibid., § 15 (1).

from the beginning, because there can have been no true consent to be bound. Parties wholly or partly incapable of contracting are pupils, minors, and persons labouring under mental derangement or intoxicated.

Pupils.—Pupils are persons under the age of puberty, which is 12 in the case of girls, 14 in the case of boys. A contract by a pupil alone is void if challenged by him, or in his interest, at any time within the forty years of the negative prescription.[1] But if it is for his advantage and he acts on it the other party is bound to perform it. Indirectly a pupil by contracting may incur obligations. Thus where necessaries, *i.e.* such as food and clothing, are bought by a pupil he must pay a reasonable price for them,[2] and where money is lent to a pupil and spent on his estate he will be liable in so far as he has been thereby enriched.[3]

Pupils' contracts are properly made on their behalf by their guardians or tutors, and these are good subject to certain limitations. The natural guardian or tutor of a pupil child is his or her father. On the father's death the mother, if surviving, may be tutor or guardian either alone or jointly with anyone appointed tutor by the father.[4] Tutors may be appointed by Will of the father or mother and by the Court.[5]

Contracts made on behalf of a pupil by his tutor or guardian are not void from the beginning, but may be reduced by the pupil after he or she attains majority and during four years thereafter (the *quadriennium utile*) on proof of lesion, *i.e.* loss and injury, provided the loss is considerable, and the contract was not proper and reasonable at the time it was made. When the contract is so reduced it is set aside as from the beginning, and there must be *restitutio in integrum, i.e.* the pupil must restore to the other party all benefit he has derived.

The Betting and Loans (Infants) Act, 1892, the Moneylenders Act, 1900, and the Moneylenders Act, 1927, contain special provisions for the protection of pupils (and minors) against money-lenders. The main provision is to the effect

---

[1] *Q.v. infra*, p. 57.   [2] Sale of Goods Act, 1893, § 2.
[3] Scott's Tr. *v.* Scott, 1887, 14 R. 1043.
[4] Guardianship of Infants Act, 1886, § 2.   [5] *Ibid.*

that where any minor or pupil who has contracted a loan which is void in law agrees after he comes of age to repay it, such agreement is absolutely void.[1]

Minors.—Minors are persons above the age of pupilarity and under the age of 21. , They have capacity to contract, but subject to certain qualifications. If the minor has a guardian or curator contracts by him, as a rule, require the consent of such guardian or curator and are null if made by him alone. He may, in certain circumstances, validly contract alone. Thus (1) if a minor enters into a profession, trade, or business the contracts made by him in the ordinary course thereof are fully binding on him.[2] There is a presumption that bonds, bills of exchange and other such documents granted by a minor engaged in business are granted by him for the purposes of his business. This would not hold of a cautionary obligation, a gamble on the stock exchange, or a bill to a money-lender. (2) If a minor holds himself out as of full age so as actually to deceive parties with whom he contracts the contract is binding on him. (3) Contracts by a minor for necessaries are valid and he must pay a reasonable price for them as in the case of pupils. In the case of a minor contracting with consent of his guardian or, where he has none, by himself alone the contract may be reduced during the *quadriennium utile* as in the case of pupils.

These principles are well illustrated by the case of partnership. Thus a minor who is partner in a firm cannot plead minority and lesion in a question with creditors, but can in questions with his co-partners.

The law as to money-lending transactions by pupils applies also to minors.

Insane Persons.—As a general rule a person while insane is incapable of entering into a contract for he is incapable of giving the necessary consent.[3] His contract is void. Whether a person was or was not at the time of his undertaking a legal obligation of any kind so insane as to be incapable of entering into a contract is a question of fact

[1] Betting and Loans (Infants) Act, 1892, § 5.
[2] M'Feetridge *v.* Stewarts & Lloyds, 1913 S.C. 773.
[3] Stair, i. 10, 13 ; Ersk. i. 7, 51 ; Bell's Prin., §§ 10, 2105, *et seq.*

and degree. A person may be sane at one time and not at another, sane on one subject and insane on another, sufficiently sane to enter into a simple contract but not a complex one. Until proved insane his sanity is presumed. When a person has been legally declared insane he is as regards capacity to contract in the same position as a pupil, and his tutor-at-law alone can contract for him. When he has not been legally declared insane the Court will on petition, and on being satisfied that he is unable to manage his own affairs, appoint a *curator bonis* to do so. Insanity supervening during the currency of a continuing contract entered into during sanity may not end the contract, *e.g.* if it be between agent and client,[1] or a contract of partnership.[2] The Court may, however, dissolve a partnership on this ground.[3]

Intoxicated Persons.—Intoxication may produce temporary incapacity to give the consent requisite to make a contract.[4] The contract, however, is not void from the beginning.[5] The intoxicated person must, to undo it, as soon as he recovers and realises what he has done, repudiate it.[6] It is a question of fact to be ascertained by proof whether a person was so intoxicated as to be unable to make a particular contract.[7]

Married Women.—By the Married Women's Property Act, 1920, the law as to the capacity of a married woman effectually to contract on her own behalf has undergone a radical change. Prior thereto the general rule was that without the consent and concurrence of her husband in his capacity as her curator and administrator-in-law she could not effectually contract. In some cases even his consent was not sufficient to render the contract effectual against her separate estate. Her personal obligation was a nullity. Thus she could not effectually sign a bill as guarantor or undertake a personal obligation.[8] By that

[1] Wink *v.* Mortimer, 1849, 11 D. 995 ; Pollok *v.* Paterson, 10th Dec. 1811, F.C.
[2] Partnership Act, 1890, § 35.
[3] *Ibid.*
[4] Stair, i. 10, 13 ; Ersk. iii. 1, 18.
[5] Wilson & Fraser *v.* Nisbet, 1736, M. 1509.
[6] Pollok *v.* Burns, 1875, 2 R. 497.
[7] Taylor *v.* Provan, 1864, 2 M. 1226.
[8] Galbraith *v.* Provident Bank, 1900, 2 F. 1148.

Act [1] the husband's right of administration over his wife's estate has been " wholly abolished." If she is of full age she can without her husband's consent, or even against his wish, dispose of her estate. She can contract, sue and be sued as if unmarried, and her husband is not liable on any contract she makes on her own behalf.[2] Should she be in minority the husband, if of full age, is her curator,[3] and consequently the rules applicable to minors who have curators apply to her case. If her husband be a minor her father or other guardian is her curator.

The consequence of the above change is that the wife is alone and personally liable in all her contracts. When, of course, she is acting not for herself, but as her husband's agent as *præposita negotiis domesticis*, he is liable, as under the former law, but this is not a question of her capacity to contract as principal.

(b) **Error or Mistake, Misrepresentation, and Fraud.**—A contract otherwise completely constituted may in the next place be reduced as invalid on the ground that there was no genuine consent to be bound.

(i.) **Error or Mistake.**—What is the effect of error on a contract ?

A contract may be affected by error in two cases : first, an error in expression where by some slip or blunder the contract is concluded or recorded in terms other than those to which the parties to it consented ; second, an error of intention, that is where, though the contract accurately represents the immediate intention of the parties, that intention was formed by one or both of them owing to a misapprehension as to some matter regarded as material in determining whether they should enter into the contract.[4]

Error of Expression.—The Court has a wide equitable power to rectify a mistake in the execution of an obligatory document so as to give effect to the real intention of the parties. If the mistake

---

[1] Married Women's Property Act, 1920, § 1.   [2] *Ibid.*, § 3.
[3] *Ibid.*, § 2.
[4] Gloag on Contract, 2nd ed., p. 435.

is admitted there is no difficulty, or where it is obvious on inspection of the document. Where a mistake is not admitted by one party nor obvious it can only be established by extrinsic proof.[1] And where a clerical error is not discovered until the interests of third parties have become involved rectification is still competent. The Court will not, however, supply the want of statutory formalities necessary to the validity of an instrument as a probative deed.

An offer containing an error in expression, even though accepted, may not be binding on the offerer. It will not be binding if the acceptor knew that a mistake had been made.[2] If the acceptor has no knowledge of the mistake and accepts in *bona fide* there is some conflict of authority whether the offerer is bound or not.[3] Where an offer is incorrectly transmitted, as by mistake of a telegraph operator, and the offer is read by the recipient in terms materially different from those in which it was made, his acceptance does not conclude a contract.[4]

Error of Intention.—One party may be in error, or both. The case of error by one party induced by the misrepresentation of the other is dealt with later.[5]

Error of One Party.—There is error of intention when it can be shown that one of the parties would not have entered into the contract, or would not have assented to its particular terms, if he had been aware of the true state of the facts. The general rule is that mere error of one party has no legal effect. If a man buys too dear or sells too cheap he is not by reason of his mistake protected from

---

[1] Krupp *v.* Menzies, 1907 S.C. 903.

[2] Webster *v.* Cecil, (1861) 30 Beav. 62 ; Steuart's Trs. *v.* Hart, 1875, 3 R. 192.

[3] Sword *v.* Sinclair, 1771, M. 14241 ; Seaton Brick and Tile Co. *v.* Mitchell, 1900, 2 F. 550 ; Wilkie *v.* Hamilton Lodging House Co., 1902, 4 F. 951.

[4] Verdin Bros. *v.* Robertson, 1871, 10 M. 35 ; *cf.* Falck *v.* Williams, [1900] A.C. 176.

[5] *Vide* p. 22.

loss.[1] Essential error of one party is not enough in itself to nullify a contract. " It must further be proved that the error was mutual, *i.e.* common to both parties, or that it was induced by misrepresentation, either innocent or fraudulent, made by the other party to the contract, or that it was induced by fraudulent concealment." [2] It is immaterial that the error was due to a man's own fault or that of a third party, and he has no remedy unless he can charge the other party with misrepresentation.[3] It is also clear that where the error alleged is as to some circumstance external to the contract itself that will not release the person in error, as where a party leased a theatre and afterwards discovered that the plays he meant to produce were illegal.[4] The rule applies where the contract is onerous, but not when it is gratuitous, or in substance so.[5]

The above general rule does not, however, apply where the error is so fundamental or substantial as to exclude any agreement, that is, where there is really no contract to enforce. That is, errors in substantials may invalidate consent, whereas error in regard to collateral matters, " error concomitans," leaves the parties as they are.

Where there is error in the substantials of a contract it is void, and even third parties can acquire no rights. The cases of error in substantials avoiding a contract are exceptions to the general rule that the intentions of parties are to be derived from the words in which they express themselves. Errors in substantials may be (1) as to the party contracted with, (2) as to the contract entered into, (3) as to the subject-matter of the contract, (4) as to the price or consideration. Examples may be given.

[1] Bell's Prin., § 11.
[2] Lord Skerrington in A. B. *v.* C. B., 1914, 2 S.L.T. 107.
[3] Wallace's Factor *v.* M'Kissock, 1898, 25 R. 642.
[4] Cloup *v.* Alexander, 1831, 9 S. 448.
[5] Macandrew *v.* Gilhooly, 1911 S.C. 448.

(1) *Error as to Party.*—The identity of the
other party must be material. In a case in England
one Blenkarn ordered goods from a manufacturer.
They were supplied in the belief the order came
from Blenkiron, a well-known dealer who had
premises in the street from which Blenkarn wrote
and whose credit they knew to be good. Having
got the goods Blenkarn resold them. Blenkarn
failing to pay for the goods the manufacturers
sought to recover the goods from the purchasers to
whom Blenkarn sold them, and it was held, owing
to the manufacturer's mistake as to Blenkarn's
identity, there was no contract and Blenkarn
could not give a title to the purchasers from
him.[1]

(2) *Error as to Contract.*—The usual case is
where a person signs an obligatory document thinking he is signing as a witness on a different document. So where a person signs a bill of exchange
thinking he is signing as a witness the bill cannot
be enforced by a holder in due course.[2]

(3) *Error as to Subject-matter.*—This covers
both the case where the parties are at variance as
to the particular thing about which they contract
and where they differ materially about the qualities
the thing is supposed to possess. Thus, in the
former case, there were two ships both called the
Peerless and both sailing with cotton on board from
Bombay, though at different dates. Where a party
bought the cotton on board the *Peerless* thinking
of the one ship, and the seller thinking of the other,
it was held there was no contract.[3] In the latter
case there is no contract if the difference in quality
amounts to a difference in kind, but not otherwise.

[1] Cundy *v.* Lindsay, (1878) 3 App. Cas. 459 ; *cf.* Morrison *v.* Robertson, 1908 S.C.
332 ; Lake *v.* Simmons, [1927] A.C. 487 ; Said *v.* Butt, [1920] 3 K.B. 497.

[2] Foster *v.* Mackinnon, (1869) L.R. 4 C.P. 704 ; Buchanan *v.* Duke of Hamilton,
1878, 5 R. (H.L.) 69 ; Ellis *v.* Lochgelly Iron and Coal Co., 1909 S.C. 1278, per Lord
Dunedin at p. 1282.

[3] Raffles *v.* Wichelhaus, (1864) 2 H. & C. 906 ; *cf.* Wallis *v.* Pratt, [1911]
A.C. 394.

Thus a purchaser of new oats, thinking they were old, failed to reduce the contract.[1]

(4) *Error as to Price or Consideration.*—Where in a verbal sale of cattle one party thought the price had been fixed and the other thought it was to be settled after, there was held to be no completed contract.[2]

The above examples are all errors of fact. Where there is error by one party as to the legal effect of a contract the legal import of it does not as a rule affect his obligation.[3] But this does not apply where the parties stand in a fiduciary relation to one another, as, for example, between partners, nor in gratuitous obligation, nor where money has been paid unnecessarily, as in the case of over-payments.[4]

Mutual Error.—Where both parties have contracted on the mistaken assumption of the existence of a certain state of facts the contract may be void or at least voidable.[5] Thus, under the Sale of Goods Act, 1893, § 6, " where there is a contract for the sale of specific goods and the goods without the knowledge of the seller have perished at the time the contract was made, the contract is void " ; or where one purchases a thing which already belongs to him, neither party being aware of the fact [6] ; or where a discharge is given under a material error as to the nature or extent of the right in question.[7] The only remedy is reduction.[8] Mutual error will not, on the other hand, avoid a contract where the error is one of opinion, or as to the value of a thing which is the subject-matter of a sale.

---

[1] Smith *v.* Hughes, (1871) L.R. 6 Q.B. 597.
[2] Wilson *v.* Marquis of Breadalbane, 1859, 21 D. 957.
[3] Muirhead *v.* Turnbull & Dickson, 1905, 7 F. 686, per Lord M'Laren.
[4] Henderson & Co. *v.* Turnbull & Co., 1909 S.C. 510.
[5] Hamilton *v.* The Western Bank, 1861, 23 D. 1033.
[6] Magistrates of Inverness *v.* Highland Railway Co., 1893, 20 R. 551.
[7] Purdon *v.* Rowat's Trs., 1856, 19 D. 206.
[8] Pender-Smith *v.* Kinloch's Trs., 1917 S.C. 307.

(ii.) **Misrepresentation.**—Error due to misrepresentation by one party inducing the other to contract may be either innocent or fraudulent. In both cases where the misrepresentation touches the substantials of the contract it is void, otherwise it is merely voidable.

A distinction should be noted, that between a representation and a warranty, for they are not always easily distinguished and have different legal effects. A representation is a statement which induces a party to contract but is not part of the contract. The misrepresentation does not, therefore, give rise to a breach of contract, but to a right to rescind it. A warranty, however, is something which a party has undertaken to fulfil as part of the contract, and breach of it is, therefore, a breach of the contract, and the legal remedy is damages for breach of the contract, not rescission. Thus, statements as to the description of goods sold are not representations but warranties.[1] It is generally a question of the intention of the parties whether a statement is a representation or a warranty, and much will depend on the nature of the contract. In determining whether a statement is of the one character or the other, if it refers not to the subject-matter, but to something collateral, it is usually merely a representation.

Innocent Misrepresentation and Concealment.—A misrepresentation may consist in failure to disclose a material fact or in an actual statement or in an act. The legal effect of misrepresentation without fraudulent intent is to render the contract voidable unless touching the substantials, when it is void. It seems to be settled that an innocent misrepresentation can render a contract voidable.[2] It undoubtedly does so where the contract is one

---

[1] Sale of Goods Act, 1893, § 13 ; Hyslop v. Shirlaw, 1905, 7 F. 875, per Lord Kyllachy at p. 881.

[2] Stewart v. Kennedy, 1890, 17 R. (H.L.) 25. See also Mair v. Rio Grande Rubber Co., 1913 S.C. (H.L.) 74 ; Westville Shipping Co. v. Abram Steamship Co., 1922 S.C. 571 ; 1923 S.C. (H.L.) 68 ; Gloag on Contract, 2nd ed., p. 471.

uberrimœ fidei, i.e. one where there is a duty on the parties, owing to the nature of the contract, to disclose all material facts with accuracy, for example, contracts of insurance or partnership agreements [1] or agreements to take shares founded on a prospectus.[2]

To render a contract voidable a representation must be material and essential, *i.e.* such as would, if known, have deterred the party deceived from entering into the contract,[3] and must have, in fact, either by itself or along with other representations, induced the contract. Therefore it has no effect if the other party knew the facts.[4] If the statement is ambiguous, proof that it was understood in the misleading sense must be led. Unless there was a duty to enquire, the fact that by enquiry the party deceived might have discovered the truth does not deprive him of his remedy.[5]

Failure to Disclose.—The general rule is that each party relies on his own means of knowledge. They are " at arm's length." [6] Thus a party need not inform the other that he has doubts of his own solvency and consequent ability to fulfil obligations undertaken. Again, he need not disclose his reasons for making an offer, even though he knew these, if disclosed, would prevent acceptance. In contracts *uberrimœ fidei,* however, *e.g.* insurance, there is a duty to disclose all material facts known.

On the other hand, conduct amounting to active concealment is a misrepresentation, and is often equivalent to fraud, *e.g.* to conceal the fact that an article is a sham antique.[7] A half truth

[1] Ferguson *v.* Wilson, 1904, 6 F. 779.

[2] Blakiston *v.* London and Scottish Banking Corporation, 1894, 21 R. 417.

[3] Menzies *v.* Menzies, 1893, 20 R. (H.L.) 108, per Lord Watson at p. 142.

[4] Cruickshank *v.* Northern Accident Insurance Co., 1895, 23 R. 147.

[5] Scottish Widows' Fund *v.* Buist, 1876, 3 R. 1078, per Lord Inglis at p. 1083.

[6] Royal Bank *v.* Greenshields, 1914 S.C. 259 ; Young *v.* Clydesdale Bank, 1889, 17 R. 231.

[7] Patterson *v.* Landsberg, 1905, 7 F. 675 ; Edgar *v.* Hector, 1912 S.C. 348 ; Gibson *v.* National Cash Register Co., 1925 S.C. 500.

may be a misrepresentation.[1] Again, if change of circumstances renders a statement untrue which was true when made, or if believed to be true when made and later discovered by the maker to be untrue, the fact must be communicated if it was such as would affect the judgment of a reasonable man.[2]

Misrepresentation by Actual Statements.—When these turn out to be incorrect it depends on the character of the statement whether it amounts to a misrepresentation. An honest expression of mere opinion is not a misrepresentation.[3] A statement as to the law, if general, is mere opinion ; if as to the legal effect of a particular document, it is a statement of fact and may amount to a misrepresentation.[4] An exaggerated or unduly laudatory statement by a seller in praise of his goods is not necessarily a misrepresentation. The law allows a certain latitude to statements of an advertising nature. Statements must be taken in their reasonable meaning. They must not be given a strained though possible construction.[5]

A misrepresentation of an agent is treated as a misrepresentation of a principal. No person can take advantage of his agent's misstatements,[6] unless the principal has explicitly and in advance disclaimed responsibility for the agent's statements.

Fraudulent Misrepresentation and Fraud.—Fraud has been defined as a false representation of fact made with a knowledge of its falseness, or in reckless disregard if it be true or false, with the intention it should be acted upon, and actually inducing the other party to the contract to act upon

---

[1] Royal Bank *v.* Greenshields, *supra* ; Crossan *v.* Caledon Shipbuilding Co., 1906, 14 S.L.T. (H.L.) 33.

[2] Gowans *v.* Dundee Steam Navigation Co., 1904, 12 S.L.T. 137 ; Shankland *v.* Robinson, 1919 S.C. 715 ; revd. 1920 S.C. (H.L.) 103.

[3] Bile Beans Co. *v.* Davidson, 1906, 8 F. 1181 ; Plotzer *v.* Isaacs, 1907, 15 S.L.T. 186.

[4] Brownlie *v.* Miller, 1878, 5 R. 1076 ; affd. 1880, 7 R. (H.L.) 66.

[5] Romanes *v.* Garman, 1912, 2 S.L.T. 104.

[6] Mair *v.* Rio Grande Rubber Estates, Ltd., 1913 S.C. (H.L.) 74.

it.[1] It may consist in a statement of what is false or a concealment of what is true. It must, of course, be material. Also it may consist of an act, as where the seller at a sale by auction bid though he made no representation that he meant to do so.[2] If a statement be honestly made, even though negligently, it cannot be fraudulent.[3] The fraud must have been successful, and the party deceived must have sustained damage thereby. The distinguishing features of a fraudulent from an innocent misrepresentation are the knowledge of its falseness and the intention it should be acted upon.

The distinction in effect between innocent and fraudulent misrepresentation is that in the former case the party deceived has only the remedy of reduction, in the latter he has also the remedy of damages. The reduction is based upon the misrepresentation, the claim of damages upon the civil wrong of fraud.[4]

The effect of fraud upon a contract is to render it voidable at the instance of the party deceived. The whole contract must be reduced. The action can only be at the instance of a party to the contract, not of a third party on the ground of fraudulent statements not made to him.[5] The sole exception appears to be where a man, from the nature of the case, is bound to contemplate that his statements will be acted upon by others than the person to whom he makes them.[6] A fraudulent representation made to the public will give a right of action to anyone who is misled by it and suffers

---

[1] Lord Herschell in Derry v. Peek, (1889) 14 A.C. 374.

[2] Sale of Goods Act, 1893, § 58.

[3] Boyd & Forrest v. Glasgow and South-Western Railway Co., 1912 S.C. (H.L.) 93 at p. 98 ; Derry v. Peek, infra ; Manners v. Whitehead, 1898, 1 F. 171.

[4] The leading case is Derry v. Peek, (1889) 14 A.C. 337.

[5] Re Discoverer's Finance Corporation, (1909) 26 T.L.R. 98 ; Edinburgh United Breweries v. Molleson, 1893, 20 R. 581 ; affd. 1894, 21 R. (H.L.) 10 ; Macfarlane, Strang & Co. v. Bank of Scotland, 1903, 40 S.L.R. 746.

[6] Langridge v. Levy, 1837, 2 M. & W. 519 ; Robinson v. National Bank, 1916 S.C. (H.L.) 154 ; see also Fortune v. Young, 1918 S.C. 1.

loss.[1] Where a fraudulent misrepresentation of a
third party has caused a person to make a contract,
he can sue the third party for damages, but cannot
insist that he take over the contract from him.

(c) **Facility and Circumvention, Undue Influence, Force and Fear
and Extortion.—Facility and Circumvention.**—A contract is
voidable and may be reduced on the above grounds. In
facility and circumvention there is presupposed a weakness
or facility of mind in the one contracting party, due for
instance to old age or severe illness, taken advantage of by
the other in order to obtain or impetrate from him a deed or
contract. It is distinguishable from insanity in respect that
the facile party has capacity to contract, and from fraud in
that the end is the more easily attained owing to the state
of mind of the defrauded party. There must have been
also the motive to mislead, which is involved in the idea
of circumvention. Consent must therefore have been improperly obtained.[2]

Undue Influence.—Where there is not facility acts of
circumvention falling short of fraud do not warrant reduction except in the special case where a party acquiring a
benefit has abused a position of trust and influence. To this
form of circumvention is given the specific name of " undue
influence." The factors going to make a case of undue
influence have been summarised as the existence of a relation
creating a dominant or ascendant influence by the one
over the other, a confidence and trust arising out of such
relation, a material and gratuitous benefit given to the
prejudice of that other and the absence of independent
advice. Undue influence may occur in contracts between
near relations, e.g. parent and child [3] ; between a clergyman
and a person over whom he exercises spiritual influence [4] ;
between a doctor and his patient.[5] Such contracts are
reducible for want of true consent.

Force and Fear and Extortion.—Bell [6] says : " Force

[1] Lees v. Tod, 1882, 9 R. 807 (Prospectus and Annual Reports) ; Peek v. Gurney,
(1873) L.R. 6 H.L. 377 (only original shareholders).

[2] Liston v. Cowan, 1865, 3 M. 1041.

[3] Smith Cuninghame v. Anstruther's Trs., 1872, 10 M. (H.L.) 39.

[4] Munro v. Strain, 1874, 1 R. 522.

[5] Dent v. Bennett, (1839) 1 My. & Cr. 269.   [6] Principles, § 12.

and fear annul engagement, when not vain or foolish fear, but such as to overcome a mind of ordinary firmness." The contract is void, not merely voidable. The threats must have been the active inducing cause of the contract, and must have been such as would have affected the mind of a reasonable person. The threat, *e.g.* of imprisonment, must not have been justified. The threat must have been a threat to the contracting, not to a third party. Where a wife signed deeds at her husband's request on being informed by him that he was in danger of imprisonment and would flee the country if she declined she was held not entitled to reduce.[1]

Closely resembling the case of contracts reduced on the ground of extortion by force or fear are certain money-lending transactions which the Court annul as manifestly and grossly extortionate. Under the Money-lenders Acts, 1900 and 1927, the Courts have power to reopen a money-lending transaction should they, looking to all the circumstances, in particular to the risk undertaken by the money-lender, consider it harsh and unconscionable, and to fix the debtor's liability at what may be adjudged to be reasonable.[2] The more general rule, however, is that persons of full contractual capacity dealing at arm's length with each other are bound by their contracts whether fair or not.[3]

(d) **Contracts Prohibited by Law.—Illegal and Immoral Contracts.—** The validity of a contract may be challenged by either of the parties on the grounds already noticed. Illegal contracts, however—known as *pacta illicita*—are all invalid to this effect, that they cannot be enforced by action, irrespective of whether the plea of illegality is taken by a party, because it is the duty of the Court at its own hand to take cognisance of the illegality.

Illegal contracts include those which are forbidden by statute and those which are illegal at common law. A particular contract may be open to objection that it is both illegal at common law and forbidden or penalised by statute.

---

[1] Priestnell *v.* Hutcheson, 1857, 19 D. 495.
[2] Young *v.* Gordon, 1896, 23 R. 419 ; Gordon *v.* Stephen, 1902, 9 S.L.T. 397.
[3] A. B. *v.* Joel, 1849, 12 D. 188 ; Caledonian Railway Co. *v.* North British Railway Co., 1881, 8 R. (H.L.) 23 at p. 31.

(i.) **Illegality by Statute.**—Under this head are considered
contracts which are unobjectionable at common law,
though prohibited or penalised by statute. In
such cases the statute may either declare an act or
agreement of a particular kind void, or may merely
impose a penalty without declaring the contract
void, or may merely declare the contract unenforceable.

Where a contract, unobjectionable at common
law, is declared void or penalised by statute, while
it cannot be enforced or damages recovered under
it, the parties to it will not be deprived of any right
enforceable by law. The Court will take cognisance
of rights incidentally arising, as where the contract
is part implemented, and intervene to prevent
one party obtaining an advantage over the other.
There is a maxim, *in turpi causa melior est conditio
possidentis*, which, if applicable, would prevent the
Court giving any such assistance, but a statutory
provision avoiding a contract would not fall within
this rule. Thus, by the Gaming Act, 1845, it was
provided that " all contracts or agreements, by way
of gaming or wagering, shall be null and void."
But where a turf commissioner, employed to make
bets, had expended money in making bets he had
lost, he was held entitled to recover these sums
from his employers, although the parties with whom
he had betted could not have enforced payment
from him or his principals by action.[1]

Where a statute, without declaring the contract
void, enforces a penalty upon a particular contract,
or upon a contract entered into without the
observance of statutory conditions or the payment
of a statutory duty, there is a general presumption
that the imposition of a penalty implies illegality.
But in exceptional cases it may be held that the
imposition of a penalty is the sole effect of the
statute, either because its object is merely the
collection of revenue, or because the circumstances

[1] Read *v.* Anderson, (1884) 13 Q.B.D. 779.

are such as to make the avoidance of contracts a
penalty greater than the legislature can be supposed
to have intended to inflict. Thus it was held that
the effect of the Companies Clauses Consolidation
(Scotland) Act, 1845, § 89, whereby if a director of
a company shall be either directly or indirectly
concerned in a contract with the company his office
shall become vacant, was that the office became
vacant but the contract was not affected. And
under the provisions of the Money-lenders Act,
1900, which imposes a penalty on infringement of
its provisions, it has been held on the one hand that
where a money-lender entered into a contract
without having registered at all the name under
which he carried on business, as required by the
statute, the contract was void.[1] On the other hand,
where the money-lender had registered, but not
under the name which was his usual trade name, he
was subject to the penalty for contracting under his
unregistered trade name, but not to avoidance of
his contracts, as being too severe a penalty in the
absence of express enactment covering such a case.[2]
Again, where a statute imposes a stamp duty on a
particular contract, with a penalty on the party
failing to affix the stamp, it has been held the
provision is merely intended for revenue purposes
and does not avoid the contract.

Where a statute, without declaring a contract
illegal, or imposing any penalty, declares it unenforceable there seems to be no general rule.[3]
Examples are to be found in the Trade Union
Act, 1871, and the Tippling Act, 1750. Under
the latter Act no action is maintainable to recover
any debt on account of any spirituous liquors
unless *bona fide* contracted at one time to the
amount of twenty shillings and upwards. It has
been held that the Act does not merely cut off the

---

[1] Sagar *v.* M'Adam, 1914, 1 S.L.T. 93.
[2] Whiteman *v.* Sadler, [1910] A.C. 514.
[3] Gloag on Contract, 2nd ed., p. 553.

right of action but renders such furnishings illegal,
to the effect, for example, of reading out of a
tradesman's account items for such furnishings
occurring at the end in a question whether the
triennial prescription applied to it.[1]

(ii.) **Illegality at Common Law.**—A contract may be illegal
at common law because its objects are the furtherance of a criminal, fraudulent, or immoral act or
of an act contrary to public policy. Gaming contracts in Scots Law require separate consideration.[2]

A contract to commit an act indictable as a
crime is *pactum illicitum*, and the Court will not
only not enforce it but will take no cognisance of
the rights of parties under it.[3]

An agreement to defraud a third party is an
unlawful contract on which no action can be based.[4]
So also is an agreement tending to induce breach
of trust, or a collusive agreement in bankruptcy to
defeat the equal rights of creditors in distribution
of a bankrupt estate.[5]

A contract having for its object the furtherance
of illicit sexual intercourse, as where a woman
sought to enforce a bond granted to reward her
for having submitted to intercourse, is an immoral
and unlawful contract.[6] Certain contracts interfering with the liberty of marriage or marital relations are illegal, such as marriage brocage contracts,
in which obligations are granted in consideration of
bringing about a marriage.[7] So also are contracts
interfering with the relation of parent and child.
Further, contracts in themselves innocent may be
treated as *pacta illicita* if entered into for the
purpose of promoting an illegal or immoral purpose,
as, for example, where money is lent for the purpose

---

[1] Macpherson *v.* Jamieson, 1901, 4 F. 218.　　　　[2] See p. 33.

[3] Macdougall *v.* Bremner, 1907, 15 S.L.T. 193.

[4] Henderson *v.* Caldwell, 1890, 28 S.L.R. 16.

[5] Macfarlane *v.* Nicoll, 1864, 3 M. 237 ; Farmer's Mart, Ltd. *v.* Milne, [1915]
A.C. 106 ; and see Munro *v.* Rothfield, 1920, 2 S.L.T. 172 ; Bankruptcy (Scotland)
Act, 1913, § 150.　　　　[6] Thomas *v.* Waddell, 1869, 7 M. 558.

[7] Hermann *v.* Charlesworth, [1905] 2 K.B. 123.

of playing an illegal game, or where a house was
let which to the knowledge of the landlord was to
be used by the tenant in order to keep a mistress.[1]
In such cases it must be shown that the party suing
was aware of the purpose.[2]

Contracts void because contrary to public
policy have been classified as those conflicting with
national foreign policy, with the administration of
the law, with individual liberty, or with freedom
of trade.[3] Thus contracts entered into with any
person residing in and making contracts from an
enemy state are illegal as conflicting with national
foreign policy. And where war is declared its
effect is to suspend the operation of contracts
between the subjects of the belligerent states until
peace is restored. A contract to interfere with the
free and responsible right to vote at an election,
or one to obstruct the course of justice such as to
bribe a judge, or one to evade the revenue laws
as by smuggling, is void as conflicting with the
administration of the law.[4]

Contracts in Restraint of Trade.—Contracts in
restraint of trade merit special mention. Restrictive covenants are usually imposed as a condition
in contracts of service or apprenticeship or in contracts for the sale of a business or analogous cases.[5]
An agreement not to exercise a particular trade or
profession may be *pactum illicitum* if it imposes a
restriction wider than is reasonably necessary to
safeguard the interests of the persons it is designed
to protect. Such is void if the circumstances of
the individual case do not justify the restriction of
individual liberty. What is reasonable depends on
the circumstances of both parties.[6] An employer

---

[1] Upfill *v.* Wright, [1911] 1 K.B. 506.

[2] Smith's Advertising Agency *v.* Leeds Laboratory Co., (1910) 26 T.L.R. 335.

[3] Gloag on Contract, 2nd ed., p. 565.

[4] *Cf.* Trevalion *v.* Blanche, 1919 S.C. 617 ; Eisen *v.* M'Cabe, 1920 S.C. (H.L.) 146.

[5] *E.g.* Trego *v.* Hunt, (1896) A.C. 7 ; Stewart *v.* Stewart, 1899, 1 F. 1158.

[6] Meikle *v.* Meikle, 1895, 33 S.L.R. 362 (Painter) ; Mulvein *v.* Murray, 1908
S.C. 528 (Traveller) ; Dumbarton Steamboat Co. *v.* Macfarlane, 1899, 1 F. 993 ;
Mason *v.* Provident Clothing, etc. Co., [1913] A.C. 724.

may legitimately protect his business connection
and his trade and professional secrets, but otherwise may not protect himself from the competition
of his former employees ; on the other hand, the
purchaser of a business may within limits protect
himself from the competition of the seller.[1] Both
the interests of the individual and of the public
are to be taken into account.[2] The restriction
must refer to a particular business or profession.[3]
There should be some limit to the restriction in
point either of area or time. If the restriction is
too wide it falls.[4] The restriction must not be
capricious,[5] and the interest to restrict must exist
at the time when it is proposed to enforce it.[6]
Where a question of construction of contract arises
the Court will prefer a construction which makes
the contract enforceable.[7]

Some examples may be given. An obligation
by a doctor to discontinue practice in a particular
district, involving an obligation to resign the post
of medical officer to local authorities, has been
held reasonable.[8] An agreement by a commercial
traveller, limited to twelve months after leaving his
employment, not to sell or travel in any of the towns
or districts traded in by his employer has been held
unenforceable on the ground that the restriction
was wider than was reasonably necessary.[9] Restrictions on a servant taking up business on the
cessation of his employment within a certain time
or distance from his place of employment are not
binding on a servant who is unwarrantably dis-

[1] Fitch v. Dewes, [1920] 2 Ch. 159 ; [1921] A.C. 158 ; Morris v. Saxelby, [1916]
A.C. 688 ; Mason v. Provident Clothing and Supply Co., Ltd., [1913] A.C. 724.
[2] Nordenfeldt v. Maxim-Nordenfeldt Gun, etc. Co., [1894] A.C. 535.
[3] Mulvein v. Murray, 1908 S.C. 528.
[4] Dumbarton Steamboat Co. v. Macfarlane, supra ; Mulvein v. Murray, supra.
[5] Hepworth Manufacturing Co. v. Ryott, [1920] 1 Ch. 1.
[6] Berlitz School of Languages v. Duchene, 1903, 6 F. 181 ; Rodger v. Herbert-
son, 1909 S.C. 256 ; General Billposting Co. v. Atkinson, [1909] A.C. 118.
[7] Watson v. Neuffert, 1863, 1 M. 1110, per Lord Cowan.
[8] Ballachulish Slate Quarries Co., Ltd. v. Grant, 1903, 5 F. 1105.
[9] Mulvein v. Murray, supra.

missed.[1] A world-wide restriction, though sustained when granted in favour of a maker of cannon,[2] is unreasonable when designed to protect a local business.[3] Restrictions imposed by an association on its members intended to promote the business of the members have been held legal. Price maintenance agreements are not necessarily illegal, *e.g.* tied houses,[4] or where a purchaser undertakes not to resell under a certain price.[5] On the other hand, in the case of patented articles, power to adjust restrictive conditions is limited by statute.[6]

(iii.) **Gaming Contracts.—Under Statute.—**There is no general prohibition of an action founded on a wager in Scotland, differing from England.[7] There are, however, several Acts which affect the enforceability of such contracts. (1) Act 1621, c. 14. It is doubtful whether this Act would now be enforced.[8] By the Act sums exceeding 100 merks won at cards, dice, or horse-racing within twenty-four hours, are to belong to the kirk session of the parish for behoof of the poor. (2) The Act 9 Anne, c. 14, provides that all notes, bills, bonds, securities, or other conveyances where the whole or any part of the consideration is for money lost in playing at any game or betting on the result of a game, or is for repayment of money advanced or lent for such betting or gaming, are absolutely void. The Act is now repealed.[9] But (3) the Gaming Act, 1835, provides that every note, bill, or mortgage which would under the former Act have been absolutely void is to be deemed and taken to have been

---

[1] General Billposting Co. *v.* Atkinson, [1909] A.C. 118.

[2] Nordenfeldt *v.* Maxim-Nordenfeldt Gun, etc. Co., *supra.*

[3] Dumbarton Steamboat Co. *v.* Macfarlane, 1899, 1 F. 1158.

[4] Noakes & Co. *v.* Rice, [1902] A.C. 24.

[5] Elliman Sons & Co. *v.* Carrington, [1901] 2 Ch. 275 ; Morton *v.* Muir Brothers, 1907 S.C. 1211.

[6] Patents and Designs Act, 1907, § 38 (1).

[7] Levy *v.* Jackson, 1903, 5 F. 1170.

[8] But see O'Connell *v.* Russell, 1864, 3 M. 89, per Lord Deas at p. 93 ; Lord Justice-Clerk Moncreiff in Calder *v.* Stevens, 1871, 9 M. 1074.

[9] Gaming Act, 1845, § 15 ; Rayner *v.* Kent & Stanisfield, 1922, S.L.T. 331.

made, drawn, accepted, given, or executed for an illegal consideration. The effect of this, applying the Bills of Exchange Act, 1882, § 30 (2), is that an indorsee of such a bill may sue upon it if he proves he gave value for the bill without notice of its origin.[1] A bond or other security or conveyance granted for a gaming debt, and therefore for an illegal consideration, could not be enforced by an assignee against the granter, but the assignee could probably recover the consideration for the assignation from the cedent.[2] (4) The Betting Acts, 1853 and 1874, make criminal the keeping of a house or room for the purpose of betting, make recoverable from the keeper any deposit or any bet, but except from the operation of the Acts stakes or deposits to be paid to the winner of a race or other lawful sport or game, or to the owner of a horse. (5) To hold a lottery is in Scotland an illegal act. This is a result of the common law and the Lotteries Act, 1823, with statutory exceptions in favour of art unions under certain conditions,[3] and advertisements of foreign lotteries are penalised unless the lottery has been authorised by Act of Parliament.[4] (6) The Gambling Act, 1774, declares void any contract of insurance in which the insured has no insurable interest in the life assured.[5]

At Common Law.—Sponsiones ludicræ.—The Courts will not decide who is the winner of a competition. They pay no regard to *sponsiones ludicræ*. But the fact that the relations of parties is due to a *sponsio ludicra* will not debar the Court from interfering to protect the rights of parties once the winner is decided.[6] Thus a broker or

[1] Woolf *v.* Hamilton, [1898] 2 Q.B. 337.
[2] Ferrier *v.* Graham's Trs., 1828, 6 S. 818 ; see Gloag on Contract, 2nd ed., p. 580.
[3] Art Union Act, 1846, 9 & 10 Vict. c. 48 ; Christison *v.* M'Bride, 1881, 9 R. 34.
[4] Lotteries Act, 1836, 6 & 7 Will. IV. c. 66.
[5] *See* Insurance, *infra.*
[6] Calder *v.* Stevens, 1871, 9 M. 1074.

agent employed to bet may recover his commission and expenditure from his principal,[1] and the principal may recover from the agent winnings actually received.[2]

Wagering Contracts.—If the Court is satisfied there is a wagering contract it will not deal with the case at all. But there may be gambling without gaming. It is a question of the intention of both the parties. Thus a mere speculator in stocks and shares, or even commodities, is not necessarily barred from maintaining an action.[3] Again, while the speculator may not mean to take up the shares or commodities, and is merely gambling on differences, and so gaming, it may not be a gambling transaction so far as his relations with the broker with whom he deals are concerned. To constitute a wagering transaction both parties must intend the transaction to be fictitious, and one must lose, neither being bound to accept delivery of the stock, shares, or goods.[4, 5]

(iv.) **Effect of Illegality in Contracts.**—Where a contract involves an element of illegality, as distinguished from the case where it is merely declared void by statute, the effect is to debar the parties from recourse to the Courts. The principle is expressed in two legal maxims, viz. *ex turpi causa non oritur actio*, that is, the parties are debarred from maintaining an action, and *in turpi causa melior est conditio possidentis*, that is, one wrongdoer may with impunity take any advantage of the other which the circumstances admit of. Thus, where a scheme by several parties to defraud a third party has proved successful, the conspirator who has obtained

---

[1] Levy *v.* Jackson, 1903, 5 F. 1170 ; Foulds *v.* Thomson, 1857, 19 D. 803 ; Knight & Co. *v.* Stott, 1892, 19 R. 959.

[2] Bridger *v.* Savage, (1885) 15 Q.B.D. 363.

[3] Mollison *v.* Noltie, 1889, 16 R. 350.

[4] Foulds *v.* Thomson, 1857, 19 D. 803 ; Universal Stock Exchange Co. *v.* Howat, 1891, 19 R. 128.

[5] For full definition of a wager as distinct from a speculative contract, see Carlill *v.* Carbolic Smoke Ball Co., [1892] 2 Q.B. 484, per Hawkins J. at p. 490.

the profit cannot be legally compelled to share it
with the others.[1] So also if an illegal transaction
results in a loss the party who has sustained the
loss will not be allowed to plead the illegality in
order to get relief from the other party.[2] The
general test of whether an action is excluded is
whether the pursuer can establish his case without
exposing that he has been guilty of illegality.

There are certain exceptions to the rule that a
party to an illegal contract is debarred from suing
on it. Thus, where the illegal purpose involves a
mere temporary right, as where property is let or
hired for an improper object, while the rent or hire
cannot be recovered,[3] the owner of the property
might sue to recover it when the temporary purpose
was over.[4] Again, where the parties are not *in pari
delicto*, *i.e.* equally blameworthy, the less blameworthy may found upon the illegality. This applies
where one party has been in a position to compel
the other in an illegal act, as where a creditor has
obtained a secret preference from the debtor as the
price of his concurrence in a composition. Again,
where the illegality arises under a statute which has
been passed to protect a particular class, in contrast
to the public interest,[5] a member of that class may
sue to recover what he has paid under the illegal
contract.[6] In England it has been held that if
money is paid for an illegal object it may be recovered if demanded before the illegal object has
been carried out, as in the case of money paid to a
matrimonial agency when no marriage followed.[7]
And if the contract is only partly illegal and is
divisible the part not tainted with the illegality
may be enforced, as in contracts not to carry on a

---

[1] Laughland *v.* Miller, Laughland & Co., 1904, 6 F. 413.
[2] Anderson *v.* Torrie, 1857, 19 D. 356.
[3] Upfill *v.* Wright, [1911] 1 K.B. 506.
[4] Gloag on Contract, 2nd ed., p. 586.
[5] *In re* Mahmoud and Ispahani, [1921] 2 K.B. 716.
[6] Phillips *v.* Blackhurst, 1912, 2 S.L.T. 254.
[7] Hermann *v.* Charlesworth, [1905] 2 K.B. 123 at p. 129.

particular trade where there are two restrictions, one permissible, the other not.[1]

Where rights under a contract tainted with illegality are assigned to a third party the general rule is that the third party takes no better title than his cedent. This does not apply to bills of exchange, promissory notes, and cheques if subsequent to the illegality the endorsee has in good faith and without notice of the illegality given value for the bill, when he may enforce payment against all parties liable on the bill.[2]

5. Construction and Interpretation of Contracts.—There has already been considered under formation of contracts the manner in which their constitution requires to be proved before they can be effectively founded on. Assuming, then, the formation of a valid contract capable of being proved as to its constitution, there now fall to be considered questions which may arise out of or in relation to the terms in which a contract is expressed. This matter may be considered under the following heads : (a) the construction of contracts generally ; (b) the interpretation of particular terms ; (c) proof in matters of construction and interpretation.

(a) **The Construction of Contracts Generally.**—Where a contract is constituted and proved verbally it is mainly a question of the credibility of the witnesses as to the meaning which they respectively put on the terms used. Where the contract is in writing, while the question is what was the intention of the parties, that question is to be determined, not from what they respectively say they intended by a particular expression, but by the sense in which an expression used by the one party would be reasonably understood by the other.[3] Or, as the matter has been otherwise put, the Court is to endeavour to place itself in the position of a reasonable and disinterested third party, duly instructed, if necessary, as to the law.[4] And in arriving at a construction the general rule is that the whole contract must be looked at.

[1] Mulvein v. Murray, 1908 S.C. 528.

[2] Bills of Exchange Act, 1882, §§ 30, 38.

[3] Fowkes v. Manchester and London Assurance Association, (1863) 3 B. & S. 917, per Lord Blackburn at p. 929 ; Muirhead & Turnbull v. Dickson, 1905, 7 F. 686, per Lord President Dunedin at p. 694.

[4] Gloag on Contract, 2nd ed., p. 398.

Mutuality of Contracts.—Where a contract is mutual, that is contains obligations by both parties, or *hinc inde* as it is called, and not merely a series of independent obligations, the general rule is that both parties must be bound or neither. This has been called the principle of mutuality. The principle may apply both when the obligations are express and when merely implied. Thus, where a school teacher was appointed without any express arrangement as to the duration of his employment or notice of dismissal, and claimed damages for dismissal without reasonable notice, it was held that as a school teacher could not be supposed to be entitled to leave without notice there was a correlative obligation on the school board to give him corresponding notice.[1] Again, the principle will be applied where the incidence of contractual obligation is altered by statute. Thus the Sale of Goods Act, 1893 (§ 58), provides that a sale by auction is complete when the auctioneer announces its completion by the fall of the hammer. It has been held on this principle that before the fall of the hammer an exposer may withdraw the article from sale.[2]

Conditions in Contracts.—A contractual obligation is termed pure when it can be enforced at once and is not subject to any condition ; future, or to a day, when it will become a pure obligation at a fixed date or on the occurrence of an event which is certain to happen ; conditional or contingent when its enforceability is dependent on an event which may not happen.[3] A debt instantly and unconditionally payable is a pure obligation. A debt which, though not presently exigible, is dependent on no other condition than the arrival of the day of payment or the occurrence of an event which is certain to happen, *e.g.* the death of a particular person, is a future debt. Where the event, on the occurrence of which the enforceability of an obligation to pay depends, may or may not happen, it is a contingent or conditional debt.

A contingent obligation may be of two kinds. When the obligation does not become exigible until the occurrence of

[1] Morrison *v.* Abernethy School Board, 1876, 3 R. 945.
[2] Fenwick *v.* Macdonald, Fraser & Co., 1904, 6 F. 850.
[3] Bell's Prin., § 53.

an uncertain event, the condition is suspensive, otherwise called a condition precedent, as in sale where there is an agreement to sell but the sale is suspended until the price is paid. Where, on the other hand, the obligation though presently exigible may cease to be so on the occurrence of an uncertain event before it is exacted, it is resolutive. In each case it is a question of the construction of the particular contract which it is.

Another classification of conditions is that of potestative, casual, and mixed. A condition is potestative where its purifying depends on the action of one party to the contract. If that party is the debtor in the obligation there is an implied obligation on him not to oppose any obstacle to its being purified, and if he does it will be held to be purified. In some cases he may be even bound to promote fulfilment, but not usually. A casual condition is one the fulfilment of which depends on chance or on the action of a third party. A mixed condition is one which depends on the combined action of one of the parties and an external agency.

Implied Conditions.—Conditions may be express or implied. Where a contract is of a well-known and usual nature the Courts will read into it as implied therein the conditions or obligations recognised by law as incident thereto, and conditions may be supplied by custom or previous similar contracts between the parties.[1] Such implied conditions may be negatived by express conditions. But where the contract is constituted by performance of the act called for or acceptance is in general terms the acceptor is not bound by special terms or conditions unless he knew or had reasonable means of knowing them. Thus, where a ticket is issued by a railway company for left luggage containing conditions limiting its liability at common law, it must give adequate notice of the special condition, as by a reference on the face of the ticket to conditions which are on the back.[2]

Joint and Several Obligations.—There may be several debtors in an obligation and there may be several creditors.

---

[1] Sale of Goods Act, 1893, § 8.

[2] Lyons *v.* Caledonian Railway Co., 1909 S.C. 1185 ; Henderson *v.* Stevenson, 1873, 1 R. 215 ; affd. 1875, 2 R. (H.L.) 71.

In such cases each debtor may be liable only *pro rata, i.e.* in a share of the obligation, and each creditor may have only the right to exact a share. Where each debtor may be made to fulfil the whole obligation each is said to be liable *in solidum,* and debtors bound " conjunctly and severally " are said to be liable *singuli in solidum.* Likewise where each creditor can exact the whole from the debtor his right is *in solidum.* Unless otherwise provided in the contract the general rule is that the rights and liabilities are *pro rata.*

In certain contracts liability *in solidum* is implied. Thus, co-acceptors in a bill of exchange and all other parties liable as drawers or endorsers are liable conjunctly and severally to a holder.[1] Each partner of a firm is jointly and severally liable for all the obligations of a firm incurred while he is partner.[2] Several persons who join in contracting for a common object are presumed to be conjunctly and severally bound in any resulting liability, as where several proprietors employed a tradesman to build a bridge.[3] And where the obligation is *ad factum præstandum, i.e.* to do something, as distinct from paying money, there is an implication of joint and several liability to perform or to pay damages.

Where there are joint creditors a discharge by one is good against the rest, and probably a decree of absolvitor against one creditor, where the question at issue was the validity of the claim, would be *res judicata* against the rest.[4] Co-obligants have, as a rule, a right of relief against each other for the other's share of a debt paid, and, accordingly, if a creditor frees one of the co-obligants from his liability, the other obligants if primarily or equally liable are freed also, unless the creditor in accepting payment expressly reserves his right against the others, in respect that, and to the extent to which, their right of relief is thereby prejudiced.[5]

(*b*) **Interpretation of Particular Terms of Contracts.**—In construing a contract the object is to ascertain the intention of the parties. Where the contract is in writing that intention is to be ascertained from the terms used, looking to the whole

[1] Bills of Exchange Act, 1882, § 85.
[2] Partnership Act, 1890, § 9.
[3] French *v.* Earl of Galloway, 1730, M. 14706.
[4] Gloag on Contract, 2nd ed., p. 204 ; Allen *v.* M'Combie's Trs., 1909 S.C. 710.
[5] Morgan *v.* Smart, 1872, 10 M. 610.

contract. As a rule it is not competent to go outside the writing for extrinsic evidence of what the parties intended. In certain circumstances that may be permitted.[1]

In construing the terms of a contract the general rule is that ordinary words are to be taken as used in their ordinary meaning if there is nothing in the context or the rest of the contract to imply the contrary.[2] Conversely, technical terms are to be given their technical sense, with the aid, if necessary, of extrinsic evidence thereasto.

Where an ambiguous expression is used it is construed *contra proferentem*, that is, against the interest of the party who used it, as where a contract is dictated in detail by one party and accepted in general terms by the other, *e.g.* in insurance policies the construction favourable to the insured is taken,[3] and similarly in a prospectus in a question with the promoters of a company,[4] or of a private Act of Parliament.[5] The principle has been held not to extend to informal guarantees *in re mercatoria*.

Another principle is that of two possible constructions the Court will generally prefer that which makes a contract, as against one which will deprive it of operative effect. If the language is very vague the Court may decide that the contract cannot be enforced.

An important rule of construction is that of *ejusdem generis*, that is, where a list of things is followed by general words such as " or any other " the general words are limited in meaning to things of the same class as those in the preceding list.[6] But the things enumerated must all be of the same *genus* or description. The general words may be so general as to exclude the principle, such as " all whatever."

Where particular cases are provided for by a contract without any general or inclusive words there is a presumption that similar cases not expressly provided for are excluded, on the principle *expressio unius est exclusio alterius*.

---

[1] *See* Proof, *infra*, p. 42.
[2] *See* Lord Wensleydale in Grey *v.* Pearson, (1857) 6 H.L.C. 61 at p. 106.
[3] Hunter *v.* General Accident, etc. Assurance Corporation, 1909 S.C. 344 ; affd. 1909 S.C. (H.L.) 30.
[4] Gluckstein *v.* Barnes, [1900] A.C. 240.
[5] Colquhoun *v.* Glasgow Procurators' Widows' Fund, 1908 S.C. (H.L.) 10.
[6] Ersk., iii. 4, 9.

(*c*) **Proof in Questions of Construction.**—The general rule is that the language used is alone to be looked to, but in certain circumstances it gives way and extrinsic evidence is allowed to explain or contradict the terms of the written contract.

Where a formal deed has been executed, not merely parole evidence of the intention of the parties, but of all prior communings between the parties, is excluded. The general rule excluding extrinsic evidence applies to all conditions which the law would imply in the absence of express stipulation by the parties. Further, it is incompetent to prove a verbal agreement to add to the terms of a written contract, though not contradictory of its terms express or implied. But in some cases such evidence has been allowed, as where the writing was merely a document *in re mercatoria*.

Where an ambiguous term is used extrinsic evidence is not admissible to explain it, if patent, *i.e.* obviously ambiguous from the context. The document must be construed as best can be. But where the ambiguity is latent, *i.e.* only disclosed by the surrounding circumstances, such evidence is admissible, for example as to the identity of the parties or the subject-matter of the contract.[1]

It is always competent to lead evidence as to the circumstances surrounding the parties at the time the contract was made,[2] but not, as a rule, as to their actings during the operation of the contract as evidence of their intention. And where something depends on the extent of the knowledge of parties at the time of entering into the contract, evidence is admissible.[3]

Extrinsic evidence is necessarily admitted where a reference to the oath of the defender or a proof by his writ subsequent to the contract [4] is permissible, for these if successful amount to an admission by defender of pursuer's case. The Court can then take evidence as to what the real bargain was.

Again, extrinsic evidence is allowed where the question

[1] Robertson's Tr. *v.* Riddell, 1911 S.C. 14 ; Macdonald *v.* Newall, 1898, 1 F. 68.
[2] Bank of Scotland *v.* Stewart, 1891, 18 R. 957, per Lord President Inglis at p. 960.
[3] Jacobs *v.* Scott & Co., 1899, 2 F. (H.L.) 70.
[4] Stewart *v.* Clark, 1871, 9 M. 616.

of the intention of the parties is with or between third parties who have an interest to prove what the real intention was, as, for instance, to prove that a transaction in the form of a sale was really by way of security.[1]

Another and important exception to the rule excluding extrinsic evidence is where a custom of trade is allowed to be proved where circumstances arise for which the parties have made no express provision, or to add an unexpressed condition or to give words a meaning they do not naturally bear. This would apply to the effect of varying the incidents which the law ordinarily applies to the contract.[2] The custom of trade must, however, be lawful and not contrary to the general law of the country. It must be known to the parties, or at least notorious, and it must be reasonably fair. A custom of trade cannot be used to contradict the express and unambiguous terms of a contract.[3]

Lastly, parole evidence is allowed by statute in the case of bills of exchange, promissory notes and cheques relevant to any question of liability thereon [4] other than payment,[5] and in the case of proof of trust, proof by writ or oath of the defender.[6]

Proof of the alteration of a written contract by subsequent verbal agreement cannot be by parole evidence, unless of actings following upon it amounting to *rei interventus* and clearly inconsistent with the written contract,[7] but may by writ or oath of the opponent.

6. Assignation of Contracts.—(*a*) **Definition.**—The assignation of an obligation means the transfer of the rights of a creditor in the obligation to a third party. The granter of an assignation is called the cedent, the grantee the assignee or cessionary. When the assignee transfers the right to a third party the deed is termed a translation, and when the assignee reassigns to the cedent the deed is termed a retrocession. Assignations include translations and retrocessions.[8]

---

[1] Sale of Goods Act, 1893, § 61 (4); Rennet *v.* Mathieson, 1903, 5 F. 591; Gavin's Tr. *v.* Fraser, 1920 S.C. 674.

[2] Bell's Comm., i. 457; Sale of Goods Act, 1893, § 55.

[3] The *Turid*, (1922) 38 T.L.R. 423.

[4] Bills of Exchange Act, 1882, § 100.

[5] Robertson *v.* Thomson, 1900, 3 F. 5.

[6] Trusts (Scotland) Act, 1696.

[7] Lavan *v.* Gavin Aird & Co., 1919 S.C. 345.

[8] The Transmission of Moveable Property Act, 1862.

An assignation in some cases requires to be in the form of a deed, in others not.

(*b*) **Form of Deed.**—The Transmission of Moveable Property Act, 1862, introduced a form of assignation which may be used by any person in right of a bond or of a conveyance of moveable estate, and a form which may be written on the bond or conveyance itself. Bonds in this connection include personal bonds of every kind, decrees of Court, policies of assurance, protests of bills or promissory notes and assignations. Moveable estate includes all personal debts and obligations and moveable or personal property or effects of every kind. The form simply states the consideration and assigns the bond or other deed described.

(*c*) **How Transfer completed.**—**By Assignation in Writing and Intimation.**—Intimation of the assignment to the holder of property transferred or the debtor in the obligation is necessary to complete the transfer of the property or rights from assignor to assignee. Such intimation has the effect both of divesting the old creditor of his right and of putting the debtor under the duty of paying to the new creditor in place of the old.

The most formal method of intimation is proper notarial intimation attested by notarial instruments. Formal intimation may be made [1] (1) by a notary delivering a certified copy of the deed to the debtor in presence of two witnesses, the evidence of which is a certificate to that effect in statutory form ; and (2) by the holder of the assignation, or anyone authorised by him, transmitting a copy by post, certified as correct, a written acknowledgment of the receipt of the copy being evidence of intimation. Anything, however, which brings home to the debtor a distinct knowledge of the assignation is equivalent. Thus, a charge upon a bond at the instance of the assignee or citation of the debtor in an action for payment is equivalent. So also any act of the debtor undertaking to pay or acknowledging the debt to the assignee, or paying interest to the assignee. But mere private knowledge, though it may put the debtor in bad faith in a question with the assignee, is not equivalent to intimation in competition with other properly completed assignations, legal or voluntary— that is, in a question between assignees. And there is a class of assignations, namely, legal and judicial, which, being themselves public, require no intimation in order to give them priority over other assignations of the same right, such as the act and warrant of the

[1] The Transmission of Moveable Property Act, 1862.

trustee in a sequestration. In this class of assignation intimation is still necessary to prevent the debtor paying to the former creditor.

By Delivery.—Writing is not in all cases required for a valid assignation. Thus, in the case of corporeal moveables and certain classes of debts the right to which runs with the voucher, as bank notes, bills payable to bearer or bills blank endorsed, transfer, whether by way of sale or security, is complete by mere delivery. It is otherwise, and writing and intimation are required, if corporeal moveables are in the hands of a third party, and in some cases where statute law requires a written transfer, as in the case of ships and patent rights.

By Indorsation and Delivery.—In certain cases the law merchant, for the convenience of traders, recognises indorsation as an equivalent to a deed of assignation. That is so in the case of a bill of exchange payable to order, a promissory note, a cheque and a bill of lading, these being negotiable documents. Where the obligation therein contained is transferred by mere indorsation and delivery, intimation is not required.

By Transfer of Document of Title.—A " document of title " is defined by the Factors Acts and Sale of Goods Act to include any bill of lading, dock warrant, warehouse-keeper's certificate, and warrant or order for delivery of goods, and any other document used in the ordinary course of business as proof of the possession or control of goods, or authorising or purporting to authorise, either by indorsement or delivery, the possessor of the document to transfer or receive the goods thereby represented.[1]

Where goods are represented by a document of title the transfer of the document coupled with intimation completes the assignation. Transfer without intimation is, however, enough in the case of a bill of lading. The transfer may be by indorsement, or where the document is by custom or by its express terms transferable by delivery, or makes the goods deliverable to bearer, then by delivery.[2] Intimation is necessary, except, as above noted, in the case of a bill of lading, in order to complete the right of the transferee.[3]

(*d*) **What Contracts are Assignable.**—Not all contracts are assignable. It is settled that a claim for payment of money is assignable.

---

[1] Factors Acts, 1889, § 4 ; 1890, § 1 ; Sale of Goods Act, 1893, § 62.

[2] Factors Acts, 1889, § 5 ; 1890, § 1.

[3] Connal & Co. *v.* Loder & Ors., 1868, 6 M. 1095, per Lord Justice-Clerk Inglis at p. 1110. Intimation to the custodier is probably not necessary in the case of pledge of documents of title to goods by a mercantile agent (Factors Act, 1889, § 3 ; Inglis *v.* Robertson & Baxter, 1898, 25 R. (H.L.) 701). .

Contracts involving mutual obligations, other than payment for goods or services rendered, are generally unassignable.[1] But where a contract involves obligations other than payment of money the question of assignability depends generally upon whether the obligations involve an element of *delectus personæ*—that is, when the personality of the contracting party may be of importance.[2] Thus, while a partner in a firm may assign his rights in the firm he cannot make the assignee a partner.[3]

The question of whether there is *delectus personæ* arises sharply in the case of executorial contracts, *i.e.* contracts containing obligations to do or not to do something, as distinct from obligations which are immediately performed as in a sale over the counter. Thus, there is *delectus personæ*, and therefore no assignability, where the contract is for personal services involving literary, artistic, or professional skill.[4] A servant cannot be transferred, without his consent, to the employment of a party he has not agreed to serve.[5] On the other hand, a contract for the execution of work to be done through the instrumentality of ordinary labourers involves no element of *delectus personæ*, and the contractor may validly assign the performance of the contract to another, but will not, therefore, free himself from liability if the contract is not performed.[6] It is a question of the intention of the parties whether both rights and liabilities may pass to an assignee. Where no *delectus personæ* is present a contracting party may undoubtedly get others to perform the services contracted for without assigning the contract.[7] And where the death of a party to an obligation takes place, his personal representatives, while liable on his contracts to the extent of the deceased's estate, are not liable for personal services undertaken by him. Where the assignation is by operation of law, as in bankruptcy, the trustee cannot carry out contracts in which the personal qualities of the bankrupt were relied on.[8]

---

[1] Kemp *v.* Baerselman, [1906] 2 K.B. 604; Grierson, Oldham & Co., Ltd. *v.* Forbes, Maxwell & Co., 1895, 22 R. 812; International Fibre Syndicate *v.* Dawson, 1901, 3 F. (H.L.) 32.

[2] Boulton *v.* Jones, (1857) 2 H. & N. 564; Cole *v.* Handasyde & Co., 1910 S.C. 68 at p. 70.

[3] Partnership Act, 1890, § 31.

[4] Cole *v.* Handasyde & Co., *supra*, per Lord President Dunedin at p. 73.

[5] Berlitz School of Languages *v.* Duchene, 1903, 6 F. 181.

[6] Shanks' Exrs. *v.* Aberdeen Railway Co., 1850, 12 D. 781.

[7] Stevenson & Sons *v.* Maule & Son, 1920 S.C. 335.

[8] Anderson *v.* Hamilton & Co., 1875, 2 R. 355, per Lord Neaves; Caldwell *v.* Hamilton, 1919 S.C. (H.L.) 100.

(e) **Effect of Assignation.**—Where a contract involving a personal obligation is validly assigned the general rule is expressed in the legal maxim *assignatus utitur jure auctoris*—an assignee exercises the right of his cedent. The assignee has all the rights of action which the cedent had under the contract, and the debtor may plead against the assignee any defence which was available against the cedent at the time the assignation was intimated.[1] Thus if the cedent was in breach of a material condition of the contract, and so could not enforce the obligation which he assigns, the assignee has no higher right. If the debtor had a good plea of compensation against the cedent at the time of intimation of the assignation it would remain open to him against the assignee. And if the contract were reducible in a question with the cedent on the ground of misrepresentation, fraud, etc., it remains so reducible in the hands of the assignee. Thus an insurance company may reduce the policy on the ground of misstatement by the assured in his declaration, though the policy has been sold to a *bona fide* purchaser.[2]

The debtor may, however, be barred from pleading against the assignee a defence open to him against the cedent, as where the terms of intimation of the assignation show that the assignee relies on the apparent right and the debtor takes no exception,[3] or the debtor, knowing he has a defence, makes payments to the assignee.

Again, where the obligation is contained in a negotiable instrument the maxim does not apply, for a *bona fide* holder for value of such an instrument holds it free from any defects in title of a prior party to the bill.[4] This element of negotiability may be present not only in the case of bills of exchange, promissory notes, and cheques during their currency, but also in bills of lading and transferable bonds and debentures.

7. Extinction of Contractual Obligations.—A contractual obligation may be extinguished by (1) performance, or payment and discharge by certain equivalents, namely, (2) novation, (3) delegation, (4) confusion, and (5) compensation ; by (6) prescription ; (7) impossibility of performance, and (8) breach of the contract.

(1) Performance, Payment and Discharge.—**Performance.**—When

---

[1] Bell's Prin., § 1468.
[2] Scottish Equitable Life Assurance Co. *v.* Buist, 1877, 4 R. 1076 ; affd. 1878, 5 R. (H.L.) 64.
[3] Mangles *v.* Dixon, (1852) 3 H.L.C. 702, per Lord St Leonards, L.C.
[4] Bills of Exchange Act, 1882, § 29 (1) (b).

a contractual obligation has been fully performed it is, of course, at an end.

Payment and Discharge.—The obligation of a debtor to pay a debt which has become due is extinguished when he has made or tendered payment to the creditor in the appropriate manner and at the proper place. When payment is so tendered it is the duty of the creditor to accept payment.

(*a*) **Duty of Debtor to Tender Payment.**—When a debt is actually due and exigible it is the duty of the debtor to tender payment. Accordingly a party who has sold and delivered goods would be entitled, unless a period of credit is provided either expressly or by the custom of the particular trade, to raise an immediate action for the price. This he would be entitled to do without even sending in an account or making a demand for payment, although such a course is not usually to be recommended. On the other hand he may not. If, for instance, a bill of exchange for the amount of a debt has been accepted by the debtor, while there is an implied obligation on him to make payment on the day when the bill is payable, it is not dishonoured and cannot be sued upon until presented for payment.[1]

Method of Payment.—A debtor is not discharged of his obligation to pay unless he tenders payment in the appropriate manner. Thus, if a debtor disregards a stipulation by a creditor for a particular method of payment or if he adopts some method of payment not in the ordinary course of business and affording facilities for fraud, *e.g.* a cheque to bearer,[2] or a cheque sent by post, he takes the risk of his remittance being lost or stolen.[3] If there is no express provision to the contrary a creditor is within his rights in refusing to accept an offer of payment in any other form than legal tender, that is, gold coin of the realm or treasury notes and notes of the Bank of England up to any amount, silver up to forty shillings, and bronze up to one shilling.[4] But if a cheque is sent, the creditor, if he does not mean to accept it, must return it at once, otherwise he will be held to have accepted payment.[5] When payment by bill or cheque is accepted, however, it operates merely conditional

---

[1] Bills of Exchange Act, 1882, §§ 46, 47.

[2] Robb *v.* Gow Bros. & Gemmell, 1905, 8 F. 90.

[3] Pennington *v.* Crossley & Sons, Ltd., (1897) 13 T.L.R. 513.

[4] Glasgow Pavilion, Ltd. *v.* Motherwell, 1903, 6 F. 116, per Lord Young; Currency and Bank Notes Act, 1928, § 1.

[5] Pollock *v.* Goodwin's Trs., 1898, 25 R. 1051.

payment, the condition being that the cheque is honoured. The condition is resolutive and the debt is extinguished, but it revives if the cheque be not honoured.[1] But if the creditor who has accepted a cheque fails to present it for payment within a reasonable time, with resulting loss to the debtor, the debt is held to be discharged to the extent of such loss,[2] as, for instance, should the bank fail in the interval.

Place of Payment.—The legal implication is that the debtor is bound and entitled to tender payment to the creditor at his residence or place of business.[3] In the absence of arrangement to the contrary, any expenses resulting from payment elsewhere than at the creditor's residence fall upon the debtor, e.g. a difference in exchange.[4]

(b) **Obligation of Creditor to Accept Payment.**—It is the duty of a creditor to accept payment when offered. But, while he may agree to accept payment by instalments, he is not bound to accept partial payment.[5] Further, he is under no obligation to receive payment before it is due. And a creditor who is taking no active steps to enforce his debt is under no obligation to accept an offer of payment made by anyone but the debtor, or someone having his authority.[6] But if he is taking measures to enforce payment or to realise securities, he is bound to accept payment by, and to grant an assignation to, anyone who can show an interest to intervene, such as a friend of the debtor.[7] And a co-obligant who has paid the debt, or more than his proportionate share, is entitled to claim from the creditor an assignation of the debt, any securities held for it and any diligence that may have been done on it, to enable him to work out his relief against his co-obligants.[8] This only applies, however, where he has paid the debt to the creditor in full.[9]

(c) **Appropriation of Payments.—Ascription by Debtor.**—When a debtor owes more than one debt to the same creditor he is entitled on making a payment to ascribe it to any one or more of the debts which may suit him, and a creditor who has received a payment ascribed by instructions of the debtor to a particular debt has no

[1] Leggatt Bros. v. Gray, 1908 S.C. 67.
[2] Bills of Exchange Act, 1882, § 74 ; Hopkins v. Ware, (1869) L.R. 4 Ex. 268.
[3] Haughhead Coal Co. v. Gallocher, 1903, 11 S.L.T. 156.
[4] Shrewsbury v. Shrewsbury, (1907) 23 T.L.R. 277.
[5] Wilson's Trs. v. Watson & Co., 1900, 2 F. 761, per Lord Moncreiff at p. 770.
[6] Smith v. Gentle, 1844, 6 D. 1164, per Lord Mackenzie.
[7] Ibid.
[8] Fleming v. Burgess, 1867, 5 M. 856.
[9] Ewart v. Latta, 1865, 3 M. (H.L.) 36.

right to apply the payment to meet some other liability of the debtor to him.[1] A creditor may, however, decline to accept payment of principal when interest is due and unpaid. Thus, if there is only one debt, with arrears of interest, and the debtor, in making a remittance, ascribes it to part payment of the principal, this is not a proposal which the creditor is bound to accede to, but if he keeps the money he must apply it in accordance with the debtor's instructions.[2] Where money is sent, either by someone on behalf of the debtor, as a compromise in settlement of the whole debt, the creditor has no right to take it as part payment, and, if he keeps the money, the inference will be that he has agreed to the proposed compromise, and that the debt is discharged.[3]

Unappropriated Payments.—Rights of Creditor.—If a debtor makes a payment without any direction or previous agreement as to the debt to which it is to be ascribed, he impliedly leaves it to the creditor to ascribe it as he pleases.[4] Accordingly the intention of the creditor, express, implied, or presumed, governs the application of the money.[5] Thus he may ascribe it to an unsecured debt, leaving a debt for which he holds a security unpaid. This he may do in a question not merely with the debtor himself, but, for instance, with a cautioner for the debtor.[6] He may ascribe it to interest, leaving principal unpaid.[7] Again the creditor may ascribe indefinite payments to a debt which does not bear interest, rather than to a debt which does.[8] But indefinite payments cannot be ascribed by the creditor to a debt in which the party who made them is merely a cautioner in preference to one in which he is principal debtor,[9] to a debt which is known to be disputed,[10] to a debt of which the debtor was unaware,[11] to a debt which, under statutory provisions, cannot be enforced,[12] nor contrary to general understanding between the parties.[13] The creditor may render

[1] Bell's Prin., § 563 ; Brenes & Co. v. Downie, 1914 S.C. 97.
[2] Wilson's Trs. v. Watson & Co., 1900, 2 F. 761, per Lord Moncreiff.
[3] Punamchand v. Temple, [1911] 2 K.B. 330.
[4] Jackson v. Nicoll, 1870, 8 M. 408.
[5] Long Bros. v. Owners of the *Mecca*, [1897] A.C. 286 ; Deeley v. Lloyds Bank, Ltd., [1912] A.C. 756.
[6] Anderson v. North of Scotland and Town and County Bank, 1909, 2 S.L.T. 262.
[7] Watt v. Burnett's Trs., 1839, 2 D. 132.
[8] Bremner v. Mabon, 1837, 16 S. 213.
[9] Dickson v. Moncrieff, 1853, 16 D. 24.
[10] Dougall v. Lornie, 1899, 1 F. 1187.
[11] Couper v. Young, 1849, 12 D. 190.
[12] Maitland v. Rattray, 1848, 11 D. 71.
[13] Scott v. Sandeman, 1851, 1 Macq. 293.

an account containing separate items of debt without making any appropriation, without barring himself from appropriation afterwards.[1]

Where there is an account current on which payments are made without any appropriation by the debtor, the general rule, at least between banker and customer, is that payments on the credit side of an account are held to extinguish the items on the debit side in the order of their date. This is known as the rule in Clayton's case.[2] The rule probably only applies to accounts between banker and customer or where the account substantially involves the relation of banker and customer between the parties.[3] It does not apply to separate accounts kept at a bank.[4] It does not apply to a tradesman's account where partial payments have been made but the element of advances made by the creditor is absent.[5]

(d) **Proof of Payment.**—Where no receipt or discharge can be produced to prove the extinction of a debt the general rule, to which, however, there are numerous exceptions, is that the extinction of the claim must be effected in the same way as it was constituted. A debt may be one which is constituted or proved by a document, or it may be one which, without being so constituted, is sued for as the result of a contract between the parties, or it may have been constituted verbally.

Where the creditor founds on a document of debt, e.g. a bond, bill, or I.O.U., proof of payment is limited to the writ, such as a discharge or receipt, or to the oath of the creditor.[6] But proof by parole evidence may be allowed of grounds for holding the debt to be extinguished in other ways than by actual payment, and that the creditor has no proper right to have the document of debt with him [7]; for example, evidence of some transaction or settlement between the creditor and the debtor subsequent to contraction of the debt which necessarily leads to the conclusion that the debt was discharged,[8] such as a settlement of accounts, followed by a discharge in general terms.[9]

---

[1] Hay & Co. v. Tarbet, 1908 S.C. 781.
[2] Devaynes v. Noble, 3 Ross' Leading Cases, 643 at p. 654 ; cf. Royal Bank v. Christie, 1838, 1 D. 745 ; affd. 1841, 2 Rob. 118 ; Deeley v. Lloyds Bank, Ltd., [1916] A.C. 756.
[3] M'Laren v. Bradley, 1874, 2 R. 185.
[4] Bradford Old Bank v. Sutcliffe, [1918] 2 K.B. 833.
[5] Hay & Co. v. Tarbet, supra.
[6] Bishop v. Bryce, 1910 S.C. 426 ; vide Reference to Oath, infra, p. 60.
[7] Bishop v. Bryce, supra.
[8] Chrystal v. Chrystal, 1900, 2 F. 373.
[9] Neilson's Trs. v. Neilson's Trs., 1883, 11 R. 119.

Where the money debt arose under a contract *ad factum præstandum*, *e.g.* to supply goods or render services, if the contract was in writing proof of the payment of money becoming due under it must be by writ or oath of the creditor.[1]

If the debt has arisen under a verbal contract the method of proof of payment depends on the nature of the contract. Thus parole evidence is admissible to prove payment of a loan which is not vouched by any writing,[2] and of wages due under a verbal contract of service, at least if under £100 Scots (£8, 6s. 8d.).[3] But where there has been a substantial interval between the delivery of goods and the alleged payment, or if the sale was on credit, proof is limited to the writ or oath of the seller, even although the sale was purely verbal.[4]

Proof of Payment by Writ of the Creditor.—Where a debtor proposes to prove payment by the writ of the creditor, the writ produced need not be probative.[5] A receipted account, however, only lays the onus of proof of non-payment on the creditor, and such proof may be by parole evidence.[6] But where an acknowledgment of the receipt of money has been made in a formal and probative deed, such as acknowledgment of the receipt of the price in a disposition of lands, the creditor is limited to proof by the writ or oath of the party founding on it, *i.e.* the debtor.[7] Where, however, a creditor avers that his acknowledgment has been obtained by fraud he may prove the averments by parole evidence.

The meaning of a discharge must be arrived at by a consideration of its terms, and parole evidence of the intention of the party who granted it is incompetent.[8] Fitted accounts, *i.e.* accounts between parties who have had business transactions, rendered by one party and docqueted as correct by the other without any express discharge, raise a presumption, which the party who avers an outstanding account must overcome, that all claims were settled.[9] But a general discharge is not binding, if granted on a specific payment when both parties were unaware that any further claim

---

[1] Foggo *v.* Hill, 1840, 2 D. 1322, per Lord Fullerton at p. 1334.
[2] Newlands *v.* M'Kinlay, 1885, 13 R. 353.
[3] Brown *v.* Mason, 1856, 19 D. 137.
[4] Young *v.* Thomson, 1909 S.C. 529.
[5] Paterson *v.* Paterson, 1897, 25 R. 144.
[6] Henry *v.* Miller, 1884, 11 R. 713.
[7] Grant's Trs. *v.* Morison, 1875, 2 R. 377, per Lord President Inglis at p. 380.
[8] M'Taggart *v.* Jeffrey, 1830, 4 W. & S. 361, per Lord Wynford at p. 367.
[9] Struthers *v.* Smith, 1913 S.C. 1116.

was maintainable. A bank passbook made up and initialed by the officers of the bank as correct does not preclude parole evidence that a particular entry has been made by mistake.[1]

Presumption of Payment.—Certain debts are presumed to be paid, so as to put the onus of proof of non-payment on the creditor, e.g. tavern bills, after the guest has left.[2] The production of receipts for three consecutive instalments of a termly payment, such as feu-duty, rent, or interest, raises a presumption (*apocha trium annorum*) that all prior instalments have been paid. The presumption of payment is mainly inferred from the reiteration of discharges without reservation of the creditor's claim to prior unpaid instalments, which no prudent man is presumed to do, not from a single discharge for the amount due for several terms.[3]

If a document of debt is in the hands of the debtor, although *ex facie* undischarged, the debt is presumed to be paid, as expressed in the legal maxim *chirographum apud debitorem repertum præsumitur solutum*. But the creditor may prove by parole evidence that the document got into the hands of the debtor by mistake, or by some method which gives him no right to retain it, and that the debt has not in fact been paid.[4]

The proof of payment may also be affected by the operation of one or other of the shorter prescriptions.[5]

(2) Novation.—A debt, though not expressly discharged, may be extinguished by novation when a new obligation by the same debtor is substituted for it. If a debt for which a new debt is substituted is regularly discharged no claim can be founded upon it, in the absence of any grounds for impeaching the validity of the discharge.[6] The general presumption, however, is that if there is no discharge, but a new obligation is undertaken, the original obligation is not extinguished, and the new one is to be regarded as a security for it, or as the addition of a more convenient way of enforcing payment.[7] Thus where one document of debt is given in place of another, as where a bill is renewed, or a new promissory note given for one in danger of prescribing, but the original document is not given up or

---

[1] Commercial Bank of Scotland v. Rhind, 1857, 19 D. 519 ; revd. 3 Macq. 643.
[2] Barnet v. Colvil & Henderson, 1840, 2 D. 337.
[3] Dickson, Evidence, § 177.
[4] Henry v. Miller, 1884, 11 R. 713.
[5] *Vide* Prescription, p. 56 *et seq.*
[6] Jackson v. MacDiarmid, 1892, 19 R. 528.
[7] Anderson v. M'Dowal, 1865, 3 M. 727.

cancelled, the presumption is that any rights depending upon it are still preserved. So where several parties are liable on a bill, and a new bill for the same debt is granted by one or more of them, but the old bill is retained by the creditor, those who are parties to the old bill may be made liable on it in the event of the new bill not being met, and if the granters of the new bill have paid it, the others are liable in relief to them.[1] It is probably competent to prove by parole evidence that the arrangement was that the original debt, with all claims depending upon it, was given up.[2] But where a bill or note is given up, on a new one being granted, this does not raise any presumption that a claim for interest arising *ex lege* on the original document is abandoned.[3] And when a document of an obligatory character, such as a bill or cheque, is given for a debt resting upon open account, as distinguished from one where the balance between the parties has been agreed upon, the presumption is strongly against novation. Hence a bill or cheque, unless paid at maturity, does not extinguish the debt for which it is taken.[4] The principle of novation applies to other obligations besides payment of a money debt, but is best illustrated by the latter.

(3) **Delegation of Debt.**—A debt, though not expressly discharged, may be extinguished by delegation when the obligation of a new party is substituted for that of the original debtor. Delegation is a form of novation. There is a strong presumption against delegation.[5] It is not as a general rule in the option of a debtor to substitute the obligation of another party, who may be a person of no means, for his own.[6] The consent of the creditor must in some way be obtained. It may be given at the time when the obligation was constituted, or a custom of trade may create an implied condition that delegation is permitted.[7] When consent is not given at the time when the obligation is constituted, the debtor must prove that the creditor assented to his discharge. The consent is not to be inferred merely from the fact that the creditor accepts a new obligant. *Prima facie* he is accepted as a further security. Thus when a partner in a firm retires, and the business is carried on by the remaining partners

---

[1] Stevenson v. Campbell, 1806, Hume 247.
[2] Hope Johnstone v. Cornwall, 1895, 22 R. 314.　　　　[3] *Ibid.*
[4] Leggatt Brothers v. Gray, 1908 S.C. 67.
[5] M'Intosh & Son v. Ainslie, 1872, 10 M. 304, per Lord President Inglis at p. 309.
[6] University of Glasgow v. Yuill's Trs., 1882, 9 R. 643.
[7] North v. Basset, [1892] 1 Q.B. 333.

without the introduction of a new one, it will not be presumed that a creditor of the original firm has voluntarily given up the liability of a retiring partner for a debt due by the firm at the time he retired and accepted the liability of the firm as newly constituted in substitution for his original claim. But where a creditor who is in possession of a document of debt gives it up, at the same time obtaining the obligation of a new debtor, there is a presumption that the real agreement between the parties was that the liability under the original document of debt is discharged.[1]

(4) Confusion.—Confusion arises where the same person comes to be both debtor and creditor under the obligation. Thus where the right of a creditor in a debt is assigned to the debtor, or the creditor undertakes liability on the debt, the debt is said to be extinguished *confusione*, for no person can be creditor or debtor to himself.[2] The fusion of creditor and debtor may also arise where the debtor succeeds to his creditor. Confusion only operates, however, where a party becomes both debtor and creditor in the same capacity. If, for example, the debtor becomes the executor of his creditor on the latter's death, the debt is not extinguished. If the debtor is not the primary obligant, but is, for example, merely a cautioner and becomes the creditor, the debt is not necessarily extinguished by confusion. It may be enforced against the principal debtor.[3]

(5) Compensation.—Compensation is the term used in Scotland for the right to set one claim off against another, with the result that if equal in amount both are extinguished ; if not equal, that the larger claim is extinguished *pro tanto*.

The law of compensation is founded on the Act 1592, c. 143, which in effect provides that compensation operates only by way of exception. That is to say, compensation does not, *ipso facto*, extinguish a debt. To have that effect it must be pleaded in an action. Accordingly, a debt which might have been extinguished earlier by the fact that the debtor had a claim against the creditor, and on which compensation, if pleaded, would have been sustained, cannot in any subsequent question be regarded as having been extinguished.[4] If, therefore, a creditor will not admit a claim by the debtor to set off a debt due by the creditor to him, the only course for the debtor is to refuse payment, and so compel the creditor to bring an action for the debt, in which compensation can be pleaded.

---

[1] Stevenson *v.* Lord Duncan, 1805, Hume 245.
[2] Ersk., iii. 4, 23.
[3] *Ibid.*, iii. 4, 24.
[4] Bell's Prin., § 575.

Requisites of Compensation.—(*a*) The debtor must plead compensation before a decree against him for the debt. Otherwise he will have to sue for it in a special action. (*b*) In a pure question of compensation arising between parties who are both solvent, the debts in respect of which compensation is pleaded must be both liquid, that is, actually due and the amount ascertained.[1] Thus a debt not yet payable by the pursuer, or on which his liability is only contingent,[2] or a claim of damages arising from a separate contract or other relations between the debtor and creditor, or a claim which is disputed, unless instantly verifiable, cannot relevantly be pleaded in defence to an action for payment. (*c*) There must be *concursus debiti et crediti*, *i.e.* the parties must be debtor and creditor in the same legal capacity and at the same time. Thus a party sued for a private debt could not set off a debt due to him as an executor.[3] On the other hand, the death of a party and the confirmation of his executor do not affect rights of compensation.[4] The *concursus* must have existed before bankruptcy of either party, and the plea must not be inconsistent with the good faith of the contract under which the claim arose. When compensation is pleaded and sustained it dates back to the period when the concourse of debtor and creditor took place, with the result that no interest is due *ex lege* from that date, even though the debt was not originally liquid, and therefore not pleadable during part of the period of concourse. In short, both compensation and liquidation draw back to the date of concourse.

(6) Prescription.[5]—Contractual obligations may, under the rules of prescription, be extinguished by lapse of time. On the other hand, the effect of these rules may be merely to alter the onus and method of proof. In so far as the rules of prescription relate to mercantile contracts, obligations are extinguished by the negative prescription, but the shorter prescriptions, or, more properly, limitations—the triennial, the quinquennial, the sexennial, and the vicennial—merely alter the onus or the mode of proof. The general rule in the construction of the shorter prescriptions is that they introduce no presumptions, but enact certain specific and imperative rules on the subject of probation. Only indirectly therefore can they be said to extinguish obligations.

---

[1] Bell's Comm., ii. 122.   [2] Paul & Thain *v.* Royal Bank, 1867, 7 M. 361.

[3] Stuart *v.* Stuart, 1869, 7 M. 366.

[4] Globe Insurance Co. *v.* Mackenzie, 1849, 11 D. 618 ; affd. 7 Bell's App. 296 ; Mitchell *v.* Mackersy, 1905, 8 F. 198, overruling Gray's Trs. *v.* Royal Bank, 1895, 23 R. 199.

[5] For Septennial Prescription of Cautionary Obligations, see Chap. XI.

The Negative Prescription.—Obligations prescribe, *i.e.* cease to be enforceable, after the expiry of forty years—a rule referred to as the negative prescription. It applies generally to all contractual rights and obligations except such as amount to a real right of property in lands. Thus the lapse of forty years excludes the enforcement of a right contracted for, such as an obligation to restore moveable property lent or given in security, and is a bar to the reduction of a contract even on the ground of fraud or any other extrinsic ground,[1] or to a claim of repetition of money paid by mistake.[2] On the other hand, the negative prescription does not bar the challenge of a right which can only be defended by founding on a nullity, such as a forged deed,[3] or a deed entirely unauthenticated,[4] or possession traceable to theft,[5] or on a sale of property which is *extra commercium*, and so could not have been lawfully acquired.[6] In the case of annuities, where there is no direct claim to the capital sum, the negative prescription only applies to the claim for each term's payment, in contrast to ordinary bonds where it extinguishes the principal sum, and, with it, any further claim for interest. Again, where the right is one which the creditor may exact or not at pleasure (*res meræ facultatis*), the negative prescription is excluded, *e.g.* a contractual right such as the right to alter a common stair.

The prescriptive period starts from the day when it first became possible for the creditor to enforce his right by action.[7] Thus a bond prescribes from the date of payment, not from the date of granting.[8] Where the party who has for the time being the right to enforce the claim is in minority, the years during which the minority lasts are to be deducted in reckoning the forty years. But the minority of one of a body of creditors has no effect. Years during which the creditor is unable to assert his right must also be deducted, at least where there is a legal impediment to action by the creditor,[9] not due to his own act, *e.g.* insanity, but not to cases of mere physical incapacity to sue, as where he was ignorant of his rights.[10]

[1] Cubbison *v.* Hyslop, 1837, 16 S. 112, per Lord Corehouse at p. 119.
[2] Magistrates of Edinburgh *v.* Heriot's Trust, 1900, 7 S.L.T. 371.
[3] Graham *v.* Watt, 1843, 5 D. 1368 ; affd. 1846, 5 Bell's App. 172.
[4] Kinloch *v.* Bell, 1867, 5 M. 360.
[5] Stair, ii. 12, 10.
[6] Magistrates of Dumbarton *v.* Edinburgh University, 1909, 1 S.L.T. 51.
[7] Simpson *v.* Melville, 1899, 6 S.L.T. 355.
[8] Ersk., iii. 7, 36.
[9] Bell's Prin., § 627.
[10] Buchanan *v.* Bogle, 1847, 9 D. 686.

If the running of the forty years is interrupted before it has expired, the period prior to the interruption ceases to count, as where a debtor makes a written acknowledgment of the existence of the claim, or makes payment of part of the principal sum or interest,[1] or where there is judicial interruption, such as an action against the debtor, or diligence if regularly effected,[2] or a petition by the creditor for the debtor's sequestration.

The Short Prescriptions.—The Triennial Prescription.—By the Act 1579, c. 83, all actions of debt for house maills, *i.e.* the rent of a house, men's ordinaries, *i.e.*, for example, accounts for board and lodging, servants' fees, *i.e.* wages, merchants' accounts, and other the like debts that are not founded upon written obligations, must be pursued within three years, otherwise the creditor shall have no action, except by proof by the writ or oath of the debtor. The terms of the Act have been held to cover, *inter alia*, the accounts of a law agent, architect, engineer, stockbroker, or a surgeon, but not cases of mercantile agency,[3] nor the account of insurance brokers for disbursements in respect of policies.[4] " Merchants " means shopkeepers or other persons engaged in trade analogous to that of a shopkeeper, such as builders or contractors. It does not apply generally to mercantile transactions. The general principle is that it applies to accounts between trader and consumer, not to accounts between manufacturer or producer and retailer, or between a merchant and his correspondent. There is some doubt as to whether it applies to an account for the supply of a single article.[5]

Where payments should have been made termly each separate term runs a separate course of prescription, *e.g.* servants' wages.[6] In other cases prescription runs from the close of the account between the parties,[7] when it is calculated from the date of the last item which is enforceable, even where the items vary in character.[8] Prescription begins to run on the account as soon as it is definitely closed, though a new one be opened between the same parties.[9]

The triennial prescription does not extinguish the debt. But

[1] Briggs *v.* Swan's Trs., 1854, 16 D. 385.
[2] Bell's Prin., § 621.
[3] Brown *v.* Brown, 1891, 18 R. 889 ; see Mercantile Agents, Chap. II.
[4] Lamont, Nisbett & Co. *v.* Hamilton, 1904, 12 S.L.T. 624.
[5] Millar on Prescription, p. 128 ; Gobbi *v.* Lazaroni, 1859, 21 D. 801.
[6] Douglas *v.* Duke of Argyll, 1736, M. 11102.
[7] Bell's Prin., § 631.
[8] Ross *v.* Cowie's Exrx., 1888, 16 R. 224.
[9] Christian *v.* Knowles, 1901, 3 F. 480.

whereas within the three years the onus is on the debtor to prove payment, after the three years the creditor must prove not only that the debt was incurred but that it is still resting owing, and he is limited to proof by the writ or oath of the debtor. But constitution and resting owing being established, the burden of proof of subsequent payment reverts to the debtor. The principle of interruption is not properly applicable to cases of triennial prescription. But the assertion of the debt in a legal process, even though not that in which prescription has been pleaded, excludes the prescription, e.g. where the plea was one of compensation.[1] Time during which the creditor is in minority is not deducted.

The writ of the debtor relied on to redargue the effect of the triennial prescription need not be probative,[2] or addressed to the creditor.[3] Thus an entry in the debtor's books amounting to an explicit statement of the debt is proof by his writ.[4] The writ of the debtor if adduced as proof either of constitution or of resting owing may be dated within the three years.[5] The amount of the debt may, after proof of constitution and of resting owing, be proved by parole evidence.[6]

The Quinquennial Prescription.—The quinquennial prescription, introduced by the Act 1669, c. 9, applies to rents after the tenant has left, and bargains concerning moveables provable by witnesses, i.e. verbal bargains not requiring writing for their constitution. In the case of rents it applies only after the tenant has removed, and is excluded by action or diligence within the five years.[7] In the case of bargains concerning moveables the Act applies to all sales, locations and other consensual contracts concerning moveables to the constitution of which writing is not necessary.[8] It applies to the sale of a single article.[9] In the case of the quinquennial prescription the years during which the creditor is in minority are to be deducted. After the five years proof of constitution and resting owing are limited to writ or oath of the debtor.

The Sexennial Prescription.—The sexennial prescription applies

---

[1] Sloan v. Birtwhistle, 1827, 5 S. 742 ; Millar on Prescription, p. 117.
[2] Dickson, Evidence, § 512.
[3] Wilson v. Scott, 1908, 15 S.L.T. 948.
[4] Neilson v. Magistrates of Falkirk, 1899, 2 F. 118.
[5] Johnson v. Tillie, Whyte & Co., 1917 S.C. 211.
[6] Fife v. Innes, 1860, 23 D. 30.
[7] M'Donald v. Jackson, 1826, 5 S. 28.
[8] Ersk. Inst., iii. 7, 20.
[9] Kennard & Sons v. Wright, 1865, 3 M. 946.

to bills of exchange, and was introduced by the Bills of Exchange (Scotland) Act, 1772. By the Act diligence or action upon a bill of exchange, or inland bill, or promissory note, is excluded unless diligence be raised and executed or action commenced thereon within six years after the terms at which the sums in the notes or bills became exigible. The bill then ceases to exist as an enforceable document of debt and proves nothing, although it may be used along with other evidence to set up the debt. But proof of the constitution of the debts contained in the bills or notes, and of the resting owing, by writ or oath of the debtor thereafter are permitted. If the creditor can vouch the debt in some other way he may prove the constitution in the manner applicable to the particular debt, notwithstanding that he has taken a bill or note which has prescribed. The prescription is interrupted by the years of minority of the creditors. Bank notes are excluded from the operation of the Act.

When proof by writ of resting owing is attempted the general rules as to the character of the writ required are the same as those applicable in the case of the triennial prescription.

The Vicennial Prescription.—The Act 1669, c. 9, provides " that holograph letters and holograph bonds and subscriptions in compt books without witnesses not being pursued for within twenty years shall prescribe in all time thereafter, except the pursuer offer to prove by the defender's oath the verity of the said holograph bonds and letters and subscriptions in the compt books." The Act has been held to extend to all holograph writings on which an obligation can be founded,[1] except probably bills and notes.[2] After the expiry of twenty years the creditor has to establish the genuineness of the writing, not merely of the signature, by the debtor's oath. Once he has done so he need not establish the resting owing. The only admissible exception to the operation of the Act is action or diligence by the creditor within the twenty years. Hence mere payment of interest by the debtor will not exclude the operation of the Act.[3] The years of the creditor's minority fall to be deducted.

Reference to Oath.—When liability is sought to be set up by a reference to the oath of a debtor he is not entitled to resort to a general denial, and must answer all relevant questions. If a defender denying liability in his oath qualifies the denial, the qualification, if it nega-

---

[1] Mowat v. Banks, 1856, 18 D. 1093 ; Macadam v. Findlay, 1911 S.C. 1366.
[2] Drummond v. Lees, 1880, 7 R. 452.
[3] Macadam v. Findlay, 1911 S.C. 1366.

tives liability, is said to be intrinsic of the oath, but if it does not necessarily negative liability it is said to be extrinsic and liability may be inferred. Thus if the defender in his oath qualifies his denial of liability by saying that the debt was compensated or the goods supplied were not according to contract, the qualification is extrinsic, and the oath amounts to an admission of the debt. When, however, the qualification is, for example, that money which is sued for in repayment of a loan was received by the debtor in payment of services rendered, that is an intrinsic qualification and is therefore negative of the receipt of a loan.

(7) **Impossibility of Performance.**—Where it is impossible for an obligant to perform a contractual obligation the contract may or may not be terminated in consequence. It may, on the one hand, never have been possible to perform it, or it may have become so, so as finally, on the occurrence of the event which renders it impossible, to put an end to all rights and duties present or future between the contracting parties. On the other hand, the result may be merely to relieve a contracting party from being compelled to perform in terms of his obligation, but leave him liable in damages to the other for failure so to perform.

Impossibility Personal to the Obligant.—Where the impossibility is personal to the obligant the obligation continues. Thus it is no defence that performance is " commercially impossible," e.g. the obligant has not enough money or that a loss will result to him,[1] or that it cannot be done within the time stipulated,[2] or that performance depends on some third party over whom the obligant has no control, as where a person becomes cautioner or gives a guarantee for the payment of a debt or fulfilment of a contract.[3]

Impossibility at Date of Contract.—Where an obligation at the time the contract was made was impossible of performance either then or in the future, the contract is void. This is so where the impossibility of performance is due to the mutual error or mistake of the parties, the parties having contracted on the assumption of the existence of a certain thing or state of things.[4] There is then no real consent between the parties. This is so also, and there is held to be no real consent, where, though the element of mutual

---

[1] Hong-Kong and Whampoa Dock Co. v. Netherton Shipping Co., 1909 S.C. 34.
[2] Steel v. Bell, 1900, 3 F. 319 ; cf. Milligan v. Ayr Harbour Trs., 1915 S.C. 937.
[3] Stevenson v. Wilson, 1907 S.C. 445, per Lord Dunedin at p. 455.
[4] Vide Error or Mistake, supra, p. 21.

mistake is not present, the thing intended to be done is known by all reasonable men to be physically and legally impossible. The rule also extends to cases where both deem performance possible but its impossibility is part of the stock of knowledge of the average man, *e.g.* an agreement to discover treasure by magic.[1] On the other hand, an obligation impossible of performance at the time of contracting, but expected to have become possible at the date fixed for performance, *e.g.* by an advance in scientific knowledge or a change in the law, may be binding.[2] In such cases, performance not being manifestly impossible, the party who undertook the obligation takes the risk of its impossibility. Where there is legal impossibility, as in a case of something *extra commercium* and therefore not saleable, such as a seat in a parish church, there is no contract. Such contracts are to be distinguished from contracts which can be performed but only by the commission of an illegal act.[3]

Supervening Impossibility.—Where, on the other hand, an obligation possible at the time of contracting becomes impossible by an alteration in the circumstances before the date of performance, the legal effect may be affected by the nature of the circumstances from which the impossibility results. These circumstances may be (1) a change in the law, (2) a change in circumstances material to the contract, and (3) a change in the condition of the obligant.

(1) If, before the time fixed for performance, a change in the law has made the act prestable under the contract either impossible [4] or illegal,[5] performance is excused. The validity of a contract is, however, not affected by a change in the law which merely alters the nature of the rights conferred or the burden of the obligation imposed. Accordingly, an obligation may be enforceable although subsequent legislation has made it more difficult or expensive to perform. Thus a party who has undertaken to supply goods must do so although the imposition of a duty may have made his contract unprofitable.[6] Where the contract is of extended or indeter-

---

[1] Indian Contract Act, 1877, § 56.
[2] Clifford *v.* Watts, (1870) L.R. 5 C.P. 577, per Willes J. at p. 585.
[3] *Vide* Illegal Contracts, *supra*, p. 27 *et seq.*
[4] Shipton Anderson & Co. *v.* Harrison, [1915] 3 K.B. 676 ; Metropolitan Water Board *v.* Dick Kerr & Co., [1918] A.C. 619 ; Marshall *v.* Glanvill, [1917] 2 K.B. 87 ; Leith School Board *v.* Rattray's Trs., 1918 S.C. 94.
[5] Trinidad Shipping Co. *v.* Alston, [1920] A.C. 888.
[6] Maclennand *v.* Adam, 1795, M. 14247.

minate duration and the supervening illegality of a temporary
nature, as where the contract is affected by a declaration of
war, the effect seems to depend on the probability or otherwise of the illegality ceasing during the currency of the
contract.[1]

(2) Where a contract involves anything to be done in the future,
and something occurs to render fulfilment by one party
impossible, the contract may be terminated, and both parties
freed from their obligations. On the other hand, while
specific performance may no longer be claimable, damages
for non-fulfilment may be due. The occurrence may, on
the one hand, have been foreseen and expressly provided
against in the contract. The contract may nevertheless
be at an end. For example, where the contract provides
against non-fulfilment due to delay from specified and excepted causes, the party so protected by the contract may
not be entitled to insist on the other party performing
his part, and so the contract may be at an end. It is an
implied condition that if performance after delay would
in a business sense be a different thing from performance at
the proper time, delay, though due to an excepted cause,
will entitle the other party to rescind the contract. For
example, if a ship is chartered to convey goods, but is
prevented from proceeding to the port of loading by perils
of the sea excepted in the contract of affreightment, the
charterer may be entitled to declare the contract at an end
in respect that, taking into consideration the object for which
the ship was required, the offer of the ship came too late
for the implement of the original contract.[2] The occurrence
may, on the other hand, not have been expressly provided
against, and the rights of the parties will then depend on
the nature of the occurrence. Both these cases are known
as cases of " frustration of the adventure." The theory is

---

[1] Leiston Gas Co. v. Leiston Urban Council, [1916] 2 K.B. 428 ; Tamplin
Steamship Co. v. Anglo-American, etc. Co., [1916] 2 A.C. 397 ; Modern Transport
Co. v. Duneric Steamship Co., [1917] 1 K.B. 370 ; Bank Line Co. v. Capel, [1919]
A.C. 435 ; Trevalion v. Blanche, 1919 S.C. 617. As to effect of change in foreign
law, see Aurdal v. Estrella, 1916 S.C. 882 ; Kurll v. Timber Operators, [1927]
1 K.B. 298.

[2] Jackson v. Union Marine Insurance Co., Ltd., (1874) L.R. 10 C.P. 125 ;
cf. The Penelope, [1928] P. 180.

that the basis of the contract is gone, and neither party can enforce performance. Again a common case for which there is not usually an express provision is the accidental destruction of some particular thing to which the contract relates and without which it cannot be performed. This is known as *rei interitus*. It thus depends on whether the continued existence of the thing was an implied condition whether the contract is ended or not. As a general rule if a thing essential to the contract perishes without fault of either party the party whose obligation is thereby rendered impossible is excused from performance or payment of damages.[1] In England these principles have been applied to cases where an unexpected change of circumstances renders the thing contracted for useless to the party who has bargained for it, though the thing itself is not destroyed or in any way affected, and though it was perfectly possible that the contract might have been carried out in its exact terms.[2]

(3) Lastly, performance of an obligation may be rendered impossible by a change in the condition of an obligant, such as his death, insanity, serious illness, and, in certain cases, his bankruptcy. Thus if a man has been chosen for a contract in reliance on his personal qualities, his continuance in life is an implied condition of the contract and his death annuls it, as in the case of contracts of service, partnerships, agency, and cautionary obligations. If the contract is for personal service of a kind which can only be rendered by the sane, the insanity of the obligant must determine it.[3] If a musician is engaged for a particular occasion and is too ill to perform, neither party is under any liability.[4] The bankruptcy of a partner dissolves the partnership, subject to any agreement to the contrary.[5]

(8) Breach of Contract.—The breach of a contract by one party may entitle the other party to rescind and so put an end to it. That is, however, only one of the remedies which may be open to the

[1] Taylor *v.* Caldwell, (1863) B. & S. 826 ; London Shipping Co. *v.* The Admiralty, 1920 S.C. 309.
[2] Taylor *v.* Caldwell, (1863) 3 B. & S. 826 ; Krell *v.* Henry, [1903] 2 K.B. 740 ; Chandler *v.* Webster, [1904] 1 K.B. 493.
[3] Liddell *v.* Easton's Trs., 1907 S.C. 154.
[4] Robinson *v.* Davison, (1871) L.R. 6 Ex. 269.
[5] Partnership Act, 1890, §§ 33, 47.

party not in breach. The primary right of a creditor in a contractual obligation is to secure performance by invoking the assistance of the Court to compel it, known as specific implement, or, where that remedy is inappropriate, to obtain compensation in damages. But in many cases the law also confers on the creditor the right to adopt defensive measures to enable him to minimise loss which the default of the debtor threatens to entail. He may on the one hand have the right of withholding performance of obligations incumbent on him until those in which he is creditor are performed or secured, or he may on the other hand have the right of rescinding and so of putting an end to the contract. The competency of such defensive measures is based on the principle that obligations in a contract are as a rule interdependent and conditional on each other. Accordingly, where one party has refused or failed to perform his contract, or has failed to perform any material or substantial part of it, the other is entitled to insist for implement, claiming damages for breach, or to rescind it altogether.

Anticipatory Breach.—If one party to a contract intimates by word or act, amounting to a definite and distinct refusal, that he will not implement the obligation he has undertaken, the other is entitled to treat this as a repudiation of the contract, and to avail himself at once of the remedies that may be open, although the time for performance has not arrived, and there has therefore been no actual breach.[1] The contract entitles him not merely to performance when due, but to the expectation of performance. Such repudiation does not amount to a rescission of the contract, for one party to a contract cannot by his own act rescind it, but it puts it in the power of the other party to agree to a rescission subject to his claim of damages. The party entitled to rescind may, on the other hand, refuse to rescind, and, when the date of performance arrives, sue for damages calculated on the loss inflicted as at that date. An act by which a party voluntarily puts it out of his power to perform a contract when the time for performance arrives may be treated as equivalent to an immediate refusal to perform it.[2]

Materiality of Breach.—To justify rescission a breach of contract must be material. A minor breach may give rise to a claim of damages and that only. What is material is a pure question of the construction of the contract and the intention of the parties. Where there is

[1] Hegarty & Kelly v. Cosmopolitan Insurance Corporation, 1913 S.C. 377; Forslind v. Bechely-Crundall, 1922 S.C. (H.L.) 173.
[2] North British Railway Co. v. Benhar Coal Co., 1886, 14 R. 141.

a total failure of performance or a refusal to perform by one party, the other is entitled to treat it as a repudiation of the contract, and rescind. Where there is a refusal or failure to perform one of several stipulations the question of the materiality of that stipulation arises. Where a comedian engaged to perform in a theatre in the following year and undertook to give fourteen days' notice accompanied by bill matter before the date he was engaged to appear and failed to do so, and the theatre manager cancelled his engagement, it was held that the comedian was entitled to damages in respect that his own breach was not so material as to justify the other party in rescinding the contract.[1] On the other hand, where a dictionary of English and Gaelic was published by subscription, and in the proposals it was stated it would contain a glossary of proper names and an historical account, and contained neither when published, it was held the subscribers were entitled to return their copies and refuse payment of the price ; in other words, to rescind the contract of sale in respect of material breach by the other party.[2]

Where a contractual obligation has been performed but the performance is defective, provisions as to the character or quality of the work to be done are in general material conditions of the contract, and the question of the right to rescind depends on the degree of failure. Thus under the Sale of Goods Act, 1893,[3] the delivery of a smaller quantity than that ordered, or of a larger quantity, or of the goods ordered mixed with goods of a different description, are all failures of a character sufficiently material to justify rejection. On the other hand, in the case of a sale of machinery a remediable defect probably does not justify rejection, and the buyer's remedy is to have the defect cured at the expense of the seller.[4]

Where the failure is in respect of time of performance, its materiality depends on the nature of the contract. Stipulations as to time of payment are not treated as material conditions of the contract, except in very special cases.[5] On the other hand, in contracts for the sale or supply of goods which vary in price from day to day, *prima facie* stipulations as to time of giving or taking delivery are of the essence of the contract. But even in mercantile contracts there is only a presumption that time is of the essence of the contract. It

---

[1] Wade *v.* Waldon, 1909 S.C. 571.
[2] Shaw *v.* M'Donell, 1786, M. 9185.   [3] § 30.
[4] Morrison & Mason *v.* Clarkson Bros., 1898, 25 R. 427, per Lord M'Laren at p. 437 ; *vide* Sale of Goods, *infra*, p. 111.
[5] *E.g.* Sale of Goods Act, 1893, § 10 (1).

is not an absolute rule that a short delay either in giving or accepting delivery of goods will justify repudiation. That course may be justifiable if the market for goods is subject to sudden fluctuations in price, or if the conduct of the party in delay was such as to cause a reasonable apprehension that he had no intention of fulfilling his contractual obligations. Otherwise a party must wait for a time reasonable in the circumstances before he takes the extreme step of declaring the contract rescinded.[1] In each case it is a question of degree.

8. Damages for Breach of Contract.—General Damages.—When

damages are claimed for breach of contract it is the aim of the law to ensure that a person whose contract has been broken shall be placed as near as possible in the same position as if it had not.[2] Accordingly, as damages are intended as compensation for loss, it is irrelevant, for example, to consider what profit was made by the party in breach by breaking his contract,[3] except in so far as that profit may be evidence of the profit the other party would have made had the contract been fulfilled [4] ; or to consider the means of defender, and his consequent ability to meet the damage without serious loss to himself ; or injury to pursuer's feelings, or to his credit or reputation, as in a sudden dismissal from service. On the other hand, a party whose contract has been broken is bound to take all reasonable means to minimise the resulting loss, and can only recover the amount which the adoption of such means would have failed to avert. Thus when a buyer delays to purchase goods in place of those with which he ought to have been supplied, and the price continuously rises, he cannot demand more than the loss he would have sustained if he had bought at once.[5] And if a buyer has refused to take delivery the seller must resell, no matter what the state of the market, if he is to claim the difference between the contract price and the market price from the buyer. But it would not be reasonable, for example, to require a purchaser whose contract has been broken to supply himself with goods if these can only be obtained with difficulty and in remote markets.[6]

[1] Carswell v. Collard, 1892, 19 R. 987, per Lord M'Laren ; affd. 20 R. (H.L.) 47.

[2] Fletcher Moulton L.J. in Chaplin v. Hicks, [1911] 2 K.B. 786 at p. 794.

[3] Teacher v. Calder, 1898, 25 R. 661 ; affd. 1899, 1 F. (H.L.) 39.

[4] Watson, Laidlaw & Co. v. Pott, Cassels & Williamson, 1913 S.C. 762.

[5] Ireland & Son v. Merryton Coal Co., 1894, 21 R. 989 ; Sale of Goods Act, 1893, §§ 50, 51.

[6] Gunter & Co. v. Lauritzen, 1894, 31 S.L.R. 359 ; Clippens Oil Co. v. Edinburgh Water Trs., 1907 S.C. (H.L.) 9.

Where a breach of contract is proved, even in respect of time, an award of damages must follow. If no inconvenience has been suffered the damages will be nominal. If trouble and inconvenience have been caused, though no specific damage is proved, the damages will be substantial.[1]

Remoteness and Special Damage.—Assuming that a party has taken all reasonable means to minimise the consequences of a breach of contract, it does not follow that he will necessarily be entitled to recover his loss or the whole of it. The general rule as to the items of damage for which a party who has broken his contract may be held responsible has been authoritatively laid down.[2] Where two parties have made a contract, which one of them has broken, the damages which the other party ought to receive in respect of such breach of contract should be either such as may fairly and reasonably be considered as arising naturally, *i.e.* according to the usual course of things, from such breach of contract itself (general damages), or such as may reasonably be supposed to have been in the contemplation of both parties at the time they made the contract as the probable result of the breach of it (special damages). The claim may accordingly be limited on two grounds : (1) that the loss is too remote a consequence of the breach of contract ; or (2) that though the loss is the direct result of the breach, yet it arises from some exceptional circumstances of which the party in breach was not aware, and the effect of which he could not be expected to foresee, known as special or consequential damage. As to remoteness of damage, it has been held that a party who fails to carry or supply goods will be liable in damages found due, or for loss of profit, on a subcontract by which the other party may have disposed of them, provided that neither damage nor loss were exceptional.[3] Expenses reasonably incurred in consequence of a breach of contract may also be recovered as damages, and possibly the expenses of litigation with a third party if the ordinary and natural result of the breach. As to special or consequential damage, this frequently arises where a party has undertaken to do or supply something by a particular date and fails to observe it, with the result that delay has caused the loss of opportunity of using the goods or disposing of them to exceptional advan-

---

[1] Webster & Co. *v.* Cramond Iron Co., 1875, 2 R. 752.

[2] Hadley *v.* Baxendale, (1854) 9 Ex. 341.

[3] Ströms Bruks Aktie Bolag *v.* Hutchison, 1904, 6 F. 486 ; revd. 1905, 7 F. (H.L.) 131.

tage, or where the delay in supplying or conveying a particular thing has caused loss due to the fact that the particular thing was wanted for a larger enterprise.

Damages for Delay in Payment.—It is a general rule that no damages are due for the consequences of delay in payment of money,[1] although in certain cases interest may be demanded. An exception is the breach of contract involved in the failure of a banker to honour his customer's cheque. The customer may recover damages for the resulting injury to his credit.[2]

The question whether interest is due *ex lege*, where there is no express provision for it, depends on the nature of the contract out of which the debt arises. It can only be demanded in virtue of a contract express or implied, or by virtue of the principal sum of money having been wrongfully withheld and not paid on the day when it ought to have been paid. It is due as liquidated damages on a dishonoured bill of exchange,[3] on promissory notes, and on a loan,[4] on a balance in the hands of a mercantile agent or owing to him, and on the price of land sold and of which possession has been given.[5]

Interest is, however, not due on arrears of feu-duty, nor probably of rent ; nor on open account unless action has been raised, or intimation given that interest will be claimed in the event of non-payment [6] ; nor on damages arising out of a breach of contract until the date of decree.

Compound interest is a demand which can only be maintained either in the case of a fixed usage in commercial dealings such as an overdrawn bank account or where there has been an abuse by a party entrusted with funds and violating his trust. So it has been refused on arrears of interest on a bond.[7]

---

[1] Stephen *v.* Swayne, 1861, 24 D. 158, per Lord President M'Neill.
[2] King *v.* British Linen Co., 1899, 1 F. 928 ; but *vide* Gloag on Contract, p. 801.
[3] Bills of Exchange Act, 1882, § 57.
[4] Hope Johnstone *v.* Cornwall, 1895, 22 R. 314.
[5] Grandison's Trs. *v.* Jardine, 1895, 22 R. 925.
[6] Somervell's Tr. *v.* Edinburgh Life Assurance Co., 1911 S.C. 1069 at p. 1071.
[7] M'Neill *v.* M'Neill, (1830) 4 W. & S. 453.

CHAPTER II

THE LAW OF AGENCY

1. Definition.—Agency is a contract, express or implied, whereby one person, the principal, authorises another, the agent, to act on his behalf in a legal relationship between the principal and a third party.

2. Capacity.—Who may Appoint and be Appointed as Agent.—The capacity of a principal to contract or otherwise act through an agent is co-extensive with the principal's own capacity to act for himself. Thus a person under full age, *e.g.* a minor, when acting through an agent can bind or be bound by a third party only to the same extent that a minor can himself bind, or be bound by, one with whom he contracts. On the other hand a person with limited or no capacity can be appointed by, and act as, agent of another person to the fullest extent. But such an agent has no personal liability or rights beyond what a person of his limited capacity ordinarily has.[1]

3. How Agency Constituted.—The relationship of principal and agent exists by virtue of the express or implied assent of both principal and agent, and, it may be added, in certain cases arises out of necessity. There is no special form for the constitution of agency. It may be constituted by express appointment by the principal, by implication of law from the actings of the parties, or by subsequent ratification by the principal of acts done on his behalf by the person acting as agent.

(*a*) **Express Appointment of Agent.**—Where an appointment is express it may be oral [2] or in writing. The writing may be formal or informal. When, however, the contract is written the writing is the measure of the authority conferred, and it will not be extended to anything which the terms of

---

[1] *Vide* Capacity to Contract, *supra*, p. 13 *et seq.*
[2] Pickin *v.* Hawkes, 1878, 5 R. 676.

the writing do not expressly or impliedly warrant. The formal writing usually takes the form of a power of attorney, frequently granted for the management of affairs abroad, or by a person abroad for the management of his affairs at home ; or it may take the form of a factory and commission, a deed generally granted by a landed proprietor leaving Scotland and committing the charge of his estate to a friend or his law agent. Less formal writings may take the form, for example, of letters of mandate or powers of procuration.

(b) **Implied Appointment as Agent.**—Again, an authority to act as agent may be constituted by implication, as where a man is put into a shop as manager or shopkeeper or permitted to take charge of an office or business and remains in charge with possession of the goods and documents. That will be enough to signify to the public that the man is held out as agent and all the usual powers follow.

Holding Out.—The principle of holding out applies chiefly in connection with the dealings of merchants and commission agents. The principle is this, that when one permits another to act for him in a certain course of business repeatedly he is barred *personali exceptione* from denying a grant of authority in a question with a third party with whom the alleged agent has transacted within the scope of such business.[1] Thus, where a buyer paid for goods by cash to the sellers' agents without challenge and in good faith in a series of transactions and the agents embezzled the money, it was held, in an action for payment at the instance of the sellers against the buyer, that the payments made to the agent were valid in respect that the buyer had no reason to believe that he was not entitled to receive the payments in that form.[2] In Scotland a wife has a presumed mandate, while she remains in family with her husband, to provide things proper and necessary for the family, for the price of which the husband is liable. Again, a person may so act as to be precluded from denying the agent's authority, no matter what instructions he gave the agent. Thus, in *Pickering* v. *Busk*,[3]

---

[1] Barnetson v. Petersen Bros., 1902, 5 F. 86.
[2] International Sponge Importers, Ltd. v. Watt & Sons, 1911 S.C. (H.L.) 57.
[3] (1812) 15 East 37.

a broker was employed by a merchant to buy hemp. The broker did so, and at the request of the buyer the hemp was left at the broker's wharf. The broker sold the goods. The sale was held good on the principle that if the owner of goods permits a person whose ordinary course of business it is to sell that class of goods to have possession of the goods or of the documents of title to the goods, and the goods are sold to a person who buys them in the belief that the holder has authority to sell, the owner is bound by the sale.[1]

Procuration to sign Bills of Exchange.[2]—Procuration is deserving of special attention, where it is procuratory to draw, accept, or endorse bills of exchange. The power of procuratory may be granted in so many words : " I, A. B., constitute you, C. D., my procurator to draw, accept, or endorse bills for me in the course of my business." Or it may be implied. It may, for example, arise out of the position in which a man is placed—for example, his being at the head of a business where the power is absolutely necessary for conducting the business.[3] A mere mandate to act as managing clerk and pay and discharge debts does not amount to a procuration to sign bills. Again, procuration by implication will be inferred where there is a course of dealing by the principal recognising the acts of his agent relative to bills, *i.e.* where the agent has no express power, but has for some time been in the habit of drawing, accepting, and endorsing his principal's bills, and the principal has paid or passed the bills in his accounts. Another case where the implication would arise would be where one man has signed the name of another on a bill at his request, and a succession of bills so signed have been presented in the course of business and been paid by the man whose name they bear.

It should be observed that a bill drawn, accepted, or endorsed " per pro " is a warning to everybody taking it that it is drawn or endorsed by a person having limited power for special purposes, and a warning to them to see that the bill is being used for the special purposes to

---

[1] This is now statutory under § 2 (1) of the Factors Act, 1889, applied to Scotland by the Factors (Scotland) Act, 1890. *Vide* Mercantile Agents, *infra*, p. 86.

[2] And *vide* Bills of Exchange, *infra*.

[3] Edmonds *v.* Bushell & Jones, (1865) L.R. 1 Q.B. 97.

which the procurator had a right to apply it. Thus, in *Union Bank* v. *Makin & Sons*,[1] an English firm gave their manager in Scotland a procuratory to sign bills limited to those " necessary to the conducting of our business." The manager got discounted at the bank bills endorsed by him " per pro Makin & Sons," the drawers, the acceptances of various firms with which he or his firm were in the habit of dealing having been forged by him on the bills. The bank discounted the bills in ordinary course and in good faith. The manager absconded with the money. It was held, however, that the bank was entitled to recover the money from Makin & Sons as the principals, but only because the bank had exercised all reasonable care, and had no warning that the money was not for the purposes of the business of Makin & Sons.

(c) **Ratification of Agency.**—Agency may further be constituted by subsequent ratification where authority to act has not been created expressly or impliedly, or the agent has exceeded his authority. Such ratification may be express or implied.

The effect is as if at the date of the contract between the agent and the third party the authority had existed, except that the rights of third parties acquired before ratification cannot be prejudicially affected by the ratification. There can be no ratification, however, if the act was in its inception void, nor if the contract was not made as on behalf of the principal who seeks to ratify it,[2] nor if the principal was not in existence at the date of the contract,[3] as where the promoters of a company enter into a contract on behalf of a company before its incorporation. The company, after formation, would require to enter into a new contract on the same terms as the old. Again, ratification of an act may be impossible after a certain time if time is essential to the validity of an act and has expired [4] and third parties would be prejudiced, *e.g.* ratification of an unauthorised stoppage *in transitu* after the transit was at an end.[5] Otherwise ratification may be at any time.

[1] 1873, 11 M. 499. [2] Keighley, Maxsted & Co. *v.* Durant, [1901] A.C. 240.
[3] Tinnevelly Sugar Co., Ltd. *v.* Mirrlees, Watson & Yaryan Co., Ltd., 1894, 21 R. 1009.
[4] Goodall *v.* Bilsland, 1909 S.C. 1152 at p. 1182.
[5] Bird *v.* Brown, (1850) 4 Ex. 786.

(*d*) **Agency of Necessity.**—Lastly, agency may arise out of necessity
though not otherwise implied. Thus, a common carrier may
be agent of necessity for the care of goods sent under his
charge, if there is no one to receive the goods at their destination.[1] And a shipmaster, when he cannot communicate with
the owners, may if necessary make them liable in cases to
which his ordinary powers as agent would not extend.[2]

4. The Agent's Powers or Authority.—(*a*) **Extent as regards Third
Parties.**—**General and Special Agency.**—The extent of the authority of
an agent varies in different circumstances. Thus, an agent's authority
may be general ; he may act for the principal in all his affairs in any
particular business, *e.g.* the master of a ship or a solicitor. On the
other hand, the authority may be special, in which case he is employed
to act in regard to a particular matter only. With regard to special
and general agents, it is of importance to observe the different rules
as to the care which third parties transacting with them must take as
to the power which these agents respectively have. In the case of a
man employed to act in a particular piece of business, he will not bind
the principal if he oversteps the special powers with which he is
invested. In dealing with him, accordingly, care should be taken to
ascertain precisely the terms of his commission. On the other hand,
in the case of a general agent it is safe to trust him in all matters
within his functions according to the usage of his particular trade.
To that extent he has an ostensible authority and may bind his
principal. For example, a stockbroker is entitled to act in accordance
with the rules and customs of the Stock Exchange, and accordingly will
bind his principal in any contract he makes for him in accordance
with the rules. And an auctioneer, as he may not sell on credit,
will not bind his principal if he does so. The general agent has full
powers according to his ostensible authority. As a general rule,
however, a general agent has no implied power to borrow, though a
partner may borrow when necessary to meet an emergency in the
business of his firm.[3]

Delegation of Authority of Agent.—The relation of agency is of a
personal character. The personal nature of the relationship is expressed in the maxim *delegatus non potest delegare.* In other words, a

---

[1] G.N. Rly. Co. *v.* Swaffield, (1874) 43 L.J. Ex. 89.
[2] *Vide* Merchant Shipping, *infra* ; The Atlantic Mutual Insurance Co. *v.* Huth,
(1879) 16 Ch. D. 474.
[3] Sinclair, Moorhead & Co. *v.* Wallace & Co., 1880, 7 R. 874.

person with delegated authority cannot delegate that authority to anyone else. He must do what he was commissioned to do himself, unless expressly or impliedly authorised to delegate it. Where the principal may reasonably be held to have relied on the personal skill or discretion of the agent selected by him delegation is excluded, *e.g.* in the case of a law agent. But authority to delegate may be implied from the usage of the particular trade, or the nature of the employment may be such as to render the employment of a sub-agent necessary. Thus, an architect has been held entitled to employ a surveyor, to whom the principal is liable,[1] for when delegation proper takes place the contract is then between the principal and the sub-agent.[2]

(*b*) **Extent as between Principal and Agent.**—As between principal and agent the actual authority must be followed to the letter, and deviation from it may involve the agent in damages.[3] If the terms of the authority are ambiguous, and are capable of two constructions, an agent acting honestly on one construction is deemed to have been duly authorised.[4]

5. The Duties and Liabilities of Agent to Principal.—(*a*) **Duties.**— The relationship of agency is of a fiduciary character. It is a relation of personal confidence. The agent must give his best exertions in his principal's interests. And he must not seek his own profit at all, beyond the commission or salary that has been stipulated.

To carry out Instructions.—The agent's first duty is to carry out the principal's instructions, whether express, or implied by the usage of trade or a previous course of dealing between the parties. Only necessity will excuse non-compliance with express or implied instructions. Thus, if he was instructed to insure goods and does not do so he will be responsible for any loss.[5] In the absence of instructions or special usage the agent must act to the best of his judgment in the interests of the employer. The standard of care required is such care and diligence as would be shown by a man of ordinary prudence in the same line of employment.[6] Even a person who acts gratuitously may be liable in damages if he fails to exercise reasonable care.[7] When an agency is undertaken requiring special skill for its performance the

---

[1] Black *v.* Cornelius, 1879, 6 R. 581.
[2] De Bussche *v.* Alt, (1878) 8 Ch. D. 286, per Thesiger L.J.
[3] Bank of Scotland *v.* Dominion Bank, 18 R. (H.L.) 21.
[4] Ireland *v.* Livingston, (1872) L.R. 5 H.L. 395.
[5] Smith *v.* Lascelles, 1788, 1 R.R. 187.
[6] Bell's Prin., § 221.
[7] Stiven *v.* Watson, 1 R. 412.

standard is the ordinary skill of a person in the particular profession or trade. Failure to use the skill or care required renders the agent liable in damages to the principal. Thus, if a law agent, from want of proper care or skill, passes a bad title, and a security which he takes over the property is in consequence lost, he will be liable to the principal for the amount of the bond. As a general rule the law agent is responsible for a good title, but not for sufficient value in the security. The agent is liable in damages even though the loss would have occurred independently of his failure of duty, for it is a matter of contract between him and his principal.

To keep Accounts.—The agent is bound to keep accounts and to account punctually.

To act solely in Interests of Principal.—It is an agent's duty to make an effectual contract and to give his principal the full benefit of the contract he has made. This arises out of the fiduciary character of the relationship. He is not entitled to any benefit over and above the commission or salary stipulated for. If he pays accounts he must account for any discount. It is illegal for him to take a secret profit or commission, as, for example, when purchasing on behalf of his principal to get something off the order from the seller for bringing it to him.[1] If employed to sell goods for his principal he may not buy them himself without permission from the principal. The principal would be entitled to take back the goods, or, if the agent had resold at a profit, to debit the agent with the profit on the resale.[2] So also an agent may not buy for his principal, he being himself the seller, without the principal's knowledge and consent. The principal can refuse to take the goods or may debit the agent with the profit he has made. Again, a law agent may not take a gift from a client without neutral advice and assistance for the client, nor can he draw a client's will in his own favour, unless he proves it was made deliberately and without undue influence on his part.[3] The law agent's account must be according to the fixed scale for law agents' business as taxed by the Auditor of Court.[4] It is an implied term of the contract of agency that the agent will not, without his principal's consent, make use, to his principal's detriment, of any information or materials which he has acquired in the course of his agency.[5]

[1] Pender v. Henderson & Co., 1864, 2 M. 1428; Gray's Trs. v. Drummond & Reid, 8 R. 956.

[2] De Bussche v. Alt, (1878) L.R. 8 Ch. D. 286.

[3] Weir v. Grace, 1898, 1 F. 253.　　　[4] Anstruther v. Wilkie, 1856, 18 D. 405.

[5] Liverpool Victoria Legal Friendly Society v. Houston, 1900, 3 F. 42.

An agent is further liable to criminal prosecution if he corruptly accepts or obtains, or agrees to accept or obtain from any person, for himself or for any other person, any gift or consideration as an inducement or reward for doing or forbearing to do any act in relation to his principal's affairs or business. A person who corruptly endeavours to induce an agent to do so is also liable to prosecution. Further, if an agent knowingly uses, with intent to deceive his principal, any receipt, account, or other document in respect of which the principal is interested, and which contains any statement which is false or erroneous or defective in any material particular and intended to mislead the principal, he is liable to prosecution.[1]

(b) **Liabilities.**—As a general rule an agent incurs no personal liability to his principal in respect of a contract entered into by him on his principal's behalf. The exceptions are *del credere* agents and insurance brokers. A *del credere* agent is one who by arrangement with his principal guarantees that the other party to the contract will fulfil it, *e.g.* when selling for his principal guarantees that the buyer is solvent, and undertakes to pay the principal in the event of his insolvency. An insurance broker is an agent who is employed to negotiate a policy of marine insurance. He is agent for both parties. But he is liable to the underwriter for payment of the premium, and has a lien over the policy of insurance against the assured for the premiums.

In accounting or paying money the agent must follow the instruction of his principal. If he remits money in some other fashion he takes the risk.[2] If he has no directions he should remit through a bank of good repute or a chartered bank, or according to the usage of the trade.[3]

6. Rights of Agent against Principal.—The rights of an agent against his principal are (a) remuneration for the services rendered, either as commission, brokerage, salary, or *quantum meruit*; (b) reimbursement of necessary expenses incurred in furtherance of the principal's business; (c) indemnity from all responsibilities and liabilities come under towards third parties; (d) a right of retention over goods in his hands belonging to the principal in order to make good his claims.

(a) **Remuneration.**—In the case of commission or brokerage the

---

1 Prevention of Corruption Acts, 1906 and 1916.
2 Warwicke *v.* Noakes, 1790, 3 R.R. 653.
3 Mackenzie's Trs. *v.* Jones, 1822, 2 S. 75.

rate is settled by stipulation or usage. Where the remuneration is settled by contract or stipulation, custom or usage cannot come in to modify the agreed rate, but may be invoked to explain any ambiguity in the terms of the contract. Remuneration is presumed to be due in the case of a mercantile agent,[1] and also where the agent makes such duties as he has undertaken to perform the trade or profession by which he earns his livelihood. Where a person is not, for instance, a professional broker, but does broker's work so as to entitle him to remuneration, his commission is a *quantum meruit* depending upon the circumstances.[2]

Commission is generally due only where the agent's duty has been completely fulfilled ; and if fulfilment is prevented by some cause for which the principal is not responsible no claim for commission emerges. Where there is an agreement under which commission is payable, the question whether commission has been earned depends upon the construction of the agreement. If the agent can show that the transaction in respect of which the commission is claimed is the result of his intervention commission is due.

A broker, who is an agent to sign for both buyer and seller, and whose business it is to introduce the principals to each other, is entitled to a commission if a contract follows. The commission is usually paid by the principal who first employs the agent. He may be a mercantile agent within the meaning of the Factors Acts, and commission is therefore presumed to be due. Custom has made a law whereby shipbrokers and house agents are entitled to a commission for the mere introduction of buyer and seller.

(b) **Reimbursement of Expenses.**—The agent, being entitled to be reimbursed his expenses as far as properly incurred, may set these off against what comes into his hands on behalf of his principal.

(c) **Indemnity against Third Parties.**—The principal must take the burden of all liabilities and obligations necessarily assumed by the agent in order to discharge his duties towards the

---

[1] See Mercantile Agents, *infra*, p. 86.
[2] Kennedy *v.* Glass, 1890, 17 R. 1085.

principal.[1] Thus, where a principal refused to implement
a contract entered into by an agent on his behalf, thereby
rendering the agent liable to a claim of damages, the principal
was held bound to relieve him.[2]

(d) **Right of Retention.**—Where property of the principal is in
the hands of the agent the latter has a right of retention
or lien over it, whether goods, documents of debt, or moneys
coming into his hands in the course of the agency, to the
effect of securing payment of his commission and indemnity
from any obligations undertaken by him on behalf of the
principal.[3] The lien is termed in law a " possessory " one,
and is lost when the goods are parted with. Retention may
be special or general. Special retention is a security to the
agent for the fulfilment by the principal of his part of the
obligation connected with the goods retained. General retention, however, is a security for a general balance due
by the principal. It may arise either from custom or contract. Thus a banker has a lien over all unappropriated
moneys and documents of debt of his customer in his hands
for the general balance of the customer's account, although
not to bills sent to him to be discounted which he has refused
to discount.[4] Again, a mercantile factor has a lien over
the goods in his possession for a general balance due him by
the principal.[5] And a law agent has such a lien over the
writs and titles of his client for payment of his business
account, though not for cash advances, salary, or commission.[6] A stockbroker also has a general lien.[7]

7. Relations between Agent and Third Parties.—An agent is liable
to third parties for his own negligence, misrepresentation, or fraud,
whether his principal is bound or not, and whether the wrongful act
was authorised by his principal or not. Apart from such cases it
is, generally speaking, a question of the intention of the parties and
the authority of the agent what are the rights and liabilities between
an agent and third parties with whom he contracts. On the other

---

[1] Erskine, Oxenford & Co. v. Sachs, [1901] 2 K.B. 504.
[2] Stevenson & Sons v. Duncan and Ors., 1842, 5 D. 167.
[3] Glendinning v. Hope, 1911 S.C. (H.L.) 73, per Lord Kinnear at p. 78.
[4] Lang v. Brown, 22 D. 113.
[5] Gairdner v. Milne & Co., 1858, 20 D. 565.
[6] Drummond v. Muirhead & Guthrie Smith, 1900, 2 F. 585.
[7] Glendinning v. Hope, supra.

hand, the rights of a third party may depend not so much on what was the actual as on what was the apparent authority of the agent. Three classes of case may occur : (*a*) The agent may be acting for a disclosed principal ; (*b*) he may be acting for an undisclosed principal ; (*c*) the supposed principal may be non-existent.

(*a*) **Where Principal disclosed.**—Where the agent has contracted expressly as agent on behalf and on account of a named principal the agent is not liable on the contract, for the contract is then between the principal and the third party.[1] The agent may, of course, when contracting as agent, agree to be made liable on the contract,[2] or a custom of trade may make him liable. That case apart, he cannot competently sue or be sued on the contract ; but as, when he contracts as agent, he warrants his authority, should he exceed his powers he is liable in damages to the third party for any loss caused by a breach of the implied warranty of authority,[3] and he does not, as a rule, bind his principal.[4] He has failed to perform the duty he undertook to perform, namely, to make an effectual contract, and the measure of damages in such a case is the loss sustained by the third party as a natural and probable result of the agent's failure.[5]

While an agent may in general agree to be made liable on a contract, or be so by custom of trade, there are certain classes of agents who are bound to contract only in the name of their principal. These are brokers, such as shipbrokers, marine commission agents, stockbrokers,[6] and others. They are mere middlemen or negotiators whose business is to bring the contracting parties together.

Foreign Principal.—In one case an agent may be liable on the contract even where he truly contracts on behalf of a disclosed principal, namely, when the principal is resident abroad. There is a presumption that a foreign principal does not as a rule give an agent in this country authority

---

[1] Stone & Rolfe *v.* Kimber Coal Co., 1926 S.C. (H.L.) 45.

[2] *E.g.* Lindsay *v.* Craig, 1919 S.C. 139.

[3] Anderson *v.* Croall & Sons, Ltd., 1904, 6 F. 153.

[4] Wylie & Lochhead, Ltd. *v.* Hornsby, 1889, 16 R. 907.

[5] Firbank's Exrs. *v.* Humphreys, (1886) 18 Q.B.D. 54 ; Meek *v.* Wendt, (1888) 21 Q.B.D. 126.

[6] Stockbrokers are in a special position, and by the rules of the Stock Exchange act as principals *inter se*.

to pledge his credit to those with whom he contracts.[1] The presumption is rebutted if the agent has in fact express authority to bind the principal and the third party is made aware of the authority. Further, if it can be shown that the third party knew the agent to be the established agent of the foreign principal in the country, and not merely a commission agent acting on special orders, the third party is bound to the foreign principal and the agent free.[2]

(b) **Where Principal undisclosed.**—Here the agent contracts in his own name. He may contract as principal, or expressly for a principal whose name he does not disclose. In this case he cannot at his own hand by disclosing the principal escape liability under the contract, and similarly he can himself sue as a principal on the contract. On the other hand, as in fact he is an agent, the third party, if he discovers there is a principal behind the agent, can go against the concealed principal. The only condition is that no prejudice shall thereby be suffered by the principal. If, for example, the third party, whether in knowledge of the concealed principal or not, has continued dealing with the agent and on his credit, and the principal has in the meantime altered the state of accounts between himself and the agent, as for instance by paying to the agent the price due to the third party for goods bought from him, so that it is to the principal's prejudice to have to pay again to the third party, the third party may not be able to go against the principal.[3] The decisions have varied. In some cases the courts have held that the third party is not barred from going against the principal unless the third party has himself produced the prejudice to the principal by keeping only to the agent's credit.[4] Accordingly, it would appear that, in order to preserve recourse against the principal, the third party must, as soon as he discovers there is a principal, find out who he is and claim recourse against him.[5] It follows that the

[1] Armstrong v. Stokes, (1872) L.R. 7 Q.B.D. 598; Hutton v. Bulloch, (1874) L.R. 9 Q.B.D. 572; Millar v. Mitchell, 1860, 22 D. 833.
[2] Bennett v. Inveresk Paper Co., 1891, 18 R. 975; Girvan, Roper & Co. v. Monteith, 1895, 23 R. 129.
[3] Armstrong v. Stokes, supra.
[4] Irvine v. Watson, 1880, 5 Q.B.D. 414.
[5] M'Intosh v. Ainslie, 10 M. 304.

6

undisclosed principal may sue the third party on the contract, and in that case the third party, having been in
ignorance that there was a principal behind the agent,
is entitled to plead against the principal compensation
on the state of accounts between him and the agent, but
not if the third party knew there was an undisclosed
principal.[1]

When a third party discovers who is the undisclosed
principal he is entitled to elect whether he will hold the
agent or the principal liable. He cannot be compelled to
elect immediately, but when his election is made the other
party is exempt from liability.[2] What constitutes election
is a question of fact.[3]

(c) **Where Principal non-existent.**—Where an agent contracts
ostensibly for a disclosed principal who does not exist or is
unable to contract, he is personally liable on the contract.
Thus, where A., B., and C. signed a promissory note in the
name and on behalf of a particular congregation, it was held
that, as a congregation could not be bound by a promissory
note, A., B., and C. were liable as contracting parties.[4]

8. Relations between Principal and Third Parties.—Where a contract has been made by an agent for a disclosed principal the principal
alone has a title to sue on the contract.

Every act done by an agent professedly on behalf of his principal
and within the scope of his authority is binding upon the principal,
whether the authority be express, or implied from his acting on behalf
of the principal in the course of his employment and within the
apparent scope of his authority, as where the agent is a general agent
or is held out by the principal as having authority. But if the agent
is acting in excess of his actual authority, whether apparent or not,
and the person dealing with him has notice or has reason to believe
that in doing such act he is exceeding his authority, the principal is
not bound.[5]

When an agent becomes bankrupt with the money or goods of the

---

[1] Matthews *v.* Auld & Guild, 1874, 1 R. 1224 ; Wester Moffat Colliery Co. *v.*
Jeffrey, 1911 S.C. 346.

[2] Morel *v.* Earl of Westmorland, [1904] A.C. 11.

[3] Lamont, Nisbett & Co. *v.* Hamilton, 1907 S.C. 628.

[4] Kelner *v.* Baxter, (1866) L.R. 2 C.P. 174.

[5] Walker *v.* Smith, 1906, 8 F. 619; Forman *v.* The Ship *Liddesdale*, [1900]
A.C. 190.

principal in his possession the principal is entitled to recover them if distinguishable from the agent's private funds or goods. The principal has a higher right than any third party creditor of the agent.[1]

A principal is liable for the wrongful acts of his agent in carrying out the transaction entrusted to him or committed within the scope of his employment. Where the principal has taken benefit from his agent's wrong, there is no doubt that this is so,[2] unless he is not only himself innocent of the fraud but also has acquired its results for a valuable consideration.[3] The principal is also liable in respect of the negligence of his agent in carrying out the transaction entrusted to him or in the ordinary course of his employment.[4] If, on the other hand, the principal employs an independent agent or contractor to do a lawful thing from which, if properly done, no injurious consequences would follow, the employer is not liable for his negligence or dishonesty in carrying out the contract. It would be different if the contractor were merely a servant of the principal, or if, for example, without special stipulation a railway company contracts to carry goods from one place to another, and employs another company as sub-agents to perform part of the contract. The contracting company would then be liable for any loss due to the negligence of the sub-agents.[5]

9. Termination of the Contract of Agency.—The contract of agency may be determined either by the act of the parties or by operation of law.

(*a*) **By Act of the Parties.**—(i.) **By Mutual Agreement.**—The parties may terminate the agency by mutual agreement.

(ii.) **By Act of Principal.**—Agency may be terminated by the principal by express recall or by appointment of a new agent to do the same act.[6] The principal may terminate the contract of agency at any time in most kinds of mercantile agency.

Relations with Agent.—He must then pay the agent any remuneration to which he is entitled. The agent will further be entitled to relief from the principal of obligations incurred, even though exigible only after the termination of the agency.

---

[1] Macadam *v.* Marton's Tr., 11 M. 33.
[2] Clydesdale Bank *v.* Paul, 1877, 4 R. 626.
[3] Gibbs *v.* British Linen Co., 1875, 4 R. 630.
[4] Citizens' Life Assurance Co. *v.* Brown, [1904] A.C. 423.
[5] Metzenburg *v.* Highland Rly. Co., 7 M. 919.
[6] Patten & Carruthers, 2 Paton 238.

The principal is not entitled to revoke at such time as to prejudice the agent. Accordingly the agent is entitled to go on and complete any transaction in which he is engaged, and where the agent's authority is " coupled with an interest " it cannot be revoked by the principal at pleasure. Thus, when brokers agreed to take, and took, shares in a ship on condition of being appointed sole chartering brokers, their agency was held not terminable by the principal at will, but only on showing reasonable cause.[1] If a time was fixed in the contract for the duration of the agency, the principal may not dismiss him before such time, or he will be liable in damages for terminating it without just cause. And where the principal expressly or by implication agrees to continue to carry on business during the term for which the relations of agency subsists, he is liable as for breach of contract if he fails. On the other hand, where an agent is employed for a definite term, say five years, there is no necessary breach of the agreement if, say, after one year, the principal finds it impossible to carry on the business.[2] Where, however, the principal undertakes to employ the agent for a certain term independently of change of circumstances, failure to do so infers a breach of contract.[3]

Relations with Third Parties.—When a principal recalls an agency, if he wishes to keep himself safe from the further actings of his agent he is bound to give notice to the customers with whom the agent has dealt, and when the authority of the agent is derived from " holding out " on the part of the principal, he must intimate that the agent's ostensible authority is at an end [4] by notice to customers and by advertisement in the *Gazette* and newspapers to the public.

(iii.) **By Act of Agent.**—The agent may renounce his agency at any time, but not in the middle of a transaction.

(*b*) **By Operation of Law.**—Agency is terminated where the special object for which it is created is accomplished, or, as in any

---

[1] Galbraith & Moorhead *v.* " Arethusa " Ship Co., Ltd., 1896, 23 R. 1011 ; Rhodes *v.* Forwood, (1876) 1 App. Cas. 256 ; Turner *v.* Goldsmith, [1891] 1 Q.B. 544 ; Ogdens, Ltd. *v.* Nelson, [1904] 2 K.B. 410 ; affd. [1905] A.C. 109.

[2] Patmore & Co. *v.* B. Cannon & Co., Ltd., 1892, 19 R. 1004.

[3] Turner *v.* Goldsmith, *supra*.

[4] Ferguson & Lillie *v.* Stephen, 1864, 2 M. 804.

other contract, by destruction of the subject-matter, *e.g.* if an article which an agent is employed to sell is destroyed. In addition, it may be terminated by death, bankruptcy, or insanity.

By Death.—The death of the principal terminates the agency,[1] but so long as the agent continues to act *in bona fide* in ignorance of the death of the principal his acts are good against his principal's estate.[2] And the agent, as in the case of revocation by the principal, may complete any transaction in which he is engaged. The death of the agent also, necessarily, terminates the agency.

By Bankruptcy.—Bankruptcy of the principal terminates the agency to the same effect as in the case of death. That is, the agent may complete a transaction and will bind the principal's estate if he continues to act in ignorance of the bankruptcy. The bankruptcy of the agent does not necessarily terminate the agency.

Death and bankruptcy are public facts, and no notice of the death or bankruptcy of the principal is required, so that, after a reasonable time, the knowledge will be supposed to have reached the customers.

By Insanity.—Insanity of the agent terminates the agency. Insanity of the principal, if of a temporary character, does not of itself interrupt the agent's power to act.[3] If of a permanent character, the agency seems to subsist until the third party contracting is put in bad faith by having knowledge of the principal's insanity.[4]

10. Classes of Agents.—The best-known classes of agents in mercantile affairs are auctioneers, bankers, factors, and brokers, and in addition may be mentioned the agencies of partners and shipmasters. With the exception of bankers, factors, and brokers, these are all dealt with elsewhere in this work.

(*a*) **Bankers.**—The relationship of banker and customer is substantially that of debtor and creditor, or lender and borrower, respectively, but the banker is the agent of the customer to pay sums of money as ordered. At common law he has

---

[1] Life Association of Scotland *v.* Douglas, 1886, 13 R. 910.
[2] Campbell *v.* Anderson, (1829) 3 W. & S.C. 384.
[3] Wink *v.* Mortimer, 1849, 11 D. 995.
[4] Bell's Prin., § 228 ; Pollok *v.* Paterson, 10th Dec. 1811, F.C.

a general lien or right of retention over all unappropriated negotiable instruments belonging to and deposited with him as banker by a customer for the amount of a general balance due by such customer on banking transactions, but not, apart from express contract, for debts due to the banker in any other capacity. The owner can sell the subjects over which the lien extends without the consent of the bank, but the purchaser is not entitled to enforce delivery unless and until the debt due to the bank is paid.

(b) **Mercantile Agents, Factors, and Brokers.**—Factors and brokers are mercantile agents. A factor has been defined as an agent employed to sell for a compensation goods or merchandise consigned or delivered to him by or for his principal. A broker has been defined as an agent employed to make bargains and contracts in matters of trade, commerce, or navigation between other parties for a compensation, usually called brokerage. The chief points of difference between a factor and a broker are that, whereas a factor has possession of the principal's goods, a broker has not, and that a factor may sell in his own name, whereas a broker may not. Brokers on the Stock Exchange, however, usually transact among themselves with personal liability according to the rules of the Exchange. The broker is a mere middleman, who, for a commission, introduces the two principals to each other. Thus, when a man wishes to buy or have built a ship, but does not know to which shipbuilder to go, he goes to a shipbroker who knows which shipbuilder is likely to suit him. The broker charges a percentage commission to the shipbuilder for the introduction. The shipbuilder adds the commission to the price payable by the purchaser, and with it pays the broker.

The factor may pledge the goods of the principal in his possession, and has a lien on any goods that have come to him *qua* factor, and on the proceeds of such goods, for the general balance of his charges.

The position of a mercantile agent having in the customary course of his business as such agent authority either to sell goods, or to consign goods for the purpose of sale, or to buy goods or to raise money on the security of goods, has been defined by the Factors Act, 1889, and the Factors

(Scotland) Act, 1890, in his relation with third parties. These Acts lay down that where such an agent is, with the consent of the owner, in possession of goods or of the documents of title to goods, any sale, pledge, or other disposition of the goods made by him, when acting in the ordinary course of his business as a mercantile agent, shall be as valid as if he were expressly authorised by the owner to make the same : provided that the person taking under the disposition acts in good faith, and has not at the time of the disposition notice that the person making the disposition has not authority to make the same.[1] These provisions do not apply to a broker, as he has not possession of the goods. They are an application of the doctrine of holding out or ostensible authority. While a third party acting in good faith and without notice of the agent's want of authority gets a good title to the goods, the rights of the true owner as against the agent are preserved. The main exception to the statutory rule is that the pledge of the goods shall not be for an antecedent debt of the agent. That is to say, if a mercantile agent pledges goods or documents of title to goods belonging to his principal in security for a debt due by himself before the date of the pledge, the pledgee does not acquire a good title to the goods as against the true owner, the principal. It is only where the pledge is given for an advance made to the agent at the time, or to be made to him thereafter, that the statutory rule applies. Corresponding provisions are contained in the Sale of Goods Act, 1893.[2]

[1] Factors Act, 1889, § 2 (1).   [2] § 25.

CHAPTER III

THE LAW OF SALE OF GOODS

The Sale of Goods Act, 1893.—The law of sale in the United Kingdom is now governed principally by the Sale of Goods Act, 1893. That statute codified the law existing prior to its passing and assimilated the laws of England and Scotland. In the assimilating process certain distinctive characteristics of the law of Scotland have been retained and apply still only to Scotland, while certain principles of the law of England have been extended to and made applicable to Scotland. Two examples may be given. In Scotland prior to the Act the property in the article sold did not pass to the purchaser until delivery. Now the property in the goods may pass irrespective of delivery, when the parties intend it to pass. Again the *actio quanti minoris, i.e.* a claim of damages in diminution or extinction of the price of goods bought by a buyer who retains the goods although the seller has failed to perform a material part of the contract,[1] is now recognised to an extent which, before the Act, was unknown in Scotland.[2]

Parties to a contract of sale, as to all legal contracts, are free to make their own terms, and effect will be given to the bargain thus made. Recourse to the statute is only justified where no specific contract has been made or the intention not clearly defined. In construing questions arising under the statute the language of the Act must receive its natural meaning uninfluenced by what may have been the interpretation of the law prior to its coming into operation.

The Sale of Goods Act is applicable only to the United Kingdom, and sales in a foreign country are in general regulated by the law

---

[1] Act, § 11 (2) ; see *infra*, p. 113.

[2] As to law of Scotland before the Act, see M'Cormick & Co. *v.* Rittmeyer & Co., 1869, 7 M. 854, per Lord President Inglis at p. 858 ; Pearce Bros. *v.* Irons, 1869, 7 M. 571.

of the country where the sale takes place. If the law of a foreign country regulates the contract, but an action on the contract takes place in the United Kingdom, effect will be given to the foreign law if it be proved to be different from the law as codified in the Sale of Goods Act.[1]

1. Formation of the Contract of Sale.—(a) Sale and Agreement to Sell.

—A contract of sale of goods is a contract whereby the seller transfers or agrees to transfer the property in goods to the buyer for a money consideration, called the price.

Where under the contract of sale the property in the goods is transferred from the seller to the buyer the contract is called a sale. The contract is called an agreement to sell where the transfer of the property in the goods is to take place at a future time or subject to some condition thereafter to be fulfilled. But an agreement to sell becomes a sale when the time elapses or the conditions are fulfilled subject to which the property in the goods is to be transferred.[2]

It should be noted, however, that there may be an unfulfilled condition and yet be a sale. Conditions in Scotland are either suspensive or resolutive. A suspensive condition holds the sale in suspense until the condition is fulfilled. Until the condition is so fulfilled the contract between the parties is merely an agreement to sell. A resolutive condition, however, implies that a sale has taken place, but that in a certain event the contract will be resolved or dissolved and each party restored as nearly as possible to his former position. The rights of parties are affected differently by the two kinds of condition. Where there is an unfulfilled suspensive condition the property in the goods has not passed to the buyer, and the seller may accordingly maintain his right to the property as against other parties whose only right is derived from the buyer, even though the buyer has obtained possession of the goods. A resolutive condition, on the other hand, does not affect the passing of the property from seller to buyer, and accordingly does not prevent the buyer from giving a title to others which will prevent the seller from reclaiming the property on the occurrence of the event which constitutes the condition. Thus where goods are sold by weight or measure, the weighing and measuring, and, if sent on approval, the buyer's approval, constitute suspensive conditions.[3] But if goods be sold by auction

---

[1] The *Parchim*, [1918] A.C. 157, per Lord Parker at pp. 160, 161.
[2] Act, § 1.   [3] *Ibid.*, § 18 (4).

with a condition that they may be resold if not paid for within
a stated time, the condition is resolutive.

By an agreement to sell a *jus in personam*, *i.e.* a claim against
the seller, is created ; by a sale a *jus in rem*, *i.e.* a right of property
in the goods themselves, is transferred. Where an agreement to sell
is broken by the buyer, the seller's remedy is only an action of
damages ; but where goods have been sold and the buyer makes
default in paying the contract price, the seller may sue for it.

(*b*) **How the Contract of Sale is Constituted and Proved.**—A contract
of sale may be made in writing or by word of mouth, or partly in
writing and partly by word of mouth, or may be implied from the
conduct of the parties. Writing is not necessary, even for the sale
of a ship, although writing is essential to enable the purchaser to
become the registered owner of the vessel.[1]

Being a mutual or consensual contract the sale of goods may be
proved either by writing or parole testimony. If, however, the
parties stipulate for writing, the contract is not complete without it.[2]
A verbal contract of sale falls under the quinquennial prescription
introduced by the Act of 1669, cap. 9, and if action is not brought
within five years can only be proved by writ or oath.[3]

(*c*) **Subject-matter.—What the Contract Includes.**—The Act applies
to the sale of goods. Goods include in Scotland all corporeal moveables except money, *e.g.* machinery, parts of machinery, horses,
cattle, articles of vertu, etc. It embraces industrial growing crops,
and things attached to or forming part of the land which are agreed
to be severed before sale or under the contract of sale, *e.g.* standing
trees[4] and ships.[5] It does not apply to incorporeal moveable property such as stocks and shares. It necessarily excludes money,
because in sale the goods and the price are contrasted.

The goods which form the subject of a contract of sale may be
either existing goods owned or possessed by the seller, or future
goods, *i.e.* goods to be manufactured or acquired by the seller after
the making of the contract of sale.[6] Existing goods may be either
(*a*) specific, *i.e.* identified and agreed on at the time the contract
of sale is made ; or (*b*) generic or unascertained, *e.g.* a portion of

---

[1] M'Connachie *v.* Geddes, 1918 S.C. 391.
[2] See Contract, *supra*, p. 5.
[3] See Prescription, *supra*, p. 59.
[4] Morrison *v.* Lockhart, 1912 S.C. 1017.
[5] Behnke *v.* Bede Shipping Co., [1927] 1 K.B. 649.
[6] Act, § 5 (1).

a larger quantity of goods lying in a store or forming the cargo of a ship.[1]

Specific goods may be the subject either of a sale or of an agreement to sell. In the case of a sale, however, if at the time the contract was made the goods, without the knowledge of the seller, have perished, the sale is void.[2] Thus where a cargo of corn at sea was sold and it was afterwards discovered that the cargo, having got heated, had been sold at a foreign port before the date of the contract, the contract was held void.[3] Similarly, where there is merely an agreement to sell specific goods, as where goods though specific are not in a deliverable state or the price is not ascertained,[4] or the parties have agreed to postpone the passing of the property in the goods,[5] the contract is void if at the time it was made the goods, without the knowledge of the seller, have perished, or if subsequently and before the agreement to sell becomes a sale the goods, without any fault on the part of seller or buyer, perish.[6] The contract is in each case void because of impossibility of performance.

Both these cases of impossibility are peculiar to the law of sale, but there are, of course, cases common to the whole field of contract where performance of a contract of sale is excused on that ground. Thus a declaration of war by this country operates as an Act of Parliament prohibiting all intercourse with the enemy. If a contract of sale made before war involves intercourse with the enemy for its due performance, the contract is dissolved.[7]

Where, however, the contract is for the sale of generic or unascertained goods the seller fulfils his contract by delivering any goods which answer to the description in the contract.[8]

Future goods may form the subject of an agreement to sell, as where the seller has still to acquire the goods he presently contracts to sell,[9] but not of a sale so as to pass the property.

[1] See Hayman v. M'Lintock, 1907 S.C. 936.
[2] Act, § 6.
[3] Couturier v. Hastie, (1856) 5 H.L.C. 673.
[4] Act, § 18, Rules (2) and (3).
[5] Sibson & Kerr v. Ship " Barcraig " Co., Ltd., 1896, 24 R. 91.
[6] Act, § 7.
[7] Ertel Bieber v. Rio Tinto Co., [1918] A.C. 260 ; Claddagh Steamship Co., Ltd. v. Steven & Co., 1919, 1 S.L.T. 31 ; 1919, 2 S.L.T. 170 ; see Impossibility of Performance, supra, p. 61.
[8] Blackburn Bobbin Co. v. Allen, [1918] 2 K.B. 467.
[9] Act, § 5 (3).

(*d*) **The Price.**—This must consist of money, else the contract is one of exchange or barter, not sale.¹ If required by the seller payment must be made in legal tender.

The price may be ascertained in three different ways : (1) fixed by the contract ; (2) fixed in manner specified in the contract ; (3) determined by the course of dealing between the parties.² Failing these, the buyer must pay a reasonable price.³ A reasonable price may or may not be the market price, according to circumstances. The course of dealing between the parties has no necessary connection with the usages of trade. Trade usage, however, may be implied so as to fix the price or mode of payment.⁴ Thus in some trades a large proportion of the price, *e.g.* 20 or 30 per cent., is allowed as discount if the price is punctually paid when due. Again, sometimes part of the price is prepaid by way of security when the contract is entered into. This money is called a deposit. Unless otherwise agreed, if the sale goes off through the buyer's fault, the deposit is forfeited.

Proof of Payment of the Price.—Proof of payment of the price differs in Scotland and England. In England parole evidence is allowed, but in Scotland written evidence only is permitted, except in ready money transactions, or where the amount is under £8, 6s. 8d. The receipt must, if the sum exceeds £2, be stamped with a 2d. stamp. It does not require to be witnessed, nor to be holograph.

(*e*) **Conditions and Warranties.**—A contract of sale may be conditional.⁵ The Act ⁶ states the effect in a contract for the sale of goods of failure to comply with a condition, lays down the law as to conditions or stipulations as to time, and provides that certain conditions as to title, description, and quality or fitness are to be held as implied.

Condition and Warranty.—A condition is a stipulation which goes to the root of the contract, and breach of which on the part of the seller entitles the buyer to reject the goods and treat the contract as void. A distinction between a condition and a warranty is made in the Act. It is really one of English law, and hardly exists in the Scottish law of sale, for in Scotland a breach of warranty, which is defined ⁷ as a failure to perform a material part of the contract,

---

¹ Act, § 1 (1).　　　　² *Ibid.*, § 8 (1).　　　　³ *Ibid.*, § 8 (2).
⁴ Athya *v.* Powell, 1856, 18 D. 1299.
⁵ Act, § 1 (2).
⁶ *Ibid.*, §§ 10, 11 (2) (3), 12–14, 62.　　　　⁷ *Ibid.*, § 62 (1).

entitles the buyer [1] to reject the goods, although he may retain them and claim damages.[2]

Stipulations as to Time.—The Act expressly says that stipulations as to time of payment are not deemed to be of the essence of the contract.[3]   The contract may, however, expressly make them so.   As to other stipulations as to time they may or may not be of the essence of the contract, but time is usually of the essence of the contract in mercantile transactions.[4]

Implied Undertaking as to Title.—Unless the contract shows a contrary intention the seller impliedly undertakes that in the case of sale he has the right to sell the goods, and in the case of an agreement to sell that he will have a right to sell the goods at the time when the property is to pass, that the buyer will have and enjoy quiet possession, and that the goods are free from any charge or encumbrance unknown to the buyer when the contract is made. Thus where a horse was sold by mistake and the purchaser was afterwards, though on the same day, informed of the mistake, he was held entitled to damages for loss of the bargain.[5]

Sale of Goods by Description.—There is an implied condition that the goods shall conform with the description ; but in sales by description it is to be noted that there is no implied warranty of quality or fitness, except in purchases from a seller who deals in the goods that they shall be of merchantable quality.[6]   The two things—description and quality—are distinct. Description means that the buyer has not seen the goods.[7]   A description may consist of a single word, *e.g.* an adjective, as " flax "-yarn or " oxalic " acid, or " ship," which includes all necessary sailing gear.[8]   If, of course, the name of the article indicates its purpose it must also be fit for the purpose.[9] The buyer is not bound to take an article which does not correspond with the description, even where the sale is by sample as well as by description and the bulk of the goods correspond to the sample.[10]

---

[1] Act, § 11 (2).

[2] As to English law, see the Act, § 11 (1) ; Wallis *v.* Pratt, [1910] 2 K.B. 1003 ; Baldry *v.* Marshall, [1925] 1 K.B. 260.

[3] Act, § 10 (1).

[4] Hartley *v.* Hymans, [1920] 3 K.B. 475.

[5] Anderson *v.* Croall & Sons, Ltd., 1903, 6 F. 153.

[6] Act, § 14 (2).   [7] Varley *v.* Whipp, [1900] 1 Q.B. 513.

[8] Armstrong & Co. *v.* M'Gregor & Co., 1875, 2 R. 339.

[9] *Vide* Quality or Fitness, next paragraph ; Van Offen *v.* Arbuckle, 1855, 18 D. 113.

[10] Bowes *v.* Shand, (1877) 2 App. Cas. 455 at p. 480.   Act, § 13.

Quality or Fitness.—There is no implied condition as to quality or fitness of the goods for any particular purpose, except (1) where the buyer expressly or by implication makes known to the seller the particular purpose for which the goods are required, so as to show that the buyer relies on the seller's skill or judgment, and the goods are of a description which it is in the course of the seller's business to supply (whether he be the manufacturer or not), when there is an implied condition that the goods shall be reasonably fit for such purpose ; (2) where goods are bought by description from a seller who deals in goods of that description (whether he be the manufacturer or not), when there is an implied condition that the goods shall be of merchantable quality ; provided that if the buyer has examined the goods, there shall be no implied condition as regards defects which such examination ought to have revealed.[1]

These are exceptions to the general rule of *caveat emptor*, which means that the buyer must take care when he purchases a specific thing that it is of good quality or fitness, *e.g.* a picture or a horse. The real question which distinguishes the rule from the statutory exceptions is whose judgment was relied on in making the purchase. Knowledge of the seller of the purpose for which the goods are required may be gathered by implication from any circumstances tending to show his knowledge. Thus the known occupation or trade of the buyer may be important, as where flour is sold to a baker. And where the goods sold can only be used for one purpose, that purpose is a particular purpose in the sense of the Act according to English decisions and is sufficiently made known to the seller simply by asking for it. Thus milk must be fit for consumption as food.[2]

The implied condition as to merchantable quality is present only when the sale is a sale by description. The fact that goods are sold under a patent or other trade name does not exclude the implied warranty of merchantable quality.[3] An ordinary sale over the counter where the buyer merely asks for the article by its usual name is not a sale by description.[4] Merchantable means something which

---

[1] Act, § 14.

[2] Frost *v.* The Aylesbury Dairy Co., Ltd., [1905] 1 K.B. 608 ; *cf.* Preist *v.* Last, [1903] 2 K.B. 148 (water bottle) ; Knutzen *v.* Mauritzen, 1918, 1 S.L.T. 85 (ship's mutton).

[3] M'Millan *v.* Dick & Co., 1903, 11 S.L.T. 210 ; Bristol Tramway Co. *v.* Fiat Motors, Ltd., [1910] 2 K.B. 831 (C.A.) ; Pommer *v.* Mowat, 1906, 14 S.L.T. 373.

[4] Wren *v.* Holt, [1903] 1 K.B. 610, per Vaughan Williams L.J. at p. 615.

is merchantable when the tender of the article is made by the seller, not something which can be made merchantable by the expenditure of labour upon it.[1]

(*f*) **Sale by Sample.**—A sale is said to be a sale by sample where there is a term in the contract, express or implied, to that effect.[2] The exhibition of a sample does not necessarily make it a term of the contract.[3] It is of no consequence that samples have been shown at entering into the bargain, and have induced it, unless the sale has been made distinctly in reference to them.[4]

A sample has been defined as a description wanting words. In one respect, however, there is a marked difference between description and sample. In a sale by description the seller (except as above where he buys from a dealer in goods of a particular description) takes the risk of defects in quality or fitness of the goods. Sample, however, involves quality. The Act assumes that the bulk of the goods corresponds in description with the sample.

In a sale by sample there is an implied condition (*a*) that the bulk shall correspond with the sample in quality ; (*b*) that the buyer shall have a reasonable opportunity of comparing the bulk with the sample ; (*c*) that the goods shall be free from any defect, rendering them unmerchantable, which would not be apparent on reasonable examination of the sample. If the sale be also by description, the bulk must correspond not only with the sample but also with the description.[5]

2. Effects of the Contract.—Two questions fall to be considered : first, when do the goods which form the subject-matter of the contract cease to be the property of the seller and become the property of the buyer, and what are the considerations which, in various circumstances, determine the time at which the property passes ? In most cases the risk of loss of the goods passes with the property,[6] and accordingly the question may be otherwise put thus, when does the risk of the loss or destruction of the goods pass from the seller to the buyer ? Secondly, when a seller who is not the true owner of goods transfers the property in them to a buyer, what is the effect of the

---

[1] Jackson *v.* Rotax Motor and Cycle Co., [1910] 2 K.B. 937, per Kennedy L.J. at p. 950.

[2] Act, § 15 (1).

[3] White & Co., Ltd. *v.* Dougherty, 1891, 18 R. 972.

[4] Bell's Comm., i. 470 ; Magistrates of Glasgow *v.* Ireland & Son, 1895, 22 R. 818.

[5] Act, § 13.   [6] *Ibid.*, § 25.

contract on the right of the buyer to the goods ?—*i.e.* is there a transfer of title ?

(*a*) **Transfer of Property as between Seller and Buyer.**—The kind of property here referred to is the general property, not merely, in the phraseology of English law, a special property. An example of a special property is the right of a pledgee, which is an interest rather than a property, viz. a security interest. Again, property must be distinguished from a mere right to present possession, an example of which is a lien or right of retention. A carrier or warehouseman who is in possession of goods has a right to retain them till his charges are paid, but has no right of property in them.

Formerly the property could only pass by means of delivery, now by the Act it may pass independently of delivery. The passing is now merely a question of intention. The parties may by express agreement regulate the passing of the property.[1] The Act is concerned with determining when in the absence of express agreement such an intention is to be inferred. To ascertain such intention regard is had to the terms of the contract, the conduct of the parties, and the circumstances of the case.[2] The time at which the property, and therefore in the general case the risk, passes is the time when both parties, expressly or impliedly, consent that it passes. A statutory exception to the rule that the risk passes when the property passes is where there has been delay in delivery. There the party, buyer or seller, who is in fault takes the risk.[3]

Different rules apply as to the time the property passes when the goods are specific, *i.e.* identified and agreed upon at the time the contract was made, from the case where the goods were not at the time the contract was made ascertained. There can be no transfer of the property until the goods are ascertained.[4]

The times when the property is held to pass are as follows :—[5]

(1) When the contract is for the sale of specific, or ascertained, goods.[6]

---

[1] *Act*, § 20.   [2] *Ibid.*, § 17 (4).   [3] *Ibid.*, § 20.   [4] *Ibid.*, § 16.
[5] *Ibid.*, § 18, Rules 1, 2, 3, 5.   [6] *Ibid.*, § 17.

(*a*) If the contract is unconditional and the goods are in a deliverable state, the property passes at the time the contract is made. When the goods are not in a deliverable state the property passes only when the seller has put them in a deliverable state and the buyer has notice thereof. Thus where a farmer sold his growing crop of potatoes, they were held to be in a deliverable state when pitted.[1] The same holds good when the seller has, in order to ascertain the price, to do something with reference to the goods, such as to weigh, measure, or test them.

(*b*) When specific goods are delivered to the buyer on approval or on sale or return, or other similar terms, the property passes when the buyer signifies his approval or acceptance to the seller, or does any other act adopting the transaction. If he wishes to reject the goods he must do so within the time for doing so if there is a time stated, or within a reasonable time, otherwise he may be held to have accepted them at such times.

(2) When the contract is for the sale of unascertained or future goods by description.

If goods of a particular description and in a deliverable state have been unconditionally appropriated to the contract by either party with the consent of the other, the property is transferred at the time of such appropriation.[2] It is not sufficient to pass the property that the goods are sufficiently described to be identified by the seller on acquisition. Until appropriation a second purchaser from the seller might obtain the legal property in the goods first.[3]

The commonest mode of appropriating goods to the contract is by delivering them to a carrier or other custodier, and then, if so delivered in pur-

---

[1] Gowans *v.* Bowe & Sons, 1910, 2 S.L.T. 17.
[2] Act, § 18, Rule 5; Langton *v.* Higgins, (1859) 28 L.J., Ex. 252 (a sale of future crop).
[3] Joseph *v.* Lyons, (1884) 15 Q.B.D. 280 (C.A).

suance of the contract and the seller does not
reserve the right of disposal, the moment the goods
which have been selected in pursuance of the contract have been delivered to the carrier he becomes
the agent of the buyer, and such a delivery amounts
to delivery to the buyer.[1]

(3) When the seller reserves a right of disposal.

The seller may, whether in the case of specific
goods, or goods appropriated to the contract,
reserve, in the contract or at the time of appropriating, the right of disposal until certain conditions are fulfilled. In such case there is transfer
of the property only when such conditions are
fulfilled.[2]

When goods are shipped and the seller in the
bill of lading makes the goods deliverable to the
order of himself or his agent, he is *prima facie*
deemed to reserve the right of disposal.

When the seller of goods draws on the buyer
for the price, and transmits the bill of exchange
and bill of lading to the buyer together to secure
acceptance or payment of the bill of exchange, the
buyer is bound to return the bill of lading if he
does not honour the bill of exchange, and if he
wrongfully retains the bill of lading the property
in the goods does not pass to him.[3]

(*b*) **Transfer of Title.**—A seller impliedly warrants to the buyer
that he can give him a good title and quiet possession.[4] No
title can, however, pass from the true owner of goods without
his consent, express or implied. In certain circumstances
the consent of the true owner to a sale by an apparent owner
is implied.

There are three cases. The first case is where the
true owner by his conduct bars himself from denying the
seller's authority to sell.[5] Thus A., a timber merchant,
instructed the dock company with whom his timber was
warehoused to accept delivery orders signed by his clerk.
The clerk had a limited authority to sell to known customers.

---

[1] Act, Rule 5 (2).   [2] *Ibid.*, § 19 (1).   [3] *Ibid.*, § 19.
[4] *Ibid.*, § 12.   [5] *Ibid.*, § 21 (1).

The clerk in an assumed name sold some of the timber to
B., who knew nothing of A., or of the clerk under his real
name. The clerk carried out the fraud by giving the dock
company delivery orders to his assumed name, and then in
that name giving delivery orders to B. It was held that A.
could recover the value of the timber from B.[1] If, however,
the facts had been that A. had represented his clerk to be
invested with disposing power, and B., supposing the clerk to
be invested with the power, had bought from him, A. would
have been barred from denying that the clerk had authority
to sell to him.

The second case is that while a seller without any title
(*e.g.* the clerk in the example given) cannot confer on a
third party any higher right than his own,[2] a seller with
a voidable title can give a good title to a third party
who takes the goods in good faith. Thus a contract of sale
induced by the buyer's fraud is voidable (*i.e.* good until set
aside), not void, and accordingly until set aside the buyer
can give a good title to a purchaser from him.[3] Where,
however, the buyer's fraud has not only induced the contract, but has also led to certain kinds of error, viz. error
in substantialibus [4] on the part of the seller, the contract is
void, and the buyer, having no title, cannot give a title
even to a third party who takes in good faith. Thus in
Morrisson, T. pretended to the seller that he was the son
of W., and had authority from him to buy two cows. W.
was known to the seller to be of good credit, and he accordingly sold to T. T. resold them to a third party, who
took them in good faith. It was held that the seller could
reclaim the cows from the third party, T.'s title being void
on the ground that the seller was under essential error as
to the party with whom he was contracting.[5] When the
true owner has recovered the goods from a *bona fide* third-
party purchaser, the latter would be entitled to recover their
value from the person from whom he bought them, under the
rule, already stated, that a seller warrants his title to sell.

[1] Farquharson Bros. *v.* King & Co., [1902] A.C. 325.   [2] Act, § 21 (1).
[3] Cundy *v.* Lindsay, (1878) 3 App. Cas. 459 ; Henderson & Co. *v.* Williams,
[1895] 1 Q.B. 521. Act, § 23.
[4] See Contract, *supra*, p. 20.
[5] Morrisson *v.* Robertson, 1908 S.C. 332.

The third case embodies a species of reputed owner-ship.[1] It applies in two instances : (*a*) A seller who, having sold goods, continues in possession of the goods or a document of title to the goods, can give a good and indefeasible title without the authority of the true owner to a purchaser from him in good faith. A document of title means a document used in the ordinary course of business as proof of the possession or control of the goods, or authorising the possessor of the document to transfer it or the goods or receive the goods, *e.g.* a bill of lading, warehouse-keeper's certificate, dock warrant, or order for the delivery of goods.[2] (*b*) A buyer or person who has agreed to buy goods which are still subject to a lien or other right of the original seller over the goods, and who, with the consent of the seller, is in possession of the goods or of the documents of title to them, and who transfers them or the documents of title to a purchaser who has no notice of the lien or other right of the original seller, is, as regards purchasers from him, in the same position as a mercantile agent in possession of the goods or documents of title with consent of the owner. Instances of mercantile agents are factors and auctioneers. A sale by such an agent, when acting in the ordinary course of his business as such an agent, is as valid as if he were expressly authorised by the owner to make the same, provided that the person to whom he has sold acts in good faith and has no notice that the agent has not authority to sell.[3] This case is well illustrated by a hire-purchase agreement, or any agreement to sell as distinguished from a complete sale. A person who obtains goods on sale or return is not in possession of the goods under an agreement to buy them within the meaning of the above rules.

Sale in Market Overt.—A specialty of the law of England may be referred to, viz. sale in market overt. The general rule is that a man cannot make a valid sale of goods that do not belong to him. But where goods are sold in market overt (*i.e.* in the country at the particular spot of ground set

---

[1] Act, § 25.

[2] The Factors Act, 1889, § 1 (4), and the Factors (Scotland) Act, 1890, § 1.

[3] Factors Acts, 1889, § 2 (1) ; 1890, § 1 ; and *vide* Mercantile Agents, *supra*, p. 86.

apart by custom for the sale of particular goods, not including shops, and in London every shop in which goods such as the owner openly professes to trade in are exposed publicly for sale), according to the usage of the market, the buyer acquires a good title to the goods, provided he buys them in good faith and without notice of any defect or want of title on the part of the seller.[1] This does not apply to the sale of horses, to which special rules are applicable owing to the peculiar facility with which these animals when stolen can be removed from the neighbourhood of the owner and disposed of in markets and fairs.[2] And a sale by sample is not a sale in market overt.

3. Performance of the Contract.—It is the duty of the seller to deliver the goods and of the buyer to accept and pay for them in accordance with the terms of the contract.[3] These are concurrent conditions, unless otherwise agreed ; that is, to paraphrase the words of the Act, the seller is liable to deliver the goods whenever they are demanded upon payment of the price, but the buyer has no right to have possession of the goods until he pays the price. Where these conditions are not concurrent, as in sale on credit, the buyer is entitled to immediate delivery, though the right is liable to be defeated if he becomes insolvent before he obtains possession.[4]

(*a*) **Seller's duty to Deliver.**—The contract may or may not regulate the manner, place, and time in or at which delivery is to be given and taken. If delivery of the goods is not given in accordance with the terms of the contract, express or implied, the buyer is not under obligation to accept them. On the other hand, where delivery is properly offered, the buyer must take delivery.

Manner of Delivery.—The delivery may be actual or constructive. " Where goods are ponderous and incapable of being handed over from one to another there need not be an actual delivery ; but it may be done by that which is tantamount, such as the delivery of the keys of a warehouse in which the goods are lodged, or by delivery of other *indicia* of property." [5] Thus delivery may be made by transfer of a document of title, *e.g.* a bill of lading. The transfer of a

---

[1] Act, § 22 (1).   [2] *Ibid.*, § 22 (2).   [3] *Ibid.*, § 27.
[4] *Vide* Rights of Unpaid Seller against the Goods, *infra*, p. 104 *et seq.*
[5] Per Lord Ellenborough in Chaplin *v.* Rogers, (1801) 1 East 192.

bill of lading operates as a delivery of the goods themselves, because while goods are at sea they cannot be otherwise dealt with. But the transfer of, for example, a delivery order or dock warrant operates only as a token of authority over the goods or possession until intimation of the transfer to the storekeeper or other custodier of the goods, when it operates as a transfer of possession.[1]

When it is arranged that the seller is to send the goods to the buyer, the delivery of the goods to a carrier, whether named by the buyer or not, is *prima facie* deemed to be a delivery of the goods to the buyer.[2] The carrier is the agent of the buyer to receive goods. (He is not his agent to accept them as in conformity with the contract.) But it is the seller's duty to exercise due care and diligence in making the contract with the carrier, otherwise the buyer, if the goods are lost or damaged in transit, may decline to treat the delivery to the carrier as a delivery to himself, or may hold the seller responsible in damages.[3] Where the goods are sent by sea or rail, under circumstances in which it is usual to insure, the seller must give such notice to the buyer as may enable him to insure them during their sea transit. Otherwise the goods are at the seller's risk during the sea transit.[4] This does not apply where the contract between seller and buyer is either c.i.f. (*i.e.* at a price to cover cost, insurance, and freight) or ex-ship (*i.e.* delivery to be from a ship at the port of delivery), for the seller is then the insurer. Where, however, the contract is f.o.b. (free on board) or f.o.r. (free on rail), it does apply, for after the seller has delivered the goods on board ship the goods are at the buyer's risk, and the seller must give him notice if he has not already sufficient information to enable him to insure. Where the seller is at fault in omitting to give notice the buyer may refuse to pay for the goods, the concurrent condition of delivery not having been fully satisfied.

Unless otherwise agreed the buyer of goods is not bound to accept delivery thereof by instalments.[5]

---

[1] Blackburn on Sale, p. 302 ; Hayman *v.* M'Lintock, 1907 S.C. 936 ; Price & Pierce, Ltd. *v.* Bank of Scotland, 1910 S.C. 936.

[2] Act, § 32 (1).

[3] Buckman *v.* Levi, (1813) 3 Camp. 414.

[4] Act, § 32 (3).   [5] *Ibid.*, § 31 (1).

Place of Delivery.—Unless otherwise stipulated in the contract the place of delivery is the seller's place of business, or if he has none, his residence, or if the parties when making the contract know the goods in the case of specific goods [1] to be in some other place, that place.[2] Where the seller of goods agrees to deliver them at his own risk at a place other than where they are when sold the buyer must, nevertheless, take any risk of deterioration to the goods necessarily incident to the course of transit.[3] The seller would have to stand the risk of any extraordinary or unusual deterioration, and in the case of perishable goods, such as fish, flesh, and the like, they must, when sent off by the seller, be in such condition as to continue saleable for a reasonable time.

Time of Delivery.—When the seller is bound to send the goods to the buyer and the time for delivery is not fixed he must do so within a reasonable time,[4] and both demand and tender of delivery may be treated as ineffectual unless made at a reasonable hour. Where the goods at the time of sale are in the possession of a third party there is no delivery by the seller to the buyer unless and until such third party acknowledges to the buyer that he holds the goods on his behalf. This is a case of constructive delivery. The section saves the effect of the issue or transfer of any document of title to goods, *e.g.* a bill of lading or a delivery order.

(b) **Buyer's Duty to Accept.**—It is the duty of the buyer to accept goods of which delivery in accordance with the contract has been tendered. If he neglect or refuse to take delivery of goods of which he is bound to take delivery he is liable for loss occasioned to the seller thereby.[5]

When goods are delivered to the buyer which he has not previously examined he is not deemed to have accepted them unless and until he has had a reasonable opportunity of examining them for the purpose of ascertaining whether they are in conformity with the contract. If he has not such opportunity he is entitled to demand it.[6] On the

---

[1] Act, § 62 (1).   [2] *Ibid.*, § 29 (1).
[3] *Ibid.*, § 33.   [4] *Ibid.*, § 29 (2).   [5] *Ibid.*, § 37.
[6] Castle *v.* Sworder, (1860) 29 L.J., Ex. 25 at p. 238.   Act, § 34.

other hand, the buyer is deemed to have accepted the goods (*a*) when he intimates to the seller that he has accepted them (unless of course he accepts them conditionally)[1]; (*b*) when the goods have been delivered to him and he does any act in relation to them which is inconsistent with the ownership of the seller, as, for example, where feed tanks were purchased by shipbuilders to fit into a tug they were building, subject to their being passed by the Admiralty, and they were fitted in without being so passed and were subsequently condemned[2]; or (*c*) when, after the lapse of a reasonable time, he retains the goods without intimation to the seller that he has rejected them.

The question of acceptance is material where there is a right to reject. In Scotland a buyer may in certain circumstances reject goods which he has accepted if he do so timeously.[3]

4. Rights of Unpaid Seller against the Goods.—An unpaid seller is one to whom the whole price has not been paid or tendered, or who has been conditionally paid by means of a negotiable instrument, such as a bill of exchange or cheque, which has been subsequently dishonoured.[4] Seller includes any person in the position of a seller, *e.g.* an agent for the seller to whom the bill of lading has been endorsed.[5]

The unpaid seller of goods has means of securing himself against the buyer's failure to pay the price until the goods are actually or constructively in the possession of the buyer, even though the property in the goods has passed to the buyer. And even when the goods are constructively in the possession of the buyer if they are in course of transit to the buyer the seller has a special remedy should the buyer be insolvent, *i.e.* has ceased to be able to pay his debts in the ordinary course of business, or cannot pay his debts as they become due.[6] These are remedies against the goods, as distinct from remedies by action against the buyer, and exist only so long as the seller is unpaid.

The unpaid seller's rights against the goods are (1) a lien or right

---

[1] Heilbutt *v.* Hickson, (1872) L.R. 7 C.P. 438.
[2] Mechan & Sons, Ltd. *v.* Bow, M'Lachlan & Co., Ltd., 1910 S.C. 758; *cf.* Woodburn *v.* Andrew Motherwell, Ltd., 1917 S.C. 533.
[3] *Vide* Rejection, *infra*, p. 111 *et seq.*
[4] Act, § 38 (1).
[5] Feise *v.* Wray, (1802) 3 East 93; Gunn *v.* Bolckow, Vaughan & Co., (1875) L.R. 10 Ch. App. 491. Act, § 38 (2).
[6] Act, § 62 (3).

of retention for the price, (2) stoppage *in transitu*, (3) a limited right of resale, and (4) attachment of the goods by arrestment or poinding.

Lien or right of retention and stoppage *in transitu* are analogous rights, but are to be kept distinct, for they are in certain respects governed by different considerations. The seller's lien attaches when the buyer is in default in payment of the price, whether he is solvent or insolvent. The right of stoppage *in transitu* arises only where the buyer is insolvent. Moreover, it does not arise until the seller's lien is gone, for it presupposes that the seller has parted with the possession as well as the property in the goods.[1]

The unpaid seller's rights apply where the property in the goods has passed to the buyer. Where the property has not passed the unpaid seller has, in addition to his other remedies, a right of withholding delivery similar to, and co-extensive with, his rights of lien and stoppage *in transitu* where the property has passed.[2] He is still the owner, and cannot, properly speaking, have a lien over his own goods. Moreover, he has the more extensive rights of an owner, and in Scotland an owner's right of retention entitles him to retain the things sold not only for the price, but for any debt or general balance owing to him by the buyer.[3] Where, however, the property passes before delivery the seller is no longer owner, but, on the other hand, he acquires the inferior right of a lien for the price.

Unpaid Seller's Lien.—This remedy is available to the seller only where he has possession of the goods, but irrespective of whether the property has passed or not. The unpaid seller is entitled to retain possession of the goods until payment or tender of the price (1) where the goods have been sold without any stipulation as to credit ; (2) where the goods have been sold on credit, but the term of credit has expired ; and (3) where the buyer becomes insolvent ; and all these even where he is in possession of the goods as agent or custodier of the buyer. The lien is more than an interference with the buyer's right of possession. It also interferes with his right of property.[4] While it does not amount to treating the contract as rescinded, it does enable the seller, should he resell or pledge the goods, to confer a title on a third party.[5] The lien is a lien for the price only, and not for charges for keeping the goods.[6] A sale on credit excludes the lien during the

---

[1] Chalmers, Sale of Goods Act, 1893, 8th ed., p. 95.
[2] Act, § 39 (2).
[3] Black *v.* Incorporation of Bakers, Glasgow, etc., 1867, 6 M. 136.
[4] Blackburn on Sale, 3rd ed., p. 482.   [5] Act, § 48 (2).
[6] Field *v.* Lelean, (1861) 30 L.J., Ex. 168.

currency of the credit, but not in instalment contracts if the price of instalments already delivered is due and unpaid.[1] Where an unpaid seller has made part delivery he may exercise his right of lien on the remainder in his hands.[2] Where the buyer has been sequestrated his trustee in bankruptcy may affirm the contract and obtain the goods by tendering the price within a reasonable time.[3]

The unpaid seller's lien comes to an end (a) when he delivers the goods to a carrier or other custodier for the purpose of transmission to the buyer without reserving the right of disposal ; (b) where the buyer or his agent lawfully obtains possession of the goods ; and (c) by waiver. Waiver may be express or by implication. Thus the seller may assent to a subsale by the buyer, or part with the documents of title so as to exclude his lien if the documents get into the hands of a holder for value taking them in good faith.[4] The mere obtaining of a decree for payment of the price against the buyer does not terminate the lien, unless and until the buyer pays the price.[5]

Stoppage in transitu.—Where the buyer is insolvent the unpaid seller, though he has lost his lien by parting with the possession of the goods, has a right of resuming possession of them so long as they remain in transit, and retaining them until payment.[6] Transit embraces not only the carriage of the goods to the place where delivery is to be made, but also delivery of the goods there according to the terms of the contract of carriage.[7]

The following rules [8] as to duration of transit show that the right of stoppage ceases after the goods have been delivered into the actual or constructive custody of the buyer, or his agent other than a carrier conveying the goods to the buyer, or in terms of the contract :—(1) Goods are deemed to be in course of transit from the time when they are delivered to a carrier by land or water, or other bailee or custodier for the purpose of transmission to the buyer, until the buyer, or his agent in that behalf, takes delivery of them from such carrier or other bailee or custodier. This applies even where the contract makes the goods deliverable at the port of loading.[9] (2) If the buyer or his agent in that behalf obtains delivery of the goods before their arrival at the appointed destination the transit is at an end. (3) If, after the arrival

---

[1] *Ex parte* Chalmers, (1873) L.R. 8 Ch. App. 289.
[2] Act, § 42.   [3] *Ex parte* Stapleton, (1879) 10 Ch. D. 586 (C.A.).
[4] Act, § 47.   [5] *Ibid.*, § 43 (2).   [6] *Ibid.*, § 44.
[7] Kemp *v.* Falk, (1882) 7 App. Cas. 588.
[8] Act, § 45.
[9] M'Dowall & Neilson's Trs. *v.* Snowball Co., 1904, 7 F. 35.

of the goods at the appointed destination, the carrier or other bailee or custodier acknowledges to the buyer, or his agent, that he holds the goods on his behalf and continues in possession of them as bailee or custodier for the buyer, or his agent, the transit is at an end, and it is immaterial that a further destination for the goods may have been indicated by the buyer.[1] (4) If the goods are rejected by the buyer, and the carrier or other bailee or custodier continues in possession of them, the transit is not deemed to be at an end, even if the seller has refused to receive them back. (5) When goods are delivered to a ship chartered by the buyer it is a question depending on the circumstances of the particular case whether they are in the possession of the master as a carrier or as agent of the buyer. (6) Where the carrier or other bailee or custodier wrongfully refuses to deliver the goods to the buyer, or his agent in that behalf, the transit is deemed to be at an end. (7) Where part delivery of the goods has been made to the buyer, or his agent in that behalf, the remainder of the goods may be stopped *in transitu*, unless such part delivery has been made under such circumstances as to show an agreement to give up possession of the whole of the goods.[2]

Stoppage *in transitu* is effected in the following manner [3] :—(1) The unpaid seller may exercise his right of stoppage *in transitu* either by taking actual possession of the goods, or by giving notice of his claim to the carrier or other bailee or custodier in whose possession the goods are. Such notice may be given either to the person in actual possession of the goods or to his principal. In the latter case, the notice, to be effectual, must be given at such time and under such circumstances that the principal, by the exercise of reasonable diligence, may communicate it to his servant or agent in time to prevent a delivery to the buyer. (2) When notice of stoppage *in transitu* is given by the seller to the carrier or other bailee or custodier in possession of the goods he must redeliver the goods to, or according to the directions of, the seller. The expenses of such redelivery must be borne by the seller.

Resale.—The seller may expressly reserve the right to resell should the buyer be in default, and in such case should the seller resell to another, the contract is rescinded.[4] And where the goods are of a perishable nature, or where the unpaid seller gives notice to the

---

[1] *E.g.* Muir *v.* Ranken, 1905, 13 S.L.T. 60.
[2] Mechan *v.* North-Eastern Rly. Co., 1911 S.C. 1348.
[3] Act, § 46.   [4] *Ibid.*, § 48 (4).

buyer of his intention to resell, and the buyer does not within a reasonable time pay or tender the price, the unpaid seller may resell the goods.[1] In all these cases the unpaid seller may recover from the original buyer damages for any loss occasioned by his breach of contract.[2] And should the seller exercise his right of lien or stoppage *in transitu* and resell, the buyer acquires a good title to the goods as against the original buyer.[3] The exercise by the seller of his right of lien or stoppage *in transitu* does not rescind the contract.[4] Hence the seller, if the property has passed to the buyer, exercises his right of resale as a pledgee, and is accountable to the buyer for any balance resulting from the resale.

Defeat of Unpaid Seller's Rights.—The buyer can defeat the seller's unexercised rights of stoppage *in transitu*, lien, and resale where the buyer transfers the documents of title to a third party who has taken the documents in good faith and for valuable consideration.[5] Thus, to take an instance of stoppage *in transitu*. A. sells certain coffee to B., forwarding bill of lading endorsed in blank, and bill of exchange for acceptance. B., who is insolvent, does not accept the bill of exchange. It is his duty to return it to A.,[6] but he does not. Instead he transfers the bill of lading to X. in fulfilment of a contract to supply him with coffee. X. in good faith pays the price. A. cannot stop the coffee *in transitu*.[7] Further, where a document of title has been transferred by a buyer to a person who takes the document in good faith and for valuable consideration by way of pledge or other disposition for value, such as one intended to operate as a security, the unpaid seller's right of lien or stoppage *in transitu* can only be exercised subject to the rights of the transferee.

Arrestment or Poinding.—The Act provides (§ 40) : " In Scotland the seller of goods may attach the same while in his own hands by arrestment or poinding ; and such arrestment or poinding shall have the same effect in a competition or otherwise as an arrestment or poinding by a third party." Arrestment is the appropriate diligence.[8]

5. Actions for Breach of Contract.—(*a*) **Action by the Seller against the Buyer.**—The seller has two forms of remedy against the buyer

---

[1] Act, § 48 (2) and (3).

[2] Brown, Sale of Goods Act, 1893, 2nd ed., p. 360.   Act, § 48 (3).

[3] Milgate *v.* Kebble, (1841) 3 Man. & Gr. 100.

[4] Act, § 48 (1).   [5] *Ibid.*, § 47.   [6] *Ibid.*, § 19 (3).

[7] Cahn & Mayer *v.* Pockett's Bristol Channel Steam Packet Co., Ltd., [1899] 1 Q.B. 643.

[8] Wyper *v.* Harvey, 1861, 23 D. 606.

for breach of the contract, namely, (1) an action for the price, and (2) an action for damages for non-acceptance of the goods. These are remedies, not against the goods as in the case of lien and stoppage *in transitu* and resale, but against the buyer by action.

If the property in the goods has passed to the buyer the seller may, if the buyer makes default in payment, bring an action for the price,[1] or, if the buyer neglects or refuses to accept, he may bring an action for damages for not accepting the goods.[2] On the other hand, if the property in the goods has not passed, as where it is to pass on delivery, the action is usually one for damages for not accepting. But where the price is payable on a day certain, irrespective of delivery, and the buyer wrongfully neglects or refuses to pay the price, the seller may maintain an action for the price, although the property in the goods has not passed, and the goods have not been appropriated to the contract.[3] Where the contract is to deliver by stated instalments, refusal by the buyer to accept or to pay for one or more instalments may entitle the seller to treat the contract as wholly repudiated, or it may give a right to sue only for damages arising from the particular default.[4] A similar principle would probably apply where the instalments were not specific.[5]

Action for the Price.—In Scotland the seller can, as a rule, sue for the price and interest from the date when the money should have been paid. " I think it is a rule of law that interest is only due where there is either a contract to pay interest, or a duty to invest, or in respect of a *morata solutio*." [6] The only damages for delay in payment of money is the interest.[7]

Damages for Non-acceptance.—The damages for non-acceptance may be general or special.[8] General damages are measured as the estimated loss directly and naturally resulting, in the ordinary course of events, from the buyer's breach of contract.[9] The object is to put the injured party, so far as money can do it, in the same position as if the contract had not been broken.[10] Thus where there is an available market for the goods in question the measure of damages

---

[1] Act, § 49 (1).   [2] *Ibid.*, § 50 (1).
[3] Stein, Forbes & Co. *v.* County Tailoring Co., (1916) 115 L.T. 215.   Act, § 49 (2).
[4] Act, § 31 (2).
[5] Jackson *v.* Rotax Motor and Cycle Co., [1910] 2 K.B. 937 (C.A.).
[6] Lord M'Laren in Ross *v.* Ross, 1896, 23 R. 802 at p. 805.
[7] Roissard *v.* Scott's Trs., 1897, 24 R. 861.   [8] Act, § 54.
[9] *In re* Vic. Mill, Ltd., [1913] 1 Ch. 465.
[10] British Westinghouse Electric Co. *v.* Underground Railways of London, Ltd., [1912] A.C. 673 ; Gunter & Co. *v.* Lauritzen, 1894, 1 S.L.T. 435 ; 31 S.L.R. 359.

is *prima facie* to be ascertained by the difference between the contract price and the market or current price at the time when the goods ought to have been accepted.[1] Special damages means the particular damages beyond the general damage which result from the particular circumstances of the case.[2] Should the contract provide for liquidate damages, *i.e.* a pre-estimate of the loss which a breach of contract is likely to involve, that is the measure of damages.[3]

Damages for Delay in taking Delivery.—The seller has also a remedy for delay in taking delivery. When the seller is ready to deliver the goods, and requests the buyer to take delivery, and the buyer does not within a reasonable time after such request take the goods, he is liable to the seller for any loss occasioned by his neglect or refusal to take delivery, and also for a reasonable charge for the care and custody of the goods.[4]

(*b*) **Actions by the Buyer against the Seller.**—The buyer has the following remedies when the seller fails to perform his duty to deliver the goods according to the contract:—(1) An action of damages for non-delivery[5]; (2) an action for specific performance[6]; (3) the right, where the seller fails to perform any material part of the contract (*a*) to reject the goods within a reasonable time after delivery and treat the contract as repudiated; or (*b*) to retain the goods and claim damages.[7]

Damages for Non-delivery.—Where the seller wrongfully neglects or refuses to deliver the goods to the buyer he may sue the seller for damages for non-delivery.[8] This remedy is always open to the buyer. It would lie when goods are tendered and rejected as not in conformity with the contract.[9] If the agreement was to deliver by stated instalments, to be separately paid for, and the seller fails to deliver one or more instalments, it is in each case a question depending on the terms of the contract whether the buyer is entitled to repudiate the contract, or has merely a right of damages.[10] The measure of damages is the same as in the case of non-acceptance,[11] and where there is a claim for delay in delivery damages are estimated at the loss occasioned by the delay.

---

[1] Act, § 51 (2) and (3).
[2] Agius *v.* Great Western Colliery Co., [1899] 1 Q.B. 413 ; Hammond & Co. *v.* Bussey, (1888) 20 Q.B.D. 79 ; Hadley *v.* Baxendale, (1854) 9 Ex. 341.
[3] Diestal *v.* Stevenson, [1906] 2 K.B. 345.
[4] Act, § 37.   [5] *Ibid.*, § 51.   [6] *Ibid.*, § 52.
[7] *Ibid.*, §§ 11 (2), 53.   [8] *Ibid.*, § 51 (1).   [9] *Ibid.*, § 39.
[10] *Ibid.*, § 31 (2).   [11] *Ibid.*, § 51 (2).

Where there is an anticipatory breach, *i.e.* where the seller intimates in advance a refusal to deliver, the buyer may bring an action
at once without waiting until the time fixed for delivery.

Specific Performance.—In case of non-delivery of specific or ascertained goods the buyer can sue for, and in Scotland demand as of
right wherever it is practicable, the delivery of the goods in terms of
the contract. The goods must, however, be specific or ascertained.
In England the granting of specific implement is entirely in the
discretion of the Court.[1]

Rejection on Repudiation, or Retention and Damages.—The buyer
may, where the seller fails to perform a material part of the contract,
either (1) within a reasonable time after delivery reject the goods
and treat the contract as repudiated [2]; or (2) retain the goods and
claim damages.[3] Examples of a material failure are delivery of a
short quantity, of a quantity larger than ordered, or of goods ordered
mixed with goods of a different description. Where the defect is not
material the buyer's remedy is a claim of damages.[4] A remediable
defect in machinery has been held not to justify rejection. The buyer's
remedy then is to have the defect cured at the expense of the seller.[5]
Where there is a contract for the sale of goods to be delivered by
stated instalments, which are to be separately paid for, and the
seller makes defective deliveries in respect of one or more instalments, it is a question in each case, depending on the terms of the
contract and the circumstances of the case, whether the breach of
contract is a repudiation of the whole contract or whether it is a
severable breach giving rise to a claim for compensation but not to
a right to treat the whole contract as repudiated.[6]

Rejection.—The right to reject the goods and treat the contract
as repudiated may be exercised although the property in the goods
has passed to the purchaser.[7] If the buyer rejects he must do so
within a reasonable time, otherwise he may be held to have accepted
the goods. If the breach is patent, *i.e.* apparent on inspection of the
goods, he must do so on delivery; if latent, *i.e.* not discoverable by

[1] Stewart *v.* Kennedy, 1890 17 R. (H.L.) 1 at pp. 10 and 11.
[2] Aird & Coghill *v.* Pullan & Adams, 1904, 7 F. 258 ; Nelson *v.* William Chalmers
& Co., 1913 S.C. 441 (yacht).
[3] Act, § 11 (2).
[4] Webster & Co. *v.* Cramond Iron Co., 1875, 2 R. 752.
[5] Morrison & Mason, Ltd. *v.* Clarkson Bros., 1898, 25 R. 427, per Lord M'Laren
at p. 437.
[6] Act, § 31 (2).   [7] Nelson *v.* William Chalmers & Co., *supra.*

mere inspection, on discovery of the defect. The subject-matter of
the contract has an important bearing on timeous or non-timeous
rejection. Thus, in the case of seeds, the defect cannot generally be
ascertained before the crop appears above ground, or in the case of
machinery, before it is tried, perhaps for some time.[1] The buyer is
not bound to return the goods in order to reject them. He may
reject them by returning them, or offering to return them on stating
that they are not according to contract and are at the seller's risk. It
is sufficient if he do any unequivocal act showing that he rejects them.

Where part of a consignment of goods is in conformity with the
contract and the rest of inferior quality the buyer may reject the
whole, but may not keep the part and reject the rest.[2] On the other
hand, where goods ordered are sent mixed with goods of a different
description the buyer may accept the goods which are in accordance
with the contract and pay the contract price for those he has retained,
or he may reject the whole.[3] So also if a larger quantity is delivered
than ordered.[4]

The right to reject will be barred when the buyer accepts the goods
as being in fulfilment of the contract, and if he does any act in relation
to the goods inconsistent with the seller's right of ownership he is
held to have accepted them.[5] A buyer who has ineffectively elected
to reject the goods and treat the contract as repudiated may subsequently fall back upon the alternative remedy of retaining the goods
and claiming damages.[6] A buyer who rejects goods may also have
a claim for damages for consequential loss,[7] but is not entitled to
retain the goods in respect of damages and expenses.[8] He may, after
due notice to the seller, retain in security of repayment of the price.[9]

Retention and Damages.—The buyer, where the seller fails to
perform a material part of the contract, has, alternatively to his right
to reject the goods, the right to retain them and treat the breach as
giving rise to a claim of damages in diminution or extinction of the

---

[1] Morrison & Mason, Ltd., *supra*, at p. 434 ; Aird & Coghill, *supra*.
[2] Aitken, Campbell & Co. *v.* Boullen, 1908 S.C. 490.
[3] Act, § 30 (3).   [4] *Ibid.*, § 30 (2).
[5] Mechan & Sons, Ltd. *v.* Bow, M'Lachlan & Co., Ltd., 1910 S.C. 758 ; Strachan
& Co. *v.* Marshall & Co., 1910, 2 S.L.T. 108 ; Woodburn *v.* Motherwell, 1917 S.C.
533 ; Hardy *v.* Hollins, [1923] 2 K.B. 490 (resale). Act, § 35.
[6] Pollock & Co. *v.* Macrae, 1922 S.C. (H.L.) 192, disapproving Electric Construction Co. *v.* Hurry & Young, 1897, 24 R. 312.
[7] See p. 68.
[8] Lupton *v.* Schultze, 1900, 2 F. 1118.
[9] Laing *v.* Westren, 1858, 20 D. 519.

price.[1] In England he has no such option.[2] This remedy, the *actio quanti minoris*, is to some extent new. Prior to the Act it was confined in its application to defects of title or quality discovered when matters were no longer entire.[3] Unless restoration was impossible, the buyer had immediately on discovery of the defect to restore the goods to the seller, or be held to have waived the breach and be liable to pay the full contract price.

The buyer's claim for damages does not depend on his having given the seller notice of his claim before acceptance of the goods, even if he knew of the defects before taking delivery and paying the price, although he might be barred from rejecting them. He must, however, inspect the goods within a reasonable time, otherwise he may be barred from claiming damages. Thus if he resells and exports the goods before inspecting them he will be barred.[4]

In Scotland, where a buyer has elected to accept goods which he might have rejected, and to treat a breach of contract as only giving rise to a claim of damages, he may, in an action by the seller for the price, be required by the Court to consign or pay into Court the price of the goods, or part thereof, or to give other reasonable security for the due payment thereof.[5] This acts as a check upon frivolous complaints and claims by the buyer.

Where a buyer has set up a breach in diminution or extinction of the price he is not thereby prevented from suing on the same breach if he has suffered further damage.[6]

6. Sales by Auction.—The law of Scotland as to sales of goods by auction has by the Sale of Goods Act been made to differ to some extent from the common law still applicable to sales of incorporeal moveables and heritage, so as to bring it into conformity with the law of England.

Where goods are put up for sale by auction in lots each lot is *prima facie* deemed to be the subject of a separate contract of sale.[7]

A sale by auction is complete when the auctioneer announces its completion by the fall of the hammer, or in other customary manner. Until such announcement is made any bidder may retract his bid,[8]

---

[1] Act, § 53.   [2] *Ibid.*, § 11 (1).
[3] Louttit's Trs. *v.* Highland Rly. Co., 1892, 19 R. 791, per Lord M'Laren.
[4] Strachan & Co. *v.* Marshall & Co., 1910, 2 S.L.T. 108.
[5] Act, § 59.
[6] Bostock *v.* Nicholson, [1904] 1 K.B. 725 (C.A.). Act, § 53 (4).
[7] Act, § 58 (1) ; Couston *v.* Chapman, 1872, 10 M. (H.L.) 74 ; contrast Aitken *v.* Doulton, 1908 S.C. 490 (part of goods of defective quality).   [8] Act, § 58 (2).

and the seller can likewise withdraw the article from sale.[1] Prior to the Act the rule in Scotland was that a subject exposed for sale by public auction, and for which even a single bid had been made, could not be withdrawn from the sale, nor could the bidder withdraw his offer.[2]

Where a sale by auction is not notified to be subject to a right to bid on behalf of the seller, the seller may not bid himself or employ any person to bid at such sale, and the auctioneer may not knowingly take any bid from the seller or any such person. Any sale contravening this rule may be treated as fraudulent, and so reducible by the buyer.[3] A person employed by a seller to bid so as to raise the price is known as a " puffer " in England and a " white-bonnet " in Scotland. The right of a seller to bid by express reservation is a novelty in Scotland. The Court will take care that knowledge of the reservation is clearly made known to all intending offerers.

A sale by auction may be notified to be subject to a reserved or upset price. In the case of a reserved price, common in English practice, it is in writing, sealed up, and its amount unknown even to the auctioneer until the hammer has fallen on the last bid and the writing opened. The practice in Scotland is to have an upset price, which is made known to intending offerers before the sale has begun.

7. Hire-purchase Agreement.—The idea of a hire-purchase agreement is that instead of the price for, for example, furniture which is supplied being paid in one sum, that price should be paid by instalments, in respect of those instalments the intending purchaser having the use of the furniture in the meantime, and the matter being so calculated that, when the last instalment is paid, the furniture then should become the property of the hirer and purchaser. The instalments will be so calculated as to provide for interest on so much of the principal as is not paid.[4] The advantage of an agreement of this sort is that it more readily enables sellers to obtain a sale of their goods, and at the same time to get security for their debts.

Questions frequently arise on the terms of such agreements whether they are ordinary sales by instalments, in which the hirer contracts to buy the goods, or whether they are merely hires until the full price

---

[1] Cree v. Durie, 1st Dec. 1810, F.C. ; Lord Trayner in Fenwick v. Macdonald, Fraser & Co., Ltd., 1904, 6 F. 850 at p. 854.

[2] Lord Young in Fenwick, *supra*.

[3] Act, § 58 (3).

[4] Lord Dunedin in Taylor v. Wylie & Lochhead, Ltd., 1910 S.C. 978.

is paid. The difference becomes of importance when the buyer who
has the possession and is the apparent owner sells to a third party.
The question then arises whether the third party gets a good title
to the goods as against the original seller. A contract of hire purchase
has been held to be a sale to which the Sale of Goods Act, 1893,[1]
applies, whereby, where a person having bought or agreed to buy
goods, obtains, with the consent of the seller, possession of the goods
or the documents of title to the goods, the delivery or transfer by that
person or a mercantile agent acting for him, of the goods or documents
of title under any sale, pledge, or other disposition, to any person
receiving the same in good faith and without notice of any right of
the original seller in respect of the goods, shall have the same effect
as if the person making the delivery or transfer were a mercantile
agent in possession of the goods with the consent of the owner, and
so having authority to sell them. But this provision and its legal
effects may be evaded by, for example, the insertion in the agreement
of an option to the buyer to return the article without further penalty
than payment of the proportion to date of the current instalment
and forfeiture of the instalments already paid. Thus in one case the
owner of a piano agreed to let it on hire, the hirer to pay a rent by
monthly instalments, on the terms that the hirer might terminate
the hiring by delivering up the piano to the owner and remaining
liable for all arrears of hire ; also that if the hirer should punctually
pay all the monthly instalments, the piano should become his sole
and absolute property, and that until such payment the piano should
continue the sole property of the owner. The hirer received the piano,
paid a few of the instalments, and pledged it with a pawnbroker as
security for an advance. It was held he was under no legal obligation
to buy, and that the owner was entitled to recover the piano from the
pawnbroker.[2] Where the buyer has merely an option he may assign
his right to the effect of entitling the assignee to acquire the article
by completing the instalments.[3] Articles the subject of a hire-
purchase agreement fall under the landlord's hypothec.[4]

[1] Act, § 25 (2).
[2] Helby v. Matthews, [1895] A.C. 471.
[3] Whiteley v. Holt, [1918] 2 K.B. 208.
[4] Rudman v. Jay, 1908 S.C. 552.

CHAPTER IV

THE LAW OF CARRIAGE OF GOODS

1. Nature of the Contract.—The contract for the carriage of goods (*locatio operis mercium vehendarum*) is a species of the consensual contract of hiring. A carrier is one who undertakes to convey for hire goods, animals or passengers from a place within the realm to a place within or without the realm. The contract for the carriage of goods is for the safe carriage of commodities and their delivery in good condition in consideration of a hire. The carriage may be gratuitous. The contract may be express, when the carrier's rights and obligations depend upon the terms of the agreement, or implied from his receipt of goods.

2. Rights of a Carrier.—The rights of a carrier are to have the goods to be carried delivered to him and his remuneration paid. He has a lien over every parcel of goods carried by him for the price of the carriage of it, but he has no lien over a parcel for the price of the carriage of a previous parcel, *i.e.* his lien is a special not a general lien.[1]

3. Obligations of a Carrier.—If a carrier carries gratuitously he is only liable for gross negligence. If he carries for hire his obligations are determined (*a*) under the contract, or (*b*) in the case of common carriers, under certain rules of public policy.

(*a*) **Obligations under the Contract.**—The responsibility of a carrier commences when he is charged with the goods by their complete delivery to him to be forwarded. In the absence of agreement to the contrary the carrier is held to undertake (1) that the vehicle shall be sufficient for safely carrying the goods. This extends also to the accessories. Thus in land carriage the tackle, harness, horses, drivers, etc., and in railway carriage the permanent ways, signals, signalmen, etc., must be sufficient; and in sea carriage not only must

---

[1] Stevenson *v.* Likly, 1824, 3 S. 291.

116

the vessel be tight, staunch and strong for the voyage, but it must be properly manned and navigated and provided with all stores and documents necessary for the voyage. The carrier is not, however, liable for latent defects, *i.e.* such as the eye cannot discover. The carrier is held to undertake (2) that the goods shall be properly packed and placed in the vehicle so as to withstand the necessary movement and concussion of the journey. The consignor may himself undertake the responsibility, in which case only ordinary diligence to notice and correct any defect is required of the carrier. In the case of dangerous goods the sender's duty is to specify their nature. The carrier is held to undertake (3) that ordinary care and the regular course of the journey shall be observed in the transit. The carrier is not bound to take precautions involving any unusual expenditure, nor is he responsible for damage arising from wholly unusual and unexpected causes. Should he deviate from the route he professes to carry or his usual route unnecessarily and the goods be lost, even by inevitable accident, he is liable.[1] If he receives goods to be conveyed to a place beyond his terminus he is responsible for their safe carriage during the whole of their transit, even though during part of the way they should be carried by another carrier, the latter being regarded as the agent of the original carrier.[2] The carrier is held to undertake (4) that he will forward the goods in due course, *i.e.* with reasonable speed, especially in the case of perishable goods. He is justified in delay if delay be necessary for safe carriage. But if he has knowledge of any unusual cause of delay he is bound to advise the sender on receiving the goods.[3]

The carrier's responsibility ceases with the delivery of the goods according to the undertaking. His undertaking must be exactly fulfilled. Thus the goods must be delivered to the person indicated in the contract or according to the address, unless the address be defective.[4] Their delivery on board a wrong vessel subjects the carrier to liability.[5]

---

[1] Polwarth *v.* North-Western Rly. Co., 1908 S.C. 1275.

[2] Caledonian Rly. Co. *v.* Hunter, 1858, 20 D. 1097 ; Metzenburg *v.* Highland Rly. Co., 1869, 7 M. 919.

[3] M'Connachie *v.* Great North of Scotland Rly. Co., 1875, 3 R. 79.

[4] Caledonian Rly. Co., *supra.*   [5] Gilmour *v.* Clark, 1853, 15 D. 478.

Should the carrier be unable to find the consignee, or the latter refuse delivery, the carrier is liable for the safe custody of the goods while waiting the consignor's orders and for their redelivery according to his orders.[1] If before the carrier has parted with the goods to the consignee the consignor orders him to retain the goods or deliver them elsewhere he is bound to do so. The obligation to deliver under his contract is discharged by the destruction or loss of the goods from a cause for which he is not responsible, or even where by his own act he is compelled to sacrifice them by manifest necessity, e.g. to save life.

(b) **Obligations of a Common Carrier.**—A common carrier is one who undertakes for hire to convey the goods or money of all who think fit to employ him in the business which he professes to ply, i.e. a public carrier. He need not profess to carry all kinds of goods but may limit his business to the carriage of any particular class of goods. A common carrier is subject to the Edict Nautæ, Caupones, etc., adopted in Scotland from the Roman Law, whereby he is held to insure the safe delivery of goods committed to his charge, and is responsible for any loss or damage, though no neglect on his part be proved, if such loss do not arise from natural and inevitable accident, the act of God or of the King's enemies. The larger responsibility of the common carrier is due to the supposed dangers of collusion and carelessness in his case.

As an insurer of the goods a common carrier is, at common law and apart from special agreement, liable for all injury to them whatever except, in addition to the exceptions under the Edict, (1) where due to neglect of the owner without negligence on the part of the carrier ; (2) where due to an inherent vice in or natural deterioration of the goods, e.g. a restive horse becoming alarmed and hurting itself during the journey [2] ; and (3) injury due to the nature of the goods requiring special care of which he was ignorant through not being informed.[3] He is thus liable for loss due to robbery or theft, to accidental fire,[4] and to the fraud or negligence of

---

[1] Metzenburg, *supra*.
[2] Ralston v. Caledonian Rly. Co., 1878, 5 R. 671.
[3] Baldwin v. London, Chatham, and Dover Rly. Co., (1882) 9 Q.B.D. 582.
[4] Mercantile Law Amendment Act, 1856, § 17.

his servants. The liability for loss through fire is different in sea carriage.[1]

The common carrier may by special agreement exclude his liability as such, as where he delivers a ticket or other notice to the person from whom he receives the goods specifying the terms upon which he agrees to carry.[2] But the evidence of the sender's knowledge of the notice must be clear.[3]

While carriers of persons are not common carriers, the obligations under a contract upon a carrier of passengers with respect to their luggage are the same as those of a common carrier during the transit,[4] but to the full extent only when the luggage has been delivered to the carrier's servants for carriage under his exclusive custody and control. He is not liable where the passenger takes his luggage with him in the carriage and loss is due to the passenger's negligence. The luggage must be the passenger's own and must be personal luggage. Personal luggage means such as is ordinarily and usually carried by passengers as their luggage, the taking of which has arisen from the fact of their journeying [5]—e.g. clothes, the fishing apparatus of the sportsman, the books of the student, but not what is carried for the purpose of business or household goods. The carrier is bound to receive and take charge of the usual amount of luggage allowed to a passenger, and he has a lien upon the luggage both for the passenger's fare and the charge for luggage.

4. Measure of Liability.—The consignor of goods is entitled to fair compensation from the carrier for loss of the goods. The general rule as to the measure of damages is the market price of the goods at the place of delivery. The facts of each case must be looked to.[6]

Valuable Goods.—Land Carriers Act, 1830.—In the case of valu-

---

[1] *Vide infra,* p. 123.

[2] Wood *v.* J. & J. Burns, 1893, 20 R. 602.

[3] Macrae *v.* Hutchison, 1886, 14 R. 4, and *vide* Henderson *v.* Stevenson, 1875, 2 R. (H.L.) 71 ; Watkins *v.* Rymill, (1883) 10 Q.B.D. 178 ; Richardson & Co. *v.* Rowntree, [1894] A.C. 217 ; Hood *v.* Anchor Line, [1918] A.C. 837.

[4] Campbell *v.* Caledonian Rly. Co., 1852, 14 D. 806.

[5] Hudston *v.* Midland Rly. Co., (1869) 4 Q.B. 366.

[6] Ciceri *v.* Sutton, 1889, 16 R. 814 ; Keddie, Gordon & Co. *v.* N.B. Rly. Co., 1886, 14 R. 233.

able goods the severity of the responsibility put upon common carriers led to the passing of the Land Carriers Act, 1830.

By that Act [1] no common carrier by land for hire is liable for loss or injury to certain articles when the value exceeds £10, unless when they are received the value is declared and an increased charge accepted by, or agreed to be paid to, the carrier. The articles include gold or silver coin, precious stones, jewellery, watches, bills, bank notes, title-deeds, paintings, glass, china, silks, lace and furs, and others.

The increased rate of charge must be notified by the carrier to the public by a notice conspicuously affixed in every place where such articles are received,[2] and the carrier must give a receipt for such increased charge or lose the benefit of the Act.[3] Other than as provided for by the Act no public notice can limit or affect the liability of a common carrier.[4] The carrier can still enter into special contracts limiting his responsibility, but these will not deprive the carrier of the protection of the Act, unless their terms are inconsistent with the goods having been received by him in his capacity of common carrier.[5] A sender entitled to damages may in addition to the value of the parcel receive the increased charges.[6] The carrier is not relieved by the Act of liability for the felonious acts of his servants.[7] The Act applies to a passenger's ordinary personal luggage which a railway company by its published regulations entitles him to have carried free of charge.[8]

While railway companies and carriers by sea are at common law subject to the rules affecting the liability of common carriers, their liability is in some respects determined by rules more special to themselves, statutory and other.

5. Railway Companies as Carriers.—Apart from statutes imposing obligations the obligations of a railway company are to receive and carry such goods as they profess to carry, and in this regard their responsibility is that of insurers. Their obligations have been extended by the Railway and Canal Traffic Acts to the effect that they are bound to convey every class of goods or animals which they have facilities for carrying, their liability, however, in this connection

---

[1] Act, § 1.   [2] Ibid., § 2.
[3] Ibid., § 3.   [4] Ibid., § 4.
[5] Baxendale v. Great Eastern Rly. Co., (1869) L.R. 4 Q.B. 244. Act, § 6; Great Northern Rly. Co. v. N.E.P. Ltd., [1922] 2 K.B. 742.
[6] Act, § 7.   [7] Campbell v. N.B. Rly. Co., 1875, 2 R. 433.
[8] Casswell v. Cheshire Lines Committee, [1907] 2 K.B. 499.

not being that of common carriers.[1] They are not bound to carry dangerous goods.[2]

Regulation of Contracts.—Prior to the passing of the Railway and Canal Traffic Act, 1854, the limitation of liability by special contract was stretched to extravagant lengths, and owing to the practical monopoly of land carriage by railway and canal companies and the danger of oppression to traders the Act was passed regulating the matter. The Act saved the operation of the Carriers Act, 1830, with respect to the articles of the descriptions affected by it, but *quoad ultra* affirmed the liability of a railway company for loss of or injury to goods, etc., occasioned by the default or neglect of the company or its servants, and declared any notice, etc., limiting such liability void. The Act of 1854, however, permitted the making of such conditions as should be adjudged just and reasonable by the Court before whom the question is raised, and further laid down conditions necessary to bind persons entering into special contracts with a view to certiorating that the special conditions have actually been brought under the notice of and consented to by the consignor.[3] These conditions are (1) a written contract ; and (2) signature by the consignor ; and the agreement must in addition be reasonable. These are concurrent conditions.[4]

As to what is a reasonable condition, that is a question of circumstances. Unreasonable conditions are, for example, exemptions from fraud and direct negligence,[5] or subjection of the goods to general lien.[6] Reasonable conditions are, for example, a condition providing against the consequences of loss of market, except where due to gross negligence,[7] or one requiring a claim for loss to be made within a certain time.[8] The offer of an alternative rate without condition, or of an alternative mode of carriage, may render conditions reasonable. The alternative rate must not be prohibitory, and the alternative mode must be reasonable.[9]

---

[1] Dickson *v.* Great Northern Rly. Co., (1886) L.R. 18 Q.B.D. 176.

[2] The Railway Clauses Act, 1845, § 98.

[3] Peebles & Son *v.* Caledonian Rly. Co., 1875, 2 R. 347.

[4] Peek *v.* Directors, etc. of North Staffordshire Rly. Co., (1863) 10 H.L.C. 473 ; Wilkinson *v.* Lancashire and Yorkshire Rly. Co., [1907] 2 K.B. 222.

[5] Ashendon *v.* L.B. & S.C. Rly. Co., (1880) L.R. 5 Ex. D. 190.

[6] Scottish Central Rly. Co. *v.* Ferguson & Co., 1863, 1 M. 750.

[7] Beal *v.* South Devon Rly. Co., (1864) 3 H. & C. 337.

[8] Lewis *v.* Gt. Western Rly. Co., (1860) 29 L.J., Ex. 425.

[9] M'Connachie *v.* Great North of Scotland Rly. Co., 1875, 3 R. 79 ; Lloyd *v.* Waterford Rly. Co., (1862) 15 Ir. C.L.R. (N.S.) 37.

The Act of 1854 is only applicable to traffic on a company's own line and does not affect loss on a foreign line.[1] By the Regulation of Railways Act, 1868,[2] it is enacted that where a company, by through booking, contracts to carry any animals, luggage, or goods from place to place, partly by railway and partly by sea, or partly by canal and partly by sea, a condition exempting the company from liability from any loss or damage arising from the act of God, the King's enemies, fire, accidents from machinery, boilers and steam, and all and every other dangers and accidents of the seas, rivers, and navigation, shall be good and shall be considered to be incorporated in the contract if printed legibly on the receipt or freight note and published in a conspicuous place in the booking-office.

Carriage of Animals.—The liability of carriers for live stock is not so absolute as in the case of inanimate articles. They are not insurers to the extent that if the animal die in the course of transit the value or loss must fall on them.[3] The Act of 1854[4] contains a special provision limiting the sums recoverable for certain animals unless their value has been declared, in which case the company may charge a further reasonable percentage on the value to be notified as in the Land Carriers Act. The contract need not be in writing, and the declaration must be made with the intention that it shall be understood as for the purpose of insurance. The values recoverable in the absence of declaration of high value are £50 for a horse, £15 per head of neat cattle, and £2 per head for sheep or pigs.

Regulation of Rates.—Railway carriers must forward goods without delay or partiality, and cannot give preferential rates so as to handicap any other company or persons. Powers are given by the Railway and Canal Traffic Acts, 1873 and 1888, to a Commission, " The Railway and Canal Commission," to hear complaints, and to make such orders as may, in the circumstances, be right. The Railways Act, 1921,[5] regulates still further both the conditions of railway carriage and also the charges that may be made by the companies. Certain rates known as " Standard Rates " are fixed for each company. Within limits certain exceptional rates may be arranged, but they must be submitted for approval to the Minister of Transport.

Passengers' Luggage.—A railway company is not a common

---

[1] Gill v. Manchester, etc. Rly. Co., (1873), L.R. 8 Q.B.D. 186.   [2] Act, § 14.
[3] Hodgkinson v. London and North-Western Rly. Co., (1884) 14 Q.B.D. 228.
[4] Act, § 7.   [5] 11 & 12 Geo. V. c. 55.

carrier of passengers, but is of their personal luggage so long as in the control of the company. Personal luggage has been described as " whatever a passenger takes with him for his personal use and convenience." [1] The luggage is deemed not to be in the company's possession if it be given to a porter an unreasonable time before the train starts, nor if a reasonable time has elapsed since the passenger arrived at the journey's end and the luggage was placed at his disposal.[2]

6. Carriers by Sea.—(a) **Common Law.**—A shipowner is deemed to be a common carrier only in respect of such ships as are employed as general ships, i.e. ships intended on a particular voyage for a miscellaneous cargo composed of goods of any person that chooses to ship. When goods are shipped a special contract (contract of affreightment) is almost always made, and this may vary the liability of the carrier to any extent. The responsibility of the shipowner has, however, been limited in some respects by statute.

(b) **Liability under the Merchant Shipping Acts, etc.**—By the Merchant Shipping Act, 1894,[3] the owner of a British sea-going ship is not liable for any loss or damage happening without his actual fault or privity (1) where any goods are lost or damaged by reason of fire on board the ship ; (2) where any gold, silver, diamonds, watches, jewels or precious stones, the true nature and value of which have not at the time of shipment been declared by the owner or shipper to the owner or master of the ship in writing, are lost or damaged by reason of any robbery, embezzlement, making away or secreting thereof, or (3) in contracts of carriage falling within the provisions of the Carriage of Goods by Sea Act, 1924,[4] a limit of £100 per package or unit is imposed unless the nature and value of such goods has been declared by the shipper before shipment and inserted in the bill of lading.[5] By agreement another maximum may be fixed provided that it is not less than the figure above mentioned.

By the Act [6] the owner of a British or foreign ship is not liable without his actual fault or privity beyond certain limited amounts, (1) for loss of life or personal injury to anyone being carried on the ship ; (2) for damage to or loss of goods on board ; (3) for loss of life or personal injury caused by improper navigation of the ship to any

---

[1] Jenkyns v. Southampton Steam Packet Co., [1919] 2 K.B. 135.
[2] Paxton v. N.B. Rly. Co., 1870, 9 M. 50.
[3] Act, § 502.
[4] 15 & 16 Geo. V. c. 22
[5] Pendle & Rivet, Ltd. v. Ellerman Lines, Ltd., 33 Com. Cas. 70.
[6] Act, § 503.

person carried in any other vessel ; (4) for loss or damage to any other vessel or goods on board of it by improper navigation of the ship. The owner's liability in these cases is limited (1) in respect of loss of life or personal injury, either alone or together with damage to vessel and goods, to £15 for each ton of the ship's tonnage ; and (2) in respect of loss or damage to a vessel or goods, to £8 for each ton.

By the Pilotage Act, 1913,[1] the owner's liability is no longer affected by the ship being compulsorily in charge of a pilot.

By the Carriage of Goods by Sea Act, 1924, the responsibilities and liabilities, and the rights and immunities, of carriers by sea under bills of lading are defined.[2]

(c) **The Contract of Affreightment.**—This contract is for the carriage of goods in vessels for a price or freight. There is no general rule of law which requires it to be in writing, but it usually is. Contracts of carriage embodied in charter-parties are occasionally entered into verbally,[3] and this as a general rule would appear to be permissible in contracts normally embodied in bills of lading. The Carriage of Goods by Sea Act, 1924,[4] however, appears to require contracts falling within its scope to be embodied in writing.[5]

(i.) **Forms of the Contract.**—The contract of affreightment has two forms : (1) charter-party ; (2) bill of lading.

(1) *Charter-party.*—Affreightment by charter-party is a contract whereby an entire ship, or some principal part thereof, is let by the owner for the specified purposes of the merchant or charterer who hires it during a specified term (time charter) or for a specified voyage (voyage charter), in consideration of a certain sum of money, called freight, per ton, or per month, or for the whole period of the adventure described.

A charter-party may operate in two ways : (1) It may confer on the charterer simply the right to have his goods carried by a particular vessel. In this case the possession and control of the ship are not transferred to the charterer. The master and crew are the owner's servants. The owner is

---

[1] Act, § 15.
[2] See Carriage of Goods by Sea Act, 1924, *infra*, p. 138.
[3] Nordsjernan *v.* Salvesen, 1903, 6 F. 69 at p. 75.
[4] 14 & 15 Geo. V. c. 22.
[5] Act, Art. III., Rules 3, 7 ; Art. VI.

responsible for the goods shipped and has a lien over the goods for freight. (2) It may amount to a " demise " or lease of the ship. The possession and control of the ship in this case are in the charterer. The master and crew are his servants and the master is the agent of the charterer. Demise is not very common and need not be further dealt with.

(2) *Bill of Lading.*—A bill of lading is a receipt for goods shipped, signed by the person who contracts to carry them, or his agent, and stating the terms on which the goods were delivered to and received by the ship. It is not the contract, for that has been made before the bill of lading was signed, but it is excellent evidence of the contract.[1]

The charterer may himself supply the cargo, or he or the owner where the ship is not chartered may advertise the ship for a specified voyage to carry for any persons who wish to send goods to places mentioned. In the latter case the ship is said to be employed as a general ship and the contract with the shippers of goods is embodied in a bill of lading given to each shipper when the goods are put on board. Where the charterer himself supplies the cargo he usually obtains bills of lading signed by the master as evidence that the goods have been shipped. In such case the bill of lading is generally merely a receipt for the goods shipped, and the rights of shipowner and charterer will be governed by the charter-party. Where the shipper is not the charterer the rights of the shipper will not be subject to the terms of the charter-party unless there is a clear stipulation in the bill of lading to that effect,[2]—*e.g.* " freight and all other conditions as per charter-party," and, under such a clause, only in so far as the stipulations in the charter-party affect the delivery of the goods. It

---

[1] Scrutton on Charter-parties, 12th ed. ; Sewell *v.* Burdick, (1884) 10 A.C. 74 at p. 105.

[2] Pearson *v.* Goschen, (1864) 33 L.J., C.P. 265.

has been stated that such a clause will not import into the bill of lading a clause in the charter-party exempting the carrier from the consequences of his negligence,[1] but this rule has been questioned.[2] If, in consequence of discrepancies between the terms of the charter-party and the bill of lading, the shipowner incurs liability in excess of that which he would have incurred had the charterer incorporated into the bill of lading the clauses which he was bound to insert, the charterer will be liable to relieve the shipowner.[3]

A bill of lading differs from a charter-party in being a receipt and a document of title.[4] They resemble each other in embodying the terms of the contract, although, while the charter-party is the contract, the bill of lading is merely evidence of its terms. Where, however, the shipper, whether he be charterer or another, assigns the bill of lading, with the intention to pass the property in the goods, the bill of lading is the contract as between the assignee and the shipowner.[5]

When a ship is put up and advertised as a general ship for a particular voyage the person who wishes to send goods communicates with the master or shipowner's agents and with him or them fixes the quantity of goods to be sent for carriage and the rate of freight. The goods are delivered at the quay or in lighters alongside the ship to the custody of the person in charge of the ship in exchange for a receipt called the mate's receipt. The bills of lading are then filled up by the shipper stating the quantity of goods sent for shipment and describing their identification marks. The goods are then put on board and checked with the figures in the bill of lading by the master, who then

---

[1] Delaurier *v.* Wyllie, 1887, 17 R. 167; Rodocanachi *v.* Milburn Bros., (1886) 18 Q.B.D. 67.

[2] Scrutton on Charter-parties, 12th ed., p. 56.

[3] Kruger *v.* Moel Tryvan Ship Co., [1907] A.C. 272.

[4] *Vide infra*, p. 146.

[5] Leduc *v.* Ward, (1888) 57 L.J., Q.B. 379.

signs the bill and returns it to the shipper in exchange for the mate's receipt.

Usually the bill is signed in triplicate, " bills in a set." One copy is retained by the master, the shipper takes the other two—one to retain as a protection against fraud on the part of the master, and the other to transmit to the consignee. For, the bill of lading being a document of title to the goods mentioned in it, the master will deliver the goods only to a person who presents a proper bill of lading. He is entitled to deliver the goods to the person who first presents one of the bills to him on payment of freight, unless he has notice that there is another party holding a bill and claiming the goods, in which case he must not deliver until the true owner is ascertained.

The master is presumed to be the servant of the registered owner of the ship, but if he signs bills of lading or a charter-party without words showing he is merely acting as agent for the owners, the other party may treat either him or the owners as the person liable on the contract, and the master likewise may himself sue on the contract.

(ii.) **Construction of the Contract.—Implied Undertakings by Shipowner.**—In all contracts for the carriage of goods by sea the shipowner impliedly undertakes (1) that the vessel is seaworthy ; (2) that the ship shall proceed with reasonable dispatch ; and (3) that it shall not unjustifiably deviate. Under the laws of the United Kingdom the above undertakings may be excluded or varied to any extent by express contract. It is otherwise in the United States and most continental countries, and in contracts to which the Carriage of Goods by Sea Act, 1924, and similar Acts apply. The Water Carriage of Goods Act, 1910 (Canada) [1] ; Sea Carriage of Goods Act, 1929 (Australia) [2] ; and the Indian Act (No. 26 of 1925) are examples of similar Acts within the British Empire. This becomes of importance where the contract is to be construed with reference to the law of another

[1] 9 & 10 Ed. VII. c. 61, and 1 & 2 Geo. V. c. 27.
[2] No. 22 of 1924.

country. For instance, by the Harter Act, 1893, of the
United States, a clause in the contract exempting the
shipowner from liability for the negligence of himself and
his servants, or a clause exempting him from liability to
provide a seaworthy ship, would be void as enabling the
shipowner to escape his liability to exercise due diligence
under his otherwise implied undertaking.

(1) *Seaworthiness.*—This means seaworthy for the particular voyage and for the cargo carried. It is
an absolute undertaking, but relates merely to the
ordinary perils likely to be encountered on such a
voyage with the cargo agreed on.[1] The ship must be
in a fit state as to repairs, equipment, crew, and
in all other respects.[2] The implied warranty of seaworthiness relates to the time of sailing from the
port of loading. It is a condition precedent.[3]
Accordingly if the charterer prior to the commencement of the voyage discovers that the ship is
unseaworthy, and the defect cannot be remedied
within a reasonable time, he may rescind the contract. After the voyage has begun he cannot
rescind, but can claim damages for loss. On the
other hand, a clause in a charter-party that the ship
is to be " tight, staunch and strong, and in every
way fitted for the voyage," refers to the time the
contract is made or to the time of sailing for the
port of loading, and so may relate to the preliminary
voyage to the port of loading. The clause, therefore, does not displace the implied undertaking.[4]
While a breach of the implied warranty of seaworthiness entitles the charterer to refuse to load,
a breach of the express warranty, relating as it
does to the time the contract was made, does not,
unless it is such as to frustrate the object of the
charterer.[5] Accordingly an unseaworthiness exist-

---

[1] Kopitoff *v.* Wilson, (1876) 34 L.T. 677.
[2] Dixon *v.* Sadler, (1891) 5 M. & W. 495 at p. 414 ; The " Gunford " Ship Co.,
Ltd., 1911 S.C. (H.L.) 89 ; Rio Tinto Co. *v.* Seed Shipping Co., 1925, 42 T.L.R. 381.
[3] Stanton *v.* Richardson, (1874) 45 L.J., C.P. 78.
[4] Lindsay *v.* Klein, [1911] A.C. at p. 205.
[5] Tarrabochia *v.* Hickie, (1856) 26 L.J., Ex. 26,

ing when the contract was made, but cured before arrival at the port of loading, would not suffice to entitle the shipper to refuse to load. The burden of proving unseaworthiness is on those who allege it. Where, as under the Harter Act or the Carriage of Goods by Sea Act, 1924, and similar Acts, the obligation is to use reasonable diligence to provide a seaworthy ship, this does not displace the common law warranty but gives immunity in certain cases if it is shown that due diligence has been used to make the vessel seaworthy.[1]

(2) *Undertaking of Reasonable Dispatch.*—The shipowner impliedly undertakes that the ship shall proceed on the voyage with reasonable dispatch.[2] Failure may entitle the charterer to repudiate the contract if such as to frustrate the venture as a commercial enterprise, otherwise he has merely a claim for damages. On the other hand, a clause in the contract expressly exempting the shipowner from liability for loss due to a peril of the sea is a good defence to a claim of damages for delay due to such a peril. Thus in *Jackson* v. *Union Marine Insurance Co.*,[3] a ship was chartered in November 1871 to proceed to Newport and there load iron rails for San Francisco. She sailed for Newport on 2nd January 1872, but was stranded on the way and could not be repaired for some months. On 15th February the charterers repudiated the contract. It was held that they had a right to do so ; but as the delay arose from the perils of the sea, which were excepted by the charter-party, the shipowner was not liable in damages for failure to perform his contract.

(3) *Deviation.*—The shipowner undertakes that the ship shall proceed on the voyage without unnecessary deviation, *i.e.* he must follow the prescribed route, or, if none be prescribed, the ordinary route. The

---

[1] M'Fadden v. Blue Star Line, [1905] 1 K.B. 697.
[2] Sutuki & Co. v. Benyon & Co., 1925, 42 T.L.R. 269.
[3] (1873) L.J., C.P. 284.

general presumption is that the route to be followed
will be the shortest geographical sea track between
the two points, but that presumption may be dis-
placed by the existence of alternative routes or of
a customary route.[1] The contract may of course
give liberty to call at ports out of the ordinary
course. But a general permission will not permit
a vessel to call at ports off the course altogether.[2]
And liberty to deviate will not be sanctioned so as
to defeat the object of the contract.[3] Apart from
express contract deviation is justifiable (1) for purposes necessary to the prosecution of the voyage
or to the safety of the adventure, *e.g.* to put into
the nearest port for necessary repairs, even though
this involves deviation[4] ; (2) to save life, but not
property.[5] The implied undertaking not to deviate
is regarded as a vital term of the contract. Breach
of it sweeps aside the whole of the special contract
in the charter-party or bill of lading. If the ship
deviates the shipowner is liable for any loss, whether
it arose out of the deviation or not, and whether it
occurred before or after the deviation, subject only
to the common law exceptions, *i.e.* the shipowner's
liability becomes in effect that of a common
carrier.[6]

Form of Charter-party.—The following is a
simplified form of charter-party :—

" It is this day mutually agreed between the
Steamship Company, Limited,
owners of the good steamship
of　　　　　　　tons net register or there-
abouts, *now lying* in the Port of London,
and　　　　　　　Merchant : That the

---

[1] Frenkel *v.* MacAndrews & Co., Ltd., (1927) 45 T.L.R. 311, per Lord Dunedin
at p. 314.

[2] United States Shipping Board *v.* Bunge & Born, Ltd., 1925, 42 T.L.R. 174.

[3] Glynn *v.* Margetson, [1893] A.C. 351.

[4] Phelps *v.* Hill, [1891] 1 Q.B. 605.

[5] Scaramanga *v.* Stamp, (1880) 5 C.P.D. 295.

[6] Thorley *v.* Orchis Steamship Co., [1907] 1 K.B. 660 ; International Guano
Co. *v.* McAndrew, [1909] 2 K.B. 360 ; Cunard Steamship Co. *v.* Buerger, 1925, 42
T.L.R. 653.

said *ship being tight, staunch and strong, and
in every way fitted for the voyage*, shall *with
all reasonable dispatch proceed to*
and *there load a full and complete cargo of
                      and/or other lawful merchan-
dise*, and, being so loaded, *shall proceed to
                      , or so near thereto as she
may safely get, and deliver the same*, on being
paid freight at the rate of
per bale of 100 lbs., with liberty to call at
any port or ports on the way (*the Act of God,
the King's enemies, restraints of princes, fire
and all and every other peril of the sea always
mutually excepted*).

" Ten days to be allowed for loading and discharge and five days on *demurrage* over and
above the said *lay days* at £10 per working
day."

Terms Common in Charter-parties.—Some usual
terms of a charter-party may be explained :—

" Now lying at." The shipowner agrees to provide a ship. The position of the ship at the
time the contract is made is generally a
material part of the contract. If the position is falsely represented the charterer can
rescind, for on the whereabouts of the ship
depends the time it will be available at the
port of loading. Thus a charter was made
on a certain date for a ship described as
" now in the port of Amsterdam " to proceed with all possible dispatch to Newport
and there load a cargo. She did not in fact
arrive at Amsterdam till four days later.
The charterer was held justified in refusing
to load.[1]

" And there load a full and complete cargo of
                      and/or other lawful merchan-
dise." The charterer is under obligation to
provide a full cargo, corresponding to the

[1] Behn *v.* Burness, (1863) 32 L.J., Q.B. 204.

shipowner's duty to provide a ship and to
receive it. The shipowner must give notice
to the charterer that the ship is ready to
load. The charterer must thereafter provide the cargo before the expiry of the lay
days, *i.e.* the time agreed to be allowed for
loading, by bringing it to the place where
the ship is lying. If there is a custom at
the port of loading it will bind the parties
unless inconsistent with the written contract. Thus it may be customary at the
port of loading to ship coal cargo direct
from the colliery.[1] The fact that it has
become impossible to provide a cargo does
not as a rule excuse the charterer, but he is
excused where events have rendered performance of the contract illegal,[2] or the shipowner has broken a condition precedent, *e.g.*
to provide a seaworthy ship, or there are
express provisions in the contract relieving
him in certain circumstances. Thus in one
case a cargo of wheat was to be loaded at
Odessa. Before the ship arrived there war
broke out between Britain and Russia. The
charterer was relieved from liability to load
a cargo.[3] If a full cargo is not provided
the charterer must pay not only freight on
the goods shipped but also damages, known
as " dead freight," at the same rate for the
unoccupied space.[4] " Other lawful merchandise " means goods of a similar kind
ordinarily shipped from the port of loading.[5]
The shipowner becomes responsible for the
goods directly they are handed over to the
person authorised to receive them, *e.g.* the
mate.

[1] Ardan Steamship Co. *v.* Weir, [1905] A.C. 501.
[2] Esposito *v.* Bowden, (1857) 27 L.J., Q.B. 17.
[3] Esposito, *supra.*
[4] Mikkelsen *v.* Arcos, Ltd., 42 T.L.R. 3.
[5] Vanderspar *v.* Duncan, (1891) 8 T.L.R. 30.

" Shall proceed to or so near thereto as she may safely get." In the case of a general ship the port of discharge is stated in the bill of lading. Where the ship is chartered by one merchant the port may be agreed on or named in the charter-party, in which case the obligation to go to the named port is absolute. If not named in the charter-party the charterer must name a safe port, *i.e.* safe enough to enable ships to load and unload there by taking reasonable precautions. " Or as near thereto as she may safely get " refers to obstacles which are regarded as permanent, not temporary obstacles such as an unfavourable state of the tide. Thus in one case delivery was to be made at Taganrog, in the Sea of Azov. In December when the vessel arrived the Sea of Azov was closed by ice and would not be open for five months. It was held that the shipowner was not entitled to freight by delivering as near as he could get.[1] The question really is what may be regarded as contemplated incidents of the voyage.[2]

" And deliver the same." It is the duty of the holders of the bills of lading to look out for the arrival of the ship. The reason is that the master may not know who is entitled to the goods, for the bills of lading may have been assigned during the voyage. But a reasonable time must be allowed for claiming the goods, and until that time has elapsed the shipowner's liability as a carrier continues. The custom of the port may, in place of personal delivery, recognise another method, *e.g.* delivery to a dock company.[3]

[1] Metcalfe *v.* Britannia Ironworks Co., (1877) 46 L.J., Q.B. 443.
[2] Cf. *Matheos* (Owners of) *v.* Dreyfus Co., [1925] A.C. 654.
[3] Grange *v.* Taylor, (1904) 20 T.L.R. 386.

In questions of discharge weight is given to the custom of the port in interpreting the various terms used in the contract.[1] The shipowner may limit his liability for safe custody of the goods to that of an ordinary custodier by notice, accepted by the consignee, that he has warehoused the goods. The shipowner's liability is ended by refusal of the consignee to take delivery within a reasonable time, or under the Merchant Shipping Act, 1894,[2] in the case of imported goods, if the owner fails to make entry of the goods at the customs house or having made entry fails to take delivery, by warehousing the goods at any time after that fixed for delivery in the bill of lading or charter-party, or, if none is fixed, after the expiration of three working days from the time when the master reports the ship at the customs house.

" The act of God, the King's enemies, restraints of princes, fire, and all and every other peril of the sea mutually excepted." These are the " excepted perils." They apply to the preliminary voyage to the port of loading, to the loading, to the voyage itself and to the unloading ; but not, unless expressly, to any detention of the ship beyond the agreed period for loading and unloading. The effect of the excepted perils clause is to relieve the shipowner from liability for delay, but not for failing to perform an obligation he is bound to perform, e.g. to deliver the goods at the port of destination. Therefore no freight is payable if the ship is prevented from completing the voyage even by excepted perils. Since the decision in the

---

[1] The *Turid*, [1922] A.C. 397 ; Hillas & Co. v. Rederi Aktiebolaget Acolus, 1926, 43 T.L.R. 67 ; Smith, Hogg & Co. v. Louis Bamberger & Sons, [1929], 1 K.B. 150.
[2] Act, § 493.

Xantho,[1] it has been the law that a collision
due to the negligence of the other vessel is a
peril of the sea. If, however, the carrying
ship is alone to blame the shipper can sue
the ship on the contract, and if both ships
were to blame the shipper can recover
damage from each in proportion to the
degree of blame attributable to each.[2]

" Lay days " and " demurrage." The earning
power of a ship depends upon her continuous
employment with as little delay as possible
beyond the time occupied by the voyage.
The charter-party generally specifies a
certain number of days, called " lay days,"
within which the ship is to be loaded and
discharged. Lay days are presumed to
mean running days, *i.e.* all days whatsoever,
but by the contract they may be only working days, *e.g.* excluding Sundays and customs house holidays. Lay days begin to run
when the ship is actually ready to receive
or to discharge the cargo, and the charterer
has notice from the shipowner that the ship
is ready to load.[3] When no provision is
made for lay days a reasonable time is
allowed for loading and unloading. When
the ship is detained beyond the lay days or a
reasonable time the shipowner may have a
claim of damages for detention of the ship.
The contract may stipulate for a sum,
usually *per diem* for so many days, called
" demurrage," as damages for detention
beyond the lay days. Where no provision is
made in the contract the shipowner has a
claim of unliquidated damages.[4]

Where no period of lay days is fixed the

---

[1] (1887) 12 A.C. 503.
[2] Maritime Conventions Act, 1911, § 1.
[3] United States Shipping Board *v.* Strick & Co., [1926] A.C. 545.
[4] Aktieselskabet-Reidar *v.* Arcos, Ltd., 1925, 42 T.L.R. 737.

circumstances of the case are taken into consideration in determining whether there has been an unreasonable detention of the ship. For example, where a strike of dock-labourers caused delay the shipowner was held to have no claim.[1] *Prima facie* the measure of damages is the rate, if any, agreed on as demurrage, but either party may show this is not a correct measure of the damages sustained.[2]

When lay days are specified there is an absolute obligation on the charterer to complete the loading or unloading within the specified time. A strike of dock-labourers causing detention beyond the lay days would not in this case excuse the charterers.[3] On the other hand, if delay is caused by the default of the shipowner, whose servants usually load and unload the cargo, as by failing to supply sufficient labour, the charterer will not be liable.[4]

Shippers or consignees who are not parties to the charter-party may be made liable for charter-party demurrage by a stipulation in the bill of lading, usually " freight and all other conditions as per charter-party." [5]

Form of Bill of Lading.—The following is a simplified form of a bill of lading :—

" Shipped in good order and condition by
in and upon the good ship called
the   , whereof   is
the master for this present voyage, now riding at
anchor in the port of   and bound
for   , [*here specify goods*] marked

---

[1] Hick *v.* Raymond, [1893] A.C. 22.

[2] Moorsom *v.* Bell, (1811) 2 Camp. 616.

[3] Budgett *v.* Binnington, [1891] 1 Q.B. 35 ; Dampskibsselskabet Svendborg *v.* Love & Stewart, 1915 S.C. 543.

[4] Hansen *v.* Donaldson, 1874, 1 R. 1066 ; *cf.* Houlder *v.* Weir, [1905] 2 K.B. 267, and Thiis *v.* Byers, (1877) 1 Q.B.D. 244.

[5] Gardner *v.* Trechmann, (1885) 15 Q.B.D. 154.

and numbered as in the margin, and are to be delivered in the like good order and condition at aforesaid (the Act of God, the King's enemies, fire, and all and every other dangers and accidents of the seas, rivers, and navigation of whatever nature and kind soever excepted) unto or to his assigns, he or they paying freight for the same at the rate of with primage and average accustomed. In witness whereof the master or agent of the said ship hath affirmed to   bills of lading all of this tenor or date, the one of which bills being accomplished the others to stand void.

"Dated at   the   day of   .
"[*Signature*]."

Admissions in the Bill of Lading.—The bill of lading usually contains an admission as to the quantity, quality, and condition of goods shipped. The shipowner undertakes to deliver all the goods put on board "in like good order and condition," provided freight is paid as agreed and he is not prevented by any of the excepted perils. When the goods are not in good order when shipped a note should be made to that effect in the margin of the bill. A bill without such a note is known as a clean bill of lading. Broadly such admissions are evidence against the shipowner, for the master is his agent to make all admissions ordinarily made in a bill of lading,[1] but are not conclusive. The master's signature only admits the receipt of a certain number of packages, and that the goods or packages were externally in good condition. Accordingly the onus of proving that goods mentioned in the bill of lading were not shipped is on the shipowner.[2] He may escape liability by proving that the master had exceeded his authority by

---

[1] Evans *v.* Webster & Bros., Ltd., 1929, 45 T.L.R. 136.
[2] Smith *v.* Bedouin S.N. Co., [1896] A.C. 70 ; Mantoura & Sons *v.* David, 32 Com. Cas. 4.

signing for goods not actually shipped,[1] or that
the master incorrectly stated the quality marks in
the bill of lading,[2] or that defects in the condition
of the goods were not apparent on reasonable
inspection,[3] or if the bill of lading contains a qualification such as " weight, quality, quantity and
contents unknown." [4] And where the consignee is
also shipper he must show that damage was due
to fault on the part of the shipowner or else that
the goods were in fact shipped in good condition.[5]
Where the bill of lading has got into the hands of
a consignee or endorsee for value the bill is conclusive evidence as against the person signing it
that the goods represented to have been shipped
have been actually shipped, unless the holder of
the bill knew when he took it that the goods had
not been shipped or the person signing can show
that the misrepresentation was due to the fraud of
the shipper, holder of the bill of lading, or someone
under whom the holder claims.[6]

The Carriage of Goods by Sea Act, 1924.—(1)
General.—The Act gives the force of law to the
" Rules relating to Bills of Lading " set out in
articles in the schedule to the Act. The object in
view was to secure uniformity so that shippers and
consignees might know the exact extent of the
obligations and liabilities of shipowners carrying
their goods. Acts in similar terms have been
passed in other parts of the British Empire.[7]
The general intention of the Act is that the carrier
of goods is to be subject to the responsibilities and
liabilities set forth in Article III. of the schedule,
while at the same time he is to be entitled to the

---

[1] Grant *v.* Norway, (1851) 20 L.J., C.P. 93.
[2] Cox *v.* Bruce, (1886) 56 L.J., Q.B. 121.
[3] Martineaus, Ltd. *v.* R.M.S. Packet Co., (1912) 28 T.L.R. 364.
[4] Craig Line Steamship Co., Ltd. *v.* North British Storage and Transit Co.,
1921 S.C. 114.
[5] The *Ida*, (1875) 32 L.T. 541.
[6] Bills of Lading Act, 1855, § 3 ; Parsons *v.* New Zealand Shipping Co., [1901]
1 Q.B. 548.
[7] Australia (Sea Carriage of Goods Act, 1924) ; India (Act No. 26 of 1925).

rights and immunities contained in Article **IV**. The responsibilities and liabilities imposed on the carrier are *minimum* responsibilities which he may not reduce, while the rights and immunities represent a *maximum* which he cannot enlarge.

(2) **The Scope of the Act.**—The Act deals only with " Carriers under Bills of Lading." It does not affect carriers under a charter-party beyond requiring them if they issue bills of lading to issue them in conformity with the requirements of the Act.[1] By § 1 of the Act it is provided that the Rules shall have effect in relation to and in connection with the carriage of goods by sea in ships carrying goods from any port in Great Britain or Northern Ireland to any other port. They do not, however, apply to contracts of carriage either of live animals or of deck cargoes which are in fact carried on deck. The Rules have a modified effect in relation to the coastal trade and shipments of particular goods made otherwise than in the ordinary course of trade. The Rules apply only to outward bills of lading. Every bill of lading or similar document of title, including " Received for Shipment Bills of Lading," [2] issued in Great Britain or Northern Ireland, which contains or is evidence of any contract to which the Rules apply, must contain an express statement that it is to have effect subject to the provisions of the Rules as applied by the Act.[3]

The following definitions are contained in the Act :—

Carrier includes the owner or the charterer who enters into a contract of carriage with a shipper.

Ship means any vessel used for the carriage of goods by sea.

Carriage of goods covers the period from the time when the goods are loaded on board to the time when they are discharged from the ship. It is accordingly advisable that shippers should make

[1] Article V.   [2] See *infra*, p. 146.   [3] § 3.

provision to cover the periods before shipment and after discharge if the goods are to be in the hands of the carrier during these times.

Contract of carriage is defined as " contracts of carriage covered by a bill of lading or similar document of title in so far as such document relates to the carriage of goods by sea, including any bill of lading or similar document as aforesaid issued under or pursuant to a charter-party from the moment at which such bill of lading or similar document of title regulates the relations between a carrier and a holder of the same." It is not quite certain if these words mean contracts of carriage which are in fact embodied in a bill of lading or contracts of carriage which are usually and normally so embodied. From the general intention of the Act the latter would appear to be the correct meaning.

Particular Goods.—The carrier is permitted to enter into a special agreement with the shipper in certain circumstances.[1] This agreement may be upon any terms selected by the parties provided that (*a*) it is not contrary to public policy, and (*b*) does not exempt the carrier from liability for want of care and diligence on his own part or on that of his servants. The special circumstances in which such agreements may be entered into require that the shipments shall be other than ordinary commercial shipments made in the ordinary course of trade and that they be shipments where the character or condition of the property, or the circumstances, terms, and conditions of carriage are such as to justify a special agreement. These special agreements are subject to three conditions :—

(1) No bill of lading may be issued.

(2) The terms of the agreement shall be embodied in a receipt.

(3) This receipt is to be marked " Non-negotiable."

---

[1] Article VI.

The term " particular goods " is not defined in the Act, but it is thought to be intended to cover new types of cargo or shipments involving a risk the extent of which cannot be accurately foretold.

Coasting Trade.—Carriers and shippers in the coasting trade are at liberty to enter into special agreements covering the shipment of goods of any class or description.[1] The coasting trade is defined as trade between any port in Great Britain or Northern Ireland and any port within the same limits or in the Irish Free State.

(3) **The Effect of the Rules.**—(*a*) *General.*— The responsibilities and liabilities of the carrier set out in the Act [2] cannot be reduced in any way whatsoever.[3] His responsibilities cover the loading, handling, stowage, carriage, custody, care, and discharge of the goods.[4] His liabilities are, however, subject to the provisions giving to him certain rights and immunities.[5] He may surrender any or all of these rights and immunities.[6]

(*b*) *Responsibilities and Liabilities of Carriers.*— *Seaworthiness.*—The Act makes a change of great importance in regard to the warranty of seaworthiness. The common law warranty that the vessel is seaworthy at the beginning of the voyage or stage of a voyage is abolished in any case to which the Rules apply,[7] and it is replaced by the less onerous obligation to exercise due diligence before and at the beginning of the voyage to make the vessel seaworthy, properly man, equip, and supply the ship and make the holds, refrigerating and cool chambers, and all other parts of the ship in which the goods are carried, fit and safe for their reception, carriage, and preservation. Neither the carrier nor the ship will be liable for loss or damage arising from unseaworthiness, unless caused by want of due diligence in these respects on the part

---

[1] Act, § 4.   [2] Article III.   [3] Rule 8 of Article III.
[4] Article II.   [5] Article IV.   [6] Article V.   [7] Act, § 2.

of the carrier.[1] This obligation upon the carrier,
while less onerous than that imposed by common
law, applies to a period before the voyage commences as well as to the commencement of the
voyage. The onus of proving that he has in fact
used due diligence is laid upon the carrier.

Loading and Discharge.—The common law rule,
that the carrier took over the goods and the liability
for them at the ship's rail upon loading and was
relieved from liability whenever he delivered at
the ship's rail, was frequently altered by private
agreement so as to place upon the shipper the duty
of stowing on board or of unloading from the hold.
The Act [2] requires the carrier properly and carefully
to load, handle, stow, carry, keep, care for, and
discharge the goods carried. This would appear
to strike at agreements under which the responsibility for loading and discharging goods on board
is placed upon the shoulders of the shipper. The
carrier obtains some measure of protection under
the Act.[3]

The Bill of Lading.—The carrier must,[4] on
demand of the shipper, issue to the shipper a bill
of lading. This bill of lading must show three
things : (1) The loading marks necessary for the
identification of the goods as the same are furnished in writing by the shipper before loading.
(2) Either the number of packages or the quantity
of goods or the weight, according to the method of
measurement employed to record the *quantum* of
goods. The particulars are to be as furnished by
the shipper in writing. (3) The apparent order
and condition of the goods.

The carrier is not bound to state or show in the
bill of lading any marks, number, quantity or
weight which he has reasonable grounds for
suspecting not accurately to represent the goods

---

[1] Article IV., Rule 1 ; Angliss & Co. (Australia) Proprietary *v.* P. & O. S.N. Co.,
[1927] 2 K.B. 456.
[2] Article III., Rule 2.   [3] Article IV., Rule 2.   [4] Article III., Rule 3.

actually received or which he has no means of checking.

The bill of lading is *prima facie* evidence of the receipt of the goods.[1] The shipper is deemed to have guaranteed to the carrier the accuracy of the marks, number, quantity, and weight as furnished by him and is liable to indemnify him against loss resulting therefrom.[2] It should be noted that the apparent order and condition of the goods is not one of the particulars to be furnished by the shipper. By the terms of the Bills of Lading Act, 1855, a consignee under a bill of lading acquires the same rights and liabilities as the shipper. It is a question whether such a person would not be liable under this section as well as the shipper.

Notice of damage must be given in writing to the carrier or his agent at the port of discharge before or at the time of the removal of the goods or, if the loss and damage be not apparent, within three days.[3] Failing such notice, removal of the goods is deemed to be *prima facie* evidence that the goods were removed in the condition as described in the bill of lading. The carrier and the ship are discharged unless suit is brought within one year after delivery of the goods or the date when the goods should have been delivered.

(c) *The Carrier's Rights and Immunities.*— *General.*—Nothing in the rules is to prevent a carrier or shipper from entering into any agreement as to liability for loss and damage to or in connection with the custody, care, and handling of goods prior to the loading on and subsequent to the discharge from the ship on which the goods are carried.[4]

The provisions in the Rules are not to affect the rights and obligations of the carrier under any statute for the time being in force relating to the

---

[1] Article III., Rule 4.   [2] *Ibid.*, Rule 5.
[3] *Ibid.*, Rule 6.   [4] Article VII.

limitation of the liability of owners of sea-going vessels.[1]

Particular Immunities.—In addition to the provisions dealing with Seaworthiness,[2] Deviation,[3] Limitation of Liability,[4] and Dangerous Goods,[5] the Act provides [6] that neither the carrier nor the ship shall be responsible for loss and damage arising or resulting from certain enumerated causes. These are : (1) Act, neglect or default of the master, mariner, pilot, or the servants of the carrier in the navigation or in the management of the ship.[7] (2) Fire, unless caused by the actual fault or privity of the carrier. (3) Perils, dangers, and accidents of the sea or other navigable waters. (4) Act of God. (5) Act of war. (6) Act of public enemies. (7) Restraint or arrest of princes, rulers or people, or seizure under legal process. (8) Quarantine restrictions. (9) Act or omission of the shipper or owner of the goods, his agent or representative. (10) Strikes or lockouts or stoppage or restraint of labour from whatever cause, whether partial or general. (11) Riots and civil commotions. (12) Saving or attempting to save life or property at sea. (13) Wastage in bulk or weight or any other loss or damage arising from inherent defect, quality, or vice of the goods. (14) Insufficiency of packing. (15) Insufficiency or inadequacy of marks. (16) Latent defects not discoverable by due diligence.[8] Failure to prevent theft is not an act of management.[9] (17) Any other cause arising without the actual fault or privity of the carrier or without the fault or neglect of the agents or servants of the carrier.[10] The burden of proof is on the person claiming the benefit of this

[1] Article VIII.   [2] *Supra*, p. 141.   [3] *Infra*, p. 145.
[4] *Infra*, p. 145.   [5] *Infra*, p. 145.   [6] Article IV.
[7] Goosse Millard v. Canadian Government Merchant Marine, [1929] A.C. 223.
[8] The *Dimitrios Rallias*, (1923) 128 L.T. 491.
[9] The *Touraine*, [1928] P. 58 ; The *Glenochil*, [1896] P. 10 ; Forman v. Ellans, 1928, 44 T.L.R. 250 ; *City of Baroda* (Owners) v. Hall Line, Ltd., 1925, 42 T.L.R. 717.
[10] Broun & Co. v. Harrison, 1926, 43 T.L.R. 633.

exception to show that neither the actual fault or privity of the carrier nor the fault or neglect of the agents or servants of the carrier contributed to the loss or damage. Stevedores are agents or servants of the carrier within the meaning of this section.[1]

The shipper is not to be responsible for loss or damage sustained by the carrier or the ship arising or resulting from any cause without the act, fault or neglect of the shipper, his agents or his servants. The effect of this provision would appear to be far reaching and there might be cases in which it would exempt an assignee from payment of a demurrage claim.

Deviation.—Deviation in saving or attempting to save life and property at sea, or any other reasonable deviation, is not to be deemed to be an infringement or breach of the Rules or of the contract of carriage, and the carrier is not to be liable for any loss or damage resulting therefrom.[2]

Limitation of Liability.—Neither the carrier nor the ship is, in any event, to be liable for loss or damage in an amount exceeding £100 per package or unit unless the nature and value of the goods shall have been declared by the shipper before shipment and inserted in the bill of lading. By agreement this figure may be increased.[3]

Dangerous Goods.—Goods of an inflammable, explosive, or dangerous nature, to the shipment whereof the carrier has not consented with knowledge of their nature and character, may be landed at any time or place and destroyed or rendered innocuous by the carrier without compensation.[3] The shipper of such goods is liable for all damages and expenses directly or indirectly resulting from such shipment.

If such goods are shipped with the knowledge and consent of the carrier and they become a danger to the ship or cargo they may be likewise

---

[1] Heyn v. Ocean Steamship Co., 1926, 43 T.L.R. 358.
[2] Article IV., Rule 4.   [3] *Ibid.*, Rule 6.

landed, destroyed, or rendered innocuous by the carrier without liability on the part of the carrier except to general average, if any. These powers in regard to dangerous goods are in addition to the powers conferred upon him by the Merchant Shipping Act, 1894.[1]

The Bill of Lading as a Document of Title.—By the custom of merchants the bill of lading operates to pass the property in the goods when endorsed and delivered with that intention to a *bona fide* endorsee for value,[2] and the endorsee has all the rights of action which the consignee had as if the contract contained in the bill of lading had been made with himself.[3] If the bill is drawn " to order or assigns," the person to whom the bill is made out may transfer his rights under it by endorsing and delivering it to the assignee. He may merely endorse it in blank (*i.e.* without specifying any endorsee), in which case his rights are transferred by mere delivery, the holder being entitled to fill up the blank as he chooses. If made out to a specified person without the addition of the words " to order or assigns," it is not negotiable to any extent. A bill of lading is not a negotiable instrument in the full sense like a bill of exchange,[4] for a *bona fide* endorsee for value of a bill of lading cannot get a good title from a transferor whose title is defective. The transfer of a bill of lading to a *bona fide* endorsee for value does, however, defeat the lien and the right of stoppage *in transitu* of an unpaid vendor.[5]

In recent times a form of bill of lading, known as a " Received for Shipment Bill of Lading," has come into general use. It is in the same form as an ordinary bill of lading, but instead of acknow-

---

[1] 57 & 58 Vict. c. 60, §§ 446–450.

[2] Lickbarrow *v.* Mason, (1793) 6 East 19 ; Sewell *v.* Burdick, (1884) 10 A.C. 74 ; Hayman *v.* M'Lintock, 1907 S.C. 936.

[3] Bills of Lading Act, 1855, § 1.

[4] *Vide* Bills of Exchange, *infra*.

[5] *Vide* Sale of Goods, *supra*, p. 106.

ledging receipt of goods on board it merely acknowledges that the goods have been received for shipment either by a named ship or by any ship of a particular description.[1] It is not clear if such a document is the same as a true bill of lading or is more of the nature of a storekeeper's warrant. The Carriage of Goods by Sea Act, 1924, seems to assume that it is a true bill of lading, and this is in accordance with the view taken in *The Malborough Hill*,[2] but in the case of *Diamond Alkali* v. *Bourgeois* [3] it was held that in the absence of a custom of trade or express provisions in the contract such a bill of lading is not a good tender under a contract of sale on c.i.f. terms.

(iii.) **Freight.**—Freight is the consideration paid to the shipowner for the carriage of goods in his ship. Payment of freight and delivery of the goods are, unless otherwise agreed, concurrent conditions. Unless non-delivery is caused by the fault of the shipper alone freight is payable only on delivery of the goods in terms of the contract of affreightment. The excepted perils may excuse the shipowner from liability for non-delivery, but will not entitle him, generally speaking, to earn freight, as where the master has to abandon the voyage. He must still forward the goods in order to earn freight.

Advance Freight.—Freight may be made payable in advance, *e.g.* on shipment, or at a definite time thereafter. In that case, in England, payment does not depend on delivery and is due though the ship is lost or the voyage abandoned and the cargo never delivered. In Scotland an advance of freight is recoverable if the consideration fails.[4] Sometimes the charterer agrees to make payments in advance to meet the current expenses of the ship and to be deducted from the freight when it becomes payable. Such advances are merely a loan and can be recovered if delivery is not made.

Pro rata Freight.—The parties may agree, or it may be

---

[1] Weis & Co. *v.* Produce Brokers Co., (1921) 74 L.R. 211.
[2] [1921] A.C. 444.
[3] [1921] 3 K.B. 443.
[4] Watson & Co. *v.* Shankland, 1871, 10 M. 142 ; Cantiere San Rocco *v.* Clyde Shipbuilding and Engineering Co., 1923 S.C. (H.L.) 105.

implied, that delivery at an intermediate port is to be accepted as part performance of the contract. In that case freight is payable *pro rata*, *i.e.* in proportion to the part of the voyage completed. To raise an implication that *pro rata* freight is due the shipowner must have been able and willing to carry the cargo to its final destination. Mere acceptance by the merchant of delivery of the goods at an intermediate port where the master insisted on leaving them will not imply an obligation to pay *pro rata* freight. The merchant must have had a real option to have the goods conveyed to their destination.[1]

Lump Sum Freight.—Sometimes the charterer agrees to pay " lump sum freight " for the use of the ship, payable on delivery of the cargo. The full sum is payable when the shipowner has delivered or is ready to deliver the full cargo, or such part of it as has not been lost by reason of excepted perils,[2] but probably subject to deduction where part of the cargo has been lost through the negligence of the master. As already stated, the excepted perils do not, generally speaking, affect the shipowner's rights as to freight, whether payable on delivery, in advance, or lump sum.

Dead Freight.—Where a merchant undertakes to supply a given quantity or weight of goods and fails to supply the specified quantity the shipowner is entitled under a claim for dead freight to receive freight in respect of the goods not supplied. It is the shipmaster's duty to try to obtain additional cargo and so lessen the claim to be borne by the charterer.[3]

Cesser Clause.—A charterer is primarily liable for freight, and the fact that he has sublet the services of the ship to persons who have put goods on board under bills of lading reserving the same freight does not release him. Sometimes the charterer is merely an agent or broker to fill the ship with the goods of other persons. A clause is then inserted in the charter-party called a " Cesser Clause," making his liability to the shipowner for freight to cease when the goods are shipped, and giving the shipowner a

---

[1] Metcalfe *v.* Britannia Iron Works Co., (1887) 46 L.J., Q.B. 443.
[2] Harrowing Steamship Co. *v.* Thomas, [1913] 2 K.B. 171 ; affd. [1915] A.C. 58.
[3] Wallems Rederi A/s. *v.* Muller & Co., Batavia, [1927] 2 K.B. 99.

lien on the cargo for freight and other claims, *e.g.* demurrage, under the charter-party. The clause may run, " charterer's liability to cease when the ship is loaded, the captain having a lien on the cargo for freight, dead freight, and demurrage." There is a general presumption that the extent of the shipowner's lien is the measure of the charterer's exemption.[1]

Lien for Freight.—The shipowner has at common law a lien over goods shipped for the freight. This is a possessory lien, and so can only be enforced by retaining the goods. It arises only when freight is payable on delivery. Therefore if freight is payable in advance or after delivery there is no lien at common law. The lien is presumed not to extend to or be enforceable against persons not parties to the charter-party. Accordingly in their case, apart from clear indication in the bill of lading, the lien will be enforceable only as regards freight reserved by the bill of lading.

If the goods on delivery are damaged or deteriorated the merchant cannot deduct from the freight. He may sue for the amount of the damage.

(iv.) **Average.**[2]—If in the course of the voyage it is necessary to sacrifice the ship or cargo the loss will generally fall on the owner of what is sacrificed. But where to avert a common danger the ship or part of the cargo is intentionally sacrificed, or extra expenditure is incurred to avert the danger, the loss or expenditure will be apportioned among the various interests in proportion to their saved values. This is called a " general average " sacrifice. An interest sacrificed and claiming contribution will not, however, be entitled to it if the danger has arisen from the fault of that interest. Thus the shipowner cannot recover in respect of extra expenditure to further the adventure where such expenditure was due to the ship's own unseaworthiness.[3] If, however, the fault is excepted in the contract of carriage, contribution may be claimed. Thus in one case the charter-party excepted negligence of the shipowner's servants. By reason of negligence on the part of the ship's engineers water got into the ship and the shipowners claimed against the

---

[1] Jennenson, Taylor & Co. *v.* Secretary of State for India, [1916] 2 K.B. 702.
[2] *Vide* also Marine Insurance, *infra.*
[3] Schloss *v.* Heriot, (1863) 32 L.J., C.P. 211.

cargo owner in respect of expenditure necessary to remove it and was held entitled to contribution.[1] The sacrifice or expenditure must have effected the preservation of the ship or cargo or part thereof, otherwise there is no case for general average contribution.

Common instances of general average sacrifice are jettison of the cargo in order to lighten the vessel, sacrifice of the ship or its tackle, stranding of the ship to avoid its sinking, and deviation to put into a port of refuge to save the ship and cargo.

The shipowner has a lien on the cargo for general average contributions, and must retain the goods until contributions due in respect of them to other persons are paid.[2]

[1] The *Carron Park*, (1890) 59 L.J., Adm. 74.
[2] Strang *v.* Scott, (1889) 14 A.C. at p. 606.

CHAPTER V

THE LAW OF MERCHANT SHIPPING

THE law maritime as administered in Scotland is in substance that of the United Kingdom. To a great extent it is codified in the Merchant Shipping Acts, 1894 to 1921, the principal Act being the Act of 1894. The principal amending Acts are the Act of 1906, the Maritime Conventions Act, 1911, and the Pilotage Act, 1913. The Act of 1911 largely altered the law of liability in cases of collision.

1. British Ship.—A British ship is a vessel that belongs wholly to (1) natural born British subjects, unless they have become citizens or subjects of a foreign state ; (2) naturalised British subjects or denizens who, while they are owners, continue resident within His Majesty's dominions or are partners in a firm actually carrying on business within His Majesty's dominions, and have, since naturalisation or denization, taken the oath of allegiance ; and (3) bodies corporate established under the laws and having their principal place of business in these dominions, even though there be alien shareholders on the register.[1]

With unimportant exceptions every British ship must be registered.[2] Registers of Shipping are provided at ports in the United Kingdom and colonies and, in certain cases, foreign ports.[3] Preparatory to registration the ships have to be surveyed, measured, tonnage ascertained, a certificate of survey produced identifying the ship,[4] and, in the case of the first registration, a builder's certificate produced giving particulars as to the build and tonnage and of the sale to the person desiring to be registered as owner.[5] The name of the vessel must be marked on the bows and her name and the name of the port of registry on the stern, the official number and tonnage cut on her main beam, and her draught painted on the stern or sternpost.[6]

[1] Reg. v. Arnaud, (1846) 9 Q.B. 806.   [2] M.S.A., 1894, § 3 ; Ibid., 1921, § 1.
[3] Ibid., 1894, § 87.   [4] Ibid., § 6.
[5] Ibid., § 10.   [6] Ibid., § 7.

The applicant for registration must make a declaration of his qualification to own a British ship, the time and place of building, and the name of the master.[1]

An entry of the above particulars is then made in the registry by the principal officer of customs of the port of registration, and a certificate of registration given containing similar particulars.[2]

If the ship is lost or ceases to be a British ship the certificate of registry must be given up.[3] If the ownership changes hands, or there is a change of master, an endorsement to that effect must be placed on the certificate at the port of registry.[4]

2. Property in a British Ship.—The property in a British ship is divided into sixty-four shares and no more.[5] No person is entitled to be registered as owner of a fractional part of a share. But a share may be held by joint owners, not exceeding five in number, who will be considered as constituting one person. And any number of persons may have a beneficial title in a single share, the registered individual representing them. A corporation may be registered as owner by its corporate name. No notice of any trust may be entered in the register book, or received by the registrar, and the registered owner of a ship or share has accordingly absolute power to deal with his interest in the manner provided by the Act.

All deeds relating to the ownership of ships must be on printed forms, which can be obtained at the Customs House of a port of registry.

3. Acquisition of Ownership.—While a contract for the sale of a ship may be made verbally,[6] ships or shares of ships must be transferred by bills of sale in the form prescribed by the Act.[7] These have to be entered on the register by the registrar. If two bills of sale are granted by a registered owner, *i.e.* to two different transferees, the first one produced to the registrar, even though second in date, takes preference, assuming *bona fides* on the part of the transferee.[8] The transferee is not entitled to be registered without making a declaration of transfer stating his qualification to own a British ship and that no unqualified persons have any legal or beneficial interest in the ship or any share.[9] A statement of the entry in the register is endorsed on the bill of sale itself.[8]

---

[1] M.S.A., 1894, § 9.   [2] *Ibid.*, § 14.
[3] *Ibid.*, § 21.   [4] *Ibid.*, § 20.   [5] *Ibid.*, § 5.
[6] M'Connachie *v.* Geddes, 1918 S.C. 391.
[7] M.S.A., 1894, § 24 *et seq.*   [8] *Ibid.*, § 26.   [9] *Ibid.*, § 25.

Where the property in a registered ship or share therein is transmitted on the marriage, death, or bankruptcy of a registered owner, or otherwise by means other than bill of sale, a declaration of transmission must be made containing statements as in a declaration of transfer, and a statement, accompanied by the appropriate evidence, of the manner in which and the person to whom the property has been transmitted.[1] When the person to whom a ship or share is so transmitted is a person not qualified to own a British ship, the Court may, on application by the unqualified person within four weeks (or one year if extension allowed) of the transmission, order a sale of the property so transmitted, the proceeds to be paid to the person entitled. In ordering a sale the Court names a person in whom it vests the right to transfer the ship or share.[2] If no application is made or no order for sale is pronounced the ship or share so transmitted is subject to forfeiture.[3]

4. Mortgages.—A registered ship or share therein may be the subject of a security for debt. The security instrument is called a mortgage. The mortgage must be in the statutory form prescribed by the Act and must be entered in the register to have effect.[4] Mortgages enter the register in the order of time in which they are produced to the registrar, irrespective of their date. The registrar notes on the mortgage the fact, the time, and the date of registration.[5] Similarly, the discharge of a mortgage must be entered on the register.[6]

The mortgage confers on the mortgagee a power of sale of the ship on non-payment of the debt.[7] If there are several recorded mortgages, a subsequent mortgagee cannot, without the order of the Court, sell the ship or share without the concurrence of every prior mortgagee.[8]

The Act [9] also contains provision for the issue by the registrar of certificates of sale and mortgage whereby the ship may be sold or mortgaged while out of the country or colony where the ship is registered.

The mortgagor remains the owner of the ship,[10] and can continue to use the ship in a reasonable and ordinary way. But he cannot do unusual acts whereby the security is impaired.[11] Should he do so,

---

[1] M.S.A., 1894, § 27.   [2] Ibid., § 29.
[3] Ibid., § 28.   [4] Ibid., § 24.
[5] Ibid., § 31.   [6] Ibid., § 32.
[7] Clydesdale Bank v. Walker & Bain, 1926 S.C. 72.
[8] M.S.A., 1894, § 35.   [9] Ibid., §§ 39–46.   [10] Ibid., § 34.
[11] The Heather Bell, [1901] P. 272 ; Law Guarantee Trust Society v. Russian Bank of Foreign Trade, [1905] 1 K.B. 815.

or should he be in default in payment, the mortgagee may take possession of the ship in order to enforce his security, as by placing someone on board to represent him, such as a new captain. He is then entitled to any freight which is in course of being earned. The mortgagee of a majority of shares in the ship, but not the mortgagee of a minority, may enter into possession.

5. The Master.—The master is presumed to be the servant of the registered owner of the ship. He has authority to do all acts usual and necessary for the employment of the ship, unless persons dealing with him have notice to the contrary. He is also in certain circumstances the agent of the cargo-owner to take special measures to preserve the cargo or minimise loss in cases of necessity—this as part of his general authority as servant of the shipowner. Thus he may, when in a foreign port and unable to communicate with the owners, make contracts for the hire of the ship, or enter into agreements to carry goods for freight. He may sign bills of lading for goods shipped, sell the cargo at an intermediate port in order to prevent loss to the cargo-owner when it has become unfit to be carried farther, make a general average sacrifice of ship, freight or cargo, or hypothecate the ship or cargo in security of money borrowed by him in foreign ports for necessary expenses. On the other hand, he cannot cancel or alter contracts already made by the owners.

6. Bottomry and Respondentia.—When it is necessary for purposes essential to the prosecution of the voyage to raise money the master has power to do so by hypothecating the ship and cargo in security for the loan, *e.g.* to pay for repairs. When both ship and cargo are given in security the contract of loan is embodied in a " bottomry bond." When only the cargo is hypothecated a " respondentia bond " is given. The master cannot hypothecate the cargo unless the interests of the cargo-owner require it and the ship and freight are an insufficient security for the sum required.[1]

The purpose of a bottomry bond being to enable the ship to complete the voyage and of a respondentia bond to secure the safe arrival of the cargo, if the ship does not arrive at her destination the lender loses his money. Where several bonds have been given at different times on the same voyage, the later bond, being given at a time of necessity when the earlier hypothecation would otherwise fail of its purpose, is entitled to be satisfied before the bond of earlier date.

A bottomry bond confers on the creditor a maritime lien on the

[1] The *Onward*, (1873) 42 L.J. Adm. 61.

ship, freight, and cargo. It therefore attaches to the property even
if that has passed into other hands. The Court will if necessary
sell the property charged to satisfy the bond. The cargo cannot
be resorted to unless the ship and freight are insufficient to satisfy
the charge.

Resort to borrowing by hypothecation is rarely necessary nowadays
owing to the facilities for communicating with the owners by telephone
or telegraph. It should only be resorted to when no better way can
be adopted of obtaining the money required.

7. Salvage.—The term " salvage " is used to mean either salvage
services or the reward for such services. A salvor is " a person who,
without any particular relation to a ship in distress, proffers useful
service and gives it as a volunteer without any pre-existing covenant
that connected him with the duty of employing himself for the preservation of that ship." [1]

The subjects of salvage are a ship, its apparel, and cargo, including
such when in the form of jetsam, flotsam or lagan,[2] or life.[3] Salvage
is payable by ship, cargo, and freight " at risk," *i.e.* if it has not been
paid in advance and its payment is dependent on delivery ; but not
the personal effects of master and crew or the wearing apparel of
passengers.

In order that services may be rewarded as salvage they must be
voluntary. Thus the crew cannot be salvors unless and until the ship
has been abandoned with the authority of the master or person in
command.[4] The services must also have been successful.[5]

In estimating the amount of salvage reward the following elements
are taken into account : (1) the enterprise of the salvors and the risk
they run ; (2) the degree of peril encountered by the salved ship ;
(3) the degree of labour and skill which the salvors incur and display,
and the time occupied ; (4) the value of the ship salved.[6]

The right to salvage reward, while it arises independently of contract, may be the subject of contract.[7] An agreement between those
in charge of a ship and the salvors as to the amount of the salvage

---

[1] Lord Stowell in the *Neptune*, (1824) 1 Hagg. Adm. 227 at p. 236.
[2] The Gas Float *Whitton No. 2*, [1896] P. 42 ; affd. H.L., [1897] A.C. 337.
[3] M.S.A., 1894, § 544.
[4] The *Warrior*, (1862) Lush. 376.
[5] *Melanie* v. *San Onofre*, [1925] A.C. 246.
[6] Owners of the *Vulcan* v. Owners of the *Berlin*, 1882, 9 R. 1057, per Lord
Deas at p. 1062.
[7] Nicholson v. Leith Salvage and Towage Co., 1923 S.C. 409.

award will in general be upheld by the Court.[1] It may, however, be disregarded if, in the opinion of the Court, it would be inequitable to enforce it. An agreement to pay an exorbitant sum made where the master was acting under stress of circumstances will be regarded as inequitable.[2]

The salvor has two forms of action to recover his salvage reward. He has a personal action against the shipowner and each cargo-owner. In addition he can proceed against the ship and cargo themselves, *i.e. in rem.*[3] If the property salved is in the salvor's possession he has a right of retention or lien over it until he is paid what is due him. If not in his possession he has a maritime lien (hypothec) over it which he can enforce no matter in whose hands the property is.[4]

[1] The *Arthur*, 1862, 6 L.T. (N.S.) 556.
[2] The *Port Caledonia* and the *Anna*, [1903] P. 184.
[3] Bell's Comm., i. 592 ; ii. 103.
[4] Currie *v.* M'Knight, 1896, 24 R. (H.L.) 1.

CHAPTER VI

PATENTS AND DESIGNS

THE law regarding patents is to be found chiefly in the Patents and Designs Act, 1907. This is an amending and consolidating statute which repealed all prior statutes except portions of the Statute of Monopolies,[1] which still forms the foundation of the law. An important amending statute was passed in 1919 and is cited along with the principal Act, an Act of 1914, and a further amending Act passed in 1928, as the Patents and Designs Acts, 1907 to 1928.

1. Principles of Law of Patents.—So far as the principles of the law are concerned the Scottish and the English laws of patents are the same. " In Scotland prior to the Union we had no special statute legalising patents ; and none of our institutional writers before Professor Bell allude to the subject except Bankton, in whose work (published in 1751) some doubt is thrown out (vol. i. p. 411) as to the validity of exclusive privileges granted by the Sovereign in Scotland to private individuals or companies in matters of trade or manufacture. But it was found that the validity of these rights was incontestable, not only under the King's prerogative, but under the Articles of Union which provided (Art. 6) ' that all parts of the United Kingdom for ever after the Union shall have the same allowances, encouragements and drawbacks, and be under the same prohibitions, restrictions and regulations of trade.' In virtue of that compact the Statute of Monopolies legalising patents for limited terms became law in Scotland." [2]

The Statute of Monopolies enacted, thereby declaring what was the common law of England, all monopolies void, but excepted patents for new inventions.[3] Such a patent is a grant by letters patent of the

[1] 21 Jac. I. c. 3.
[2] Lord Cunninghame in Neilson v. Househill Coal and Iron Co., 1842, 4 D. 470 at p. 475.
[3] Act, § 6.

sole right of making, using, exercising, and vending the invention therein described during a certain term, enabling the grantee to prevent all persons, other than himself and those whom he authorises, from doing all these things. Letters patent are *open* letters from the Crown, sealed and recorded, so that all subjects of the realm may read and be bound by their contents.

What is the principle of the grant of letters patent for new inventions ? It may be noted first what are the elements necessary as conditioning the grant under the Statute of Monopolies. They are granted to the true and first inventor, *i.e.* there must be novelty —such manufacture " which any other at the time of making such letters patent did not use." Further, the privilege must not be contrary to law, nor mischievous to the State by raising the prices of commodities at home, and must not be to the hurt of trade, nor generally inconvenient. With these elements in mind, the principle of the grant is summed up as follows :—" The only thing which a patentee gives to the public is a knowledge of his invention, and a patent is in effect a bargain between the patentee and the public in which the public, in consideration of an inventor communicating to them a knowledge of his invention, so that they may afterwards be enabled to practise it, grant to him the sole use of his invention for a limited time." [1] It follows accordingly that the invention must be novel, and want of novelty in any material part is sufficient to invalidate the grant, and prior publication of an invention in a book, pamphlet, etc., or in a specification of a prior invention, will invalidate the patent, as will also prior use of an invention in public, or by the inventor himself. It follows also that the invention must be useful and beneficial to the public.

2. Who can Apply.—An application for a patent may be made by any person who claims to be the true and first inventor of an invention, whether he be a British subject or not, and whether alone or jointly with any other person.[2] And if the person claiming to be the inventor of an invention dies without making an application for a patent for the invention, application may be made by and a patent for the invention granted to his legal representative.[3] The person who first imports an invention into this country is in law the true and first inventor of that manufacture in the realm, and may patent it. He may be a mere clerk or agent for another. But it is necessary that he

---

[1] Edmunds on Patents, p. 32.
[2] P. and D. Act, 1907, § 1.
[3] *Ibid.*, § 43 (1).

should himself have learned the invention abroad, or by direct communication thence, not from a returned traveller.[1] If a foreign inventor or other person entitled has already applied for a patent in a State with which we have entered into international arrangements for the mutual protection of inventions he may apply within twelve months of his foreign application.[2] A corporation or company cannot be an inventor in the ordinary sense, but it may import an invention and may then be sole patentee.[3] In any other case a body corporate can only apply for a patent jointly with the individual inventor.

3. The Register of Patents.—There is kept at the Patent Office a book called the Register of Patents, wherein must be entered the names and addresses of grantees of patents, notification of assignments and of transmission of patents, of licences under patents, and of amendments, extensions and revocations of patents, and such other matters affecting the validity or proprietorship of patents as may from time to time be prescribed.[4] No notice of any trust, express, implied, or constructive, may be entered in the register.[5]

4. Application for a Patent.—An application in the proper form (to be had at the Patent or Inland Revenue Offices, or any money order office) must be made. This is done by lodging the application at the Patent Office in London.[6] It may be made through a registered patent agent, who may sign it. The application contains a declaration that the applicant is in possession of an invention, and that he claims to be the true and first inventor. The application must be accompanied by a provisional or a complete specification, dated and signed by the applicant or his agent.

The Provisional Specification.—The provisional specification describes the nature of the invention. Its object is to ascertain the identity of the invention, not to detail it in its entirety. The provisional specification was introduced for the benefit of the patentee. The consideration for the grant of a patent is by good authorities thought to be the disclosure of the invention and the manner of performing it, whereby the public is instructed how they may, after the expiration of the monopoly, enjoy the invention for themselves. If accordingly the Officers of the Crown consider the nature of the invention properly stated they accept his application, thereby

---

[1] Marsden v. The Saville Street Foundry and Engineering Co., Ltd., (1878) L.R. 3 Ex. D. 203.

[2] P. and D. Act, 1907, § 91. [3] Carey's Application, (1889) 6 R.P.C. 552.

[4] P. and D. Act, 1907, § 28. [5] *Ibid.*, § 66. [6] *Ibid.*, 1902, § 1 (2).

authorising the applicant to use the invention publicly without making a publication which would render the patent, if granted afterwards, invalid. During this period of protection the applicant is enabled to make further experiments and improve the means of carrying out his invention before filing his second and complete specification, in which he is required to state " the manner in which the same shall be performed." The comptroller, on the report of an examiner, may refuse the application if it or the specification are not properly prepared, or the invention not fairly described or the title does not sufficiently indicate the subject-matter. Or he may require amendment before proceeding.

The Complete Specification.—The complete specification contains a full and detailed description of the invention, also the manner in which it is to be performed, and concludes with a distinct statement of the invention claimed.[1] It must be lodged within nine (extendable to ten) months from the date of the application, which is otherwise deemed to be abandoned.[2] The complete specification must be of an invention substantially the same as that described in the provisional specification. If the comptroller, on a report of an examiner, finds anticipations in prior specifications he may require amendment or may require a reference to prior specifications to be inserted in the applicant's specification by way of notice to the public. If satisfied that the invention has been wholly and specifically claimed in a prior specification he may refuse to grant a patent.[3] There is a right of appeal to one of the law officers of the Crown for England.

The complete specification must be accepted by the comptroller within fifteen months of the date of application (extendable to eighteen), otherwise (except where an appeal is lodged) it becomes void.[4] The acceptance is advertised in the Illustrated Official Journal and the patent becomes open to public inspection. Within two months of the advertisement any person having an interest may give notice of opposition on the ground (1) that the applicant has obtained his invention from him or from a person whose legal representative he is ; (2) that the invention has been anticipated by a prior specification of a patent granted within the fifty years preceding within the United Kingdom, or by publication in any document, other than a British specification, published in the United Kingdom, or is claimed by a complete specification published subsequently in pursuance of an

---

[1] P. and D. Act, 1907, § 2 (4).   [2] Ibid., 1907, § 5 ; 1919, § 20, Sched.
[3] Ibid., 1907, § 7.   [4] Ibid., 1907, § 6 (5) ; 1919, § 20, Sched.

application for a patent of prior date ; (3) that the nature of the invention or the manner in which it is to be performed is not sufficiently or fairly described ; (4) that the applicant in his complete specification claims something other than what is described in the provisional specification, and that such other invention forms the subject of an application made by the opponent in the interval between the dates of the provisional and complete specifications ; or (5) that, where an applicant has taken advantage of the provisions for the reciprocal protection of patents between the United Kingdom and a foreign State or British possession and has lodged a specification in this country which describes an invention other than that for which protection has been applied for in a foreign State or British possession, the opponent has made an application for that other invention between the dates of the applicant's application abroad and his application in the United Kingdom.[1] The comptroller hears and determines the questions, subject to an appeal to the law officer.

The grant of a patent is completed by its being sealed with the seal of the Patent Office, and dates from the date of the application. But no proceedings for infringement committed before the publication of the complete specification can be taken.

5. Duration of a Patent.—The term of duration of a patent has by the Act of 1919 been extended from fourteen to sixteen years.[2]

A patentee may, after advertising his intention to do so, petition the Court, at least six months before the expiration of the term, for an extension of his patent for a further term, and persons giving notice of objection, and the comptroller, may be heard in opposition. And if the Court considers that the patentee has been inadequately remunerated by his patent it may extend the term for a further term of five or, in exceptional cases, ten years, or order the grant of a new patent for such terms and under such conditions as it thinks fit.[3] The Act also provides for the restoration of patents which have lapsed through non-payment of fees,[4] and for the amendment of specifications.[5]

6. Patents of Addition.—Where a patent has been applied for or granted, a further patent, called a patent of addition, in respect of any

[1] P. and D. Act, 1907, § 11 ; 1919, § 4 ; see *In re* Ucar's Patent, [1922] 2 Ch. 220.

[2] P. and D. Act, 1919, § 6 (1).

[3] *Ibid.*, 1907, § 18 ; 1919, § 7 ; see *In re* Société Chemique des Usines du Rhônes Patent, [1922] 1 Ch. 258 ; *In re* Summers Brown's Patent, [1922] 2 Ch. 759.

[4] P. and D. Act, 1907, § 20.

[5] *Ibid.*, § 21.

improvement in or modification of the invention may be applied for and granted.   It remains in force as long as the original patent.[1]

7. Property in and Transfer of Patents.—A patent is moveable property and passes to personal representatives.[2]   A patent may be assigned in whole or in part, and the assignation may be limited to use in any particular place or part of the country.[3]   Assignations and other transmissions should be promptly registered.

Licences.—A patent licence authorises another person than the patentee to exercise the privilege granted by the Crown, and the grant of a patent being of a personal nature, the licence can probably not be granted unless the power to grant such licence was expressly given by the letters patent themselves which create the monopoly.[4]

Licences to use patented inventions may be express or implied. The sale of an article without any restriction as against the vendor gives the purchaser an implied licence to deal with the article during its natural life in any way he thinks fit.[5]   Licences may also be voluntary or compulsory.

   (a) **Voluntary Licences.**—These are grants, not of the patent, but merely of the right to use the invention for the whole term or any part thereof.   They should be registered.[6]   They may be (1) exclusive, granting the whole right ; (2) general, leaving the licensor right to grant other licences ; or (3) limited as to time, place, or manner of use.

   Licences of Right.—The patentee may also voluntarily arrange for the public obtaining " licences of right."

   At any time after the sealing of a patent the comptroller shall, if the patentee so requests, cause the patent to be endorsed with the words " licences of right," and a corresponding entry to be made in the register.   Thereafter any person shall at any time be entitled as of right to a licence under the patent.   The patentee and such person may agree as to terms.   In default of agreement the comptroller may settle the terms on the application of either.   In so settling terms the comptroller should endeavour to secure (1) the widest possible user of the invention in the United Kingdom consistent with the patentee deriving a reasonable advantage

---

[1] P. and D. Act, 1907, § 19.
[2] Lord Advocate v. Oswald, 1848, 10 D. 969.
[3] P. and D. Act, 1907, § 14 (1).
[4] Frost on Patents, 4th ed., ii. 178.   [5] *Ibid.*, p. 181.
[6] P. and D. Act, 1907, § 71 (2).

from his patent rights, (2) the maximum advantage to the patentee consistent with the invention being worked by the licensee at a reasonable profit in the United Kingdom, (3) equality of advantage among the several licensees.[1]

(b) **Compulsory Licences.**—These also take the form of licences of right, but are obtained as the result of the exercise by the comptroller of his powers for the prevention of the abuse of monopoly rights, and are so treated of below.

8. Revocation and the Prevention of Abuse of Monopoly Rights.—Revocation.—Proceedings for the revocation of a patent may be taken on the following grounds :—(1) Fraud ; (2) that the person seeking revocation was the true inventor ; (3) that such person had publicly manufactured, used or sold, within the realm, before the date of the patent, anything claimed by the patentee as his invention. The proceedings are in the form of an action of reduction and shall be at the instance of the Lord Advocate, or a party having interest with his concurrence.[2] The comptroller may also revoke a patent on application within two years of the date of the patent by a person who would have been entitled to oppose the grant, or the successor of such person. The grounds of revocation in such case are the same as the grounds that could have been urged in opposition.[3] There is a right of appeal from the comptroller to the Court.

Abuse of Monopoly Rights.—Any person interested may at any time apply to the comptroller alleging that there has been an abuse of the monopoly rights under a patent and asking for relief.[4] Monopoly rights are deemed to be abused (a) if after the expiration of three years from the date of the grant of a patent the patented invention (being one capable of being worked in the United Kingdom) is not being worked within the United Kingdom on a commercial scale, and no satisfactory reason can be given for such non-working, or (b) if such working on a commercial scale is being prevented or hindered by the importation from abroad of the patented article by the patentee, persons claiming under him, or persons against whom he might take action for infringement, or (c) if the demand for the patented article in the United Kingdom is not being met to an adequate extent and on reasonable terms, or (d) if trade in the

---

[1] P. and D. Act, 1919, § 2.
[2] Ibid., 1907, §§ 25 and 94 (3).
[3] Ibid., § 25.
[4] Ibid., § 27 (1), as amended 1919, § 1 ; 1928, § 1.

United Kingdom is being prejudiced by the refusal of the patentee to grant licences, it being in the public interest that licences should be granted, or by his attaching conditions to the hire, licence, or use of the patented article or process. In such cases the comptroller, subject to an appeal to the Court, may (1) order the patent to be endorsed " licences of right," and he may settle the terms of licences ; (2) he may order the grant of a licence to an applicant ; (3) he may order the grant of an exclusive licence to an applicant providing capital for the working of the invention on a commercial scale within the United Kingdom ; or (4) failing the above means of preventing abuse he may order the patent to be revoked.[1]

9. Infringement of Patents.—The right of the patentee is not to the invention he has made, but only to what he has claimed. The infringement of a patent is the doing of that which the patent prohibits being done. Infringement must be by making, using, exercising, or vending the invention without permission, by oneself, one's agents or servants.[2] But the purchaser of an article from the patentee has an implied right to resell.[3]

The proprietor of a patent can raise an action for infringement. Threatened as well as actual infringement will be sufficient ground for the action. There is no action for infringement committed before the actual date when the patent was granted. Unless damages or an account of the profits is sought the proceedings take the form of a note of suspension and interdict against the respondents during the continuance of the patent making, using, exercising, or vending the invention within the United Kingdom without leave of the complainers, and for interim interdict. Where damages are sought, the action may be for interdict with conclusions for damages or an account of profits. Where, however, the patent was granted after 1st January 1908, a patentee may not recover damages from an infringer who proves that he was not aware, and had no reasonable means of making himself aware, of the existence of the patent.[4] Defences to the action may be, among others, that the grant was irregular or not subsisting, that there was no infringement, or on the ground of objection to the validity of the patent.

10. Rights of the Crown.—A patent has to all intents the like effect

---

[1] P. and D. Act, 1907, § 27 ; 1919, § 1 (2) ; 1928, § 1.
[2] Sykes v. Hogarth, (1879) L.R. 12 Ch. D. 537.
[3] Thomas v. Hunt, (1864) 17 C.B. (N.S.) 183.
[4] P. and D. Act, 1907, § 33 ; Wilderman v. F. W. Berk & Co., [1925] 1 Ch. 116.

against the King as it has against a subject.[1] But any Government Department may, by themselves, their agents, contractors, or others, at any time after the application, use the invention for the services of the Crown on such terms as may, either before or after the use thereof, be agreed on, or in default of agreement be settled by the Treasury after hearing all parties interested. Inventors of improvements in instruments or munitions of war may assign their inventions and patents, obtained or to be obtained, to the Secretary of State for War, or the Admiralty, and agreements to keep the invention secret may be enforced by the Secretary.[2]

11. Designs.—Design means only the features of shape, configuration, pattern or ornament applied to any article by any industrial process or means, whether manual, mechanical or chemical, separate or combined, which in the finished article appeal to and are judged solely by the eye, but does not include any mode or principle of construction, or anything which is in substance a mere mechanical device.

A Register of Designs is kept at the Patent Office, in which are recorded the names of the registered owners of designs, assignments and transmissions thereof. Designs are registered for articles in a variety of classes and the same design may be registered for more than one class.

The registered proprietor of a design has copyright in the design (*i.e* an exclusive right to apply a design to any article in any class in which the design is registered) during five years from the date of registration, and application may be made for an extension of the period for an additional five years, and later for a third period of five years.

The registered owner must, before delivery on sale of an article to which a registered design has been applied, furnish the comptroller with a specimen of the design, and unless he marks the article with the prescribed mark and words or figures denoting the registration, cannot recover damages for infringement of his copyright from a person who had no knowledge of the copyright in the design.

An appeal to the Court lies against a refusal of the comptroller to register a design.

---

[1] P. and D. Act, 1919, § 8.   [2] *Ibid.*, 1907, § 30.

CHAPTER VII

TRADE MARKS AND NAMES

1. Nature of Trade Marks.—A trade mark has been defined as " the mark under which a particular individual trades, and which indicates the goods to be his goods—either goods manufactured by him, or goods selected by him, or goods which in some way or other pass through his hands in the course of trade." " It is a mode of designating goods as being the goods which have been in some way or other dealt with by the person who owns the trade mark." [1] Such a person obtains a property in the mark which he so affixes to his goods, and he is protected by the law in his right of property.

When the owner of a trade mark is asserting exclusive rights, " monopoly is not the thing for which the one party struggles and which the other resists. On the contrary, fair trading is all for which the protection of the law is invoked, and the public, as well as the manufacturer or merchant, are concerned that infringement of trade marks and trade designations should be prevented. For there is a double wrong : the public are or may be deceived, and the trader whose trade mark or trade designation is infringed is or may be injured." [2]

2. Registration of Trade Marks.—At common law there is a right of action for interdict and damages against any person who " passes off " goods as those of another person by, for instance, adopting or imitating the trade mark by which the other person identifies his goods. Since the year 1875, however, when the Trade Marks Registration Act was passed, a person has been able, by registering a mark, to obtain the exclusive right to the use of the trade mark (subject to certain qualifications in respect of *bona fide* concurrent user by another

---

[1] Kay, J., *In re* Australian Wine Importers, Ltd., 41 Ch. D. 278 ; and see Trade Marks Act, 1905, § 3.

[2] Per Lord Craighill in Dunnachie *v.* Young & Sons, 1883, 10 R. 874.

person),[1] and may protect his right by action for infringement by way of interdict and damages. The present statutory law as to trade marks is contained in the Trade Marks Acts, 1905 to 1919.

Register of Trade Marks.—The Act of 1905 provides for the keeping of a Register of Trade Marks under the control and management of the Comptroller-General of Patents, Designs, and Trade Marks, who is known as the Registrar. Special registers are kept by the Cutlers' Company at Sheffield, and by a Manchester Branch of the Trade Marks Registry at Manchester in respect of cotton goods. The registers are open to the inspection of the public, and certified copies of any entry may be obtained.[2]

What Marks Registrable.—A trade mark is registrable only in respect of particular goods or classes of goods.[3] But associations of persons who undertake to certify the origin, material, mode of manufacture, etc., of goods by marking the goods (called standardisation marks) may with leave of the Board of Trade register their marks.[4] A mark must, to be registrable, contain or consist of at least one of the following essential particulars :—(1) The name of a company, individual, or firm represented in a special or particular manner ; (2) the signature of the applicant for registration or some predecessor in his business ; (3) an invented word or words [5] ; (4) a word or words having no direct reference to the quality or character of the goods and not being according to its ordinary signification a geographical name or a surname ; (5) any other distinctive mark, but not a name, signature, or word or words, other than as above, except upon evidence of its distinctiveness, and in this connection " distinctive " means adapted to distinguish the goods of the proprietor of the trade mark from those of other persons, *e.g.* by extent of user.[6]

Application for Registration.—In order to obtain registration of a trade mark application in the prescribed manner must be made to the registrar. He may refuse the application or accept it absolutely or subject to conditions or amendments, limitations as to mode or place of user,[7] or to disclaimer of right to the exclusive use of matter common to the trade or otherwise of a non-distinctive character.[8] In case of refusal the applicant may appeal to the Board of Trade

[1] T.M.A., 1905, § 21 ; 1919, § 12, 2nd Sched.
[2] *Ibid.*, 1905, §§ 4–7.   [3] *Ibid.*, § 8.
[4] *Ibid.*, § 62 ; 1919, 2nd Sched.
[5] *In re* Eastman Photographic Materials Co., Ltd., [1898] A.C. 571.
[6] T.M.A., 1905, § 9 ; *In re* Crosfield, (1909) 26 R.P.C. 561, 837.
[7] T.M.A., 1905, § 12 ; 1919, § 12, 2nd Sched.   [8] *Ibid.*, 1905, § 15.

or Court.[1] If an application is accepted (or before acceptance in the case of a distinctive mark under § 9 (5)), advertisement is made by the registrar, and any person may give notice to the registrar of opposition to the registration. The registrar decides the matter after hearing the parties, subject to appeal to the Court. If registration is permitted it dates from the date of application, and a certificate by the registrar is issued to the applicant. The registration endures for fourteen years and may be renewed for further periods of fourteen years.

Effect of Registration.—The effect of a valid registration of a person as proprietor of a trade mark under the Act of 1905 is to give such person the exclusive right to the use of such trade mark upon or in connection with the goods in respect of which it is registered (subject, as already mentioned, to certain qualifications in respect of *bona fide* concurrent user by another person [2]). Registration is *prima facie* evidence of the validity of the original registration and all assignments, and registration for seven years is conclusive evidence of validity unless the original registration was obtained by fraud, or the mark is in any particular calculated to deceive or otherwise disentitled to protection in a Court of justice or contrary to law or morality or of a scandalous design.[3]

By the Act of 1919 the register was divided into two parts, A and B. In part A are included all marks registered or registrable under the provisions of the principal Act of 1905. In part B are included marks for which application for registration in that part are made, being marks which have been *bona fide* used for not less than two years in the United Kingdom. Registration in part B is merely *prima facie* evidence that the proprietor has the exclusive right to the trade mark, and an alleged infringer may resist an application by the registered owner for interdict against him by showing that his user of the mark is not calculated to deceive.

Correction and Rectification of Register.—The Act of 1905 [4] provides for the correction of the register at the instance of the proprietor, and also for its rectification at the instance of persons aggrieved by an entry, as, for example, on the ground that the proprietor never intended to use and has made no *bona fide* use of the mark in connection with the goods or has in fact made no *bona fide* use of it during the preceding five years.[5]

---

[1] T.M.A., 1905, § 12 (2).   [2] *Ibid.*, 1905, § 21 ; 1919, § 12, 2nd Sched.
[3] *Ibid.*, 1905, §§ 41, 11.   [4] *Ibid.*, §§ 32–37.   [5] *Ibid.*, § 37.

3. Transfer of Property in Trade Mark.—A trade mark when registered can be assigned and transmitted, but only in connection with the goodwill of the business concerned in the goods for which it has been registered, and is determinable with that goodwill. Where on dissolution of a partnership the goodwill is divided the registrar may permit an apportionment of the registered trade mark among the persons continuing the business.[1]

4. Trade Name.—Apart from registration, a right which at least resembles a right of property may be acquired in a trade name with which a particular business has come to be identified,[2] even though not registrable as a trade mark. Thus, it may be the name of an hotel, when it is regarded as attaching particularly to the premises.[3] Again, Bass's Ale is an instance of a name which could not safely be used by another Bass without clearly distinguishing his goods from the well-known goods of that name.

5. Merchandise Marks.—The Criminal Law in relation to trade marks is contained in the Merchandise Marks Acts, 1887 to 1926.

The Merchandise Marks Act, 1887, makes it an offence against the Act, subject to imprisonment, fine, and forfeiture of the goods, (1) to forge any trade mark; (2) falsely to apply to goods any trade mark or any mark so nearly resembling a trade mark as to be calculated to deceive; (3) to make an instrument for the purpose of forging a trade mark; (4) to dispose of or possess such an instrument; (5) to apply any false trade description to goods; or (6) to cause any of these things to be done.[4] It is likewise an offence for a person to sell, expose for sale or be in possession of for purposes of trade or manufacture goods under a false mark or description, unless such person has acted innocently.[5] Persons whose ordinary business is to make dies or to apply marks or descriptions to goods on behalf of other persons are protected from prosecution.[6] A trade mark to which the Act applies is a trade mark registered under the Trade Marks Acts, and a " trade description " means any description or statement as to quantity, place of production, manner of making, material of which the goods are made, or existing patent or copyright protecting the goods.[7] The customs entry relating to imported goods is deemed to be a trade description applied to the goods.[8] Special provision is made for

---

[1] T.M.A., 1905, §§ 22, 23.
[2] *E.g.* Singer Manufacturing Co. *v.* Loog, (1882) 2 A.C. 15.
[3] Great North of Scotland Railway Co. *v.* Mann, 1892, 19 R. 1035.
[4] M.M.A., 1887, § 2 (1).   [5] *Ibid.*, § 2 (2).
[6] *Ibid.*, § 6.   [7] *Ibid.*, § 3.   [8] *Ibid.*, 1891, § 1.

distinguishing the place of making watches and watch cases, and having the watch case stamped at an assay office.[1] The Board of Trade are empowered to undertake prosecutions in cases appearing to affect the general interests of the country.[2] Similar powers in certain cases are given to the Board of Agriculture.[3]

With a view to preventing the importation of goods liable to forfeiture, all such goods, and all goods of foreign manufacture bearing any name or trade mark purporting to be that of a trader within the United Kingdom, unless there is a clear indication that they have been manufactured abroad, are prohibited to be imported.[4] Further, it is an offence under the Act of 1887 to sell imported goods bearing a name or trade mark of a British manufacturer or trader unless accompanied by an indication of origin,[5] e.g. " foreign " or " Empire," or a definite indication of the country where they were manufactured or produced. Distribution in the United Kingdom of imported goods by way of advertising goods of some other kind is also prohibited. And power is given to the Commissioners of Customs and Excise to require information from importers of such goods as to the name and address of the person by whom the goods were consigned and of the person to whom the goods were sent. Information so obtained may be communicated to the person whose name or trade mark is alleged to have been used or infringed.[6]

A person who falsely represents that any goods are made by a person holding a Royal Warrant, or for the service of the King or Royal Family or for a Government Department, is liable to a penalty of £20.[7]

---

[1] M.M.A., 1887, §§ 7 and 8.
[2] Ibid., 1891, § 2.
[3] Merchandise Marks (Prosecution) Act, 1894, § 1.
[4] M.M.A., 1887, § 16.
[5] Ibid., 1926, §§ 1, 5.
[6] Ibid., 1911, § 1 (1).
[7] Ibid., 1887, § 20.

CHAPTER VIII

THE LAW OF COPYRIGHT

1. Principles.—The underlying principle of the law of copyright is the same as in the case of patents. Of all things the produce of a man's intellectual labour is most peculiarly distinguishable as his own, and the statutes upon which copyright now rests are intended not so much to create a right as to protect it from invasion.[1] The necessity for this protection arises from the doctrine of the common right of property in things corporeal, according to which the purchaser of a book may apply it to what use, or draw from it what advantage, it may be calculated to afford, producing, by the application of his own industry, other books exactly similar, and disposing of those by sale or by gift.[2] The legislature has sought to reconcile the interests of the author with those of the public.

The law of copyright is now purely statutory,[3] and is governed principally by the Copyright Act, 1911 (amended by the Copyright Act, 1915), an amending and consolidating statute which left unrepealed only a few provisions in existing Acts relating to copyright.[4]

2. Definition.—The word copyright is used to comprehend two different rights, viz. (1) the right of property which an author has in an unpublished production ; (2) the exclusive privilege of multiplying copies of the work. It is in the latter sense that the word is generally used ; but it has come to include also the exclusive privilege of performing a work in public. In the Copyright Act, 1911,[5] copyright is now defined as the sole right to produce or reproduce a work, or any substantial part thereof, in any material form whatsoever ; to perform, or, in the case of a lecture, to deliver, the work or any substantial part thereof in public ; or, in the case of an unpublished work, to publish the work or any substantial part thereof.[6]

---

[1] Bell's Comm., i. 108.
[2] *Ibid.*, i. 109.
[3] Copyright Act, 1911, § 31.
[4] Act of 1911, § 36, 2nd Sched.
[5] § 1 (2).
[6] Act of 1911, § 1 (2).

3. The Subjects of Copyright.—The privileges of copyright extend to every original literary, dramatic, musical, and artistic work, which, if published, was first published within the dominions to which the Act extends, or which, if unpublished, was, at the date of making, the work of a British subject, or the author was resident within those parts of His Majesty's dominions to which the Act extends for the time being.[1]

Original Work.—A work must be original in order to be the subject of copyright ; that is, it must not be copied from another work, but originating from the author.[2]   Thus a new edition of a book, if merely a reprint of an old, is not original, but may be so enlarged and improved as to constitute in reality a new work.[3]   Abridgments, under the old law, were entitled to protection if they were true abridgments in the sense of preserving the entire substance in condensed form in language different from the original.[4]   But in later cases the Courts have been inclined to view the work of an abridger as an infringement of copyright,[5] and it is doubtful if abridgments would now be permitted.   Translations are original works and entitled to protection against other translations in the same language, but this is without prejudice to the author of the work, whose copyright includes the sole right to make a translation.[6]   Very little independent labour may be sufficient to gain protection for a work as original.   Thus a compilation may be an original literary work.   Copyright may therefore be claimed by an author of a book who has taken existing materials, and arranged and combined them in a new form, and given them an application not known before.[7]   Protection is, however, not given to the component parts of a compilation independently of their arrangement and combination.   Probably the mere process of selecting passages from works readily accessible to the public is not, but difficulty in obtaining access to the originals, or skill manifested in making or arranging the selection, is sufficient to give the character of an original literary work to the selection.[8]   Again, an original artistic work means merely one not copied from another artistic work of the

---

[1] Act of 1911, § 1 (1).

[2] University of London Press, Ltd. v. University Tutorial Press, Ltd., [1916] 2 Ch. 601, at p. 608.

[3] Black v. Murray, 1870, 9 M. 341 ; Hedderwick v. Griffin, 3 D. 383.

[4] Gyles v. Wilcox, (1740) 2 Atk. 142 ; D'Almaine v. Boosey, (1835) 1 Y. & C. Ex. 288.

[5] Dickens v. Lee, (1844) 8 Jur. 183 ; Tinsley v. Lacy, (1863) 1 H. & M. 747.

[6] Act of 1911, § 1 (2) (a).

[7] Copinger on Copyright, 6th ed., p. 48.   [8] *Ibid.*, p. 56.

same character, such as an engraving copied from an engraving or a photograph from a photograph. But probably an engraving of a painting or a photograph of a picture is an original artistic work,[1] but without prejudice to the rights of the original author.

Publication.—Publication means the issue of copies of the work to the public. It does not include the performance in public of a dramatic or musical work, the delivery in public of a lecture, the exhibition in public of an artistic work, or the construction of an architectural work of art, nor the issue of photographs and engravings of works of sculpture and architectural works of art.[2] The question of whether there has been publication becomes of importance in certain cases in which the duration of the period of protection is more in the case of an unpublished than of a published work,[3] and because the work of a foreigner not resident in the British dominions will not be entitled to protection so long as unpublished.[4]

Literary Works.—What is a literary work is not defined in the Act, but it is stated to include maps, charts, plans, tables, and compilations.[5] The following may also come within the category of literary works : a tradesman's catalogue, a directory, a sheet of advertisements (but not a single advertisement), a system of electric telegraphy or shorthand. On the other hand, there is no copyright in a mere diagram, such as a scoring-sheet used in a game of cricket, in the mere plan of a work or a general subject or particular method of treating it ; in titles to books, periodicals, and newspapers,[6] or a *nom de plume*, which more resemble trade marks. There is, also, no copyright in a work which is intended to defraud the public by falsely representing, *e.g.*, that it is the work, or a translation of the work, of an author who has a real existence.[7] But there is no fraud in publishing books of amusement or instruction as translations which are in fact original works, or in publishing them under an assumed name, for in such cases there is no intent to deceive the purchaser and make a gain by the false representation.[8] Copyright is also denied to an immoral, obscene, irreligious, or libellous work, on the ground that the author is unable to acquire a

[1] Copinger on Copyright, 6th ed., p. 95 ; Graves' case, (1869) L.R. 4 Q.B. 723.
[2] Act of 1911, § 1 (3).
[3] See Duration of Ownership Rights, *infra*.
[4] Copinger, p. 23.
[5] Act of 1911, § 35 (1).
[6] Clements *v.* Maddick, (1859) 1 Giff. (Ch.) 98 ; Weldon *v.* Dicks, (1878) 10 Ch. D. 247.
[7] Wright *v.* Tullis, (1845) 1 C.B. 893.
[8] Wright *v.* Tullis, *supra*, per Tindal C.J. at p. 906.

property in such works and therefore cannot show a right to sell.[1] Protection has been refused to works as being irreligious on the ground that they contradicted scriptural doctrine,[2] but it is now considered permissible to criticise or controvert religious doctrines and beliefs, provided it is not done contumeliously or scoffingly, and in an indecorous manner.[3]

Dramatic and Musical Works.—Copyright in dramatic and musical works includes two rights, viz. (1) the right of multiplying copies of the written or printed work, and (2) the right of public representation or performance, now called play right or performing right. These two rights are quite distinct and may be vested in different individuals. Dramatic work includes any piece for recitation, choreographic work, or entertainment in dumb-show, the scenic arrangement or acting form of which is fixed in writing or otherwise, and any cinematograph production where the arrangement or acting form, or the combination of incidents represented, give the work an original character.[4] Musical work is not defined in the Act of 1911, but the Musical (Summary Proceedings) Copyright Act, 1902, which is unrepealed, defines a musical work as meaning " any combination of melody and harmony, or either of them, printed, reduced to writing, or otherwise graphically produced or reproduced." [5] A musical work may be also a dramatic work, e.g. an opera. But a song that does not require for its representation either acting or scenery is not a dramatic piece, although it is intended to be sung in appropriate costume on the music-hall stage.[6] Copyright may be secured for the adaptation of a play which is itself common property, e.g. of a play of Shakespeare, or for the adaptation of an old piece of music or the adaptation of the music of an opera to a particular instrument, e.g. the pianoforte.[7]

Artistic Works.—An artistic work may be one which is wholly or mainly produced by hand, or one entirely or mainly produced by mechanical processes. It includes works of painting, drawing, sculpture, and artistic craftsmanship, architectural works of art, engravings, and photographs.[8] These classes of artistic works are further defined in the Act of 1911.[9] Designs capable of being regis-

---

[1] Copinger, p. 59.
[2] Lawrence v. Smith, (1822) 1 Jac. 471.
[3] Story, Equity Jurisprudence, p. 938 ; Copinger, p. 61.
[4] Act of 1911, § 35 (1).   [5] Ibid., § 3.
[6] Fuller v. Blackpool Winter Gardens, [1895] 2 Q.B. 429.
[7] Copinger, p. 71 et seq.
[8] Act of 1902, § 3.   [9] Act of 1911, § 35 (1).

tered under the Patents and Designs Act, 1907, are not protected under the Copyright Act, 1911, except designs which, though capable of being so registered, are not used, or intended to be used, as models or patterns to be multiplied by any industrial process.[1] The fundamental distinction between a design and a simple artistic work lies, probably, in the applicability of the former to another article—that is to say, an artistic work is bought purely and simply for its artistic properties ; an article to which a design has been applied is bought because of the utility of the article, apart from the design.[2]

Joint Works.—Joint works are works " produced by the collaboration of two or more authors, in which the contribution of one author is not distinct from the contribution of the other author or authors." [3] They differ from collective works, in which the contributions of the various authors are distinguishable from one another. Joint authors, in the absence of agreement to the contrary, are deemed to be interested in equal shares.[4]

Existing Works.[5]—The Act of 1911 having repealed all previous statutes conferring copyright, it was necessary to make special provision with regard to works which were entitled to protection at the date when the Act came into operation. This is done by substituting the rights conferred by the statute [6] for those in existence prior to its date. In some cases these rights are greater, in others less, than those previously existing. Works in existence at the time when the Act came into force also acquire the extended term of protection granted by the Act. The Act provides for the protection of vested interests, as where persons who have incurred expense before the Act will suffer loss by reason of the increased protection.[7]

4. Ownership of Copyright.—First Owner.—Subject to certain exceptions, the author of a work is the first owner of the copyright therein.[8] In the case of artistic works other than photographs it is the person whose hands fix the picture upon the canvas, paper, stone, copper-plate, or wood who is the author. In the case of a photograph the person who was owner of the original negative at the time when such negative was made is to be deemed the author of the work, including a body corporate if it has established a place of business within the dominions to which the Act extends.[9] In the case of

---

[1] Act of 1911, § 22 (1).   [2] Copinger, p. 81.   [3] Act of 1911, § 16 (3).
[4] Jones v. Moore, (1841) 4 Y. & C. Ex. 351.   [5] Ibid., §§ 19 (8), 24.
[6] See § 24 (1) and First Schedule.
[7] See Copinger, p. 258 et seq.   [8] Act of 1911, § 5 (1).   [9] Ibid., § 21.

engravings, photographs, and portraits, if the plate or other original has been ordered by some other person and made for valuable consideration, the first owner of the copyright is, in the absence of agreement to the contrary, the person by whom the plate or other original was ordered.[1] Where the author of a work was in the employment of some other person under a contract of service or apprenticeship, and the work was made in the course of his employment by that person, that person is, in the absence of any agreement to the contrary, the first owner of the copyright. What is a contract of service is a question of fact depending on the degree of control exercised by the employer over the servant. If an author or an artist is employed by a publisher to write a book or draw a picture, he does not necessarily become the servant of the publisher; but where an author is employed by a publisher to write a book for a capital sum, the law will generally presume that it was the intention of the parties that the copyright should belong to the publisher.[2] In making the employer the first owner of the copyright in works made under a contract of service, the Act, however, provides that where the work is an article or other contribution to a newspaper, magazine, or similar periodical, the author shall be deemed to have reserved to him, in the absence of any agreement to the contrary, the right to restrain the publication of the work otherwise than as part of the newspaper, magazine, or similar periodical.[3] Other exceptions to the rule that the author of a work is the first owner of the copyright are Government publications and mechanical reproductions. In the case of the former the copyright belongs to His Majesty, subject to any agreement with the author.[4] As regards contrivances for reproducing sounds mechanically, as in the case of photographs, the person who was the owner of the original plate at the time when the plate was made is to be deemed to be the author of the work, including a body corporate if it has established a place of business within the parts of the dominions to which the Act extends.[5] Where the ownership of an author's manuscript after his death has been acquired under a testamentary disposition made by the author, and the manuscript is of a work which has not been published nor performed in public nor delivered in public, the owner-

[1] Act of 1911, § 5 (1), proviso (*a*); Con Planck Co. *v.* Kolynos Incorp., [1925] 2 K.B. 804.

[2] Lawrence *v.* Aflalo, [1904] A.C. 17; *cf.* Scottish Insurance Commrs. *v.* Edinburgh Royal Infirmary, 1913 S.C. 751; *Re* National Insurance Act, [1913] I.R. 219.

[3] Act of 1911, § 5 (1) (*b*).

[4] *Ibid.*, § 18.   [5] *Ibid.*, § 19 (1).

ship is *prima facie* proof of the copyright being with the owner of the manuscript.[1]

Duration of Ownership Rights.—The consideration which determines the duration of copyright is what protection an author can reasonably demand to ensure an adequate return for his labours.[2] The period of protection now adopted is during the life of the author and fifty years after his death (with certain minor exceptions).[3] Where copyright subsists but there has been no publication, or delivery in the case of a lecture, or performance in the case of a dramatic work, at the death of the owner of the work, copyright endures for fifty years from the date of publication, delivery, or performance.[4] At the end of twenty-five years, or in the case of a work in which copyright subsisted at the passing of the Act of 1911 thirty years, from the time the fifty years begin to run another person may reproduce the work on giving the owner the appropriate notice under the statute, and paying him royalties on the sale of the work.[5]

Special periods of copyright are, however, provided in the case of (1) photographs, (2) mechanical instruments, (3) Government publications, (4) joint works, (5) posthumous works, and (6) assignments.

(1) *Photographs.*—The period of protection for photographs is fifty years from the making of the original negative from which the photograph was directly or indirectly derived.[6] It is immaterial whether the photograph be published or unpublished.

(2) *Mechanical Instruments.*—The term of copyright is fifty years from the making of the original plate from which the contrivance was directly or indirectly derived.[7]

(3) *Government Publications.*—Where any work has been prepared or published by or under the direction or control of His Majesty or any Government Department, the copyright in the work shall, subject to any agreement with the author, belong to His Majesty, and in such case shall continue for a period of fifty years from the date of the first publication of the work.[8]

(4) *Joint Works.*—In the case of a work of joint authorship, *i.e.* a work produced by the collaboration of two or more authors in which the contribution of one author is not distinct from

---

[1] Act of 1911, § 17 (2).   [2] Copinger, p. 84.   [3] Act of 1911, § 3.
[4] *Ibid.*, § 17 (1).   [5] *Ibid.*, § 3, proviso.   [6] *Ibid.*, § 21.
[7] *Ibid.*, § 19.   [8] *Ibid.*, § 18.

12

the contribution of the other author or authors,[1] copyright shall subsist during the life of the author who first dies and for a term of fifty years after his death, or during the life of the author who dies last, whichever period is the longer.[2]

(5) *Posthumous Works.*—Literary, dramatic, and musical works and engravings (not photographs) in which copyright subsists at the date of the death of the author, and which have not been published, nor in the case of a dramatic or musical work been performed in public, nor in the case of a lecture been delivered in public before that date, are entitled to copyright until publication or performance or delivery in public, whichever may first happen, and for a term of fifty years thereafter.[3]

(6) *Assignments.*—Where the author of a work is the first owner of the copyright in it, no assignment of the copyright, unless by will of the author, is operative beyond twenty-five years from the death of the author, and on his death the reversionary interest shall, notwithstanding any agreement to the contrary, devolve on his personal representatives unless it be a collective work or a licence to publish a work or part of a work as part of a collective work.[4]

5. Transmission and Assignment of Copyright.—Copyright is personal property. It will accordingly pass to the owner's trustee in bankruptcy, at least if published.[5] Upon the death of the proprietor it will pass to his personal representatives, or under any testamentary disposition by him.

Copyright is to be distinguished from the material object which is the subject of the copyright. The assignment of the material object does not necessarily transfer the title to the copyright any more than the transfer of the copyright necessarily transfers the title to the material object.[6] Thus the purchase of a painting does not necessarily entitle the purchaser to reproduce it by such means as engravings and photographs. He can only obtain the right to reproduction of the work he has purchased by insisting upon a licence or assignment of the copyright in writing.[4]

The owner of the copyright in any work may assign the right either wholly or partially, and either generally or subject to limitations to

---

[1] Act of 1911, § 16 (3).   [2] *Ibid.*, § 16 (1).   [3] *Ibid.*, § 17.
[4] *Ibid.*, § 5 (2).   [5] See Copinger, p. 104.
[6] Philip *v.* Pennell, [1907] 2 Ch. 577.

the United Kingdom or any self-governing dominion or other part of His Majesty's dominions to which the Act of 1911 extends, and either for the whole term of the copyright or any part thereof, and may grant any interest by licence. Thus the performing rights, the translating rights, the gramophone rights, the photographic rights, the engraving rights, and so forth, are all capable of separate assignment. But the grant must be in writing, signed by the owner or his authorised agent.[1]

An author, where he is the first owner of the copyright, cannot, however, assign any interest in his copyright beyond the expiration of twenty-five years from his death.[2] This would not apply, for example, to the case of a photograph where the plate was ordered by some other person and was made for valuable consideration, or under a contract of service. Nor does it apply to the assignment of the copyright of a collective work,[3] or a licence to publish a work or part of a work as part of a collective work. Accordingly, an assignment of the copyright of the complete work may be made for the full period of protection, and a licence to publish a contribution as part of the collective work may also be granted for the like full period. But an assignment of the copyright in the contribution cannot be made for the period commencing twenty-five years after the death of the author.[4] An assignment of a posthumous work would not be affected by the limitation.

6. Licences.—The owner of a copyright may, as an alternative to assigning, grant a licence to produce and copy the work. An assignment conveys an interest in the property assigned, whereas a licence does not, but merely creates a contractual relationship between the parties, unless,[5] probably, it can be shown that the licence was both exclusive and irrevocable. As in the case of assignment, the author, where he was the first owner of the copyright, cannot grant a licence which will extend beyond twenty-five years after his death.

Compulsory Licences.—If at any time after the death of the author of a literary, dramatic, or musical work which has been published or performed in public a complaint is made to the Judicial Committee of the Privy Council that the owner of the copyright in the work has refused to republish or to allow the republication of the work, or has refused to allow the performance of the work in public, and that by

---

[1] Act of 1911, § 5 (2) (3).   [2] Ibid., § 5 (2).
[3] Defined, Act of 1911, § 35 (11).   [4] Copinger, p. 111.
[5] Ibid., pp. 113–114.

reason of such refusal the work is withheld from the public, the owner of the copyright may be ordered to grant a licence to reproduce the work or perform the work in public on such terms and subject to such conditions as the Judicial Committee may think fit.[1]

After the expiration of twenty-five years from the death of the author of a published work (and thirty years in the case of a work in which copyright subsisted at the passing of the Act), another person may reproduce the work on giving notice to the owner of his intention to reproduce and paying certain royalties.[2] This applies to posthumous works as if the author had died when the work was first published, performed, or delivered in public.[3]

7. Foreign Authors.[4]—Any foreign author not entitled to copyright on the ground of residence in the British dominions may acquire copyright in a book by first publication within the British dominions. In the same way, if an artistic work of a foreigner is first published as part of a book, copyright for the work will be obtained if the book is first published within the British dominions. The right of a foreign author to acquire copyright by first publication is, however, to a certain extent dependent upon his country's treatment of British authors. If British authors are entirely excluded from copyright in a foreign country, or are admitted only on very onerous conditions, this country may retaliate by excluding the citizens of such foreign country from all protection here. This is done by Order in Council directing that the appropriate provisions of the Copyright Act, 1911, shall not, after a certain date, apply to authors who are citizens of the foreign country and are not resident in His Majesty's dominions.

A foreigner is not entitled to copyright in his unpublished work unless he was resident in the British dominions at the date of the making of the work or unless the Act of 1911 has been applied to his country by Order in Council. But a foreign author who is unable to claim copyright for his unpublished work may yet be entitled to restrain publication of the work if made under circumstances amounting to a breach of trust or confidence.[5]

Where a British subject and a foreigner not resident at the time the work was made in any part of the King's dominions to which the Act extends jointly produce a work, and do not publish it, the British subject is to be treated as if he were the sole author, and he alone, therefore, can sue for infringement. But the foreigner will be entitled

---

[1] Act of 1911, § 4.   [2] Ibid., § 3, proviso.   [3] Ibid., § 17.
[4] Ibid., § 23.   [5] Ibid., § 31 ; Copinger, p. 27.

to enforce his contractual rights against his British co-author. The term of protection will be the same as if both authors were British subjects at the time the work was made.

8. Infringement of Copyright.—Copyright in a work is deemed to be infringed by any person who, without the consent of the owner of the copyright, does anything the sole right to do which is by the Act of 1911 conferred on the owner of the copyright.[1] The rights conferred on the owners of copyright the invasion of which constitute infringement are : (1) to produce or reproduce the work or any substantial part thereof in any material form ; (2) to perform the work or any substantial part thereof in public ; (3) to publish the work, if unpublished, or any substantial part thereof.[2] These rights include the sole right (a) to produce a translation of the work ; (b) in the case of a dramatic work to convert it into a novel or other non-dramatic work ; (c) in the case of a novel or other non-dramatic work to convert it into a dramatic work by way of performance in public or otherwise ; and (d) in the case of a literary, dramatic, or musical work to make any record, perforated roll, cinematograph film, or other contrivance by means of which the work may be mechanically performed.[2] In addition to these direct acts of infringement, copyright is infringed where one (a) sells or lets for hire, or by way of trade exposes or offers for sale or hire ; or (b) distributes either for the purpose of trade or to such an extent as to affect prejudicially the owner of the copyright ; or (c) by way of trade exhibits in public ; or (d) imports for sale or hire into any part of the British dominions any work which to his knowledge infringes or would infringe copyright if it had been made within the part of the British dominions in or into which the sale, hiring, exposure, etc., took place.[3] It is to be noted that whereas direct acts of infringement are actionable whether committed knowingly or not,[4] acts of these classes, consisting in dealing with infringing works, require proof of knowledge. The Act provides that certain acts shall not constitute an infringement of copyright. These are (1) any fair dealing with any work for the purposes of private study, research, criticism, review, or newspaper summary—what is a fair dealing will depend on the facts of each case ; (2) where the author of an artistic work is not the owner of the copyright therein the use by the author of any mould, cast, sketch, plan, model, or study made by him for the

---

[1] Act of 1911, § 2 (1).   [2] *Ibid.*, § 1 (2).   [3] *Ibid.*, § 2 (2).
[4] Scott *v.* Stanford, (1867) L.R. 3 Eq. 718 ; Mansell *v.* Valley Printing Co., [1908] 2 Ch. 441 ; Byrne *v.* Statist Co., [1914] 1 K.B. 622.

purpose of the work, provided that he does not thereby repeat or imitate the main design of that work ; (3) the making or publishing of paintings, drawings, engravings, or photographs of a work of sculpture or artistic craftsmanship if permanently situate in a public place or building, or the making or publishing of paintings, drawings, engravings, or photographs (which are not in the nature of architectural drawings or plans) of any architectural work of art ; (4) the publication in a collection, mainly composed of non-copyright matter, *bona fide* intended for the use of schools, and so described in the title and in any advertisements issued by the publisher, of short passages from published literary works, not themselves published for the use of schools, in which copyright subsists ; provided that not more than two of such passages from works by the same author are published by the same publisher within five years, and that the source from which such passages are taken is acknowledged ; (5) the publication in a newspaper of a report of a lecture delivered in public, unless the report is prohibited by conspicuous written or printed notice affixed before and maintained during the lecture at or about the main entrance of the building in which the lecture is given, and, except while the building is being used for public worship, in a position near the lecturer, but without affecting the right to make a fair newspaper summary ; (6) the reading or recitation in public by one person of any reasonable extract from any published work [1] ; (7) the publication in a newspaper of a full report of an address of a political nature delivered at a public meeting, notwithstanding any prohibition by public notice.[2] Copyright is also deemed to be infringed by any person who for his private profit permits a theatre or other place of entertainment to be used for the performance in public of the work without the consent of the owner of the copyright unless he was not aware, and had no reasonable ground for suspecting, that the performance would be an infringement of copyright.[3]

Since the Act of 1911 registration forms no part of the law of copyright.

---

[1] Act of 1911, § 2 (1).　　　[2] *Ibid.*, § 20.　　　[3] *Ibid.*, § 2 (3).

CHAPTER IX

BILLS OF EXCHANGE, CHEQUES, AND PROMISSORY NOTES

BILLS OF EXCHANGE

1. Origin and Functions.—The origin of bills of exchange, which are perhaps the most familiar and important of all our instruments of commerce, is, like many other inventions in daily use, involved in obscurity. Hence no opinion can be expressed with any confidence as to its accuracy as to when or by whom bills of exchange were first used as a circulating medium representative of money. There is no direct evidence as to when bills of exchange were first used in Great Britain. In England there is mention made of them as early as the reign of Richard II., but there is no mention of them in the regular reports until the reign of James I. In Scotland it is clear, from the provisions of an Act of 1681, that bills of exchange must have been in use prior to that time, for in that year an Act of the third Parliament of Charles II. was passed, providing for summary diligence upon foreign bills. In 1696 this provision was extended by the first Parliament of King William to inland bills. Whoever may have had the honour of introducing bills of exchange, there seems to be no doubt of this, that bills of exchange originated from the necessities of foreign trade and the difficulty of transmitting coin from one country to another. Gradually, as trade prospered, the use of such instruments naturally increased ; and while at first their use was limited to the case of foreign merchants and merchants in this country to avoid the risk and difficulty in the transmission of coin, in the course of time their use expanded until now they have become a great constituent in commercial credit and currency.

Keeping out of view for the present the question of accommodation bills, the paramount importance of ordinary trade bills is that they fix a debt ; the acceptor by signing the bill acknowledges that he is indebted to the drawer in the sum stated, and that at maturity he will pay that amount. Value is always presumed to have been given for a bill. Every party whose signature appears on the instrument is presumed to have become a party to it for value, and every

183

person who is in possession of a bill is presumed to have given value for it.[1]

Foreign bills are the most important media for the settlement of foreign debts. It is outwith the scope of our present purpose to deal with the question of foreign exchanges, but international debts are not settled by the export and import of gold. It is only the balance of indebtedness which is settled in this way. Bills of exchange and cheques are the chief media by which international payments are made. For example, a London merchant buys goods from a Paris merchant, and, in payment, sends a bill of exchange for £100, payable in London. The Paris merchant owes £100 to a Glasgow firm. It is obviously not worth his while to collect the bill due to him in London, have the proceeds remitted to Paris, and then send them back to Glasgow. What he may do is this : he sends the London bill endorsed to his Glasgow creditors, and the latter present it through the clearing-house in the ordinary way by their bankers. The whole transaction is thus settled without any movement of gold. Bills of exchange play an important part in shipping transactions. For example, a Glasgow firm buys a cargo of wheat from a Canadian firm. The goods are duly shipped, and the seller gets the bills of lading for the cargo. The only way by which the buyer can get delivery of the cargo at Glasgow is by presenting the bill of lading to the captain on the arrival of the vessel. The seller wants to make sure that the buyer, before getting the cargo, will at least admit his indebtedness for the amount of the purchase price, and what he does is this : he draws a bill of exchange for the amount on the buyer, attaches that bill to the bill of lading, and sends the two, through his bankers in Canada, to their banking correspondent in Glasgow, with instructions only to deliver the bill of lading against acceptance of the bill of exchange. As regards inland bills, their utility may thus be illustrated : one merchant sells goods to another, the bargain being a three months' credit. The seller draws upon the buyer for the amount of the price, and this bill the purchaser accepts. The seller at once has an acknowledgment for the amount due to him payable at a future date, and the means of obtaining cash at once by taking that bill to his bankers and having it discounted. We shall now proceed to consider the law applicable to such documents.

2. Definition and Essentials.—Bills of Exchange Act.—The law relating to bills of exchange, cheques, and promissory notes, is now

[1] B. of E. Act, § 30.

chiefly governed by the Bills of Exchange Act, 1882, which codified and, to some extent, modified the law existing prior to its passing. The bill as originally drafted was not intended to apply to Scotland. It was drawn solely with reference to the law of England and Ireland, and was mainly a digest of the then existing law in those parts of the United Kingdom. It was only through the strenuous endeavours of Scottish bankers and certain legal societies that the bill was subsequently made applicable to Scotland.

Statutory Definition of Bill.—The statutory definition of a bill of exchange [1] is : " A bill of exchange is an unconditional order in writing, addressed by one person to another, signed by the person giving it, requiring the person to whom it is addressed to pay on demand or at a fixed or determinable future time a sum certain in money to or to the order of a specified person, or to bearer." The following is the form of a bill in daily use :—

(*Place and date.*)

Three months after date pay to me or to my order within the Head Office of the Bank of Scotland Edinburgh the sum of FIFTY POUNDS value received.

PETER ROBINSON,   JOHN SMITH.
   141 High Street,
         Edinburgh.

It is not necessary that the bill should be in a form resembling the one quoted, for so long as the document, however inelegantly expressed, complies with the provisions of the Act, it is entitled to the benefits pertaining to a bill. A bill may be expressed in any language, and may be, although it is not desirable, written in pencil. It may also be printed or typewritten, with the exception, of course, of the signatures of the parties to it. Bills are privileged documents inasmuch as they are freed from all ordinary formalities by which instruments of value require to be authenticated. They prove their own dates without witnesses, and the designations of the drawer, acceptor, and endorser are not essential.[2]

The difference between an inland and a foreign bill, so far as mere phraseology is concerned, need not be very marked. Inland and foreign bills are defined in the Act [3] as follows : An inland bill is a bill which is or on the face of it purports to be both drawn and payable within the British Islands, or drawn within the British

---

[1] Act, § 3.   [2] See Privileged Writings, *supra*, p. 9.   [3] § 4.

Islands upon some person resident therein. Any other bill is a foreign bill. For the purpose of the Act, " British Islands " means any part of the United Kingdom of Great Britain and Ireland, the Islands of Man, Guernsey, Jersey, Alderney, and Sark, and the islands adjacent to any of them, being part of the dominions of His Majesty.

Unless the contrary appear on the face of the bill, the holder may treat it as an inland bill.

Position of Parties to Bill.—In the form of bills just quoted the creditor in the bill is called the drawer, and as the bill is made payable to him he is also called the payee. The person to whom the bill is addressed, and who is to be primary debtor on the bill, is, before he signs the bill, called the drawee, and, after he has signed the bill, the acceptor. The person to whom a bill is addressed is the only person who can sign the bill as acceptor. All other persons who thereafter sign the bill do so in subsidiary capacities, and different rules of law apply to them. Although the person to whom a bill is addressed signs his name he is not liable on the instrument so long as he keeps possession of the same, following a well-recognised rule of law that a document of debt found in possession of the debtor is presumed to have been paid.[1] It is only when the acceptor delivers the bill to the drawer, or to someone on his behalf, or gives notice that he has accepted it, that liability attaches. The drawee must be named or otherwise indicated with reasonable certainty [2] ; that is, on the bill itself, apart from any extraneous evidence, there must be a sufficient identification of the person who is to become the principal debtor. It is not necessary that the acceptor should sign on the face of the bill. It is sufficient, although unusual and inadvisable, if his name appear on the back thereof. It is competent to address the bill to two or more drawees, whether they are partners or not.[3] Thus "A. B. and C. D.," giving their addresses ; but it is not competent to address the bill to two drawees in the alternative, thus " A. B., whom failing C. D., whom failing E. F."

Order to Pay must be Unconditional.—The order to pay, such as we find in bills, " pay to me," must be unconditional.[4] Hence an order to pay out of a particular fund, or on a contingency such as " when I am in funds," or on performance by the payee of some stipulation or subject to any condition express or implied, would make the document not a bill of exchange. But an unqualified order to pay,

---

[1] See Presumption of Payment, *supra*, p. 53.
[2] B. of E. Act, § 6. [3] *Ibid.* [4] *Ibid.*, § 3.

coupled with an indication of a particular fund out of which the drawee is to reimburse himself, or of a particular account to be debited with the amount, or a statement of the transaction which gives rise to the bill, does not affect its validity, *e.g.* " Out of funds in your hands belonging to me," " debit the same to my storage account," or " being the price of goods sold and delivered by you to me." [1]

Signature of Drawer.—The bill must be signed by the person giving it ; that is, the drawer. The drawer need not sign it with his own hand, but his name may be written on the bill by someone acting by or under his authority. A bill signed by initials or by a mark may be sustained as a ground of action on proof that the party alleged to be the subscriber usually signs by initials or mark, and did sign the bill in question. The great compulsitor for the due payment of bills in Scotland, at least, is the fact that the creditor can proceed against his debtor by summary diligence ; that is, the enforcement of the bill without recourse to a Court of law to get a decree for payment ; but a bill signed by mark or by initials would not warrant summary diligence for the reason that proof would require to be given that such a mode of subscription was the usual one adopted by the debtor. It is not necessary that the drawer should sign before the acceptor.

Time of Payment.—The order to pay must be on demand or at a fixed or determinable future time, *e.g.* " three months after date pay to me or my order the sum of £50." The bill would be equally good if it bore " three months after my death," for that event is sure to happen ; but, for example, " three months after the arrival of the ship *Anchoria* in Glasgow " would be bad, for the reason that the vessel might never arrive. Further, a bill is payable at a fixed or determinable future time, which is expressed to be payable at a fixed period after date or sight. In the case of sight bills, substitute the word " sight " for " date." A bill is payable at a fixed period although it is expressed to be payable on or at a fixed period after the occurrence of a specified event which is sure to happen, though the time of happening may be uncertain. An instrument expressed to be payable on a contingency is not a bill, and the happening of the event does not cure the defect.

Bills Payable on Demand.[2]—A bill is payable on demand when it is expressed to be so payable or where no time for payment is stated. If a demand bill is post-dated—that is, if it is issued prior to the date

---

[1] B. of E. Act, § 3 (3).   [2] *Ibid.*, § 10.

it bears—payment cannot be demanded until on or after the date stated therein. Where a bill is accepted or endorsed when it is over-due (that is, in the case of all bills not payable on demand, on the expiry of the last day of grace), it is, as regards the acceptor who so accepts or any endorser who endorses it, deemed to be payable on demand.[1]

Undated Bills.—If a bill payable at a fixed period after date be issued without a date, or where the acceptance of a bill payable at a fixed period after sight is undated, any holder may insert therein the true date of issue or acceptance, and the bill is payable accordingly; but should the holder in good faith and by mistake insert a wrong date, and in every case where a wrong date is inserted, if the bill subsequently come into the hands of a holder in due course, the bill is not thereby avoided, but operates and is payable as if the date so inserted had been the true date.[2]

Bill must be for Sum certain in Money.—The bill must state as the amount to be paid a sum certain in money.[3] A document would be bad as a bill if it were stated that the acceptor were to deliver goods equal to a specified value. The amount is certain within the meaning of the Act, although it is required to be paid with interest, or by stated instalments, with a provision that upon default in payment of any instalment the whole shall become due, or according to an indicated rate of exchange, or according to a rate of exchange to be ascertained as directed by the bill.[4] In the form of bills in daily use the sum payable is expressed in words and also in figures. Where there is a discrepancy between the two, the sum denoted by the words is the amount payable.[5] Where a bill is expressed to be payable with interest, unless the instrument otherwise provides, interest runs from the date of the bill, and if the bill is undated, from the issue thereof.[5] If the bill has been issued either ante-dated or post-dated, interest runs from the date it bears.[6] Where there is no stipulation as to the rate of interest on an interest-bearing bill, interest is payable at 5 per cent. from the date of the bill.

Person to whom Bill to be Paid.—The Act[3] provides that the bill is to be paid to, or to the order of, a specified person or to bearer; in the case of " order " bills the usual phraseology is " pay to me or my order." It is, however, quite competent for the drawer to make the document run thus : " Three months after date pay to John Brown

---

[1] B. of E. Act, § 10 (2).   [2] Ibid., § 12.   [3] Ibid., § 3.
[4] Ibid., § 9.   [5] Ibid., § 9 (3).   [6] Ibid., § 13.

or order the sum of **Fifty Pounds.**" In such a case the payee of the bill would be Brown, he being the person to whom the bill is made payable. Further, a bill may be made payable to bearer thus : "Three months after date pay to bearer." Unlike the case of a drawee or acceptor, a bill may be made payable to two or more persons jointly, or it may be made payable in the alternative to one of two or one or some of several payees. A bill may also be made payable to the holder of an office for the time being.[1]

3. Non-Essentials of Bills.—A bill is not invalid by reason only that it is not dated, that it does not specify the value given, or that any value was given. Again, a bill is not invalid by reason only that it does not specify the place where it is drawn or the place where it is payable.[2] Although it is usual and advisable that a place of payment should be stated in a bill thus : " Accepted payable at the George Street Branch of the Bank of Scotland, Edinburgh," or in the body of the bill thus : " Pay to me or my order within the Bank of Scotland, George Street Branch, Edinburgh," this is unnecessary. It also is unnecessary that the word " accepted " should appear. Further, a bill is not invalid by reason only that it is ante-dated or post-dated or that it bears date on a Sunday.[3]

4. Due Date of Bill.[4]—Days of Grace.—When a bill is drawn payable at a certain specified period after date or sight, three days, called days of grace, are, in every case where the bill itself does not otherwise provide, added to the time of payment as fixed by the bill, and the bill is due and payable on the last day of grace. Originally the acceptor of a bill of exchange was not entitled to demand as a right any days of grace, but was bound to pay the bill on its due date, as appearing from the face thereof. The allowance of any days of grace was merely gratuitous and depending on the inclination of the holder of the bill. The laws of certain commercial countries have, however, long since recognised days of grace as a right of the acceptor in all cases where the bill is payable after the lapse of a certain time from its date unless the bill otherwise provides. A bill may, however, be drawn payable *ex grace, sans grace*, fixed, or the like. No days of grace are allowed on bills payable on demand ; that is, on bills expressed to be so payable or on sight or on presentation or in which no time for payment is expressed. In most countries days of grace have already been abolished ; but, besides the United Kingdom, they are recognised in the United States, Russia, Portugal, and some of the

---

[1] B. of E. Act, § 7 (2).   [2] *Ibid.*, § 3 (4).   [3] *Ibid.*, § 13 (2).   [4] *Ibid.*, § 14.

smaller States. Foreign bills are occasionally drawn at one or more usances. By usance is meant the customary time at which bills are made payable in a particular country—France, thirty days ; Hamburg, one calendar month ; and Leghorn, three calendar months. Double, treble, and half usance are terms implying corresponding alterations on the usual period.

If the month in which the bill falls due has no day corresponding to that of the issue or acceptance, the last day of that month is the day from which the days of grace are reckoned. Thus a bill drawn on the 28th, 29th, 30th, or 31st January, and payable one month after date, is due on the 3rd March. If, however, a bill be drawn on the 28th of January in leap year, payable one month after date, it will fall due on the 2nd March.

When payment of a bill is refused by the acceptor at any time on the last day of grace, the holder (although he is entitled at once to give notice of dishonour to the drawer and the endorsers) has no right of action against the acceptor or the other parties to the bill until the expiration of that day. Accordingly an action brought by the holder of a bill against the acceptor on the last day of grace was dismissed as premature.[1]

5. How Bills must be Issued.—With reference to the form of a bill, it must be drawn, except in the case to be immediately noted, upon paper appropriated to such documents, stamped with the proper impressed duty, and cannot be stamped after execution. An un-stamped or improperly stamped bill cannot be founded on as evidence in our Courts. This provision, especially with regard to foreign bills, brings about, in certain cases, unfortunate results. Suppose a bill is drawn in London on Berlin without the proper English stamp, it is negotiated in France and Germany, and is finally dishonoured in Berlin. There being no law in these countries requiring bills to be written on specially stamped paper, the result is that the German holder can sue the French endorser, but neither of them can sue the English drawer, who was the party to blame for issuing the bill un-stamped. In the case, however, of a bill payable on demand, or within three days after date, the stamp duty may be denoted by a twopenny postage stamp, and the bill may be written on any kind of paper. A curious point once arose with regard to the provision that a bill cannot be stamped after execution. All impressed bill stamps are dated. The date of the bill was, let us say, 1st February, whereas the date of

---

[1] Kennedy v. Thomas, [1894] L.R. 2 Q.B. 759.

the stamp on the bill was, say, 1st March. It is obvious that the stamp on the bill was not in existence on 1st February, but the bill was nevertheless held to be good for the reason that a bill may be post-dated or ante-dated.

6. Acceptance of Bill.—The acceptance of a bill is regulated by §§ 17, 18, and 19 of the Act. An acceptance may be either general or qualified. The form of acceptance where the acceptor simply signs his name, or even adds " accepted," is general, because it assents, without qualification, to the order of the drawer. A qualified accept-ance, on the other hand, varies the effect of the bill as drawn. When such an acceptance is taken, the words of qualification " must be incor-porated in the acceptance or at least so connected with the acceptance as clearly to form part of it ; and must also be such as to indicate clearly and unequivocally the nature of the restrictions which they are meant to introduce." A qualified acceptance may vary the effect of the bill in almost any way, but it must not promise performance by any other means than the payment of money, and it must not engage for payment of a larger sum than the one on the bill, for that would make a new contract under the Stamp Act. The acceptance may be in favour only of some one or more of the parties to the bill. The addition of the words " as cautioner " does not qualify the acceptance ; it can only affect the question of relief. The acceptor cannot in a question with a holder in due course, *i.e.* a person to whom the bill has been validly negotiated, avail himself of a qualification which does not appear in the bill. No one is bound to take a qualified acceptance. If he does take a qualified acceptance other than a partial acceptance without the concurrence of prior parties they are discharged. Although the acceptor dies before the bill is completed by the signature of the drawer his acceptance remains good. All acceptances on bills are presumed to have been made within a reasonable time after the issue of the bill and before its maturity.

7. Blank Bills.—If any person sign his name on bill paper duly stamped, and hands it to another in order that it may be converted into a bill, that operates *prima facie* as an authority to him to fill it up as a complete bill for any amount the stamp will cover, and the signature may be used for that of the drawer or the acceptor or an endorser.[1] The *prima facie* authority here conferred is not limited by a note of a sum of money in figures on the margin of the blank bill.[2] In like manner, when a bill is wanting in any material particular the

---

[1] B. of E. Act, § 20.   [2] Gurrard *v.* Lewis, (1882) 10 Q.B.D. 30.

person in possession of it has *prima facie* authority to fill up the omission in any way he thinks fit. In order that a bill when completed may be enforceable against any person who became a party thereto prior to its completion it must be filled up within a reasonable time and strictly in accordance with the authority given. If any such instrument after completion is negotiated to a holder in due course it is valid and effectual for all purposes in his hands, and he may enforce it as if it had been filled up within a reasonable time and strictly in accordance with the authority given.[1] So strong is the position of a holder for value that he is entitled to enforce the bill though it has been stolen after delivery, or though it has only been completed after unreasonable delay, or after the sequestration of the granter. Thus in one case A. delivered his blank acceptance to B., who retained it till after A. had become bankrupt and been discharged, and then filled it up, inserting a date subsequent to that of the discharge. A holder in due course was held entitled to enforce it against A. notwithstanding his discharge.[2]

8. Who may Contract by Bill.—Capacity to incur liability as a party to a bill is co-extensive with capacity to contract.[3]

9. Conditions of Liability on a Bill.—Signature.—Signature is essential to liability on a bill of exchange, and no person is liable as drawer or endorser or acceptor of a bill who has not signed it as such. But where a person signs a bill in a trade or assumed name he is liable thereon as if he had signed it in his own name.[4] The signature of the name of a firm is equivalent to the signature by the person so signing of the names of all persons liable as partners in that firm. If a bill is addressed to a firm and is accepted by a partner thereof in the firm's name, the addition of that partner's own name beneath that of the firm does not render the partner separately liable. Where a firm's name is that of an individual, if the bill is used for partnership purposes, the individual partners of the firm are liable as well as the partner who has signed it. A firm's signature to a bill by one of the partners after the dissolution of the co-partnery does not bind the firm or the other partners. If an agent sign a bill in his own name, although it is really on behalf of the principal, the principal is not liable on the bill.

Where a person signs a bill otherwise than as drawer or acceptor he thereby incurs the liabilities of an endorser to a holder in due course. This is a case which frequently happens in practice. A.

---

[1] B. of E. Act, § 20 (2).   [2] *Ex parte* Hayward, (1871) L.R. 6 Ch. 541.
[3] B. of E. Act, § 22 ; see Contract.   [4] *Ibid.*, § 23.

wants to raise money through his banker, and he gets his friend B. to accept for him. The bank are not satisfied to discount the bill on the names of A. and B. A. then gets his friend C. to endorse the bill, and then the bank discount. The bank in such a case have a good claim against A., B., and C., although in a question among these three parties A. is bound to relieve both B. and C., as he is the only person who has benefited by the bill.

Effect of Forged or Unauthorised Signature.—A forged or unauthorised signature is wholly inoperative, and no right to retain the bill, to discharge it, or to enforce payment of it can be acquired through the signature unless the party against whom it is sought to retain or enforce payment is precluded from setting up the forgery or want of authority.[1] No one can be a holder in due course who derives his title through a forged or unauthorised signature, and it does not matter that the holder had no notice of the forgery or want of authority. A payment made in due course, that is, at or after the maturity of the bill to the holder in good faith and without notice that his title to the bill is defective, discharges the liability of the acceptor. But a payment on the forged signature of the drawer is not a payment in due course and does not therefore discharge the drawee, who must deliver the bill to its true owner and pay it when it falls due. A merely unauthorised signature may be subsequently ratified so as to preclude the person so ratifying it from pleading the want of authority. But mere silence does not amount to ratification or adoption.[2] This was decided in a case where the facts were as follows : a bill bearing to be drawn and endorsed by A. was brought by the acceptor to a banker who discounted it. It was dishonoured when due and notice was sent to A., but he did not communicate with the bank. The notice was given on a Saturday, and on the following Monday the acceptor called at the bank with a similar bill for a smaller amount and arranged a renewal, paying the difference to account. The second bill was also dishonoured. The bank sent notice to A. three days before the dishonour and immediately after. A fortnight after he received the first notice A. informed the bank that the bill was forged, and refused to pay it. It was held that the bank had renewed the first bill and so enabled the forger to inform A. ; that it had been arranged before A. had had time to make inquiries ; that there was therefore no evidence that A. had authorised the signature of the second bill ; and that A.'s delay in intimating the

[1] B. of E. Act, § 24.   [2] Mackenzie v. British Linen Co., 1881, 8 R. (H.L.) 8.

13

forgery after receiving the bank's notice regarding the second bill was not sufficient to infer adoption, no prejudice having been caused to the bank thereby. In this case Lord Blackburn said : " If a person whose name is without authority used chooses to ratify the act, even though known to be a crime—as forgery is—he makes himself civilly responsible just as if he had originally authorised it."

Procuration Signature.—Bills are frequently signed not by the hand of the person who is really liable on the document, but by some other one acting by or under his authority, or as it is usually termed " by procuration." A signature by procuration operates as a notice that the agent has but a limited authority to sign, and the principal is only bound by such signature if the agent in so signing was acting within the actual limits of his authority,[1] and the taker of a bill so accepted or endorsed is bound to inquire as to the extent of the agent's authority. Where the agent has such authority his abuse of it does not affect a *bona fide* holder for value. Procuration may be conferred by verbal or written authority, or by facts and circumstances inferring implied authority.[2]

A person signing by procuration must sign *per pro.* or otherwise show that he is merely an agent, or he will not bind his principal, though he may if he actually has no authority bind himself, and if he adds words to his signature showing that he signs for and on behalf of a principal he will free himself from liability even though his principal repudiate the obligation. But the mere addition of words showing he acts in a representative capacity as " director," "trustee," or " executor " does not exempt him from personal liability.[3] In case of doubt whether a signature be that of a principal or that of the agent by whose hand it is written, the construction most favourable to the validity of the bill is adopted. In all cases an agent's authority is rigidly construed. Hence a mandate to draw bills does not authorise the agent to endorse them, and a mandate to accept bills in course of a particular business does not authorise the agent to accept them for any other purpose. A foreign firm appointed an agent in this country with general power to sign for them per procuration. Some time later this authority was withdrawn. Subsequently a bank which, as was proved, knew of the withdrawal of the mandate, but knew also that for certain purposes the agent still signed for the firm, continued to discount bills signed by him per procuration of them. It was held that the bank in so doing without inquiry had

---

[1] B. of E. Act, § 25.   [2] See Agency, *supra*, p. 72.   [3] B. of E. Act, § 26.

acted at their own peril, and that as the bills in question had in fact been granted by the agent for a debt of his own, the firm was not liable.

A mandate to act as agent for a company in certain matters, including the purchase and sale of goods, to grant bills, and for all or any of the said purposes to do whatever ought to be done, does not authorise the agent to borrow on behalf of the company.

Presentment for Acceptance.—The statutory rules are contained in §§ 39 to 44 of the Act. Where a bill is payable after sight, presentment for acceptance is necessary in order to fix the maturity of the instrument. In practice an inland bill is rarely made payable so many days after sight. The use of such bills is almost exclusively confined to foreign bills, although there is nothing incompetent in an inland bill being drawn payable at so many days after sight. On such a bill being presented to the drawee he ought to date his acceptance in order to fix the maturity of the bill. If this is not done the holder may insert the true date. If he insert a wrong date in good faith, and by mistake, or if the acceptance with a wrong date comes into the hands of a holder in due course, the bill becomes payable at the date so inserted. When a bill is duly presented for acceptance, and is not accepted within the customary time, the person presenting it must treat it as dishonoured by non-acceptance. If he do not, the holder loses his right of recourse against the drawer and endorsers.[1] The drawee may require that the bill be left with him for acceptance, and he is entitled to retain it for the customary period, which is usually twenty-four hours, but varies according to the custom of the place of presentment. In Scotland the customary period is twenty-four hours. In reckoning the period non-business days are excluded. On the lapse of this time the drawee must deliver the bill, accepted or not accepted. If it is not delivered accepted, the holder must have it noted for non-acceptance. It may be that the person with whom the bill has been left for acceptance refuses to deliver it up either accepted or unaccepted. In such a case the law provides a remedy. A formal protest can be made by a notary public on production of a copy of the bill, or, if this is not available, then on written particulars thereof.

Effect of Presentation for Acceptance.—There is a difference between the laws of England and Scotland with regard to the effect of the presentation of a bill for acceptance to the drawee. In England a

[1] B. of E. Act, § 42.

bill of itself does not operate as an assignment of funds in the hands of the drawee available for the payment thereof ; and the drawee of a bill who does not accept, as required by the Act, is not liable on the instrument. In Scotland, where the drawee of a bill has in his hands funds available for the payment thereof, the bill operates as an assignment of the sum for which it is drawn in favour of the holder from the time when the bill is presented to the drawee.[1] No person is liable on a bill until he has signed it. Consequently, to get at the funds which have been attached, it is necessary to sue for the debt due by the drawee to the drawer, and to found on the bill as an assignation of the debt and not solely on the bill, as in the case of an acceptance. Presentment of a bill of exchange does not operate as an intimated assignation when the drawee has goods in his hands belonging to the drawer which have not been realised, because the assignation in a bill is an assignation of money and not of goods. When a bill has been accepted payable at a bank, presentment to the banker operates as an assignation in favour of the payee of the bill of money in the banker's hands belonging to the acceptor. Bills are preferable according to their respective dates of presentation to the drawee.

Consideration necessary to support Bill.[2]—Between the laws of England and Scotland there is a material difference on this point. In Scotland a bill does not require to be granted for value adequate or inadequate. In England a bill is invalid unless granted for value. The consideration must be real, and this has been defined as " some right, interest, profit, or benefit accruing to one party, or some forbearance, detriment, loss, or responsibility given, suffered, or undertaken by the other." [3] In Scotland a defence of no value having been given is not of itself a sufficient defence because a person may grant a bill from goodwill or in fulfilment of some moral obligation. In the cases following the plea that the bill was granted for no valuable consideration may be a good defence, which, if proved, will preclude the holder, but not a holder who has given value for the bill, from enforcing it (a) where the bill has been signed without intention to grant an obligation, or where it has been obtained by fraud, force, or fear ; (b) where a bill has been given under an agreement that it was to be used only on a certain consideration which has failed ; (c) where it is an accommodation bill ; (d) where it is given for an immoral or illegal consideration, or one which the law

---

[1] B. of E. Act, § 53 (2).   [2] *Ibid.*, § 27.
[3] Currie *v.* Misa, (1875) L.R. 10 Ex. 153 at p. 162.

does not recognise ; as, for example, for condoning a crime, for procuring a marriage, for a gambling debt, as a consideration for concurring in or obtaining a bankrupt's discharge, or as an illegal preference in bankruptcy. In all these cases, if the person in possession of the bill has given value for it, he is entitled to enforce the bill. It is only as among the parties who have given no value for the bill that a defence on the above lines would be sustained. Valuable consideration for a bill may be constituted by (a) any consideration sufficient to support a simple contract ; (b) an antecedent debt or liability. Where value has at any time been given for a bill the holder is deemed to be a holder for value as regards the acceptor and all parties to the bill who became parties prior to such time. Where the holder of a bill has a lien on it arising either from contract or implication of law he is deemed to be a holder for value to the extent of the sum for which he has a lien. In considering the position of a holder in due course it is important to observe that no person can be a holder in due course who derives his title through a forged or unauthorised signature. When the bill is taken it must not be blank in any material particular, nor bear any sign of having been altered in a material particular. In other words, the bill must be complete and regular on the face of it, and the party taking the bill must have no notice of any defect in the title of the person who negotiated it. If the holder suspects that there is some defect in the title, and avoids taking means open to him of ascertaining whether there is or not, he will be held to have acted dishonestly and to be in the same position as if he had been informed of the defect.

Accommodation Bills.—An accommodation party to a bill is a person who has signed a bill as drawer, acceptor or endorser, without receiving value therefor, and for the purpose of lending his name to some other person.[1] Accommodation bills, or wind bills, as they are sometimes called, are drawn, accepted, or endorsed by the person who so signs his name, without having received value therefor, and for the purpose of fabricating credit by being discounted, and although they differ in no respect in form from ordinary trade bills, are yet different in their legal effect as regards the parties to them, so far as betwixt persons they do not represent a real debt. In a question therefore with third parties, an accommodation bill is in the same position as any other bill issued in the ordinary course of business, the legal presumption being that it is a bill drawn and issued for value.

[1] B. of E. Act, § 28.

Hence an accommodation party is liable on the bill to a holder for value, and it is immaterial whether, when such holder took the bill, he knew such party to be an accommodation party or not, unless in the probable case where he knew at the time of taking the bill that it was transferred to him in breach of a duty to the acceptor. It is not absolutely essential that the holder should have himself given value, for where value has at any time been given for a bill, whether in its origin an accommodation bill or an ordinary trade bill, the holder is deemed to be a holder for value as regards the acceptor and all parties on the bill who became parties prior to the time the bill came into the possession of the holder.[1] The holder is entitled to call upon all the prior parties to the bill to make payment to him, and this notwithstanding the fact that at the time such holder took the bill he knew that it was an accommodation bill. Therefore if a person takes such a bill and gives value for it, he is just doing that which the other parties to the bill intended should be done upon the security of the bill which was granted. The position of the holder is, that he is entitled to look to the various parties to the bill for payment according to the position in which their names appear on the bill, and to regard the acceptor as the primary debtor, although he may know that in a question with the drawer the drawer is bound to relieve such acceptor, he being the true debtor.

10. Negotiation of Bills.[2]—A bill is negotiated when it is transferred from one person to another in such a manner as to constitute the transferee the holder of the bill. Thus the delivery of unendorsed bills payable to order is not negotiation of them. A bill payable to bearer is negotiated by delivery. A bill payable to order is negotiated by the endorsement of the holder, completed by delivery. The following may negotiate bills for a named holder : (a) An agent having authority to do so ; (b) the executor of a deceased holder ; or (c) the trustee in bankruptcy of a holder. Where the holder of a bill payable to his order transfers it for value without endorsing it the transfer gives the transferee such title as the transferor had in the bill, and the transferee in addition acquires the right to have the endorsement of the transferor. If the transferor dies without endorsing the bill, his executor may be compelled to endorse. Where a person is under obligation to endorse a bill in a representative capacity he may endorse it in such terms as to negative personal responsibility. Thus "pay D. or order without recourse on me," or simply "without

---

[1] B. of E. Act, § 29.   [2] *Ibid.*, § 31.

recourse." Such an endorsement, while limiting the endorser's liability, leaves the transferee free to have recourse to any other party to the bill whose liability is not so limited. There is a difference between the negotiation of a bill payable to bearer and one payable to order. In the case of a bill payable to bearer anyone gets a good title to it by mere delivery even from a thief or a finder provided he gave value for the bill, and that at the time he took it he had no knowledge of any defect in the title of the person from whom he took it. No such privilege—if it can be called a privilege—attaches to bills payable to order. If a bill is stolen or is found and an endorsement forged, anyone taking such a bill from the forger or a subsequent holder even for value and in ignorance of the position of matters acquires no right in the bill as against anyone liable on the bill prior to the forged signature.

Rights and Powers of Holder of Bill.—The rights and powers of the holder of a bill are as follows [1] :—He may sue on the bill in his own name, and is entitled to maintain an action on the bill in his own name against any or all of the parties liable on it unless it can be shown that he holds the bill adversely to the interests of the true owner. If, however, a bill be payable to a specified person or persons any action on the bill must be raised in the name of such person or persons. A holder who might have sued a party to a bill is entitled to claim against such party's estate in bankruptcy. Where a person is a holder in due course he holds the bill free from any defect of title of prior parties as well as from mere personal defences available to prior parties among themselves, and may enforce payment against all parties liable on the bill. Where his title is defective, if he negotiates the bill to a holder in due course that holder obtains a good and complete title to the bill, and if he obtains payment of the bill the person who pays him in due course gets a valid discharge for the bill. On the death of a holder his rights pass to his executors, and on his bankruptcy, if he be the beneficial owner of the bill or if the bill be payable to a bankrupt for his own account, his rights pass to his trustee.

11. Payment of Bill.—Presentment.[2]—A bill must be duly presented for payment unless the delay in making presentment for payment is excused, as when the delay is caused by circumstances beyond the control of the holder and not imputable to his default or misconduct or negligence, as, for example, by his sudden illness or death, and

---

[1] B. of E. Act, § 38.   [2] *Ibid.*, § 45.

the further case where the bill has been dishonoured by non-acceptance, unless it has been after " accepted for honour." [1] In practice it is now seldom necessary to consider the question of acceptance and payment for honour, as, owing to the improvement which has of recent years taken place in the means of communication, acceptance and payment for honour have fallen almost entirely into disuse. If a bill is not duly presented the drawer and endorsers are discharged, and that although they have sustained no damage through the omission. It is otherwise, however, with the acceptor. He is liable to pay in terms of his contract. Presentment for payment is not excused although the acceptor is bankrupt. A bill must be presented for payment at the address of the drawee as given in the bill unless a specified place of payment is specified. In a case decided in 1902 [2] a bill was addressed to the drawee at his residence, no other place of payment being given. Instead of being presented at the acceptor's residence the bill was presented at his place of business, and it was decided that such presentation was invalid. Although as a matter of fact the acceptor has removed from his address as given in the bill, the bill must be presented at his old address for the reason that the debtor must attend at the place prescribed in the bill with his money, and be ready to make payment. Where a place of payment is specified in the bill, thus where the bill is accepted payable at the Glasgow Bank, Glasgow, the bill must be presented there. Where the acceptor is dead and no place of payment is specified, presentment must be made to a personal representative if such there be, and with the exercise of reasonable diligence he can be found.

Proceedings necessary to preserve Recourse against Drawer and Endorser.—Notice of dishonour [3] must be given to the drawer, and each endorser and any drawer or endorser to whom such notice is not given is discharged unless in the cases specified in § 50, which provides that the delay in giving notice is excused where the delay is caused by circumstances beyond the control of the party giving notice and not imputable to his default, misconduct, or negligence. The notice may be given in writing or by personal communication, and may be given in any terms which sufficiently identify the bill and intimate that the bill has been dishonoured. The object of

---

[1] The definition and liability of a person who accepts and pays for honour are contained in §§ 65 to 68 of the Act.

[2] Neill v. Dobson, Molle & Co., 1902, 4 F. 625.   [3] B. of E. Act, § 48.

giving notice is to inform the person receiving it not only that the bill has been dishonoured, but also that the person giving notice looks to him for payment. A bill was dishonoured in the hands of the secretary of a company. It was his duty to send notice of dishonour to another company, of which he was also secretary. He did not do so, and the Courts in England decided that his knowledge of the dishonour of the bill was not notice to the second company.[1] The notice may be given as soon as the bill is dishonoured, and must be given within a reasonable time thereafter.

Enforcement of Bill.—If it is not intended to proceed by summary diligence it is not necessary to note or protest the bill in order to preserve recourse against the drawer or endorsers. But if it is wished to proceed by summary diligence the bill may be noted on the day of its dishonour, and must be noted not later than the next succeeding business day.[2] When a bill has been duly noted the protest may be subsequently extended as of the date of the noting, but only within six months after the due date. The protest must contain a copy of the bill, and must be signed by the notary making it, and must specify the person at whose request the bill is protested, the place and date of protest, the cause or reason for protesting the bill, the demand made, and the answer given if any or the fact that the drawee or acceptor could not be found.[3] The protest bears that the notary public personally presented the bill in presence of two witnesses, but by long-established practice the Courts have decided that the presentment can be made by someone authorised by the notary. Where the services of a notary cannot be obtained at the place where the bill is dishonoured, any householder or substantial resident of the place may, in the presence of two witnesses, give a certificate signed by them attesting the dishonour of the bill. The certificate operates in all respects as if it were a formal protest of the bill.[4]

Proof of Liability on a Bill.—In any judicial proceedings in Scotland any fact relating to a bill of exchange, bank cheque, or promissory note, which is relevant to any question of liability thereon, may be proved by parole evidence.[5] Prior to the passing of the Act, unless in very special cases founded mostly on questions of fraud, it was incompetent to prove by witnesses the liabilities of parties to

---

[1] *In re* Fenwick, Stobart & Co., Ltd., [1902] 1 Ch. 507.
[2] Bills of Exchange (Time of Noting) Act, 1917, § 1.
[3] B. of E. Act, § 51 (7).   [4] *Ibid.*, § 94.   [5] *Ibid.*, § 100.

a bill, the Court holding that their liability must be determined as appearing on the face of the bill.

The only way by which the presumption of onerosity implied could, according to the general rule, be rebutted was by the writ or oath of the holder. Now, however, it is possible to prove by parole evidence that the indebtedness which *ex facie* of the bill is upon the acceptor is not upon him at all. In the case of an onerous holder of the bill any arrangement between the drawer and the acceptor is not binding upon him unless he is a party to the arrangement. The section under consideration does not make parole proof of payment of a bill competent.

Summary Diligence.—This diligence is peculiar to Scotland. By § 98 of the Act it is provided that nothing in the Act or in any repeal effected thereby shall extend or restrict or in any way alter or affect the law and practice in Scotland in regard to summary diligence. The privilege of summary diligence is of the greatest utility, and its practical effect is that the creditor gets what is equivalent to a judgment of the Court against his debtor. It is a privilege of statutory creation, and was first introduced in 1681. To obtain the necessary warrant the bill, except as against the acceptor only (see *infra*), in the case of a bill payable at a currency must be duly presented for payment, noted as of the day of its dishonour, or not later than the next succeeding business day, the protest extended and registered in the Books of Council and Session which are kept in Edinburgh, or in the books of the Sheriff Court of the county within which the persons sought to be charged reside, within six months after the date of the bill in the case of non-acceptance, and within six months after the falling due thereof in the case of non-payment. Protests of bills payable on demand are registrable within six months of the date of presentation for payment and not from the date of the bill. When the protest is registered an extract thereof is obtained which contains a warrant to charge the party liable on the bill to pay the sum due, with interest and expenses, within six days if he is resident in Scotland, and within fourteen days if he is in Orkney or Shetland or furth of Scotland. By a charge is meant a written call upon the debtor to pay within the specified time handed to him by a messenger-at-arms or sheriff-officer. If the debtor fail to pay, then proceedings for sequestration may be instituted. In addition to charging, the creditor may at once arrest any money or goods belonging to his debtor in the hands of third persons. The warrant contained in the extract can be enforced at any time within forty years from the date of the extract. Summary diligence may proceed at the instance of the holder of the bill, whether payee, endorsee, or bearer ; but his title must be clear on the face of the bill, and every link of the chain connecting the creditor with the debtor must be complete. When a bill has not been accepted, diligence may be used against the drawer and prior endorsers, but not against the drawee, though he has funds in his hands sufficient to meet the bill. If a bill is accepted payable in England, although there is no equivalent in English law to our process of summary diligence, the protest may be extended by an English notary public, and thereafter in Scotland summary diligence may proceed against any of the parties resident in Scotland.

The debtor in a bill may, if he thinks fit, take proceedings in the Court of Session to have the diligence suspended ; but will, as a condition of being allowed to do so, have to find caution or consign the sum in the bill unless it appears on the face of the bill that it has been vitiated by a material alteration or that the signatures to it have been forged, or where there is any incompetency in the protest or charge.

Summary diligence is not competent on all bills. Thus signature by mark, whether in presence of witnesses or not, will not warrant summary diligence ; but if the granter cannot write, the bill may be subscribed for him by a notary public or justice of the peace before two witnesses. Such subscription will warrant summary diligence.

Signature by initials is also insufficient for summary diligence, as extrinsic proof of their authenticity is required.

An acceptance or endorsation by procuration will not warrant summary diligence except when the procuration is notorious. The question is different as regards the drawing of a bill per procuration, inasmuch as the act of acceptance infers a recognition and adoption of the principal's right, and so it has been decided by the Court that the acceptor is precluded from objecting to diligence raised in the principal's name.

The signing of a firm's name by a partner authorises diligence against any member of the firm, notwithstanding the name of such member does not appear on the bill.

Again, to warrant summary diligence, the bill must be without alteration or vitiation in essential parts. Thus it has been decided that an obvious change in the date from 1st to 8th October, and the superinduction of a 5 in the date 25th December, it being uncertain whether there had been erasure, made summary diligence incompetent. In another case it was decided that a bill torn in three pieces and pasted together again was not a document entitled to the privilege of summary diligence, unless these alterations or vitiations have been approved by the initials of the parties.[1]

As against the acceptor, who is the primary obligant on a bill, the bill may be noted even after its due date and summary diligence proceeded with at any time within six months of the maturity of the bill.

Bills to Registered Money-lenders.—An important restriction regarding summary diligence on bills and promissory notes to moneylenders was introduced by the Moneylenders Act, 1927. Section 18 (h) provides : " Notwithstanding anything to the contrary in any Act contained, summary execution or diligence shall not be competent upon any bill of exchange or promissory note or upon any bond or obligation registered in the books of any Court where such bill, promissory note, bond, or obligation has been granted to or in favour of or is held by a money-lender."

Noting of a Bill.—By noting is meant a memorandum put on the bill by a notary public to the effect that the bill was duly presented. The following is the usual memorandum, thus : 7/7/1929 pnp., that is protest for non-payment—J. S., N.P. ; or 7/7/1929, pnac., protest for non-acceptance—J. S., N.P.

12. Lost Bills.[2]—Where a bill has been lost before it is overdue the person who was the holder of it may apply to the drawer to give him another bill of the same tenour, but as a condition of this, the person so making the request must, if required, give security to the drawer to indemnify him against all persons whatever in case the bill alleged to have been lost shall be found again. For if the bill is payable to bearer, the finder, during its currency only, may have obtained value for it, and consequently the holder would have a good right to enforce payment thereof from the acceptor.

Again, if the bill, although payable to order, had the drawer's endorsement, the finder could get the bill discounted, with the result that the acceptor would be bound to pay the onerous holder.

If there is an action proceeding in Court on a bill, or an action in which a bill is necessary as one of the productions, the judge before whom the trial is proceeding may order that the loss of the bill shall

---

[1] Thomson v. Bell, 1850, 12 D. 1184.   [2] B. of E. Act, §§ 69, 70.

not be set up provided an indemnity is given to his satisfaction against the claims of any other person upon the instrument in question.

13. Discharge of Bill.[1]—A bill is discharged (1) by payment in due course by or on behalf of the drawee or acceptor, or in the case of an accommodation bill, by the person accommodated ; (2) where the acceptor is or becomes the holder in his own right of the bill at or after maturity ; (3) when the holder at or after maturity renounces in writing his rights against the acceptor ; (4) where a bill is intentionally cancelled by the holder or his agent and the cancellation is apparent thereon ; (5) where the bill is materially altered without the assent of all parties liable on the bill ; (6) by the running of the years of prescription ; (7) by compensation, that is, where one person who is under obligation to another acquires against that other a right of the same kind, so that each is the obligee of the other, the respective obligations are said to compensate or extinguish each other ; (8) by novation, that is, the substitution with the creditor's consent of one obligation by the debtor for another, the second obligation taking the place of the first, and the position of parties remaining the same ; and (9) by delegation, that is, the substitution with the creditor's consent of one debtor for another, whereby the original debtor is discharged.

Holder not bound to accept Payment to Account.—The holder of a bill is under no obligation to accept a payment to account unless the bill is payable by instalments and he is offered an instalment when it is due.

CHEQUES

Definition and Essentials.—The statutory definition of a cheque is " a bill of exchange drawn on a banker payable on demand." [2] It is of the essence of a cheque that it is drawn on a banker— that is, addressed by name to a person or a body of persons, whether incorporated or not, who carry on the business of bankers. Part III. of the Bills of Exchange Act deals with cheques, and, except as specially provided for in that part which relates to (1) presentment for payment, (2) countermand, and (3) crossing, the provisions of the Act applicable to bills of exchange payable on demand apply to a cheque. Like a bill, and in a question between the immediate parties to it—that is, between the drawer and the person in whose favour it is granted—a cheque is invalid if granted by fraud or force

---

[1] B. of E. Act, § 59.   [2] *Ibid.*, § 73.

and fear. Unlike bills drawn at a currency, cheques do not require to be written on paper specially appropriated to their use. It is sufficient if a person draws his cheque on a sheet of notepaper or other material upon which writing is legible. It is essential, however, that in the United Kingdom the drawer affix a twopenny postage-stamp, which he cancels by writing his name across it and the date. If the cheque be presented for payment unstamped, the banker may affix a proper adhesive stamp and cancel the same, charging the drawer with the amount of the stamp. The Stamp Act only permits the stamp to be affixed and cancelled by the drawer or the banker to whom the cheque is presented for payment. If the stamp is cancelled by any other person, the cheque is not validly stamped. The other essentials of a cheque are :—

1. It need not be dated, and is not invalid by reason only that it is post-dated or ante-dated, or that it bears date on a Sunday. A post-dated cheque may validly be negotiated for value prior to the date on which it bears to be drawn [1]; but a banker is not entitled to cash a cheque prior to the date on which it purports to be drawn ; and if he does so, the payment made is at his own risk.

2. It must contain an unconditional order to pay, and must be so expressed as to imply a demand made by a person who has a right to make it on another who has a duty to obey. Thus, " debit my account " has been held as equivalent to an order to pay ; and expressions such as " deliver," " credit in cash," etc., are effectual. But a mere hope that the addressee will pay is not sufficient ; nor is a letter requesting the loan of money rather than ordering the payment of it, and not imposing any compulsion on the payee, sufficient. So a mere authority to pay which does not amount to a demand is not a cheque. An order to pay money in the form of an ordinary cheque, with a proviso that a receipt form attached should be filled up, has been held not to be a cheque within the meaning of the Bills of Exchange Act.[2]

3. It must be signed by the drawer. The signature is usually, but not necessarily, adhibited in the right-hand lower corner of the cheque. It may, however, be written on any part of the cheque. The signature must be that of the person in whose name the account is kept, or of someone authorised by him to sign that name, or the signature of a person who has authority as agreed between the

[1] Royal Bank of Scotland v. Tottenham, [1894] L.R. 2 Q.B. 715.
[2] Bavins v. London and South-Western Bank, (1899) 5 Com. Cas. 1.

banker and his customer to operate on the account. Signature does not necessarily mean subscription. It is sufficient if adequate means of the customer's identification be afforded to the banker, and a cheque which is holograph of the drawer, and which contains his name, is sufficient authority to the banker to honour the cheque. Thus a cheque holograph of the drawer in such terms as " I, John Smith, desire the Bank of   to pay " is good. A cheque is valid if initialed by the drawer, if initialing be his usual mode of signature. A cheque may also be signed on behalf of any person, whether drawer or endorser, who is unable to do so, by a notary public or justice of the peace. Where a customer's signature differs from that with which the banker is familiar, the banker is under no obligation to pay the cheque. Where a cheque is returned because the signature differs from the customer's usual or specimen signature this reason should be stated and not merely " Refer to Drawer."

4. It must be payable on demand.

5. It must be an order to pay a sum certain in money. The sum payable may be expressed in words or figures or both, and where there is a discrepancy between the two the sum denoted by the words is the sum payable. Where, however, the amount is expressed in foreign currency, or in that of some British possession, the amount is payable in British currency at the customary rate of exchange. Although common in practice and invariably accepted, a cheque drawn in Scotland for a less sum than twenty shillings is " absolutely void and of no effect, any law or custom to the contrary thereof notwithstanding." [1] Any person who issues or negotiates such a cheque is liable to " forfeit and pay for such offence any sum not exceeding twenty pounds nor less than five pounds at the discretion of the justice of the peace who shall hear and determine such offence." There is no similar law in England.

6. It must be made payable to the order of a specified person or to bearer. Cheques may also be drawn payable to the holder of an office for the time being.

Drawer of Cheque.—Any number of persons can sign as drawers of a cheque so long as the account is in their names. Their legal position is this : In 1902 [2] the Court of Session decided that joint drawers of a cheque were jointly and severally liable to a Bank for the amount paid as against the cheque. The law on this point, as decided

---

[1] The Bank Notes (Scotland) Act, 1845, § 16.
[2] Laurence Henderson, Sons & Co., Ltd. *v.* Wallace & Pennell, 1902, 5 F. 166.

in the case referred to, was overturned by the House of Lords in 1929,[1] and the law must now be taken to be that joint drawers of a cheque are only liable for a *pro rata* amount of the sum due, *i.e.* each only for a rateable amount of the sum specified. Such cheques, however, are very useful where loans are granted to certain individuals who are not partners against their personal obligation. Where it is intended that the obligation of the drawers should be jointly and severally the cheque should be drawn thus : " Pay to   the sum of £ and charge the same to an account in our names jointly and severally." The account to be debited with the amount for which the cheque is drawn should be in the names of the various drawers of the cheque, adding after their names in the ledger the words " jointly and severally."

A customer, whether his account is debtor or creditor, may wish to pay in certain sums to meet cheques which he has issued or certain bills domiciled at his bank which are about to fall due. The position of the banker in regard to such a request is that he may refuse to enter into a special bargain of this nature ; but if he accept the money then he is bound to pay the cheques and bills when presented, notwithstanding what may then be the position of his customer's account.

Presentment for Payment.—A cheque must be presented to the banker upon whom it is drawn within bank hours, on a business day, and at his place of business, by the holder or some person authorised by him to receive payment on his behalf. A cheque payable at a branch bank must be presented there, and not at the head office. A cheque is deemed to be overdue when it appears on the face of it to have been in circulation for an unreasonable length of time. The drawer, however, is liable on the cheque to an onerous holder until the expiration of six years from the date of the cheque, provided he has not suffered any loss by the delay in presentment. Assuming that the money was there to meet it, such loss can only arise through the failure of the banker upon whom the cheque is drawn. While the liability of the drawer continues for six years, it is the practice of banks to refuse payment of all cheques that have been outstanding for a longer period than six months. When payment is refused, the cheque should be marked " Out of date—requires drawer's confirmation."

---

[1] Union Bank of Scotland, Ltd. *v.* Coats, decided by House of Lords on 11th July 1929 (not yet reported).

When a banker is entrusted with a cheque for presentation and collection by the payee or holder, he has as between himself and his customer the day after receipt of the cheque to present it, unless circumstances exist from which a contract or duty on the part of the banker to present earlier or to defer presentment to a later period can be inferred. If the banker employ an agent to present the cheque on his behalf he will have the day after receipt to post it to such agent, and the agent similarly will have the day after his receipt of the cheque to present it to the banker upon whom it is drawn. By the Act, presentment is excused or dispensed with in certain circumstances.[1]

Banker's Duty towards Customer's Cheque.—A banker is bound to honour his customer's cheques if these cheques be presented to him within banking hours and he has funds belonging to his customer sufficient to meet them. Should he fail in this duty he will be liable in damages to his customer should the customer suffer loss or damage through such failure or refusal.[2]

Where a customer keeps an account at several branches of the bank, one account being creditor and the other debtor, the banker is entitled, on giving reasonable notice to his customer, to transfer all the accounts at the various branches to one account, and so extinguish any debtor balance that may be due to him. A customer, however, has not the corresponding right to combine accounts kept at different branches so as to draw cheques indiscriminately. Where there is a creditor balance on a particular account the bank are entitled to hold that creditor balance as against any debt that may be due to them under any other obligation of their customer, but they are not entitled to hold as against their customer any sum standing at his credit if the debt on the other obligation is not liquid, that is, if it cannot be immediately enforced by the bank against their customer, or in cases where there is nothing more than a presumption of liability. The law on the subject may thus be stated :—

" It is settled that a banker who opens an account current with his customer undertakes to honour his cheques as presented to the extent to which there are funds at the credit of the customer in the account. This results, I need hardly say, from no arbitrary rule of law, but it is the meaning of an account current. It is the contract into which the parties enter that the banker constitutes himself

[1] See B. of E. Act, § 46 (1).
[2] King v. British Linen Bank, 1899, 1 F. 928.

the agent of his customer for the payment of his drafts on condition that he is put in funds to make these payments as required, and it follows from the nature of the relation that if the banker refuse to honour a cheque pending the subsistence of the relation, he has committed a breach of contract, for which he will be liable in damage to such an extent as damage can be proved." [1]

Countermand of Payment.—A person who issues a cheque is entitled to countermand payment thereof before it is paid by the banker upon whom it is drawn.[2] Where a cheque is drawn by two or more persons any one of them can countermand it, and when it is drawn by a partner in the firm name, any partner can countermand it, and that notwithstanding the fact that he may not be the partner who signed the cheque. When a cheque, payment of which has been countermanded, is presented to the banker upon whom it is drawn, while such banker cannot pay the cheque he must in Scotland, although not in England, retain sufficient money to meet the cheque, as the effect of the presentation is equivalent to an intimated assignation notwithstanding the countermand.

Position where Customer becomes Bankrupt.—Where the customer of a bank becomes bankrupt, should the bank be his debtors, that is, should there be a creditor balance in favour of the bankrupt, cheques drawn by the bankrupt after his sequestration are null, for the reason that by the sequestration he is divested of his estate. The proper person to withdraw the creditor balance is the trustee. Before payment is made to the trustee, however, he should exhibit to the bank his authority from the Court authorising him to act as trustee. This authority is known as an Act and Warrant, and is issued to the trustee from the Sheriff Court in the county where the sequestration is being carried on.

Endorsation of Cheques.—A cheque being a bill of exchange payable on demand may, like any other bill, be endorsed so as to entitle the endorsee or any subsequent holder to sue prior endorsers thereon, and the ordinary rules applicable to the endorsation of bills of exchange apply to cheques, but the ordinary endorsation of a payee to a banker is not such as to subject him to any liability. Such an endorsation is really of the nature of an acknowledgment of receipt of payment and a guarantee to the drawer that the banker has paid the cheque— on the principle that when a document of debt is in the debtor's possession payment of the debt is presumed—and that he is therefore

---

[1] King *v.* British Linen Bank, 1899, 1 F. 928.   [2] B. of E. Act, § 75.

entitled to debit his customer's account with the amount. An endorsation is usually, though not necessarily, written on the back of the cheque. It may be written upon the face of the cheque, but this mode is unusual.

Negotiation of Cheques.—A cheque drawn in favour of " A. B. or bearer " is negotiated by delivery without endorsation, and may be passed from hand to hand like an ordinary bank-note. When presented to a banker for payment it requires no endorsation. A cheque drawn payable to bearer so long as it purports to be so payable cannot be restrictively endorsed by the payee or any subsequent holder so as to be payable to the order of the endorser, although the payee of such a cheque is entitled to substitute the word " order " for the word " bearer " in the body of the cheque, and thus to change the cheque from one payable to bearer to one payable to order. A cheque in favour of a person " or order " is negotiated by the endorsation of that person and delivery to the endorsee. The endorsation may be (1) general, *i.e.* blank endorsed, and a cheque so endorsed becomes payable to bearer ; (2) special, *i.e.* the endorsement specifies the person to whom or to whose order the cheque is to be payable ; and (3) restrictive, *i.e.* when the endorsement prohibits the further negotiation of the cheque, or which expresses that it is a mere authority to deal with the cheque as there directed and not a transfer of the ownership, as, for example, if it be endorsed " Pay D. only," or " Pay D. for the account of X." A banker is bound to pay an endorsed and uncrossed cheque drawn upon him which purports to be endorsed by the person to whom it is drawn payable, and so long as the endorsement is regular the banker is under no obligation to ascertain that it is *bona fide*. In the case of a crossed cheque this freedom from liability depends on his obeying the direction conveyed by the crossing. A banker who suspects on reasonable grounds an endorsation to be forged is, however, justified in taking time to inquire into its genuineness. Where a person is under obligation to endorse a cheque in a representative capacity, such as trustee, executor, director, etc., he may endorse it in such terms as to negative personal liability by the addition of words indicating that he signs merely as an agent or filling a representative capacity, thus " without recourse."

While a banker who pays a cheque *bona fide* and without negligence on an endorsement which subsequently turns out to have been forged is protected, no similar protection is afforded him in the case of the forged signature of the drawer.

Crossed Cheques.[1]—The introduction of the crossing of cheques is of comparatively recent date. The practice owes its inception to the private bankers in London, who in 1775 instituted the London Clearing-House as a means of economising their capital as well as of saving much unnecessary trouble in the collection of cheques. Cheques paid into a bank were taken to the clearing-house on the afternoon of the following day, and in order to facilitate business at the clearing-house and also to preserve a record of the channel through which the cheques came, the clerks of the several bankers were in the habit at first of writing and afterwards of stamping the names of their principals across the documents presented by them. The object of this crossing was to secure that in the event of the cheque being dishonoured, it should at once be returned to the banker who presented it. The crossing of course also afforded a way of discovering the person by whom the cheque had been paid in if a question afterwards arose as to the true ownership of it. The convenience of the system led to the other private bankers in London being admitted to the clearing-house, and merchants then found that they did not require to provide for payment of such of their cheques as were presented through a bank until the afternoon of the day on which they were drawn ; and in order to secure that all their cheques should be so presented, the practice grew up of writing the name of a banker across the cheque. Afterwards it became common instead of writing the name of a banker to cross the cheque with the words " and Company," or " & Co.," generally between parallel lines, and sometimes merely by drawing two parallel lines across the face of the document. In the first case the cheque was said to be specially crossed, and the other forms were termed general crossings. Bankers paid attention to these crossings, and generally refused payment of cheques so crossed unless presented to them through a banker. It was then seen that a great protection was by this means afforded against the risk attending the loss or theft of a cheque, as an obstacle was put in the way of the thief or finder cashing it, and it was with the view of attaining this protection that the practice became common. There have been several Acts of Parliament passed dealing with crossed cheques, but these were repealed by the Act of 1882, which now contains the statutory enactments on the subject. These are contained in § 76 and the succeeding sections of the Act. When a cheque is crossed a direction is thereby conveyed to the banker upon whom it

---

[1] B. of E. Act, § 76.

is drawn that payment can only be made in a particular way, and to the holder of the cheque that he can only receive payment in that way. The law recognises two kinds of crossings, viz. (1) general, (2) special. According to a practice introduced by the London banks, a cheque may be crossed by means of a perforating machine —an invention the legislature had not in view when the Act of 1882 was passed. The effect of a general crossing is that the banker on whom the cheque is drawn is only protected if payment is made through a banker. Should he disregard the crossing and make payment in any other way, and loss thereby ensue, he is liable to the true owner for such loss. A banker who pays an uncrossed cheque payable to bearer to a thief or a finder is protected, as there is no obligation on him to see that the person who presents the cheque for payment is the person who is entitled to it. A banker who pays an uncrossed cheque drawn upon him payable to order is protected if he pay on an endorsement which purports to be made, by or with the authority of the person to whom it is payable, even should the signature turn out to have been forged or adhibited without authority. But a banker who pays a crossed cheque to a thief or finder, or upon an unauthorised or forged signature, in disregard of a crossing, whether special or general, is in a different position in that he is liable to the true owner, whether the drawer or a subsequent transferee, if that true owner can prove that he has suffered loss by the cheque having been so paid. While this is the strict interpretation of the law, there is nothing illegal or incompetent in a banker upon whom a crossed cheque is drawn paying that cheque over the counter if he is satisfied that the person by whom the cheque is presented and endorsed is the person to whom it is payable. It is not necessary that the words " Pay in cash " should be added to the endorsement ; but if they are, as is preferable, no stamp is necessary.

Position of Collecting Banker.—A banker who collects a crossed cheque for a customer has a statutory protection conferred upon him, and this protection is an exception to the general rule as to the liability of persons receiving payment of cheques on behalf of those who have no right to them. The words of the Act are in § 82, and are as follows : " When a banker in good faith and without negligence receives payment for a customer of a cheque crossed generally or specially to himself, and the customer has no title or a defective title thereto, the banker shall not incur any liability to the true owner of the cheque by reason only of having received such payment." To bring a case within the statutory protection the three following facts must co-exist : (1) the person for whom the cheque is collected must be a customer of the bank ; (2) the bank must collect the proceeds of the cheque for that customer ; and (3) the cheque must be collected and paid without negligence, that is, without want of reasonable care in reference to the interests of the true owner.   In a case decided in 1900,[1] a cheque was drawn payable to Hannan's Lake View Central, Ltd., and crossed generally.   The secretary of that company endorsed the cheque in name of his company, subscribing his own name as secretary.   He then paid it in to the credit of his own personal account with his bankers, whose customer he was, and drew out the amount as he required it.   It was decided that, though the bankers had acted in good faith, they were liable to the company in the amount of the cheque.   The ground of the decision was that it was apparent on the face of the transaction that the secretary was using for himself a valuable document, which, on the face of it, bore evidence of having been granted for the benefit of his employers, and was their property ; that the whole course of ordinary business was opposed to the idea that the secretary of a company was likely to have been paid money due to him as salary or otherwise by the authorisation of the endorsement by himself to himself of a cheque payable to the order of the company ; and that in accepting such a cheque so endorsed for his private account the bank were guilty of negligence, and thus lost the protection of the statute.   To constitute a person a customer of a bank within the meaning of the section there must be some sort of account between them, either a current or a deposit account, or some similar relation.   For example, it has been held that a person was not a customer of a bank although the bank had for some years been in the habit of paying him cash for cheques and subsequently collecting the amounts.[2]   Again, banks are entitled to the protection given only in cases where they receive payment for a customer.

Prior to the coming into force of the Crossed Cheques Act of 1906 (which was only passed after three successive bills presented to Parliament in 1903, 1904, and 1905 had proved abortive), bankers were not entitled to the statutory protection where they received a cheque under circumstances which constituted them holders of it on their own account.   Hence, if a banker at once credited a customer with the value of a cheque drawn upon another bank and allowed

---

[1] Hannan's Lake View Central, Ltd. v. Armstrong & Co., (1900) 16 T.L.R. 236.
[2] Matthews v. Williams, Brown & Co., (1894) 63 L.J. Q.B. 494.

him to draw against the balance thus increased before the cheque was cleared, the banker became a holder for value and collected the cheque not on behalf of his customer but of himself, and was therefore not within the statutory protection. But the banker would have been within the protection of the statute if, without crediting the account of the customer with the value of the cheque, before collection he allowed him to overdraw his account in view of the anticipated credit.

Various subterfuges were adopted to get over this legal difficulty by not directly placing the proceeds of the cheque to the customer's operative account. Some banks credited suspense accounts, while others again credited cheques under sundries. The distinction drawn by the Courts was a very subtle one, and was and is difficult to understand.

Further, the protection only applies to cheques which are crossed before they come into the bankers' possession, and the bankers cannot, by afterwards crossing the cheques themselves, become entitled to the protection given by the section. Again, a banker's draft addressed by one branch of a bank to another branch of the same bank is a cheque, and is entitled to this statutory protection.

To whom does a Cheque which has been paid belong ?—The question is sometimes raised, to whom does a cheque which has been paid belong ? The law on the subject is this : When a cheque is paid the holder is bound forthwith to deliver it up to the banker paying it, in whose hands it is evidence of the payment of the amount. A cheque on payment becomes the property of the drawer, but the banker who pays it is entitled to keep it as a voucher until his account with his customer is settled or until the customer's account is docqueted.

Summary Diligence on Cheque.—Although a cheque is declared to be a bill of exchange drawn on a banker payable on demand, and although summary diligence is competent on bills payable on demand, there is no case recorded where summary diligence followed on a cheque. The opinion of legal writers on the competency of such diligence is divided.

PROMISSORY NOTES

Origin.—Promissory notes [1] had their origin in the " Goldsmith's Notes," and were an invention of the goldsmiths in Lombard Street. They were not in use until long after bills of exchange, and were not at first entitled to the special privileges of bills. By two Acts

[1] B. of E. Act, § 83.

of Parliament passed in the reign of George III. it was enacted that "the same diligence and execution shall be competent, and shall proceed upon promissory notes whether holograph or not, as is provided to pass upon bills of exchange and inland bills by the law of Scotland : that promissory notes shall bear interest as bills and shall pass by endorsation, and that endorsees of promissory notes shall have the same privileges as endorsees of bills in all points." Hence at present, although distinct in form, promissory notes are in their essentials bills of exchange, and may be described as bills in which the drawer and acceptor are the same person.

The existing statutory provisions with regard to promissory notes are contained in part iv., §§ 83 to 89 inclusive, of the Bills of Exchange Act.

Definition.—A promissory note is thus defined by the Act : " A promissory note is an unconditional promise in writing made by one person to another, signed by the maker, engaging to pay on demand, or at a fixed or determinable future time, a sum certain in money to, or to the order of, a specified person or to bearer."

The usual form of such a note is " On demand (or three months after date, etc.), I promise to pay to A. B., or order, the sum of £50 for value received." But as with bills there is no statutory form for such documents ; and as long as a writing contains the essentials of a promissory note it is immaterial how it is framed or expressed. An instrument in the form of a note payable to the order of the maker is not a note within the meaning of this section unless and until it is endorsed by the maker.[1] Again, a note is not invalid by reason only that it contains also a pledge of collateral security with authority to sell or dispose thereof. For instance, a letter in the following terms : " We beg to acknowledge receipt of yours of date covering cheque for £100 sterling, which we hereby agree to pay you in, say, two years and six months from date, with interest at the rate of 6 per cent. per annum, interest payable half-yearly. In security we now enclose policies on the Life Association of Scotland on the lives of A. B. and C. D., No.   , value £200, and No.   , value £300 sterling, which are thus to be considered as assigned to you until repayment of the loan is made," was held to be a promissory note.

A document is not invalid as a promissory note by reason only that it does not contain the name of the person to whom the amount is to be paid or the words " to bearer," if in fact the document con-

[1] B. of E. Act, § 83 (2).

tains a promise to pay and it is handed by one person to another. The mere fact that a promissory note contains a statement of facts not necessary to its validity as such does not make it any the less a promissory note. But if it contains something more than is here referred to it will not be valid as a promissory note although it may still be valid as an agreement.

The essentials of a promissory note are : (1) it must be in writing ; (2) it must contain a promise. To bring a document within the category of a promissory note some phrase expressing promise, although it need not contain the word " promise " itself, is necessary to the validity of the document ; (3) it must be stamped with the appropriate stamp duty ; and (4) it must be delivered by the maker to the payee or bearer, as, until this is done, the contract is incomplete and revocable.

Where a note runs " I promise to pay," and is signed by two or more persons, it is deemed to be their joint and several note,[1] with this result that the holder of such a document can select from among the persons who have signed it any one and ask him to pay the full sum due. Where a note runs " We promise to pay," and is signed by two or more persons, they may be liable to pay in Scotland, but not in England, jointly and severally. In all such cases the proper course is to see that the promissory note reads thus : " We jointly and severally promise to pay."

Where a promissory note is made payable at a particular place it must be presented for payment at that place in order to render the maker liable. In any other case presentment for payment is not necessary in order to render the maker liable. He is always liable on his obligation without the necessity of presentment. It was decided in a case in 1898 that presentment of a promissory note payable at a particular place on the day when payment is due is not necessary in order to render the maker liable, and that presentment for payment is necessary in order to render the endorser of a note liable.[2] Where a note is in the body of it made payable at a particular place, presentment at that place is necessary in order to render an endorser liable ; but when a place of payment is indicated by way of memorandum only, presentment at that place is sufficient to render the endorser liable, but a presentment to the maker elsewhere, if sufficient in other respects, also suffices.

The rules for the due presentment of notes and excuses for

[1] B. of E. Act, § 85 (1).   [2] Gordon v. Kerr, 1898, 25 R. 570.

non-presentment and delay, protest, and summary diligence are the same as those applicable to bills.

Stamp Duty.—The stamp duty on a promissory note in all cases is *ad valorem* and, unlike a bill of exchange, this is so whether the note is payable on demand or at a currency.

CHAPTER X

RIGHTS IN SECURITY OVER MOVEABLES

1. Nature of Rights in Security.—The term " right in security " may be defined to mean any right which a creditor may possess for the recovery of his debt in the event of non-payment, and which, in the event of the bankruptcy of his debtor, is distinct from and in addition to the right which he possesses in common with other creditors of claiming a ranking in the sequestration. Hence bankruptcy (or, in the case of a company, liquidation) is the ultimate test whether a security has been created.[1]

A security may consist of either (a) a nexus over some particular property, or (b) the corroborative obligation of some third party, i.e. a cautionary obligation.[2] There is a nexus when the creditor has a real right over the subjects of security. A real right implies either possession by or delivery to the creditor (or others on his behalf) of the subjects of security. It is thus a general principle in the law of Scotland that without such possession, or delivery (see *infra* as to delivery), neither contract nor implication of law can create an effectual right in security.[3] There are certain exceptions called hypothecs which are effectual securities without possession or delivery. A further exception is the case of securities over incorporeal moveables.

2. Hypothecs.—The term " hypothecs " is used to denote securities without possession. They are either conventional, i.e. created by express contract, or legal, i.e. implied by law.

The only conventional hypothecs recognised in the law of Scotland are bonds of bottomry and bonds of respondentia.[4]

Among the recognised legal hypothecs are certain maritime

---

[1] See Gloag and Henderson's Introduction to the Law of Scotland, p. 180.
[2] See Chapter XI., *infra*.
[3] Clark *v.* West Calder Oil Co., 1882, 9 R. 1017 ; Bell's Prin., § 1385.
[4] See Shipping Law, Chapter V., *supra*.

hypothecs or liens. These give certain creditors a right in security over a ship without possession and with the power of enforcing the right by a sale under order of the Court. Such securities have priority over all other securities created over the ship, such as mortgages.[1] Thus, seamen have a maritime lien for wages,[2] the master of a ship for his wages and disbursements,[3] a salvor for any sum due for salvage [4] ; and a maritime lien exists for repairs executed or necessaries supplied to a ship in a foreign port and, if the ship is actually detained there, in a home port.[5] There is also a maritime lien for damages suffered in a collision between ships over the ship which was to blame.

3. Securities constituted by Express Contract.—Securities may be created by express contract between the parties or implied by law.

(1) Forms and Effect.—When the security is constituted by express contract it may take one or other of two forms with different effects. It may take the form of a transfer to the creditor of a right in the subjects expressly as a security, e.g. a pledge in the case of moveable property. Possession of the subject is given but the right of property is not transferred.[6] Its effect is limited in two ways. First, an *ex facie* express security such as pledge covers only the debt for which it was granted and not debts subsequently contracted.[7] Second, transfer of possession has not the effect of giving a pledgee an implied power to sell the subjects. He must either have an express power of sale or obtain that power by application to the Court.[8]

On the other hand, the security may take the form of a transfer of the right of property in the subjects by an *ex facie* absolute conveyance, subject to a separate obligation to reconvey them on repayment of the debt. An example in the case of moveables is where a document of title to goods, e.g. a bill of lading, is transferred, although only with the intention to give a security. The result is to vest in the security-holder a right of property in the goods thereby represented and not merely a right of pledge.[9] The effect is twofold. First, the creditor has a " right of retention," *i.e.* the security will

---

[1] Harmer *v.* Bell, (1851) 7 Moore P.C. 267 ; Currie *v.* M'Knight, 1896, 24 R. (H.L.) 1.

[2] M.S.A., 1894, § 156.   [3] *Ibid.*, § 167.   [4] Harmer *v.* Bell, *supra*.

[5] Clydesdale Bank *v.* Walker & Bain, 1926 S.C. 72.

[6] Bell's Comm., 7th ed., i. 278.

[7] National Bank *v.* Forbes, 1858, 21 D. 29 ; contrast Hamilton *v.* Western Bank of Scotland, 1856, 19 D. 152.   [8] Bell's Prin., § 207.

[9] Hamilton *v.* Western Bank of Scotland, *supra* ; Hayman *v.* M'Lintock, 1907, S.C. 936.

cover any debt contracted by the debtor in the future.[1] This right of retention may be limited by express contract [2] or by notice to the holder of the security that the reversion has been assigned by the granter of the security.[3] Second, the creditor is invested with a power of sale. The power is absolute, hence he may give a good title to a purchaser notwithstanding a separate agreement with the debtor not to do so.[4]

The form of the security differs also according as the subject of security is corporeal or incorporeal in its character. A security over corporeal moveables is known as a pledge. Pawn is a form of pledge.

(2) **Securities over Corporeal Moveables.**—(a) **Pledge.**—The general rule is that in order effectually to create a security over corporeal moveables actual possession must be given to the creditor. Some moveables, however, require a written conveyance to create a security over them. This is so either on account of the titles by which they are in law transferable, e.g. ships, or on account of their situation at the time the security is constituted, e.g. consignments of goods at a distance or goods at sea, or goods in another's custody.[5]

Pledge is the contract whereby in the ordinary case corporeal moveables are transferred in security. Pledge is a real contract, by which one places in the hands of his creditor a moveable subject, to remain with him in security of a debt or engagement, to be redelivered on payment or satisfaction ; and with an implied mandate, on failure to fulfil the engagement at the stipulated time or on demand, to have the pledge sold by judicial authority.[6]

The person who gives the moveables in security is the pledger. The person who gets them in security of the obligation owing to him is the pledgee. Pledge is constituted by the delivery of the subject pledged.[7] A mere agreement to pledge not followed by actual delivery is not a right of security effectual in a question with the general creditors of the debtor.[8] *Traditionibus non nudis pactis dominia rerum transferuntur.*

Delivery.—Delivery must be actual or at least the best which the circumstances will allow.[5] It may be actual, symbolical, or constructive.

---

[1] Hamilton v. Western Bank, *supra*; National Bank v. Union Bank, 1886, 14 R. (H.L.) 1.   [2] Anderson's Tr. v. Somerville, 1896, 36 S.L.R. 833.
[3] National Bank v. Union Bank, *supra*.
[4] Duncan v. Mitchell & Co., 1893, 21 R. 37.
[5] Bell's Comm., 7th ed., ii. 11.   [6] Bell's Prin., § 203.   [7] *Ibid.*, § 204.
[8] Robertson v. Baxter, 1897, 24 R. 758.

Actual Delivery.—Actual delivery takes place (1) when goods are physically transferred from one party to another, (2) if goods are in any confined space and the complete command of that space is transferred to the pledgee, *e.g.* where the key of a yard enclosed by a fence containing barrels is given to the pledgee of the barrels.[1]

Symbolical Delivery.—The main instance of symbolical delivery is the case where it is desired to give goods which are at sea in pledge and for which a bill of lading has been taken. The bill is recognised as a symbol for the goods, and if it is transferred in pursuance of a pledge of the goods it has the same legal effect as the delivery of the goods.[2] It carries the real right in the goods without intimation to the captain of the ship in which they are situated.[3]

Constructive Delivery.—Constructive delivery is the term applied when the goods assigned in security are in a store and delivery of them is attempted by a delivery order addressed by the pledger to the storekeeper or by endorsation to the pledgee of the storekeeper's warrant. Such delivery is effectual to transfer a real as distinguished from a mere personal right in the goods if intimation of the assignation is made to the keeper of the store. On intimation being made, the custodier of the goods becomes custodier for the transferee in place of the transferor.[4] But the keeper of the store must be a person independent of the pledger, *e.g.* not a mere excise official having a key of the store of which the pledger is tenant.[5] And the goods transferred must be ascertained, *i.e.* identified, so that they are distinguishable from the general mass of goods kept by the transferor in the particular store. So where a flour merchant sold to purchasers a certain number of sacks of flour, part of a large number of sacks in a neutral store, and not separated, marked, or identified in any way or separated from the other sacks of flour in the store, and gave to the purchaser delivery orders which were intimated to the storekeeper, it was held that constructive delivery had not been effected.[6] Goods, however, which are brought into separate existence

---

[1] Gloag and Henderson's Introduction to the Law of Scotland, p. 186 ; West Lothian Oil Co. v. Mair, 1892, 20 R. 64.

[2] Bell's Prin., § 417 ; Gloag and Henderson's Introduction to the Law of Scotland, p. 186.

[3] See Hayman v. M'Lintock, 1907 S.C. 936, per Lord M'Laren at p. 962, as to unascertained goods, and contrast Sale of Goods Act, 1893, § 16.

[4] Rhind's Tr. v. Robertson & Baxter, 1891, 18 R. 623.

[5] Anderson v. M'Call, 1866, 4 M. 765.

[6] Hayman v. M'Lintock, *supra* ; contrast Price & Pierce v. Bank of Scotland, 1912 S.C. (H.L.) 19.

after the intimation of the delivery order are constructively delivered as they come into separate existence.[1]

(*b*) **Pawn.**—Pawn is a form of pledge regulated by statute, viz. the Pawnbrokers Acts, 1872 and 1922, and the Moneylenders Act, 1927. The term pawnbroker is defined as including every person who carries on the business of taking goods and chattels in pawn.[2] Such a person is further defined as " every person who keeps a shop for the purchase or sale of goods or chattels, or for taking in goods or chattels by way of security for money advanced thereon, and who purchases or receives or takes in goods or chattels, and pays or advances or lends thereon any sum of money not exceeding ten pounds, with or under an agreement or understanding, expressed or implied, or to be from the nature or character of the dealing reasonably inferred, that these goods or chattels may be afterwards redeemed or repurchased on any terms." [3]

The leading provisions of the Acts are as follows :—A pawnbroker must hold a licence, and his name with the word " Pawnbroker " must be exhibited over his door.   For every advance he must give a ticket in statutory form indicating the terms of the contract and the amount (regulated by statute) which he is entitled to charge.[4]   A loan on special terms is legal if it exceeds forty shillings.[5]   In cases to which the Acts apply all goods pledged remain redeemable for a year and seven days.   Thereafter, if the amount advanced does not exceed ten shillings, the article becomes the absolute property of the pawnbroker ; if more than ten shillings, it remains redeemable until sold by the pawnbroker.   If a pledge pawned for above ten shillings is sold a record of the price must be kept, and the pawnbroker is liable to account to the holder of the pawn-ticket within three years for the surplus over the amount advanced and the statutory charges.[6] Any sale must be by public auction and the pawnbroker is entitled to bid.[7] So long as the goods remain redeemable a pawnbroker is liable for loss of or injury to them by fire.   The value of the goods so destroyed is estimated at the amount of the loan and charges, plus 25 per cent. of the amount of the loan.[8]   It is a criminal offence for a pawnbroker knowingly to take in pledge any clothing, unfinished goods, or material entrusted to the pawner to clean, mend, or finish,[9]

[1] Black *v.* Incorporation of Bakers, 1867, 6 M. 136.
[2] Act of 1872, § 5.
[3] *Ibid.*, §§ 6, 10.
[4] 1872 Act, § 14, Sched. 3 ; 1922 Act, §§ 1, 2.
[5] 1872 Act, § 24.
[6] *Ibid.*, § 22.
[7] *Ibid.*, §§ 16, 20.
[8] *Ibid.*, § 27.
[9] § 35.

or to take anything from a person apparently under the age of fourteen.[1]

Under the Moneylenders Act, 1927, § 14, a pawnbroker must deliver or send to the pawner within seven days a note or memorandum containing all the terms of the contract with interest not over 20 per cent. and limited charges. If he does not send such a memorandum he may be, like the money-lender, not entitled to enforce his contract or make charges.

A pawnbroker obtains no title to stolen goods but has been held entitled to hold, until his advances are repaid, goods pawned by a party in a position to give a good title to purchaser and with no right to pawn.[2]

(3) Securities over Incorporeal Property.—Debts cannot, like simple moveables or cash, be corporeally delivered ; but being mere rights to demand payment of a sum of money at a stipulated time, the act by which they are to be transferred is such only as can convert the obligation to pay to the cedent into a debt to the assignee. This is accomplished by a mandate empowering the assignee to demand payment, accompanied by intimation to the debtor that henceforward he is to hold the money for behoof of the assignee.[3] Mere possession of the document of debt, e.g. a policy of insurance, without any assignation confers no right to any claim arising in respect of it. Without intimation no effectual security is created in Scotland except in the case of a negotiable instrument.[4] For example, an assignation of the uncalled capital of a company is ineffectual as a security unless it is completed by intimation to each shareholder of the company.[5]

Shares in a company are frequently used as a security. The mere deposit of share certificates with the creditor cannot in Scotland create a security over them, nor is the deposit of a duly signed transfer and the share certificate with the creditor effectual to create a security. The creditor is, however, in the latter case placed in a position to complete his security by having himself registered in the books of the company as owner. Until he is so registered the security is liable to be defeated by diligence used upon the shares by another creditor or by a subsequent and fraudulent transfer of them by the debtor.[6] In Scotland, though not in England, transfers signed by

---

[1] Children Act, 1908, § 117.   [2] Bryce v. Elimann, 1904, 7 F. 5.
[3] Bell's Comm., 7th ed., ii. 15.   [4] Wylie's Exrx. v. M'Jannet, 1901, 4 F. 195.
[5] Liqrs. of Union Club v. Edinburgh Life Assurance Co., 1906, 8 F. 1143 ; Clark v. West Calder Oil Co., 1882, 9 R. 1017.
[6] Rainford v. Keith, [1905] 1 Ch. 296.

the grantee, but blank in the name of the creditor, are void under the Act, 1696, c. 25.[1] Such a security is therefore of doubtful effect.

4. Securities Implied by Law from Possession.—Lien and Retention.

—Lien is a right implied by law to retain property until some debt or other obligation is satisfied. It is a right founded on mere possession. For example, a seller of goods who has not parted with the goods which he has sold to a buyer has a lien over the goods for the unpaid price.[2] Right of retention, on the other hand, is the right of a party, whose title is one of ownership subject to an obligation to reconvey, to refuse implement until some counter-obligation due by the party entitled to a conveyance is fulfilled. The law of Scotland does not recognise any right in a mere possessor to continue in possession until all debts due to him by the owner are paid.[3]

Special and General Lien.—Liens are either special or general. A special lien is a right implied by law to retain an article until some debt arising out of a contract is paid. It is in all cases a limited right, the extent of which may depend either on the contract under which possession was obtained or on usage of trade. A general lien is a right of retention of an article until some general balance, e.g. arising out of a course of employment, is discharged.

General Lien.—A general lien is recognised by custom of certain professions and trades. Its extent depends on the usage of the particular trade. For example, a law agent has a general lien on his client's titles covering all debts due by his client from prior employment. The extent of a general lien in any particular trade must be proved by evidence showing that the dealings of parties were on the footing of a lien of the extent claimed.[4] Examples of general lien are those of a law agent, a factor or mercantile agent, and of a banker.[5]

Limits of Rights under Lien.—No lien can be asserted if it is inconsistent with the terms, express or implied, of the contract under which possession was obtained. The plea of lien is barred by the specific appropriation. Thus if a bill is sent to a banker for discount and he refuses to discount it, he cannot retain it under a general lien.[6] Further, lien is a right over which the Court may exercise an equitable control.

---

[1] See Shaw v. Caledonian Rly Co., 1890, 17 R. 466 at p. 478.
[2] Sale of Goods Act, 1893, § 39 (1).
[3] Anderson's Tr. v. Fleming, 1871, 9 M. 718.
[4] Anderson's Tr. v. Fleming, supra.
[5] See as to Bankers and Factors, Law of Agency, p. 85.
[6] Borthwick v. Bremner, 1833, 12 S. 122; see also Middlemas v. Gibson, 1910 S.C. 577.

For example, a ship may be released from a lien for repairs on terms to be fixed by the Court.[1]

Extinction of Lien.—Being founded on possession, lien is lost if possession is relinquished. But where lien covers a number of articles some may be restored to the owner without affecting the lien over the rest.[2]

5. Obligations of a Security Holder.—The right of property in the subject of security remains with the debtor. The creditor's obligation is to restore the subject of security on payment of the debt, bestowing ordinary care in the custody of the subject while in his possession.[3] Hence a creditor is not liable for the accidental loss or destruction of the security subjects before payment of the debt is tendered, nor is his right of recovering his debt affected thereby.[4] If, however, the creditor is unable to return the subjects by reason of his own fault he cannot demand payment of his debt.[5] On payment of the debt it is the duty of the creditor to restore the exact subjects given in security. Hence it was held that a bank to whom numbered shares of a company had been transferred in security were not justified in tendering in return equivalent shares of the same company.[6]

[1] Ferguson & Stewart v. Grant, 1856, 18 D. 536 ; Garscadden v. Ardrossan Dry Dock Co., 1910 S.C. 178, per Lord Ardwall.

[2] Gray v. Wardrop's Trs., 1855, 2 Macq. 435.

[3] Bell's Prin., 10th ed., § 206 ; Coggs v. Bernard, 1 Smith's L.C. 177, 191.

[4] Syred v. Carruthers, (1858) E. B. & E. 469 ; Fraser v. Smith, 1899, 1 F. 487.

[5] Ellis & Co.'s Tr. v. Dixon-Johnston, [1925] A.C. 489.

[6] Crerar v. Bank of Scotland, 1921 S.C. 736 ; 1922 S.C. (H.L.) 137.

CHAPTER XI

CAUTIONARY OBLIGATIONS

1. Definition.—A cautionary obligation is an obligation by one person not on behalf of himself but for another, to the effect that if the person primarily responsible for payment of the debt or performance of the obligation fails to implement the undertaking the cautioner will do so.

2. Constitution and Construction of Obligation.—A cautionary obligation need not necessarily be for the payment of money. It may be an obligation undertaken for the performance of some act, for the delivery of goods, or the due performance of the duties of an office. For whatever purpose the obligation is undertaken, it is essentially a collateral or accessory obligation. There must be some other person primarily responsible for the payment of the debt or performance of the obligation. While in certain cases the obligation may not be enforceable in law against the primary obligant, the cautioner is nevertheless bound in terms of his undertaking. Hence if a limited company having no power to borrow money did do so, while the creditor could not enforce payment of the debt from the company he could successfully maintain his claim against a cautioner for the debt. It has been decided that a cautioner in an indenture of apprenticeship entered into by a minor without the consent of his father was bound in terms of his obligation in the event of the minor deserting the service of his master.[1] The reason is, that the cautioner is presumed to know the position of the debtor, and the legal effect of his obligation is that, if the debtor take advantage of his inability to enter into the obligation, the cautioner shall make good the loss. In certain cases the obligation may be primary and not cautionary. " If two come to a shop, and one buys and the other

---

[1] Stevenson *v.* Adair, 1872, 10 M. 919.

227

says, ' Let him have the goods, I will be your paymaster,' this is an undertaking as for himself, and he shall be intended to be the very buyer and the other to act but as his servant." [1]

There is no special form by which a cautionary obligation may be constituted. However inelegantly a document may be expressed, it will receive effect provided it is in writing and is signed by the person undertaking the obligation.[2] A cautionary obligation, when contained in a formal bond, is strictly construed, and nothing will be inferred which the terms of the obligation do not expressly or impliedly warrant.[3] Hence, if the terms are ambiguous, the cautioner has the benefit of the doubt.[4] Such obligations must be constituted in terms of the Mercantile Law Amendment Act of 1856, which provides that "from and after the passing of this Act all guarantees, securities, or cautionary obligations made or granted by any person for any other person, and all representations and assurances as to the character, conduct, credit, ability, trade, or dealings of any person made or granted to the effect or for the purpose of enabling such person to obtain credit, money, goods, or postponement of payment of debt or of any other obligation demandable from him, shall be in writing, and shall be subscribed by the person undertaking such guarantee, security, or cautionary obligation, or making such representations and assurances, or by some person duly authorised by him or them, otherwise the same shall have no effect." Verbal representations are of no legal effect as giving a remedy to the person who may be misled by them to his detriment. Any verbal representation is ineffectual, no matter what may be the further and fraudulent design of the person who made it.[5] The writing, however, need not be executed by the granter with all the solemnities of a formal deed. If not formal, the granter may, however, resile before the guarantee has been acted upon.[6] If the document be granted in ordinary mercantile transactions it is binding, although not constituted by a probative deed, and there is no presumption either way in regard to the construction of the document. It is, however, advisable that the document should be in the handwriting of the cautioner, or that

---

[1] Selkirk (Stevenson's Tr.) *v.* Campbell & Sons, 1896, 33 S.L.R. 503.

[2] Mercantile Law Amendment Act, 1856, § 6 ; see Wallace *v.* Gibson, 1895, 22 R. (H.L.) 56.

[3] Bell's Prin., §§ 251, 285.

[4] Napier *v.* Bruce, 1840, 2 D. 556 ; affd. 1 Bell's App., 78.

[5] Clydesdale Bank *v.* Paton, 1896, 23 R. (H.L.) 22.

[6] Per Lord Eldon in Grant *v.* Campbell, 1818, 6 Dow 239.

the words " adopted as holograph " should be prefixed by him to his signature.[1]

Stamp Duty.—With the exception of mercantile guarantees, all guarantees for sums of £5 and upwards must bear a sixpenny stamp. The stamp may be denoted by an impressed or an adhesive stamp. Mercantile guarantees, *i.e.* guarantees for the payment of goods sold or to be sold, are exempt from stamp duty.

3. Kinds of Cautionary Obligations.—Cautionary obligations are divided into two classes—proper and improper. In the former class the cautioner is expressly bound as such ; but in the latter, while entitled to all the benefits of a cautioner, he is in a question with the creditor a principal obligant. A bond of credit in favour of a bank is a typical example of an improper cautionary obligation. In such a deed, while the persons who subscribe for the principal debtor are in truth cautioners, in a question with the bank they are all principal obligants, and liable as such.

4. Firms and Companies as Cautioners.—It is inadvisable to accept the obligation of a firm of two or more partners as cautioners for the reason that on the assumption of a new partner a new firm is constituted ; and such new partnership, although continuing the old name, in the absence of an express agreement to the contrary, would not be bound to implement the obligation.[2] Further, a partner of a firm by signing the firm's name cannot bind his co-partners as cautioners unless it is shown that the granting of guarantees is necessary for the purpose of carrying on the business of the firm in the ordinary way. And where a guarantee is given for the transaction of a firm, a change occurring in the constitution of the firm liberates the sureties from liability for transactions subsequent to such change.[3]

Again, a company incorporated under the Companies Act cannot validly enter into a cautionary obligation unless power to do so is either expressly or impliedly conferred on the company by its Memorandum of Association.

5. Creditor's Duty to Cautioner when entering into Obligation.— A creditor who requires a cautioner along with his principal debtor, or to whom such a security is offered, is in no way bound to make any representation to such proposed cautioner or to give him any warning or information as to the extent of the risk he is undertaking.[4]

---

[1] See Snaddon *v.* London, Edinburgh, and Glasgow Assurance Co., 1902, 5 F. 182.
[2] Partnership Act, 1890, § 18.
[3] Royal Bank *v.* Christie, 1841, 2 Rob. App. 118.
[4] Young *v.* Clydesdale Bank, Ltd., 1889, 17 R. 231.

or any portion thereof, entitled to total relief in respect of the sums paid from the principal debtor, including the payment of any necessary expenses he may have properly incurred. Further, upon payment, the cautioner is entitled to an assignation of the debt and to have transferred to him any securities or other remedies the creditor may hold for the performance of the obligation. The debt, however, must be paid in full. The payment of a dividend from the bankrupt estate of the cautioner does not entitle his trustee to an assignation of collateral securities.[1]

Position of Cautioners inter se.—Cautioners are, in a question among themselves and in the absence of any express agreement to the contrary, only liable for their rateable proportion of the obligation undertaken by them. While the creditor is entitled to proceed against one of the cautioners for payment of his debt, that cautioner is entitled to a rateable relief from his co-cautioners subject to the following qualifications, namely : (1) he must communicate to his co-cautioners any ease or deduction the creditor may make from his claim ; (2) he is entitled to charge interest against his co-cautioners from the date of his payment of the co-cautioners' share ; (3) but he is not entitled to recover from his co-cautioners any share of the expense he may have incurred without their consent in defending proceedings instituted by the creditor. The above rules apply whether the cautioners are bound in the same or separate documents, provided their obligations are substantially joint and several. The rules were accordingly held not to apply in a case where payment of a debt of £105 was guaranteed by one cautioner separately to the extent of £70, and by another to the extent of £35, on the ground that the discharge by the creditor of one of the cautioners did not affect the liability of the other for his proportion of the debt.[2]

7. Effect of Insolvency of Parties.—Principal Debtor Bankrupt.— Cautioner Solvent.—Where the estates of the principal obligant are sequestrated the creditor is entitled to rank upon his estates for the full amount of his claim and draw a dividend therefrom. He is then entitled to call upon the cautioner to make good the difference up to the limit of his obligation. Upon payment of this difference the cautioner cannot rank upon the insolvent estates of the debtor, for then there would be a double ranking for the same debt. If, however, the creditor, without ranking, calls upon the cautioner to

[1] Ewart v. Latta, 1865, 3 M. (H.L.) 36.
[2] Morgan v. Smart, 1872, 10 M. 610.

pay, the cautioner is thereafter entitled to rank for the sum he has paid and draw a dividend in respect thereof.

Where the principal debtor and the cautioners become bankrupt at or about the same time the creditor is entitled to rank upon all the estates for the full amount of his claim so as to operate payment in full.

Effect of Sequestration of Principal Obligant.—A cautioner is not entitled to get free of his obligation by the mere fact that the creditor has lodged a claim on the estate of the debtor, obtained payment of a dividend, and consented to the discharge of the bankrupt. In such circumstances the creditor is entitled to maintain his claim against the cautioner subject to any deduction in respect of dividends appropriate to the claim.

Trust Deeds.—It is otherwise in the case of trust deeds. A creditor cannot accede to a voluntary trust deed granted by the debtor so as to maintain his hold on the cautioner unless he either (1) gets the cautioner to consent to his so acceding, or (2) specially reserves his claim against the cautioner in his accession. Hence if the creditor add to his accession the following words, or words of like import, " subject to the necessary consents being received," this will enable a creditor to agree to a trust deed and draw a dividend along with the other creditors while maintaining his hold on the cautioner. It is advisable in all cases to get the cautioner specially to consent.

8. Who may Implement Obligation.—Apart from the parties to the obligation, the creditor cannot object to fulfilment by a stranger unless he is able to assign a satisfactory reason for his refusal. A stranger so paying is entitled to an assignation of the debt and of any securities held specially therefor.

9. Extinction of Cautioner's Obligation.—By extinction of the principal obligation, apart from express discharge, a cautioner may be discharged from his obligation in a variety of ways. Thus the extinction of the principal obligation involves the extinction of the accessory obligation, as by payment, novation, release, compensation.[1] So also will release of a co-cautioner release the cautioner [2] where they were bound jointly and severally.

Actings of Creditor injurious to Cautioner.—Any act of the creditor to the prejudice of the cautioner's position discharges the cautioner. Hence if the creditor gives time to the principal debtor, gives up

---

[1] Hannay & Sons' Trs. *v.* Armstrong Bros. & Co., 1875, 2 R. 399; affd. 1877, 4 R. (H.L.) 43.

[2] Mercantile Law Amendment Act, 1856, § 9.

securities held for the debt, or otherwise acts prejudicially to the interests of the cautioner without the cautioner's consent, the cautioner is freed from his obligation.

Death.—The mere fact of death does not liberate a cautioner's estate from liability for future obligations, provided that the terms of the obligation do not expressly or impliedly warrant this. It is, however, open to the representatives of a deceased cautioner to withdraw the obligation if the same be not inconsistent with the obligation.

The death of either of the principal parties to the transaction in the ordinary case frees the cautioner. The contract may otherwise provide.

Prescription.—Cautionary obligations fall under the septennial limitation or prescription introduced by the Act 1696, cap. 5. The Act is sweeping in its terms ; and as to those obligations to which it applies it provides that the cautioner is not bound for the amount in his obligation for a longer period than seven years after the date of the bond. In one case it was decided that a cautioner paying money after the seven years was entitled to get it back.[1] The Act, however, does not apply to all cautionary obligations. The following are outwith its purview, namely : (1) those in which the term of payment is beyond the seven years ; (2) those in marriage contracts ; (3) those for payment of an annuity or interest upon a loan, and cash credit bonds ; (4) bonds of corroboration, bonds of relief by one cautioner to another, and mercantile or other guarantees ; (5) those *ad facta præstanda*, bonds of caution for discharge of an office, and judicial bonds ; (6) bonds for a composition in bankruptcy ; (7) bonds for mutual relief ; (8) bonds to pay or see paid a sum already lent ; (9) bonds executed in a foreign country, since the laws of this country cannot govern those of another ; and (10) the statute does not apply to bills in which one person signs as cautioner for another. Generally stated, the Act applies to obligations by the following classes of obligants : (*first*) those who bind or engage for, or with, another in any bond or contract expressly as cautioners ; and (*second*) those who, though cautioners as between the parties who contract to pay, are principals, so far as regards the creditor, provided, however, there be a clause of relief in the bond itself, which gives the creditor notice of the character in which the party binds himself, or a separate bond of relief, of which the creditor has personal intimation at the time of receiving the bond.

[1] Stocks *v.* M'Lagan, 1890, 17 R. 1122.

CHAPTER XII

BONDS OF CREDIT AND GUARANTEES

1. Bonds of Credit.—Nature.—The commercial prosperity of Scotland, particularly during the eighteenth and early years of the nineteenth centuries, is in a large measure due to the introduction, shortly after its incorporation in 1727, by the Royal Bank of Scotland, of the bond of credit, popularly known as the cash credit bond. Difficulties were at the time experienced by the bank in getting its surplus assets made available for commercial enterprises. The system then introduced and still in operation is easily comprehended. Two or more persons interested in a third person sign along with that third person a bond for a certain specified sum in favour of a bank, or as now any financial house, under which all the persons so signing are in question with the lenders liable jointly and severally for the amount due under the credit, with interest as therein provided. The distinguishing characteristic of the bond is that although it is for a certain specified sum, the parties are only liable for, and interest is only charged upon, the amount standing from time to time at the debit of the customer's account. It is incompetent to incorporate in a bond of credit a guarantee for "ultimate loss." [1] When once signed and formally delivered, operations proceed as on an ordinary account current. No operations should be allowed until the bond has been signed by all the parties by whom it bears to be granted. Care should also be taken to see that all the parties are alive when the bond is delivered, as should one of the obligants die before the deed is delivered, although signed by him, the bond cannot be enforced against any of the obligants to it.

Terms of the Bond.—The terms of the bond are simple. The bond states that all the granters have obtained a credit for a certain specified sum, and that operations on the credit are to be by orders

[1] Veitch v. National Bank of Scotland, 1907 S.C. 554. See Guarantees, p. 236.

signed by the person on whose behalf the credit is granted. Unless specially provided for in the bond, the person named in the bond to operate on the credit is the only person who can do so, and he cannot delegate that authority to another. The bond further stipulates that any account or certificate signed by an official of the bank shall ascertain, specify, and constitute the sums or balances of principal and interest to be due, and shall warrant all executorials of law for such sums or balances and interest, whereof no suspension shall pass but on consignation only. Notwithstanding this provision, the account must be kept in accordance with usual banking practice.[1] Although doubted at first, it is now competent for the creditor to debit bills upon which the principal obligant is liable.

Interest on Sum in Bond.—The obligation of the parties to the bond includes the payment of interest from the " date or dates of advances." Where a bank is the creditor the rate is a fluctuating one in accordance with the advertised rates of the bank, usually one-half per cent. less than on overdrafts on unsecured current accounts. With other lenders the rate of interest is specified in the bond. The bank is bound once in every year to bring its books to a balance and charge interest on the debtor balance on the accounts. If the annual interest is not paid, but is, in accordance with banking practice, debited to the account, that sum thereafter loses its character as interest and becomes a principal sum itself bearing interest.[2] The result is that, if with application of interest the limit of the credit is exceeded, the cautioners are not liable for such excess. An exception to the general rule is allowed in the case where one of the parties to the bond becomes bankrupt. In such an event the bank is not bound to apply the interest to capital, but is entitled to go back to the last application of interest preceding the bankruptcy and claim interest from that date. Although the point has not yet been determined by the Court, it is thought that a like rule as regards annually applying interest by other lenders would be enforced.

Liability of Parties to Bond.—In a question with the lenders all the obligants are principal debtors, and can be individually called upon by the creditor to pay any sum due on the credit. If sums are advanced in excess of the limit specified in the credit, the obligants, apart from the principal obligant, are not liable for such excess. In a question with the obligant to whom the credit is given, the others, notwithstanding the fact that the word " cautioners " is not used,

---

[1] Gilmour *v.* Finnie, 1831, 9 S. 907.   [2] Reddie *v.* Williamson, 1863, 1 M. 228.

are indeed cautioners, and are entitled to all the equities of cautioners, and will be discharged from their obligation on like conditions as prevail in ordinary cautionary obligations.[1]

Right of Co-obligant to terminate Liability.—Subject to any express or implied agreement in the bond to the contrary, it is in the power of any one of the obligants to give notice to the creditor that he desires to terminate his obligation. On receipt of such notice the duty of the creditor is at once to stop operations on the credit and call for a settlement. Should he fail to do so, and allow operations to proceed, none of the co-obligants is liable for any sum drawn out from the credit after the date of the intimation, while any sum paid in to the credit of the account goes in reduction of the co-obligant's liability. As regards the principal debtor, the position is otherwise. He is always bound to pay in terms of his obligation.

Effect of Death of Principal Debtor or Co-obligant.—While the death of the principal obligant necessarily brings the credit to an end, there being then no person to operate on the credit, it is otherwise in the case of a co-obligant. The death of a co-obligant, subject to any provision in the bond to the contrary, does not terminate the credit or the liability of such co-obligant's estate for sums due as at the date of death or advanced subsequently.[2] The obligation continues until formally withdrawn or discharged.

Summary Diligence on Bond.—The law provides a very summary method for enforcing payment of the sums due from the obligants. An account is endorsed on the bond, certified by an official of the bank or lending corporation, and specifying the amount of principal and interest due to the date of the certificate. The bond and certificate are then recorded in the Books of Council and Session or in the Sheriff Court Books of the county in which the debtor sought to be charged resides. Thereafter an official extract is issued which entitles the creditor to at once take proceedings either by arrestment, poinding, or bankruptcy or other competent diligence to the like extent and effect as if he had obtained a formal judgment of the Court.

2. Guarantees.—These may be considered under two aspects, viz. (1) a simple guarantee, and (2) a continuing guarantee.

Simple Guarantee.—Where a guarantee is granted in the following or similar terms, " I hereby guarantee due payment of the sum of £   due to you by A.," this imports an obligation to pay the specified

---

[1] See Cautionary Obligations, *supra*, p. 232 *et seq.*
[2] British Linen Co. *v.* Monteith, 1858, 20 D. 557.

sum then due, and is discharged by payment or satisfaction by the debtor or guarantor. It does not import any guarantee for payment of a sum to become due after its date. Any words which imply that a guarantee is applicable not to a series of transactions or a continuous course of dealing, but as a guarantee from loss on one transaction or advance, will receive effect as a simple guarantee. Thus a letter in the terms, " As you have become security to the Clydesdale Bank for £150 on account of I. W., I hereby guarantee you against any loss by your doing so," was construed as a guarantee from loss on one advance of £150, and not as a continuing guarantee in security of advances on a cash credit account.[1]

Continuing Guarantee.—Where it is intended that the obligation of the guarantor should not be confined to past indebtedness, but to secure an account current, the terms of the document must clearly express the nature of the obligation undertaken. When a guarantor undertakes to pay or see paid " all sums due or to become due to you by A.," or " the price of all goods sold or to be sold by you to," such a document imports a continuing obligation, and remains good until implemented or recalled. If there is nothing in the guarantee to the contrary it is not presumed to have been granted on the faith of any specific conditions, and the guarantor is held to leave the principal debtor and creditor free to arrange the details of their transactions as they think fit, so long as these are in conformity with the ordinary custom of merchants. A guarantee is limited to the persons to whom it is addressed.[2] The obligation of a guarantor in a continuing guarantee continues until recalled, and, where his heirs, executors, or representatives are taken bound, does not fall by his death, and is binding upon his representatives.

" Ultimate Loss " Clause in Guarantees.—In guarantees in favour of banks there is usually inserted a clause to the following or similar effect which is referred to as the " ultimate loss " clause, viz. " I hereby guarantee due payment of all sums for which A. B. is or may become liable to you, the amount payable under this guarantee not to exceed   pounds, with interest from the date or dates of advance " ; or, after specifying the amount, " this guarantee shall apply to and secure any ultimate balance of the sums that shall remain due to you after applying any dividends, compositions, and payments which you may receive." In whatever way the clause is framed the interpretation of it by the Court is as follows. Assume the guarantee

---

[1] Scott v. Mitchell, 1866, 6 M. 551.   [2] Bowie v. Watson, 1840, 2 D. 1061.

to be for £500. The guarantor may think that in the event of the bankruptcy of the debtor he will be entitled to get credit for the dividend applicable to the amount of his guarantee. If at the date of the bankruptcy of the debtor he is indebted to the bank in, say, £1000, the bank, as they are entitled to do, rank for the full amount of their claim, and get a dividend thereon at the rate of, say, 10s. in the pound, thus giving them £500. They then go to the guarantor and demand payment from him of the remaining £500. The guarantor asks credit for 10s. per pound on the amount of his guarantee. The bank decline to do so, on the ground that the obligation of the guarantor is to see them paid their ultimate loss, and as that ultimate loss in the case under consideration is £500, the guarantor is bound to pay. He cannot get a ranking on the bankrupt's estate for the amount he has paid, as the bank have already got a ranking therefor. The result is that the guarantor has to make good the amount of his guarantee without any relief.[1]

[1] Harvie's Tr. v. Bank of Scotland, 1885, 12 R. 1141.

CHAPTER XIII

THE LAW OF PARTNERSHIP

THE law relating to partnership is codified by the Partnership Act of 1890 (applicable also to England and Ireland), but while this is so the rules of equity and of common law applicable to partnership continue in force except so far as they are inconsistent with the express provisions of the Act.[1] The Scots law of bankruptcy in relationship to partnership is dealt with in the Bankruptcy Acts so far as statutory.

1. Nature of Partnership.—Definition.—Partnership is the relation which subsists between persons carrying on a business in common with a view to profit. A partnership must consist of at least two partners. A business carried on by one person, although in a firm's name, is not a partnership. Societies, clubs, or other organisations not conducted with a view to profit are not partnerships. The term "business" as here used includes every trade, occupation, or profession.[2]

Any company or association registered as a company under the Companies Acts or any other Act of Parliament for the time being in force, and relating to the registration of joint stock companies or formed or incorporated by or in pursuance of any other Act of Parliament or letters patent or Royal Charter, is not a partnership within the meaning of the Partnership Act.

No partnership consisting of more than ten persons can be lawfully formed for the purpose of carrying on the business of banking, and no partnership consisting of more than twenty persons can be lawfully formed for the purpose of carrying on any other business that has for its object the acquisition of gain by the partnership or by the individual members thereof, unless such partnership is registered

---

[1] Partnership Act, 1890, § 46.　　　　　[2] *Ibid.*, § 46.

as a company under the Companies Acts, or is formed in pursuance of some other Act of Parliament or of letters patent.

Constitution of Partnership.—A partnership is usually, although not invariably, constituted by a formal deed binding the partners, usually for a certain number of years, and on certain specified terms.[1] Partnership may also be constituted verbally, or it may be implied from facts and circumstances which prove partnership.[2] The Partnership Act of 1890 [3] contains the statutory rules for determining the existence of a partnership. These are as follows : (1) Joint tenancy, joint or common property, or part ownership, does not of itself create a partnership as to anything so held or owned, whether the tenants or owners do or do not share any profits made by the use thereof. (2) The sharing of gross returns does not of itself create a partnership, whether the persons sharing such returns have or have not a joint or common right or interest in any property from which or from the use of which the returns are derived. (3) The receipt by a person of a share of the profits of a business is *prima facie* evidence that he is a partner in the business, but the receipts of such a share or of a payment contingent on or varying with the profits of a business does not of itself make him a partner in the business, although there may be a partnership in the profits of which persons not partners may share. In particular (*a*) the receipt by a person of a debt or other liquidated amount by instalments or otherwise out of the accruing profits of a business does not of itself make him a partner in the business or liable as such ; (*b*) a contract for the re-muneration of a servant or agent of a person engaged in a business by a share of the profits of the business does not of itself make the servant or agent a partner in the business or liable as such ; (*c*) a person being the widow or child of a deceased partner and receiving by way of annuity a portion of the profits made in the business in which the deceased person was a partner is not by reason only of such a receipt a partner in the business or liable as such ; (*d*) the advance of money by way of loan to a person engaged or about to engage in any business on a contract with that person that the lender shall receive a rate of interest varying with the profits or shall receive a share of the profits arising from carrying on the business does not of itself make the lender a partner with the person or persons carrying on the business or liable as such [4] ; (*e*) a person receiving by way of

---

[1] Partnership Act, § 26.
[2] Morrison *v.* Service, 1879, 6 R. 1158.
[3] Partnership Act, § 2.
[4] *Ex parte* Schofield, [1897] 2 Q.B. 495.

annuity or otherwise a portion of the profits of a business in consideration of the sale by him of the goodwill of the business is not by reason only of such receipt a partner in the business or liable as such.

The creditor for the loan of money and the seller of the goodwill in the cases (*d*) and (*e*) specified in the immediately preceding paragraph are not entitled to a ranking on the borrowers' or buyers' bankrupt estate until the claims of the other creditors for valuable consideration in money or money's worth have been satisfied.[1]

Meaning of Firm.—Distinction between Laws of Scotland and England.—There is a marked distinction between the laws of Scotland and England with regard to the meaning of " firm." In England persons who have entered into partnership with one another are for the purposes of the Act called collectively a firm, and the name under which their business is carried on is called the firm name. The partners are the firm. In Scotland, on the other hand, a firm is a legal person distinct from the partners of whom it is composed. The creditors of the firm rank along with the private creditors of the individual partners on the private estates of the partners, but the creditors of the partners have no ranking on the estate of the firm. In England, however, on the bankruptcy of a firm, the firm's creditors rank on the firm estate and the creditors of the partners on their private estates, to the exclusion of the creditors of the firm. If there be a surplus on one estate such surplus goes to meet the deficit on the other estate.

The principal consequences of this distinctive feature of the law of Scotland are as follows : (1) The funds of the partnership belong, not to the partners as joint owners, but to the firm itself as sole owner. (2) The firm itself is the primary debtor in debts owing by the partnership, and the debt must in the first place be constituted against the firm. (3) The firm may stand in the relation of debtor or creditor to any of its partners, and can sue or be sued by any of them. (4) A firm may be sequestrated without the individual partners being sequestrated, and a partner may do diligence against the firm. (5) The retirement of a partner from a firm or the addition of a new partner puts an end to the firm and creates a new one, with the result that a new partner introduced into a firm is not, in the absence of agreement to the contrary, liable for the debts of the firm prior to his admission, and a retiring partner remains liable for the debts of the firm as at

[1] Partnership Act, 1890, § 3.

16

the date of retirement.[1] Further (6) a continuing guaranty or cautionary obligation given either to a firm or to a third person in respect of the transactions of a firm is, in the absence of agreement to the contrary, revoked as to future transactions by any change in the constitution of the firm to which, or of the firm in respect of the transactions of which, the guaranty or obligation was given.[2]

Where after a partner's death the partnership business is continued in the old firm name, the continued use of that name or of the deceased partner's name as part thereof does not of itself make his executor's or administrator's estate or effects liable for any partnership debts contracted after his death.

2. Relation of Partners to Persons dealing with them.—Agency of Partner.—Every partner is an agent of the firm and his other partners for the purpose of the business of the partnership ; and the acts of every partner who does any act for carrying on in the usual way business of the kind carried on by the firm of which he is a member bind the firm and his partners, unless the partner so acting has in fact no authority to act for the firm in the particular matter, and the person with whom he is dealing either knows that he has no authority, or does not know or believe him to be a partner. If a partner of a firm pledges without the consent of his partners the credit of the firm for a purpose apparently not connected with the firm's ordinary course of business, the firm is not liable, but the partner so acting is bound in terms of the obligation granted.[3] But a firm is liable for the misapplication of money or property received for or in the custody of the firm by one of the partners if the partner was acting within the scope of his apparent authority.

If it has been agreed between the partners that any restriction shall be placed on the power of any one or more of them to bind the firm, no act done in contravention of the agreement is binding on the firm with respect to persons having notice of the agreement.[4] Where by any wrongful act or omission of any partner acting in the ordinary course of the business of the firm, or with the authority of his copartners, loss or injury is caused to any person not being a partner in the firm, or any penalty is incurred, the firm is liable therefor to the same extent as the partner so acting or omitting to act.[5]

Liability of Persons " holding out " as Partners.—Everyone who

---

[1] Partnership Act, 1890, § 17.
[3] *Ibid.*, § 7.
[5] *Ibid.*, § 10.

[2] *Ibid.*, § 18.
[4] *Ibid.*, § 8.

by words spoken or written or by conduct represents himself, or who knowingly suffers himself to be represented, as a partner in a particular firm, is liable as a partner to anyone who has on the faith of any such representation given credit to the firm, whether the representation has or has not been made or communicated to the person so giving credit by or with the knowledge of the apparent partner making the representation or suffering it to be made.[1]

3. Relation of Partners to one Another.—Partnership Property.—All property and rights and interests in property originally brought into the partnership stock or acquired, whether by purchase or otherwise, on account of the firm, or for the purposes and in the course of the partnership business, are called partnership property, and must be held and applied by the partners exclusively for the purposes of the partnership and in accordance with the partnership agreement.[2] Unless a contrary intention appears, property bought with money belonging to the firm is deemed to have been bought on account of the firm.[3]

Where a firm owns heritable property, that property, unless the contrary intention appears, is treated as between the partners (including the representatives of a deceased partner), and also as between the heirs of a deceased partner and his executors, as moveable and not heritable estate.[4]

Rights and Duties of Partners.—The partners of a firm are free to regulate their rights and duties *inter se*. Failing such arrangement the following rules apply : (1) All the partners are entitled to share equally in the capital and profits of the business, and must contribute equally towards the losses, whether of capital or otherwise, sustained by the firm. (2) The firm must indemnify every partner in respect of payments made and personal liabilities incurred by him (*a*) in the ordinary and proper conduct of the business of the firm, or (*b*) in or about anything necessarily done for the preservation of the business or property of the firm. (3) A partner making, for the purpose of the partnership, any actual payment or advance beyond the amount of capital which he has agreed to subscribe is entitled to interest at the rate of 5 per cent. per annum from the date of the payment or advance. (4) A partner is not entitled before the ascertainment of profits to interest on the capital subscribed by him. (5) Every partner may take part in the management of the partnership business.

---

[1] Partnership Act, 1890, § 10.
[2] *Ibid.*, § 20 (1).
[3] *Ibid.*, § 21.
[4] *Ibid.*, § 22.

(6) No partner is entitled to remuneration for acting in the partnership business. (7) Any difference arising as to ordinary matters connected with the partnership business may be decided by a majority of the partners, but no change may be made in the nature of the partnership business without the consent of all existing partners. (8) The partnership books are to be kept at the place of business of the partnership (or the principal place, if there is more than one), and every partner may, when he thinks fit, have access to and inspect and copy any of them.[1] The partners are bound to render true accounts and full information of all things affecting the partnership to any partner or his legal representatives.[2] If a partner without the consent of the other partners carries on any business of the same nature as and competing with that of the firm he must account for and pay over to the firm all profits made by him in that business.[3]

4. Assignation of Partnership Interest.—It is competent for a partner of a firm to assign his interest in the firm to a third person. Such third person, however, is not entitled during the continuance of the partnership to interfere in the management or administration of the partnership business or affairs, or to require any accounts of the partnership transactions or to inspect the partnership books, but the assignation entitles the assignee only to receive the share of profits to which the assigning partner would otherwise be entitled, and the assignee must accept the account of profits agreed to by the partners.[4]

5. Goodwill.—Almost every commercial business established for any material length of time acquires a goodwill which forms an asset of the firm. Goodwill has been defined as the probability that the old customers will resort to the old place. Like any other asset goodwill may be sold. If it is sold the purchaser cannot in the absence of an express provision to the contrary object to the seller setting up a rival business, but the seller is not entitled to canvass the customers of the old firm either personally or by letter or by his agent or traveller, and should he do so the purchaser can successfully take proceedings in Court to have him interdicted from soliciting any person who was a customer of the old firm prior to the sale to continue to deal with the seller or not to deal with the purchaser.

6. Dissolution of Partnership.—By Expiration of Notice.—The partners of a firm may make their own arrangement as to the dissolution of a firm. In the absence of any agreement to the contrary

---

[1] Partnership Act, 1890, § 24.   [2] *Ibid.*, § 28.
[3] *Ibid.*, § 30.   [4] *Ibid.*, § 31.

the following rules apply : A partnership is dissolved (*a*) if entered into for a fixed term, by the expiration of that term ; (*b*) if entered into for a single adventure or undertaking, by the termination of that adventure or undertaking ; (*c*) if entered into for an undefined time, by any partner giving notice to the other or others of his intention to dissolve the partnership. In the last-mentioned case the partnership is dissolved as from the date mentioned in the notice as the date of dissolution, or, if no date is so mentioned, as from the date of the communication of the notice.[1] Such a partnership is known as a partnership at will.[2]

By Bankruptcy, Death, or Charge.—Subject to any agreement between the partners every partnership is dissolved as regards all the partners by the death or bankruptcy of any partner. A partnership may, at the option of the other partners, be dissolved if any partner suffers his share of the partnership property to be charged for his separate debt.[3]

By the Court.—No majority of the partners can expel any partner unless a power to do so has been conferred by express agreement between the partners.[4] On application by a partner the Court may, however, decree a dissolution of the partnership in any of the following cases : (*a*) when a partner is found lunatic (by a legal process called cognition), or is shown to the satisfaction of the Court to be of permanently unsound mind ; (*b*) when a partner, other than the partner suing, becomes in any other way permanently incapable of performing his part of the partnership contract ; (*c*) when a partner, other than the partner suing, has been guilty of such conduct as, in the opinion of the Court, regard being had to the nature of the business, is calculated to prejudicially affect the carrying on of the business ; (*d*) when a partner, other than the partner suing, wilfully or persistently commits a breach of the partnership agreement, or otherwise so conducts himself in matters relating to the partnership business that it is not reasonably practicable for the other partner or partners to carry on the business in partnership with him ; (*e*) when the business of the partnership can only be carried on at a loss ; (*f*) whenever in any case circumstances have arisen which in the opinion of the Court render it just and equitable that the partnership be dissolved.[5]

---

[1] Partnership Act, 1890, § 32.   [2] *Ibid.*, § 26.
[3] *Ibid.*, § 33.   [4] *Ibid.*, § 25.
[4] *Ibid.*, § 35.

Notification of Dissolution to Public.—On the dissolution of a partnership or retirement of a partner any partner may publicly notify the same, and may require the other partner or partners to concur for that purpose in all necessary or proper acts, if any, which cannot be done without his or their concurrence.[1]

Winding-up.—After the dissolution of a partnership the authority of each partner to bind the firm, and the other rights and obligation of the partners, continue notwithstanding the dissolution so far as may be necessary to wind up the affairs of the partnership, and to complete transactions begun but unfinished at the time of the dissolution, but not otherwise. But the firm is in no case bound by the acts of a partner who has become bankrupt. This does not affect the liability of any person who has after the bankruptcy represented himself or knowingly suffered himself to be represented as a partner of the bankrupt.[2]

Rules for Distribution of Assets on Final Settlement of Accounts.—In settling accounts between the partners after a dissolution of partnership the following rules, failing any agreement to the contrary, apply : (*a*) losses, including losses and deficiencies of capital, shall be paid first out of profits, next out of capital, and lastly, if necessary, by the partners individually in the proportion in which they were entitled to share profits ; (*b*) the assets of the firm, including the sums, if any, contributed by the partners to make up losses or deficiencies of capital, shall be applied in the following manner and order : (1) in paying the debts and liabilities of the firm to persons who are not partners therein ; (2) in paying to each partner rateably what is due from the firm to him for advances as distinguished from capital ; (3) in paying to each partner rateably what is due from the firm to him in respect of capital ; (4) in dividing the ultimate residue, if any, among the partners in the proportion in which the profits are divisible.[3]

7. Limited Partnership.—Probably the most unsatisfactory branch of the law of partnership is that introduced by the Limited Partnerships Act, 1907. The defect of the Act is that no public notice requires to be given either at the office or on the notepaper of the company that the partnership is registered under the Act.

Definition and Constitution.—A limited partnership must not consist in the case of a partnership carrying on the business of banking of more than ten persons, and in the case of any other partnership of more than twenty persons, and must consist of one or more persons

---

[1] Partnership Act, 1890, § 37.   [2] *Ibid.*, § 38.   [3] *Ibid.*, § 44.

called general partners, who are liable for all debts and obligations of the firm, and one or more persons called limited partners, who at the time of entering into such partnership contribute thereto a sum or sums as capital or property valued at a stated amount, and who are not liable for the debts or obligations of the firm beyond the amount so contributed. General partners are liable for all the debts and obligations of the firm to the same extent as in ordinary partnerships. A limited partner, however, is liable only for the amount he has agreed to contribute. Having once paid that sum he is free from further responsibility. He cannot, during the continuance of the partnership, either directly or indirectly, draw out or receive back any part of his contribution, and if he does so draw out or receive back any such part he is liable for the debts and obligations of the firm up to the amount so drawn out or received back. A body corporate may be a limited partner.[1]

Registration of Limited Partnership.—Every limited partnership must be registered as such. If it is not so registered the partnership is a general partnership, and every limited partner is deemed to be a general partner.[2] In Scotland the registration must be with the Registrar of Joint Stock Companies in Edinburgh. The following particulars must be supplied on the appropriate form, which may be obtained from the Registrar : (a) the firm name ; (b) the general nature of the business ; (c) the principal place of business ; (d) the full name of each of the partners ; (e) the term, if any, for which the partnership is entered into and the date of its commencement ; (f) a statement that the partnership is limited and the description of every limited partner as such ; (g) the sum contributed by each limited partner and whether paid in cash or how otherwise.[3] The register may be inspected at the office of the Registrar by anyone on payment of a small fee.

Position of Limited Partner.—A limited partner cannot take part in the management of the partnership business and has no power to bind the firm. He, however, may by himself or his agent at any time inspect the books of the firm and examine into the state and prospect of the partnership business, and may advise with the partners thereon. If a limited partner takes part in the management of the partnership business he is liable for all debts and obligations of the firm incurred while he so takes part in the management as though he were a general partner. A limited partnership is not dissolved

---

[1] Limited Partnerships Act, 1907, § 4.   [2] Ibid., § 5.   [3] Ibid., § 8.

by the death or bankruptcy of a limited partner. The lunacy of a limited partner is not a ground for dissolution of the partnership by the Court unless the lunatic's share cannot be otherwise ascertained and realised. A limited partner may, with the consent of the general partners, assign his share in the partnership, and upon such an assignment the assignee becomes a limited partner with all the rights of the assignor. A person may be introduced as a partner without the consent of the existing limited partners. A limited partner is not entitled to dissolve the partnership by notice.[1]

Winding up of Limited Partnerships.—In the event of the dissolution of a limited partnership its affairs are wound up by the general partners unless the Court otherwise orders.[1]

Changes in Limited Partnership.—Any material change in the partnership must be duly registered with the Registrar of Joint Stock Companies.[2]

[1] Limited Partnerships Act, 1907, § 6.
[2] *Ibid.*, § 9.

CHAPTER XIV

THE LAW OF JOINT STOCK COMPANIES

The Companies Act, 1929.—The law regulating joint stock companies is at present in a transitory position. Prior to the passing of "the Companies Act, 1928," the law regulating joint stock companies was principally contained in the Companies Acts, 1908 to 1917. While the Act of 1928 received the Royal assent on 3rd August 1928, it is therein specially provided that, with the exception of § 92, the other provisions of the Act are not to come into operation until "such day as His Majesty may by Order in Council appoint, and different days may be appointed for different purposes and for different provisions of this Act." [1] The then Lord Chancellor undertook on behalf of the Government that the Act of 1928 would not be put in force until a Consolidating Act was introduced. The object apparently was to allow those interested in company law to have an opportunity of considering the terms of the new Act and the trend of the intention of the Government regarding the Consolidating Act, which was not merely to be an Act consolidating the law on the subject, but was to contain other provisions which the necessities of present-day company organisation required. The new provisions in the Act of 1928 relate principally to redeemable preference shares, the issue of shares at a discount, and offers for the sale of shares and debentures. Section 92 was passed to stop a practice known as "share hawking" whereby credulous people were induced to purchase shares which frequently turned out worthless. The section just referred to is with the whole Act of 1928 repealed, but like provisions are contained in § 356 of the Act of 1929.

The Consolidating Act referred to by the Lord Chancellor was duly introduced into Parliament, passed, and received the Royal assent on 10th May 1929. By an Order in Council dated 5th July 1929 it is provided that the Act of 1929 comes into force on 1st

---

[1] § 118 (4).

If, however, he does make any such representation, he must take care that it is a full and fair one ; and if he either conceals any facts which obviously are material affecting the risk, and still more if he in any way so represents those facts, whether intentionally or from mere blunder or carelessness, as to mislead the cautioner as to the hazard of his undertaking, then the cautioner will be liberated, and can never be held to an obligation substantially different from that held out to him.

6. Extent of Cautioner's Liability.—The extent of a cautioner's liability is of course determined by the terms of the deed which he has signed. If there are two or more cautioners for the same debt, unless they are taken bound jointly and severally they are only liable for a rateable proportion of the amount of the obligation. Where, however, they are bound jointly and severally, the creditor is entitled to call upon any one of them to implement the whole obligation, leaving him to operate any relief competent to him against his co-cautioners.

It is a leading principle of the law of cautionary that the cautioner can never be liable for a greater sum than that due by the principal debtor. The measure of his liability is the total actual loss sustained by the creditor from the debtor's failure to perform his obligation.[1]

Discussion of Principal Obligant.—Prior to the coming into force of the Mercantile Law Amendment Act of 1856 it was essential, before calling upon a cautioner in a proper cautionary obligation to make good his undertaking, to discuss the principal debtor. The creditor had to proceed with an action and exhaust the estate of the principal debtor before calling upon the cautioner. Now, however, and since that Act, it is competent for the creditor to proceed at once against the cautioner without taking any proceedings against the principal debtor, or he may, if he so elect, proceed against both the cautioner and the principal debtor in the one action. This statement is subject to the qualification that there be no provision in the obligation requiring the creditor to discuss the principal debtor before calling on the cautioner.

The Mercantile Law Amendment Act does not apply to obligations *ad factum praestandum, i.e.* obligations for the performance of an act within the power of the obligant. Hence the principal obligant must still first be discussed before the cautioner can be called upon.

Principal Debtor bound to relieve Cautioner.—The cautioner in a proper cautionary obligation is, upon implementing his obligation,

---

[1] Calder & Co. *v.* Cruickshank's Tr., 1889, 17 R. 74.

November 1929, and the following chapter therefore treats of the law as contained in the Act referred to, which consolidates and repeals the Companies Acts, 1908 to 1917, and the Companies Act, 1928. Under the Act of 1929 the following companies may be formed : (1) public companies limited by shares ; (2) companies limited by guarantee ; (3) unlimited companies ; and (4) private companies. The Act also contains special provisions with regard to (5) companies formed not for the purposes of gain ; and (6) foreign companies. The Act does not apply to trade unions, and the registration of any trade union under the Act is void.

1. Public Companies Limited by Shares. — (1) Constitution. — Memorandum of Association.—At common law every partner in a company incurs unlimited liability for the company's debts, no matter what the agreement between the partners as to the division of profit and loss. By the Companies Acts, joint stock companies were allowed to be formed on the footing that each member should incur liability only for a definite and limited stake in the venture, and provision was made for full notice being given to the public of the limitation of the members' liability. At the present time seven or more persons may, by subscribing their names as parties to a Memorandum of Association, and registering it in a public register kept by an official called the Registrar of Joint Stock Companies, form an incorporated company, the individual members of which have only a limited liability for the company's debts. The Memorandum is the charter, and defines and limits the powers of the company. A company may not alter the conditions contained in its Memorandum except in the cases in the mode and to the extent for which provision is made in the Act.[1] The Memorandum must now be in a statutory form provided by the Act, or as near thereto as circumstances will admit.[2]

There must be specified in the Memorandum : (1) the name of the company, with " Limited " as the last word of its name. Stringent regulations have now been made regarding the name of a company. No company can be registered by a name which (a) is identical with that by which a company in existence is already registered, or so nearly resembles that name as to be calculated to deceive ; (b) contains the words " Chamber of Commerce " unless the company is a company to be registered under a licence to be granted by the Board of Trade without the addition of the word " Limited " to its name ; (c) contains the words " Building Society." Except with the consent

----

[1] § 4.

[2] § 11 and Table B.

of the Board of Trade no company can be registered by a name which contains the words " Royal " or " Imperial," or in the opinion of the registrar suggests or is calculated to suggest the patronage of His Majesty or of any member of the Royal family, or connection with His Majesty's Government or any department thereof, or contains the words " Municipal " or " Chartered," or in the opinion of the registrar suggests or is calculated to suggest connection with any municipality or other local authority, or with any society or body incorporated by Royal Charter, or contains the word " Co-operative " ; (2) the part of the United Kingdom in which the registered office of the company is to be situate ; (3) the objects of the company ; (4) the fact that the liability of the members is limited ; (5) the amount of the share capital with which the company proposes to be registered, and the division thereof into shares of a fixed amount ; and (6) the number of shares taken by each subscriber, who must write the number opposite his name, no subscriber taking less than one whole share.

Any person who is of full age and subject to no legal incapacity may validly sign the Memorandum. It is immaterial whether the seven persons subscribing the Memorandum are relations or strangers, or are, or are not, beneficially entitled to the share or shares for which they subscribe.[1] Each signature must be attested by one witness. If the signatories sign at the same time and place one witness is sufficient, otherwise a witness must attest each signature.

Articles of Association.—It is usual, though not obligatory, for companies limited by shares to have special Articles of Association, and these are executed and registered along with the Memorandum.[2] The Articles play a part subsidiary to the Memorandum. They accept the Memorandum as the charter of incorporation, and proceed to define the duties, the rights and the powers of the governing body as between it and the general body of the members ; the mode and form in which the business of the company is to be carried on ; and the mode and form in which changes in the internal regulations of the company are from time to time to be made.

The Memorandum and Articles as contemporaneous documents must be read together, so that if there is any ambiguity in the one the other may explain or interpret it. The Articles cannot, however, extend the Memorandum to objects foreign to its scope. If the Memorandum be silent on a matter not required to be stated therein,

---

[1] Salomon v. Salomon & Co., [1896] A.C. 22. [2] § 6.

the Articles may supplement it.   If anything is done by the company which is not warranted by the Memorandum, the question will arise whether that which is so done is *ultra vires*, *i.e.* outwith the powers, not only of the directors, but of the company itself.   If anything is done, which, while keeping within the Memorandum, is a violation of the Articles, or in excess of them, the question will arise whether that is anything more than an act *ultra vires* of the directors, but *intra vires*, *i.e.* within the powers, of the company and capable of ratification by the members.

Where no Articles are registered, or where the registered Articles have become unworkable, the Articles in Table A scheduled to the Act are held to be the Articles of Association of the company.   But if Articles have been registered, and these do not exclude or modify the regulations of Table A, the latter also apply to the company.   Some companies adopt *simpliciter* the regulations of Table A ; others again provide that none of the regulations contained in the Table, except in so far as such regulations are embodied in the Articles, shall apply " to this company " ; while others again provide that " the following shall be the Articles of Association of this company to the entire exclusion of Table A."

If no Articles are registered along with the Memorandum, the Memorandum may be either printed or written or partly printed and partly written.   If Articles of Association are registered along with the Memorandum, both must be printed.

Registration.—On the registration of the Memorandum, the registrar is required to certify under his hand that the company is incorporated, and, in the case of a limited company, also that the company is limited.[1]   The certificate when issued is conclusive evidence that all the requirements of the Act in respect of registration and of matters precedent and incidental thereto have been complied with, and that the association is a company authorised to be registered, and is duly registered under the Act.[2]

From the date of incorporation mentioned in the certificate of incorporation the subscribers of the Memorandum, together with such other persons as may from time to time become members of the company, are deemed to be a body corporate by the name contained in the Memorandum, capable forthwith of exercising all the functions of an incorporated company and having perpetual succession and a common seal with power to hold lands, but with such liability on the

[1] § 13 (1).   [2] § 15.

part of the members to contribute to the assets of the company, in the event of its being wound up, as is mentioned in the Act.[1]

Publication of Name.—Every limited company must paint or affix, and keep painted or affixed, its name on the outside of every office or place in which its business is carried on, in a conspicuous position in letters easily legible, and have its name mentioned in legible characters in all notices, advertisements, and other official publications of the company, and in all bills of exchange, promissory notes, endorsements, cheques, and orders for money or goods purporting to be signed for on behalf of the company, and in all bills of parcels, invoices, receipts, and letters of credit of the company. The name of the company must be engraven in legible characters upon its seal.[2]

Alteration of Memorandum.—A company may alter or extend its Memorandum by special resolution, confirmed by the Court, if the alteration is required to enable the company (1) to carry on its business more economically or more efficiently ; or (2) to attain its main purpose by new or improved means ; or (3) to enlarge or change the local area of its operations ; or (4) to carry on some other business which may be conveniently combined with its own ; or (5) to restrict or abandon any of its objects ; or (6) to sell or dispose of the whole or any part of the undertaking of the company ; or (7) to amalgamate with any other company or body of persons.[3] The Court will not allow entirely new powers to be acquired except to a limited extent.[4]

Alteration of Articles.—The Articles can be altered by special resolution of the company to an extent [5] limited only by the provisions of the statute and conditions contained in the Memorandum,[6] and that the alteration be for the benefit of the Company as a whole.[7] It is not competent to except any Article from alteration.

(2) Promotion.—Promoters.—A promoter of a company is one who is engaged in bringing the particular company into existence. He may have heard of a property worth developing which the owners wish to sell, or a profitable undertaking from which the partners wish to retire. He may purchase the property himself, or he may make a provisional contract with the owners for the sale of the property or business with a view to getting up a company to work it. Such a person occupies, in regard to the company, a fiduciary relation. A promoter, if he sells his own property to the company, must make a

---

[1] §§ 13 (2), 14.   [2] § 93.   [3] § 5.   [4] *Re* John Brown, Ltd., [1914] W.N. 434.
[5] § 10.   [6] Andrews *v.* Gas Meter Co., [1897] 1 Ch. 361.
[7] Menier *v.* Hooper's Telegraph Works, (1874) L.R. 9 Ch. 350.

full disclosure of his interest and position with regard to that property.[1] When he is unable himself to purchase the property, and confines himself to inducing third parties, as shareholders in a company, to adopt his provisional contract, he is really their agent in the transaction, and must not deceive them into paying a price part of which is to go as a secret bonus into his own pocket. If he does not announce the precise bonus and extent of his own interest in the purchase, and directly or indirectly secures a profit of which he has not told the company, the company on being incorporated and discovering the matter can compel him to pay back the profit which he has secretly made on the sale, or the company may, in its option, set aside the bargain altogether. As an agent cannot act for a person not yet in existence, it follows that the company when formed is not bound by the contract if it does not adopt it, and cannot sue the vendor on the contract. The agent remains personally liable on the contract, unless otherwise expressly provided in the contract.

The Prospectus.—Having made the provisional contract, one of the first things the promoters usually do is to issue to the public a prospectus of the intended company, or it may be that an existing company is promoting a new, or extending an existing, undertaking. The prospectus is an advertisement depicting the advantages of the undertaking. It is the basis upon which the public are expected to make applications for and to receive allotments of shares in the company. A condition binding an applicant for shares or debentures to waive any of the statutory requirements in respect of a prospectus is void.[2] No form of application for shares or debentures should be sent to a member of the public unless accompanied by a prospectus.[3] The Act defines a prospectus as "any prospectus, notice, circular, advertisement, or other invitation, offering to the public for subscription or purchase any shares or debentures of a company," [4] and contains specific directions as to what must be stated in the prospectus.[5] These may be summarised as : (1) the contents of the Memorandum with the names, descriptions, and addresses of the signatories, and the number of shares subscribed for by them ; (2) the number of founders, or management or deferred shares, and the nature and extent of the interest of the holders in the property and profits of the company ; (3) the qualification of a director, and any provision in the Articles as to the remuneration of the directors ; (4) the names,

---

[1] *In re* Lady Forrest Gold Mine, Ltd., [1901] 1 Ch. 582.   [2] § 35 (2).
[3] § 35 (3).   [4] § 380 ; see also § 38.   [5] § 35 and Schedule 4

descriptions, and addresses of the directors or proposed directors ; (5) the minimum amount which in the directors' opinion must be raised to provide (*a*) the purchase price of any property, (*b*) preliminary expenses, (*c*) repayment of any money borrowed by the company in respect of these matters, and (*d*) working capital, and also the amounts and the sources of the amounts to be provided for these objects otherwise than out of the proceeds of the issue ; (6) the amount payable on application and allotment on each share ; (7) the number and amount of shares and debentures which have within the two preceding years been issued or agreed to be issued as fully or partly paid-up otherwise than in cash and the consideration for which they have been issued ; (8) the names and addresses of the vendors of any property purchased or acquired by the company or proposed so to be purchased or acquired, and the amount payable to each ; (9) the amount (if any) paid or payable as purchase-money in cash, shares, or debentures for any such property as aforesaid, specifying the amount (if any) payable for goodwill ; (10) the amount (if any) paid within the two preceding years, or payable, as commission for subscribing or agreeing to subscribe or procuring or agreeing to procure subscriptions for any shares in, or debentures of, the company, or the rate of any such commission ; (11) the amount or estimated amount of preliminary expenses, *i.e.* the expenses incurred in getting up and registering the company ; (12) the amount paid within the two preceding years or intended to be paid to any promoter, and the consideration for any such payment ; (13) the dates of and parties to every material contract, including verbal contracts, and a reasonable time and place at which any material contract or a copy thereof may be inspected—what is a material contract is a question of fact [1] ; (14) the names and addresses of the auditors (if any) of the company ; (15) the interest of every director, including his interest as partner of a firm, in the promotion of, or in the property proposed to be acquired by, the company, with a statement of all sums paid to him to induce him to become, or to qualify him as, a director, or otherwise for services rendered by him or by his firm in connection with the promotion or formation of the company ; (16) where the company is a company having shares of more than one class, the right of voting at meetings of the company conferred by the several classes of shares respectively ; (17) where a company or business has been carried on for less than three years, the length of time during which the company or business has been

---

[1] Sullivan *v.* Metcalfe, (1879) 5 C.P.D. 455.

carried on. A report by the auditors of the company with respect to the profits of the company for the three immediately preceding years must be given, containing certain specified particulars, and if no accounts have been made up during such period the fact must be stated. If a business is being purchased by the company a report must be set out by accountants upon the profits of the business for the preceding three years. For certain qualifications, additions, and amendments to the requirements above specified reference is made to the miscellaneous provisions of Part III. of Schedule 4 to the Act. In addition, every prospectus must state on the face of it that a copy has been delivered for registration.[1] Generally stated, a prospectus should contain every material fact which should be known to a person who is asked to apply for shares. There must be no misrepresentation and no false impression intentionally conveyed.[2] A company cannot, prior to the statutory meeting, vary the terms of a contract referred to in the prospectus except subject to the approval of the statutory meeting.[3]

Vendor to Company.—For the purposes of the above provisions every person is deemed to be a vendor who has entered into any contract, absolute or conditional, for the sale or purchase or for any option of purchase of any property to be acquired by the company in any case when (a) the purchase money is not fully paid at the date of the issue of the prospectus ; (b) the purchase money is to be paid or satisfied wholly or in part out of the proceeds of the issue offered for subscription by the prospectus ; or (c) the contract depends for its validity or fulfilment on the result of that issue.[4]

Issue of Prospectus.—A copy of a prospectus before issue must be filed with the Registrar of Joint Stock Companies. Such prospectus must be dated, and signed by every person who is named therein as a director or proposed director of the company, or by his agent authorised in writing. No prospectus should be issued until a copy has been filed for registration. If it is so issued before filing, the company and every person who is knowingly a party to the issue of the prospectus is liable to a fine not exceeding £5 for every day from the date of the issue of the prospectus until a copy thereof is so filed.[5]

Liability of Persons responsible for Issue of Prospectus.—Every person who is a director of the company at the time of the issue of the

---

[1] § 34 (4).   [2] Greenwood v. Leather Shod Wheel Co., [1900] 1 Ch. 421.
[3] § 36 (1).   [4] Act, Sched. 4, Part III, § 2.   [5] § 34.

prospectus, and every person named in the prospectus as a director or as having agreed to become a director, and every promoter of the company and every person who has authorised the issue of the prospectus is liable to pay compensation to all persons who subscribe for any shares or debentures on the faith of the prospectus for the loss or damage they may have sustained by reason of any untrue statement therein, unless he is able to prove that he had reasonable grounds to believe, and did up to the time of the allotment of shares or debentures believe, that the statement was true.[1] Where the statements in a prospectus follow on the report or valuation of an expert no liability attaches if the statement is a correct and fair copy of or extract from the report or valuation, unless in a case where it is proved that the persons issuing the prospectus had no reasonable ground to believe that the person making the statement, report, or valuation was competent to make it. A director would further escape liability if he was able to prove that he withdrew his consent to become a director before the issue of the prospectus, and that it was issued without his authority or consent, and in the further cases (a) where he is able to show that the prospectus was issued without his knowledge or consent, and on becoming aware of the issue he forthwith gave reasonable public notice that it was issued without his knowledge or consent, and (b) if after the issue of the prospectus and before the allotment thereunder, he, on becoming aware of any untrue statement therein, withdrew his consent thereto, and gave reasonable public notice of the withdrawal, and of the reason therefor.[2]

Shareholder's Remedy for Misrepresentations in Prospectus.—The prospectus is the basis of the contract between the shareholder and the company. It is to be kept in view that the offer to take shares is an offer to take them on the terms of the prospectus, and on no other terms, and the acceptance of the application by the allotment of the shares is the acceptance of the offer on those terms and on no other. Where a person has by untrue statements or the concealment of material facts in a prospectus been induced to buy shares in a public company, his remedy may, at his option, either be the rescinding of the contract or a claim for damages against those who made the representations following upon which he bought the shares. If necessary, however, for full indemnity the shareholder is entitled to have recourse to both remedies.

Statement in Lieu of Prospectus.—If a company does not issue a

[1] § 37 ; Adams *v.* Thrift, [1915] 2 Ch. 21.   [2] § 37.

17

prospectus, it must file with the registrar a statement in lieu of prospectus [1] in the form prescribed in the Fifth Schedule to the Act, containing most of the information which would be required in a prospectus. If it fails to file a statement it cannot allot any shares or debentures. This does not apply to a private company.

Underwriting Agreements.—Should there be any risk of the shares not being sufficiently subscribed for by the public so as to entitle the directors to proceed to allotment, recourse is had to the underwriting of a certain number of the shares. The commission agreed to be paid therefor is a legitimate charge against the company. To entitle the directors to charge the payment of the commission against the company, the payment of the commission and the amount or rate per cent. thereof must be authorised by the Articles of Association and disclosed in the prospectus, circular issued, or statement in lieu of prospectus.[2] The amounts so paid must appear in the annual summary and accounts of the company as separate items of expenditure. This does not, however, prevent a vendor paying to the underwriter any sum he pleases, so long as the company is not charged with the payment thereof.

(3) Commencement of Business.—A company cannot commence any business or exercise any borrowing powers unless (1) shares held subject to the payment of the whole amount thereof in cash have been allotted to an amount not less in the whole than the minimum subscription ; (2) every director of the company has paid to the company on each of the shares taken or contracted to be taken by him, and for which he is liable to pay in cash, the same amount as members of the public must pay on application and allotment ; (3) there has been filed with the registrar of companies a statutory declaration by the secretary or one of the directors in the prescribed form, that the aforesaid conditions have been complied with ; and (4) in the case of a company which does not issue a prospectus inviting the public to subscribe for its shares, there has been filed with the registrar of companies a statement in lieu of prospectus,[3] and provisions similar to those of (2) and (3) above stated have been complied with.[4]

Banking, Insurance, and other Companies.—Every company being a limited banking company, or an insurance company, or a deposit, provident, or benefit society, must, before it commences business

---

[1] § 40.
[2] § 43 ; Burrows and Matabele Gold Reefs and Estates Co., Ltd., [1901] 2 Ch. 23.
[3] § 94.   [4] *Ibid.*

(and also on the first Monday in February and the first Tuesday in August in every year during which it carries on business), make a statement in the form of the Seventh Schedule to the Act, or as near thereto as circumstances will admit. The statement includes the share capital of the company, the number of shares issued, the calls made, and a note of the assets and liabilities of the company. A copy of the statement must be put up in a conspicuous place in the registered office of the company and in every branch office or place where the business of the company is carried on.[1] Every member and every creditor of the company is entitled to a copy of the statement on payment of a sum not exceeding sixpence. The above provisions do not apply to any assurance company to which the provisions of the Assurance Companies Act, 1909, as to the accounts and balance sheet to be prepared annually and deposited by such a company apply, if the company complies with those provisions. Under the Act just referred to every such company must, before receiving a certificate of incorporation, deposit in Court a sum of £20,000 to be invested in certain defined securities. The deposit remains during the subsistence of the company.[2]

(4) The Shareholder's Contract with the Company.—(*a*) **Formation of the Contract.**—In order to become a member of a company a person desiring to do so enters into a contract of membership with the company. The contract may take the form of (*a*) signature of the Memorandum, or (*b*) an agreement to take shares. The Articles of Association are the evidence of the terms of the contract.

In the case of signatories of the Memorandum they are deemed to have agreed to become members of the company. In other cases the contract is formed by offer and acceptance. The offer takes the form of an application for shares, and the acceptance usually takes the form of an allotment of shares to the applicant. The application need not be in writing.[3] The allotment need not be formal, but knowledge of it must be brought home to the applicant in order to bind him.[4] The general rules of the law of contract as to offer, acceptance, and withdrawal, and as to capacity to contract, apply.[5] For the purpose of the withdrawal of an application, notice of withdrawal must be sent to or given at the registered office of the company. A person may become a member also by transfer of shares

---

[1] § 131.   [2] The Assurance Companies Act, 1909, § 2 (1), (2).

[3] Goldie *v.* Torrance, 1882, 10 R. 174.

[4] Curror's Tr. *v.* Caledonian Heritable Security Co., 1880, 7 R. 479.

[5] *Supra*, p. 2 *et seq.*, and p. 13 *et seq.*

from an existing member, or by transmission, *e.g.* on the death of a shareholder.

Allotment.—No allotment can be made of any share capital of a company unless the following conditions have been complied with, viz. that the amount stated in the prospectus as the minimum amount which in the opinion of the directors must be raised to provide for the matters specified in Paragraph 5 in Part I. of the Fourth Schedule to the Act [1] and the sum payable on application has been paid to and received by the company. For the purpose of this provision a sum is deemed to have been paid to and received by the company if a cheque for that amount has been received by the company in good faith and the directors have no reason for suspecting that the cheque will not be paid. The sum payable on application on each share must not be less than 5 per cent. of the nominal amount of the share.[2]

Failure to make Timeous Allotment.—If the provisions above referred to are not complied with on the expiration of forty days after the first issue of the prospectus, all money received from applicants must be forthwith paid to them without interest. If the money is not repaid within forty-eight days, the directors are jointly and severally liable to repay that money with interest at the rate of 5 per centum per annum from the expiration of the forty-eighth day. No director is liable to repay if he proves that there was loss of the money not due to any misconduct or negligence on his part. A shareholder cannot contract himself out of the benefits here conferred.[3]

Filing of Allotment with Registrar. — Whenever any company limited by shares (and this includes private companies) makes any allotment of its shares, the company must within one month thereafter file with the registrar a return of the allotments, stating the number and nominal amount of the shares comprised in the allotment, the names, addresses, and descriptions of the allottees, and the amount (if any) paid or due and payable on each share.[4]

Payment for Shares.—A company cannot issue shares at a discount, except to the limited extent and subject to the conditions specified in § 47 of the Act. The shares must be paid for in cash, unless otherwise determined by a contract duly made in writing and filed with the registrar at or before the issue of such shares. These requirements would not apply to the case of anyone not an allottee, *e.g.* a transferee.

(*b*) **The Register of Members.** — Every company must keep a

---

[1] For which see p. 255, Prospectus (5).   [2] § 39 (3).   [3] § 39 (4), (5).   [4] § 42.

register of members, and every member is entitled to be placed on
the register of members, which is *prima facie* evidence of his membership. Where a company has more than fifty members, unless the
register of members is in the form of an index, a separate index of the
names of members must be kept.[1] The following particulars must be
entered in the register, namely, (1) the names, addresses, and occupations of its members—in the case of a company having a share capital,
a statement of the shares held by each member, distinguishing each
share by its number, and of the amount paid or agreed to be considered as paid on the shares of each member ; (2) the date at which
each person was entered on the register ; (3) the date at which any
person ceased to be a member, and penalties are imposed for failure
to comply with this regulation.[2] In England no notice of any trust,
express, implied, or constructive, can be entered on the register.
Where the registered office of a company is situated in Scotland,
trustees are recognised and can be entered on the register of members,
but are liable as individuals for all the obligations of shareholders.
The register and index must be kept at the registered office of the
company, and can there be inspected by any member *gratis* and by
any other person on payment of one shilling or such less sum as the
company may prescribe for each inspection. The company may
close the register [3] for certain periods, *e.g.* prior to the close of the
financial year, but, excepting these periods, the register must be
open for not less than two hours in each day, subject to such restrictions as may be imposed by the company in general meeting.
Any member or other person may obtain a copy of the register, or
of any part thereof, or of the list and summary required by the Act,
or any part thereof, on payment of sixpence, or such less sum as
the company may prescribe for every hundred words or fractional
part thereof required to be copied. A person inspecting the register
has no right to take copies.[4] No reason need be assigned for the
inspection.[5] When the company is in liquidation the right to inspect
ceases.[6]

(c) **Share Capital.**—(i.) **What is a Share ?**—A share is the interest
of a shareholder in the company, measured by a sum of money, for
the purpose of liability in the first place and of interest in the second ;
but also consisting of a series of mutual covenants entered into by

---

[1] § 96.   [2] § 95.   [3] § 99.
[4] Balaghat Gold Mining Co., [1901] 2 K.B. 665.
[5] Holland *v.* Dickson, 37 Ch. D. 669.   [6] Kent Coal-fields, [1898] Q.B. 754.

all the shareholders *inter se* in accordance with the Companies Act.[1] A share includes a right to receive dividends, and ordinarily it confers a right to vote. Money proposed to be raised by debentures [2] should not be stated as part of the capital of the company, for it is not capital but a debt due by the company to the lender.

Limited Liability of Members.—The shareholders are liable only for the amount, if any, unpaid on the shares registered in their names.

If, however, at any time the number of members of a company is reduced in the case of a private company below two, or in the case of any other company below seven, and it carries on business for more than six months, while the number is so reduced every person who is a member of the company during the time that it so carries on business after those six months and is cognisant of the fact that it is carrying on business with fewer than two members, or seven members as the case may be, is severally liable for the payment of the whole debts of the company contracted during that time, and may be sued for the same.[3]

(ii.) **Classes of Shares.**—The Memorandum of Association must specify the amount of the capital with which the company proposes to be registered. It is sufficient compliance with the Act if the Memorandum merely states that " the share capital of the company is (say) £10,000 sterling, divided into 10,000 shares of £1 each." But any competent regulations made with reference to the capital in the Memorandum will receive effect.[4] Hence it is usual to state whether any, and what part, of the original capital is to have a preference, and to specify whether the preference applies to dividend or capital or to both. Such division is a subject of contract, and any preferences given to one class of shareholders over another class will receive effect. But, in the absence of any such contract, all the members of the company are deemed to have equal rights.

The holder of preference shares is usually entitled by the articles to a fixed dividend before any dividend is paid on the ordinary shares. Unless the preference shares are made non-cumulative, a deficiency of dividend for one year is made up in subsequent years. Interest does not, however, run on the arrears.[5] Preference shares can only claim such preference as may be conferred by the Memorandum, Articles, or resolutions of the company, and a preferable right to dividend

---

[1] Borland's Tr. *v.* Steel Bros. & Co., Ltd., [1901] 1 Ch. 279.   [2] See *infra*, p. 274.
[3] § 28.   [4] For variation of shareholders' rights, see § 61.
[5] Partick Gas Co. *v.* Taylor, 1888, 15 R. 711.

will not confer a preferable right in distribution of capital or surplus assets in winding-up the company.[1]

Founder's, or deferred shares, are shares carrying a deferred right to dividend, and only if the dividend on the ordinary shares reaches a certain amount. They were found convenient as a consideration for getting a company's capital underwritten, or as a bonus to applicants for shares, one founder's share for, say, twenty ordinary shares subscribed. Deferred shares are now frequently issued along with ordinary shares and generally have a smaller nominal value.

Conversion.—The Articles may provide that where shares have been fully paid up they may be turned into stock, and *vice versa*.[2] Stock may be transferred split up into any fractional amount, whereas a share cannot be.

Share Warrants.—When shares are fully paid the company may, if authorised by its regulations, issue share warrants under seal, stating that the bearer of the warrant is entitled to the shares therein specified.[3] The shares are transferable by delivery of the share warrant and accordingly the name of the shareholder is struck off the register. The holder is not strictly a member of the company, but the Articles may provide for his voting at meetings on production of the warrant.

(iii.) **Increase and Alteration of Capital.**—A company may increase or alter its capital if authorised to do so by its regulations.[4] Notice of any increase must be given to the registrar.[5] An increase is usually sought when a company wishes to extend its business. Capital is altered when shares are consolidated, *e.g.* ten £1 shares turned into one £10 share, or subdivided, *e.g.* when one £10 share is turned into ten £1 shares, or when the capital is reorganised to the effect of altering the rights of the different classes of shareholders, or when shares which have not been taken up or agreed to be taken up are cancelled, or when shares are converted into stock. If reorganisation does not involve consolidation or division, but requires an alteration of the Memorandum, it may be effected by an arrangement or compromise sanctioned by the Court.[6] Where no alteration of the Memorandum is required a special resolution without sanction of the Court is sufficient.[7]

Reduction of Capital.—A company may reduce its capital by

---

[1] Partick Gas Co. *v.* Taylor, 1891, 18 R. 1017 ; see also Humboldt Co., 1908 S.C. 751.   [2] §§ 50, 51.   [3] § 70.   [4] § 50.   [5] § 51.
[6] §§ 153, 154.   [7] *Re* Australian Estates Co., [1910] 1 Ch. 414.

special resolution confirmed by the Court, and power to do so must be contained in the Articles.[1] It may reduce its capital in any way.[2] It may have lost some of its capital, and be unable to pay dividends until it has replaced the lost capital, which might, if the amount lost was considerable, mean indefinitely. Or it may find it has more capital than it requires, and wish to return some of the capital to the shareholders. Capital may be reduced (1) by reducing the liability of members for uncalled capital ; (2) by writing off lost capital ; or (3) by paying off capital in excess of the wants of the company.[1] On the special resolution being passed a petition for confirmation is presented to the Court. If a return of capital or a reduction of liability for uncalled capital is involved, the Court will not confirm the resolution until all the creditors of the company consent or are paid off or secured.

Diminution of Capital means the cancelling of shares which have not been taken up or agreed to be taken up by any person, and the diminishing the amount of the capital by the amount of the shares so cancelled.

(iv.) **Company's Lien over Shares.**—In Scotland at common law a company has a lien or right of retention over the company's shares belonging to a shareholder, in security and satisfaction of debts due by him to the company. This right entitles the company not only to refuse to register a transfer but also to sell the shares in satisfaction of the debt. In England no such right exists at common law, and unless the right is conferred in the deed of incorporation the company cannot refuse to register a transfer on the ground alone that the member is indebted to them. In both Scotland and England a right of lien is usually conferred in the Articles, and is expressed in the following or similar terms : " a first and paramount lien and charge available at law and in equity upon every share for all debts due from the holder thereof." There is no right of lien over shares either in Scotland or England in respect of moneys becoming due from the shareholder to the company after notice has been sent to the company that there is a prior charge thereon.

(*d*) **Dividends.**—There is nothing in the Companies Acts about how dividends are to be paid, nor how profits are to be reckoned. For the first time, however, it is now made compulsory for a company

---

[1] § 55.

[2] British and American Trustee and Finance Corporation, Ltd. *v.* Cooper, [1894] A.C. 339 ; Poole *v.* National Bank of China, [1907] A.C. 229.

to issue a profit and loss account.[1] These are matters which are usually provided for in the Articles of Association. A dividend presupposes a profit in some shape from the use of capital. No dividend except in the case to be after mentioned can be paid out of capital, and that although the Memorandum [2] or the Articles [3] or a general meeting [4] authorise it. Capital in this connection may be referred to as either fixed or circulating. Fixed capital is that from which the return is got by holding it and drawing the income from its use or employment. Circulating capital, on the other hand, is that from which the profit is got by parting with it or turning it over, and so receiving back, if the transaction is successful, an enhanced price. If the income in any year arises from a consumption in that year of circulating capital, the division of such income as dividend without replacing the capital consumed in producing it will be a payment of a dividend out of capital. The question of what is profit available for dividend depends upon the result of the whole accounts fairly taken for the year, capital, as well as profit and loss, and, though dividends may be paid out of earned profits in proper cases notwithstanding a depreciation of capital, a realised accretion to the estimated value of one item of the capital assets cannot be deemed to be profit divisible amongst the shareholders without reference to the result of the whole accounts fairly taken.[5] The exception above referred to is where shares are issued for the purpose of raising money to defray the expenses of the construction of any works or buildings, or the provision of any plant which cannot be made profitable for a lengthened period. The company may pay interest on so much of that share capital as is for the time being paid up, and charge the same to capital as part of the cost of construction of the work or building. The sanction, however, of the Board of Trade must be obtained, and the rate of interest is in no case to exceed 4 per centum per annum.[6]

(5) Transfer and Transmission of Shares.—Transfer.—Every shareholder has the right to transfer his shares in any competent manner to whom he pleases, provided he has not undertaken to hold the shares for a specified period, or unless the directors in the exercise of a power to that effect in the Articles or deed of incorporation refuse to register a transfer. Subject to such power to refuse, so long as a company

[1] § 123.　　　[2] Verner v. General and Commercial Trusts, [1894] 2 Ch. 239.

[3] Masonic Assurance Co. v. Sharpe, [1892] 1 Ch. 154.

[4] Flitcroft's Case, (1882) 21 Ch. D. 519.

[5] Foster v. New Trinidad Lake Asphalt Co., Ltd., [1901] 1 Ch. 208.　　[6] § 54.

is a going concern a transfer will be upheld if it is an out-and-out assignation to the transferee, although the transferee is a mere pauper, and so unable to pay calls on the shares, and the transfer be made for the avowed purpose of relieving the transferor from any future liability. A director shareholder has the same power to transfer as any ordinary shareholder, and that although the shares transferred are his qualification shares.

How Transfer Completed.—When shares are sold, to complete the right of a purchaser there must be a duly executed transfer by the seller in favour of the purchaser, signed by or on behalf of the parties and stamped with the appropriate duty, delivery of the share certificate, and registration of the transfer. No transfer can be lawfully registered unless a proper instrument of transfer has been delivered to the company.[1]

Effect of Transfer.—When once a contract of sale has been made, in the absence of any agreement to the contrary the purchaser of shares is entitled to any accruing benefit from the shares, such as dividends or otherwise, after the date of the contract. The registered proprietor is bound to account to the purchaser for any benefit accruing between the date of the contract and the registration of the transfer.

Refusal to Register Transfer.—Where power to decline to register a transfer is conferred upon the directors, they are not bound to disclose their reasons for rejecting a transferee, provided they have fairly considered the question at a meeting of the board. A notice of the refusal must be given to the transferee within two months after the date on which the transfer was lodged with the company.[2]

Where a contract of sale is made in accordance with the practice of the Stock Exchange, whereby the price is payable on the seller delivering a duly executed transfer, the payment of the price on the contract does not import an undertaking by the vendor that the company will register the transfer. The risk is with the purchaser, but until registration the transferor is a trustee of the shares for the transferee.[3]

Right of Pre-emption.—It is competent for a company in the Articles of Association to provide that a shareholder willing to sell his shares should first offer them to the other shareholders, but a similar provision in favour of the company to purchase its own shares is illegal and void. A shareholder who, in terms of the Articles, has offered his shares to the other shareholders, is entitled to withdraw

[1] § 63.   [2] § 66.   [3] Stevenson v. Wilson, 1907 S.C. 445.

that offer up to the time of its acceptance, unless the Articles provide, or the selling shareholder has bound himself, that the offer remain open for a specified time.[1] There is nothing obnoxious to the bankruptcy law in Articles of Association *bona fide* providing that a shareholder shall, in the event of his bankruptcy, sell his shares to particular persons at a particular price which is fixed for all persons alike, and is not shown to be less than the fair price which might otherwise be obtained.[2]

Transmission.—The share or other interest of any member in a company is personal or moveable estate,[3] and on his death passes to the same persons and in the same proportions as his money. The transfer from the name of the deceased is accomplished in any manner provided by the regulations of the company. In the case of companies having their registered office in Scotland, on the death of a shareholder domiciled in Scotland, the title of his executor to deal with the shares is completed by confirmation granted by the Sheriff of the county in which the deceased died domiciled. Where the shareholder dies abroad, or having no fixed place of abode, confirmation is granted by the Sheriff of the County of Edinburgh. Where a shareholder dies domiciled in England, or Northern Ireland, probate is taken out by his executor in the Courts of England, or Northern Ireland, as the case may be, and on production of such probate in the Sheriff Court of the County of Edinburgh a certificate is endorsed thereon by the Commissary Clerk that it has been so produced. The probate has then the same force, effect, and operation in Scotland as if confirmation had been originally expede in the Scots Courts. Until confirmation or probate has been taken out and produced to the company an executor has no title to deal with the shares.

(6) Management of the Company.—(*a*) **Officials of the Company.**— **Directors.**—The directors are persons selected to supervise and approve of the management of a company on behalf of and as representing the whole body of shareholders. Every company other than a private company registered after the commencement of the Act must have at least two directors.[4] Except in the case of private companies and companies not having a share capital, no person can be appointed a director unless he has signed and filed with the registrar a consent in writing to act as such director, and either signed the Memorandum for

---

[1] Smith *v.* Colquhoun's Tr., 1901, 38 S.L.R. 726.

[2] Trustee in Bankruptcy of J. E. Borland *v.* Steel Bros. & Co., Ltd., [1901] 1 Ch. 279.　　　　　　[3] § 62.　　　　　　[4] § 139.

a number of shares not less than his qualification (if any), or signed and filed a contract in writing to take from the company and pay for his qualification shares (if any), or taken from the company and paid or agreed to pay for his qualification shares (if any), or signed and delivered to the registrar an undertaking to do so, or made and delivered to the registrar a statutory declaration that a number of shares not less than his qualification (if any) are registered in his name. A company is required to keep at its registered office a register containing the names and addresses and the occupations of its directors or managers. A copy thereof is sent to the registrar. Any change among the directors or managers must be duly notified to the registrar.

The mere fact that a person is a director of a company does not preclude him from selling his property to the company, nor from making the best bargain he can. He is, however, bound to disclose to the company that he is offering for sale his own property, or if it is not wholly his own, then what precisely is his interest in it. Should he not do so, the company on ascertaining the fact may rescind the contract, or in their option hold the director to it, or make him account for any profit he has made on the contract.[1] Any director who fails to comply with this provision is liable to a fine not exceeding £100.[2] Further, a director is not entitled to receive for himself any secret commission or any present in respect of anything he may do as a director of the company.[3] Directors may receive a commission if the receiving of it is made known to and approved of by the shareholders.[4]

Powers of Directors.—The management of the business and the control of the company is vested in the directors who, in addition to the powers and authority expressly conferred upon them by the Articles of Association, may exercise all such powers and do all such acts and things as may be exercised or done by the company, and are not by the Articles or the Companies Act expressly directed or required to be exercised or done by the company in general meeting. Unless specially authorised by the Articles of Association, directors cannot delegate the powers which are vested in themselves to other persons. The directors must act as a board, and cannot act without a meeting unless the Articles otherwise provide.[5]

Personal Liability of Directors.—If directors act within their

---

[1] Jubilee Cotton Mills, Ltd. (Liqr.) v. Lewis, [1924] A.C. 958.   [2] § 149.
[3] Boston Deep-Sea Fishing & Ice Company v. Ansell, (1888) 39 Ch. D. 339.
[4] Costa Rica Railway Co., Ltd. v. Forwood, [1901] 1 Ch. at p. 761.
[5] Haycroft Gold Reduction Co., [1900] 2 Ch. 230.

powers, and act with such care as is reasonably to be expected from them, having regard to their knowledge and experience, and act honestly for the benefit of the company they represent, they discharge their legal duty to the company and are not personally liable for losses which the company may suffer by reason of their mistakes or errors in judgment. Before a director can be held personally liable for his actings, he must be guilty of such negligence as amounts to negligence in law. Mere imprudence or want of judgment is not such negligence.[1]

If on the face of a bill of exchange it appears that the directors sign only for and on behalf of the company, they are not personally liable should the bill not be met. But if they sign a bill merely describing themselves as directors and not stating that they are acting on behalf of, or on account of the company, they will be personally liable.[2]

If directors pay dividends out of capital, they are jointly and severally liable to repay the whole sums so paid. They can, however, reclaim from a shareholder to whom such a dividend was paid the amount thereof, if they can prove that the shareholder knew that the dividend was so paid.[3]

Remuneration of Directors.—A director is not entitled as a matter of right to receive remuneration for any service he may render to the company. In some companies special provision is made for the way in which the directors are to be paid ; in others there is none. An authority conferred in the Articles is, so long as the company is a going concern, sufficient to justify the directors in taking payment of the amount there fixed. If there is no special provision, any payment made to the directors is of the nature of a gratuity. Where the directors take payment of fees to which they are not properly entitled the Court will order them to repay the amount received.

Loans to Directors.—The accounts to be laid before a company in general meeting must now contain particulars showing the amount of any loans which, during the period to which the accounts relate, have been made either by the company or by any other person under a guarantee from or on a security provided by the company to any director or officer of the company, including any such loans which were repaid during the period. This provision does not apply to a company the ordinary business of which includes the lending of money.[4]

[1] *In re* City Equitable Fire Assurance Co., [1925] 1 Ch. 407.
[2] Brown *v.* Sutherland, 1875, 2 R. 615. See *contra*, Brebner *v.* Henderson, 1925 S.C. 643.
[3] Moxham *v.* Grant, [1900] 1 Q.B. 88.   [4] § 128.

Secretary of Company.—Persons dealing with a company are not entitled to assume that the secretary has power to bind the company, nor can any one assume that statements made by him are necessarily to be accepted as trustworthy without further enquiry, any more than in the case of a merchant it can be assumed that one who is only a clerk has authority to make representations to induce persons to enter into contracts.[1] Where a secretary does anything in the exercise of his office and within the limit of the powers conferred upon him, although in the particular act he may be committing a fraud against the company, the company will be responsible.[2]

Auditor of Company.—Stringent statutory regulations are now in force regarding the position of auditors. At each annual meeting the shareholders must appoint an auditor or auditors to hold office until the next annual general meeting. Failing such appointment, the Board of Trade may, on the application of any member of the company, appoint an auditor for the current year. A director or officer of the company cannot be appointed auditor. Unless continuing the retiring auditor, the company cannot at the annual meeting appoint a new auditor unless notice of an intention to nominate such person to the office of auditor has been given by a shareholder to the company not less than fourteen days before the annual general meeting.[3] A copy of the notice must be sent by the company to the retiring auditor, and notice also given to the shareholders either by advertisement or in any other mode allowed by the Articles, not less than seven days before the annual general meeting.[4]

Powers of Auditor.—The duty rests upon the auditor to investigate the manner in which the business of the company has been transacted, and to report thereon to the shareholders. The auditors are required to make a report to the shareholders on the accounts examined by them and on every balance-sheet laid before the company in general meeting during their tenure of office, and their report must state (a) whether or not they have obtained all the information and explanations they have required; and (b) whether in their opinion the balance-sheet referred to in the report is properly drawn up so as to exhibit a true and correct view of the state of the company's affairs, according to the best of their information and the explanations given to them, and as shown by the books of the company. Every

[1] Barnet v. South London Tramways Co., (1887) 18 Q.B.D. 817; Whitechurch, Ltd. v. Cavanagh, [1902] A.C. at p. 124.

[2] Shaw v. Port Philips and Colonial Gold Mining Co., Ltd., (1884) 13 Q.B.D. 103.

[3] § 132.

[4] §§ 132, 133.

auditor has a right of access at all times to the books, accounts, and vouchers of the company, and is entitled to require from the directors and officers such information and explanation as are necessary for the performance of his duties. It is no part of his duty to prepare the balance-sheet. His duty only commences when the balance-sheet has been prepared and approved of by the directors. An auditor does not, however, guarantee that the books do correctly show the true position of the company's affairs. He does not even guarantee that the balance-sheet is accurate according to the books of the company. All that the auditor is bound to do is to exercise reasonable skill and care in the preparation of his report. Where suspicion is aroused more care is obviously necessary, but still an auditor is not bound to exercise more than reasonable care and skill even in a case of suspicion, and he is perfectly justified in acting on the opinion of an expert where special knowledge is required.[1] Auditors are, however, responsible if they authorise the issue of a balance-sheet which is not justified by the books of the company, on the faith of which dividends are declared and paid otherwise than out of profits available for dividend.[2] Any shareholder is entitled without charge to be furnished with a copy of the balance-sheet and auditors' report.[3]

Annual Return.—Within fourteen days after the first ordinary general meeting of the company, and every year, the company must send to the registrar a list of its members, signed by the manager or secretary, containing the names, addresses, and occupations of all the members, and the number of shares held by them. The list must also contain a summary containing, among other details, the names and addresses of present members and of past members who were members at the date of the last return, the amount of capital and shares, new shares taken up, calls on shares, debts secured, and a balance-sheet.[4]

Execution of Contracts by or on behalf of a Company.—Any contract which, if made between private persons, would be by law required to be in writing, and if made according to English law to be under seal, may be made on behalf of the company in writing under the common seal of the company, and may in the same manner be varied or discharged. If, as between private persons, it requires to be in writing, though without seal, signed by the parties, it may be

[1] Kingston Cotton Mill Co. (No. 2), [1896] 2 Ch. 279 ; *In re* City Equitable Fire Assurance Co., Ltd., [1925] 1 Ch. 407.
[2] London and General Bank (No. 2), [1895] 2 Ch. 673.   [3] § 130.   [4] § 108.

made on behalf of the company by any person acting under its authority, express or implied, or varied or discharged. In Scotland a contract may be executed in like manner, but it may also be executed by being sealed with the common seal of the company and subscribed on behalf of the company by two of the directors and the secretary of the company, and such subscription on behalf of the company is equally binding whether attested by witnesses or not.[1]

Verbal Contracts.—Any contract which if made between private persons would by law be valid although made by parole only, and not reduced into writing, may be made by parole on behalf of the company by any person acting under its authority, express or implied, and may in the same manner be varied or discharged.[2]

(*b*) **Meetings of the Company.—Statutory Meeting.—General Meeting.**—With a view to the shareholders learning the exact position of the company, the company must hold a general meeting, called the statutory meeting, within not less than one month and not more than three months from the date at which it is entitled to commence business.[3] A report must be sent to all the shareholders seven days before this meeting, stating (1) the number of shares allotted, the extent to which they are paid up, and the consideration for which they have been allotted ; (2) the amount of cash received for the shares allotted ; (3) an abstract of the receipts and payments of the company, and an estimate of preliminary expenses ; (4) the names of the officials ; (5) particulars of any contract which is to be submitted to the meeting for modification, and the proposed modification. A general meeting of every company must be held once at least in every calendar year, and not more than fifteen months after the holding of the last preceding general meeting. If it is not so held, the company and every director, manager, secretary, and other officer of the company who is knowingly a party to the default is liable to a fine not exceeding fifty pounds.[4] The above-mentioned general meetings are ordinary general meetings. All other general meetings are called extraordinary. The directors, on the requisition of the holders of not less than one-tenth of the issued share capital of the company upon which all calls or other sums then due have been paid, must forthwith proceed to convene an extraordinary general meeting of the company. The requisition must state the objects of the meeting.[5]

Resolutions of Company.—Resolutions may be either ordinary,

[1] § 29.   [2] § 29 (1) (c).   [3] § 113.   [4] § 112.   [5] § 114.

extraordinary, or special. An extraordinary resolution is a resolution
passed by a majority of not less than three-fourths of such members
entitled to vote as are present in person or by proxy (where proxies
are allowed) at a general meeting of which notice specifying the
intention to propose the resolution as an extraordinary resolution has
been duly given. A resolution is a special resolution when it has
been passed by the majority required for the passing of an extraordinary resolution, and at a general meeting of which not less than
twenty-one days' notice specifying the intention to propose the
resolution as a special resolution has been duly given.[1]

Votes of Members.—In the absence of any provision to the contrary in the Articles, every member of a company whose name is on
the register has but one vote.[2] The register is the only evidence by
which that right can be ascertained. But where the Articles provide
otherwise, effect must be given to such regulations. The Companies
Act does not provide how votes are to be given or counted when no
poll is demanded, but it has been decided that the voting in such a
case is to take place by the recognised mode, *i.e.* by counting the
persons present who are entitled to vote and who choose to do so by
holding up their hands.

Absent members who have appointed proxies vote by these
proxies. There is no common-law right on the part of a member
of a corporation to vote by proxy. The right of a shareholder to
vote by proxy depends on the contract between him and his co-
shareholders. Unless a poll is demanded the person present is only
counted once, however numerous may be the persons whom he represents,
and this notwithstanding the fact that the regulations of the company
allow voting by proxy.[3] The mere fact that a person is authorised
by proxy to attend a meeting does not entitle him to demand a poll.

(*c*) **Borrowing Powers.**—The Companies Act does not confer on
companies registered under it power to borrow money or issue
negotiable instruments. Such a power must be conferred by the
company in its Memorandum or Articles, either expressly or by implication as necessarily incident to the purposes for which the company
is incorporated.[4] An ordinary trading company has an implied power
to borrow where the regulations are silent on the subject. Where a

---

[1] § 117.   [2] § 115 (1) (*f*).

[3] Ernest *v.* Loma Gold Mines, Ltd., [1897] 1 Ch. 1 ; but see J. T. Clark & Co.,
1911 S.C. 243.

[4] Baroness Wenlock *v.* River Dee Co., 10 App. Cas. 354 ; Ashbury Co. *v.* Riche,
L.R., 7 H.L. 653.

company has upon the face of its constitution only a limited authority to borrow, a person dealing with such a company must either enquire or run the risk of the company exceeding its powers.[1]

If a company have the power to borrow, or if the power to borrow be incidental to the conduct of its business, but the Articles of Association specially provide that certain formalities must be observed in order to bind the company, such formalities must be observed in order to constitute a valid charge upon the company's property. Apart from ordinary banking overdraft facilities, companies usually borrow by means of debentures or debenture stock.

Debentures.—A debenture is merely the personal obligation of the company to repay the money lent with interest. There is no statutory form for a debenture. It may be issued without security or against security. Debentures may be issued at a discount.[2] A condition in a debenture that it is made irredeemable or redeemable only on the happening of a contingency however remote, or on the expiration of a period however long, does not render the debenture invalid.[3] Debentures to bearer issued in Scotland are valid and binding according to their terms.[4] Such debentures by companies registered in Scotland were formerly invalid under a statute of the Scots Parliament of 1696.

Position of Debenture Holder.—The position of persons holding debentures in ordinary joint stock companies is this, that they are creditors having merely the personal obligation of the company to give delivery of certain of its assets, just as the creditors for ordinary trade debts have the obligation of the company for the payment in full of the debts due to them respectively. All the creditors holding merely the personal obligation of the company are in liquidation treated alike, none being entitled to an advantage not already otherwise secured over the others. There is nothing, however, incompetent, where power to that effect is given, in a joint stock company conveying, in security, its assets to trustees for debenture holders; but such security must be given and completed according to the law of the country where the property conveyed in security is situated. Hence the ordinary joint stock company having its registered office in Scotland has not the privilege of creating securities over its moveable property or leasehold subjects of which it remains in possession.

---

[1] Per Brett L.J. in Chaples v. Brunswick Building Society, 6 Q.B.D. 715.
[2] Webb v. Shropshire Railway Co., [1893] 3 Ch. 307.
[3] § 74.   [4] § 77.

Nor can it take power in the Memorandum and Articles of Association to grant debentures, secured over its moveable property of which it retains possession, which will be effectual to the debenture holders against the ordinary creditors of the company in a winding-up.

Debenture Stock.—Debenture stock is a loan by a multitude of lenders, whose title consists of a certificate by the company that they hold specified portions thereof, under provisions as to periodical payment of interest and repayment of principal, and whose interests are entrusted to trustees, who generally hold subjects conveyed by the company in security, and are empowered and directed on default in payment of interest, or on a supervening liquidation, to enter into possession, administer the property, carry on the business, and realise the estate for the benefit of the debenture-stock holders. Unlike debenture bonds, the amount of the stock held by the different lenders need not be a round sum. It may be for any number of pounds, or fractions thereof, unless the regulations of the company otherwise provide.

(7) Winding-up.—Sequestration under the Bankruptcy Act of a company formed and registered under the Companies Acts is incompetent. While this is so a company may be made notour bankrupt, so as to equalise diligences and to enable creditors to reduce preferences.[1]

(a) **What Companies can be wound up, and Mode of doing so.**— All companies registered under the Companies Act may be wound up in the manner provided in the statutes. No restrictive condition in the Articles of Association of a company can affect the statutory privileges of winding up.[2] Companies may be wound up in the following ways, namely : (i.) by the Court, (ii.) voluntarily, and (iii.) subject to the supervision of the Court.[3]

(i.) **Winding-up by the Court.**—A company may be wound up by the Court (1) if the company has by special resolution resolved that the company be so wound up ; (2) if default is made in filing the statutory report or in holding the statutory meeting ; (3) if the company does not commence its business within a year from its incorporation, or suspends its business

[1] Clarke, etc. v. Hinde, Milne & Co., 1884, 12 R. 347 ; see Bankruptcy, *infra*.
[2] *In re* Peveril Gold Mines, 1897, 14 S.L.R. 25.   [3] § 156.

for a whole year ; (4) if the number of members is reduced below seven ; (5) if the company is unable to pay its debts,—a creditor is not entitled to a winding-up order where the company *bona fide* disputes the debt and there is no evidence of insolvency other than non-compliance with a notice to pay served under the Act.[1] In determining whether a company is unable to pay its debts, the Court must take into account the contingent and prospective liabilities of the company—or (6) if the Court is of opinion that it is just and equitable that the company should be wound up.

Jurisdiction in Winding-up.—The Courts having jurisdiction to wind up companies are, where the company is registered in England, the High Court, the Chancery Courts of the counties palatine of Lancaster and Durham, and the County Courts,[2] and, where registered in Scotland, the Court of Session.[3] A new provision has been introduced providing that where the amount of the share capital of a company paid up or credited as paid up does not exceed ten thousand pounds the Sheriff Court of the Sheriffdom in which the registered office of the company is situate shall have concurrent jurisdiction with the Court of Session to wind up the company.

Petition for Winding-up.—The application for a winding-up order must be by petition, and may be presented either by the company or by any creditor or creditors (including any contingent or prospective creditor or creditors), contributory or contributories, or by all or any of those parties, together or separately.[4]

Commencement of Winding-up.—A winding-up by the Court is deemed to commence at the time of the presentation of the petition for winding-up.[5]

Effect of Winding-up Order.—When a winding-up order has been made, no action or proceedings

---

[1] Cunninghame & Ors. *v.* Walkinshaw Oil Co., Ltd., 1886, 14 R. 87.
[2] § 163.   [3] § 166.   [4] § 170.   [5] § 175.

can be proceeded with or commenced against the company except by leave of the Court and subject to such terms as the Court may impose.[1]

Liquidators.—For the purpose of conducting the proceedings in winding-up a company, and performing such duties in reference thereto as the Court may impose, the Court may appoint a liquidator or liquidators. If more persons than one are appointed the Court declares whether any act required or authorised to be done by the official liquidator is to be done by all or any one or more of such persons. It is in the discretion of the Court to appoint a provisional liquidator before making an order for the winding-up of the company.[2]

Powers of Liquidator.—Different statutory regulations apply in the case of companies registered in England and in the case of companies registered in Scotland or Ireland.[3] Under the Act of 1929 the powers of a liquidator of a company the registered office of which is situate in Scotland may be thus summarised. For the purpose of conducting the proceedings and performing such duties in reference thereto as the Court may impose, the Court may appoint a liquidator or liquidators.[4] A provisional liquidator may be appointed at any time after the presentation of a winding-up petition [2] and may be made at any time before the first appointment of liquidators. The Court may determine whether any and what security is to be given by a liquidator on his appointment.[5] The liquidator is to be described as " the official liquidator " and not by his individual name. A liquidator appointed by the Court may resign or, on cause shown, be removed by the Court.[6] If, and so long as, there is no liquidator all the property of the company is deemed to be in the custody of the Court.[7] The liquidator has power with the sanction either of the Court or the committee of inspection (see *infra*) (a)

---

[1] § 177. [2] § 184. [3] §§ 191 *et seq.* [4] § 183.
[6] § 187. [7] § 188. [8] § 189 (2).

to bring or defend any action or other legal proceeding in the name and on behalf of the company ; (b) to carry on the business of the company so far as may be necessary for the beneficial winding-up thereof. The Court may provide by any order that the liquidator may, where there is no committee of inspection, exercise both or either of the powers just mentioned without the sanction or intervention of the Court ; (c) to appoint a solicitor or law agent to assist him in the performance of his duties ; (d) to pay any classes of creditors in full ; (e) to make any compromise or arrangement with creditors or persons claiming to be creditors ; (f) to compromise all calls and liabilities to calls, debts, etc. The liquidator has the following powers without the sanction of the Court : (a) to sell the heritable and moveable property by public auction or private contract ; (b) to do all acts and to execute on behalf of the company all deeds, receipts, and other documents, and for that purpose to use, when necessary, the company's seal ; (c) to prove, rank and claim in the bankruptcy, insolvency or sequestration of any contributory ; (d) to draw, accept, make and endorse any bill of exchange or promissory note in the name and on behalf of the company ; (e) to raise on the security of the assets of the company any money requisite ; (f) to take out in his official name letters of administration to any deceased contributory and to do in his official name any other act necessary for obtaining payment of any money due from a contributory or his estate ; (g) to appoint an agent to do any business which he is unable to do himself ; and (h) to do all such other acts as may be necessary for winding up the affairs of the company and distributing its assets.[1] The foregoing powers are subject to the control of the Court, and any creditor or contributory may apply to the Court with respect to any exercise or proposed exercise

[1] § 191.

of any of those powers. In Scotland a liquidator
has, subject to general rules, the same powers as a
trustee on a bankrupt estate.[1]

Committee of Inspection.—Where a winding-up
order has been made by the Court in Scotland, the
liquidator must summon separate meetings of
the creditors and contributories of the company
for the purpose of determining whether or not an
application is to be made to the Court for the
appointment of a committee of inspection to act
with the liquidator and who are to be the members
of the committee if appointed. Where, however,
the winding-up order has been made on the
ground that the company is unable to pay its debts
it is not necessary for the liquidator to summon
a meeting of the contributories. If there is a
difference between the determinations of the
meetings of the creditors and contributories the
Court decides the difference and makes such order
as the Court may think fit.[2] A committee of
inspection appointed in pursuance of the Act must
consist of creditors and contributories of the company, or persons holding general powers of attorney
from creditors or contributories, in such proportions
as may be agreed on by the meetings of creditors
and contributories, or as, in case of difference, may
be determined by the Court.[3] Where in Scotland
a winding-up order has been made on the ground
that a company is unable to pay its debts, the
committee must consist of creditors or persons
holding general powers of attorney from creditors.
The committee must meet at such times as they
from time to time appoint and, failing such appointment, at least once a month. The liquidator or
any member of the committee may call a meeting
of the committee as and when he thinks necessary.[4] The committee of inspection shall, in
addition to the powers and duties imposed on it by
the Act, have such of the powers and duties of

§ 191.   [2] § 198.   [3] § 199.   [4] § 199 (2).

commissioners on a bankrupt estate as may be conferred and imposed on committees of inspection by general rules.[1]

Settlement of List of Contributories and Application of Assets.—As soon as may be after making a winding-up order the Court must settle a list of contributories, with power to rectify the register of members in all cases where rectification is required in pursuance of the Act, and cause the assets of the company to be collected and applied in discharge of its liabilities.[2] In certain cases the settlement of a list of contributories may be dispensed with.

Every present and past member is bound to contribute towards payment of the debts and winding-up expenses of the company to an amount not exceeding the amount (if any) unpaid on the shares in respect of which he is liable. But a past member is not liable to contribute (a) if he has ceased to be a member for a year or upwards before the commencement of the winding-up ; (b) in respect of any debt of the company contracted after he ceased to be a member ; or (c) unless it appears to the Court that the existing members are unable to satisfy the contributions required to be made by them.[3] The contributories' liability is enforced by calls.

(ii.) **Voluntary Winding-up.**—The Act of 1929 provides for two kinds of voluntary winding-up : (1) " A members' voluntary winding-up " ; and (2) " A creditors' voluntary winding-up." Where it is proposed to wind up a company voluntarily, the directors of the company or, in the case of a company having more than two directors, the majority of the directors may, at a meeting of the directors held before the date on which the notices of the meeting at which the resolution for the winding-up of the company is to be proposed are sent out, make a statutory declaration to the effect that they have made a full enquiry into the affairs of the company and that having so done they have formed the

[1] § 201.　　　　[2] § 203.　　　　[3] § 157.

opinion that the company will be able to pay its debts in full within a period not exceeding twelve months from the commencement of the winding-up. A winding-up following on such a declaration, which must be delivered to the registrar of companies for registration, is termed " a members' voluntary winding-up." Where no such declaration is made and registered, the winding-up is referred to as " a creditors' voluntary winding-up." Different provisions apply in relation to these respective modes of liquidation.[1] A company may be wound up voluntarily (1) when the period (if any) fixed for the duration of the company by the Articles expires, or the event (if any) occurs, on the occurrence of which the Articles provide that the company is to be dissolved, and the company in general meeting has passed a resolution requiring the company to be wound up voluntarily ; (2) if the company resolves by special resolution that the company be wound up voluntarily ; (3) if the company resolves by extraordinary resolution to the effect that it cannot by reason of its liabilities continue its business, and that it is advisable to wind up.[2] A voluntary winding-up is deemed to commence at the time of the passing of the resolution authorising the winding-up.[3] When a company is wound up voluntarily, the company from the commencement of the winding-up ceases to carry on its business, except so far as may be required for the beneficial winding-up thereof.[4]

Consequences of Voluntary Winding-up.—The following consequences among others ensue on the voluntary winding-up of a company[5] : (1) the assets of the company when realised are applied in satisfaction of the liabilities of the company, subject to such preferable rights as affect the same, the surplus being distributed among the members according to their rights and interests in the company ; (2) the company in general meeting appoint

[1] § 230 et seq.   [2] § 225.   [3] § 227.   [4] § 228.   [5] § 228 et seq.

one or more liquidators and fixes the remuneration to be paid ; (3) the liquidator may, without the sanction of the Court, exercise certain powers given to the liquidator in a winding-up by the Court [1] ; (4) if there is no liquidator acting, the Court may, on the application of a contributory, appoint a liquidator ; (5) the Court may, on cause shown, remove a liquidator and appoint another liquidator.[2] The voluntary winding-up of a company does not bar the right of any creditor or contributory to have it wound up by the Court if the Court is of opinion, in the case of an application by a creditor, that the rights of the creditor, or, in the case of an application by a contributory, that the rights of the contributories will be prejudiced by a voluntary winding-up.[3]

(iii.) **Winding-up subject to Supervision of Court.**—When a company has passed a resolution for voluntary winding-up, the Court may make an order that the voluntary winding-up shall continue, but subject to such supervision of the Court, and with such liberty for creditors, contributories, or others to apply to the Court, and generally on such terms and conditions as the Court thinks just.[4]

    Effect of Supervision Order.—Where an order is made for a winding-up subject to supervision, the liquidator may, subject to any restrictions imposed by the Court, exercise all his powers, without the sanction or intervention of the Court, in the same manner as if the company were being wound up altogether voluntarily.[5]

(b) **Ranking of Claims in Scotland.**—In the winding-up of a company registered in Scotland, the general and special rules in regard to voting and ranking for payment of dividends provided in the Bankruptcy Act, so far as is consistent with the Act, apply in relation to the winding-up, and ranking for payment of dividends [6] ; and for this purpose sequestration is taken to mean winding-up, trustee to mean liquidator, and Sheriff to mean the Court.

[1] § 248.   [2] § 249.   [3] § 255.   [4] § 256.   [5] § 260.   [6] § 263.

2. Companies Limited by Guarantee.—A company limited by guarantee is one having the liability of its members limited by the Memorandum to such amount as the members may respectively thereby undertake to contribute to the assets of the company in the event of its being wound up.[1] This form of incorporation is usually adopted by clubs or associations not requiring the capital or the interests of the members to be expressed in cash terms. There is nothing impracticable or incompetent in its adoption by trading or other companies. Companies limited by guarantee may or may not have a capital divided into shares. Such companies must have a Memorandum and Articles of Association.[2] Where there is no share capital, the Memorandum must give the like particulars as in the case of companies limited by shares as to name, registered office, objects, and limited liability, and the Memorandum must also state that each member undertakes to contribute to the assets of the company, in the event of its being wound up while he is a member, or within one year afterwards, for payment of the debts and liabilities of the company contracted before he ceases to be a member, and of the costs, charges, and expenses of winding-up, and for adjustment of the rights of the contributories among themselves, such amounts as may be required, not exceeding a specified amount. Where the company has a share capital, the Memorandum must also state the amount of share capital with which the company proposes to be registered, and the division thereof into shares of a fixed amount. As in the case of a company limited by shares, at least seven members must sign the Memorandum, but a guarantee company may be a private company.

3. Unlimited Companies.—Such companies are seldom now incorporated. The shareholders of such companies are liable, according to their interest in the company, to pay all the debts and fulfil all the obligations of the concern. Unlike a company limited by shares, the Memorandum must be accompanied by Articles of Association.[3] The Memorandum must state (1) the name of the company ; (2) the part of the United Kingdom in which the registered office is to be situate ; and (3) the objects of the company. Such companies may have a share capital, and when this is so the capital requires to be stated in the Articles, but not in the Memorandum. If the company has not a capital divided into shares, the Articles must state the number of members with which the company proposes to be registered. This is done to enable the registrar to determine the fees payable

[1] § 1 (b).   [2] Table C.   [3] § 6.

on registration. A company with unlimited liability may be subsequently registered with limited liability.

4. Private Companies.—Any two or more persons may form a private limited company.[1] The incorporation of such companies has been extensively availed of. A private company means a company which, by its articles, (a) restricts the right to transfer its shares ; (b) limits the number of its members (exclusive of persons who are in the employment of the company) to fifty ; and (c) prohibits any invitation to the public to subscribe for any shares or debentures of the company.[2] In such companies it is usual to insert in the Articles of Association a power to the directors to decline to register any transfer of shares or stock to a transferee of whom they do not approve, and they are not bound to assign any reason for such refusal. It is usual not to adopt Table A, as that table does not contain certain of the provisions applicable to a private company, hence it is usual for Articles of Association to be printed along with the Memorandum. In the general working out of such companies there is no distinction made between them and ordinary limited companies. They are not compelled to make certain of the returns required from other companies, and the following are certain of the privileges to which they are entitled : (1) They do not require to include a balance-sheet in their annual summary.[3] (2) They do not require to file a report before the statutory meeting nor send a copy to the members.[3] (3) They do not require to issue a statement in lieu of prospectus.[4] (4) They may commence business immediately on incorporation, and they are not bound to obtain a certificate entitling them to commence business.[5] (5) There is no minimum restriction upon any allotment.[6] A private company may subsequently be turned into a public company. If at any time the number of members is reduced below two, and the company carries on business for more than six months thereafter, the remaining member is personally liable for the whole of the debts contracted during that period.[7]

5. Companies Formed for Purposes not of Gain.—If a company about to be formed proves to the Board of Trade that it is formed for the purpose of promoting commerce, art, science, religion, charity, or any other useful object, and intends to apply its profits (if any) or other income in promoting its objects, and to prohibit the payment of any dividend to its members, the Board may by licence direct that

---

[1] § 1.　　　　[2] § 26.　　　　[3] § 113 (10).　　　　[4] § 40.
[5] § 94.　　　　[6] § 39.　　　　[7] § 28.

the Association be registered as a company with limited liability without the addition of the word " Limited " to its name, and the association may be registered accordingly.[1] Such associations, on registration, enjoy all the privileges of limited companies, and are subject to all their obligations. They do not require to publish their names or send lists of members to the registrar of companies. Such associations cannot, without the licence of the Board of Trade, hold more than two acres of land.[2]

6. Foreign Companies.—A company, although registered abroad, may, nevertheless, carry on business in this country. Stringent regulations have been enacted to protect traders in this country, and these may be summarised as follows.[3] Every company incorporated outside the United Kingdom which establishes a place of business within the United Kingdom must, within one month from the establishment of the place of business, file with the registrar of companies (1) a certified copy of the instrument constituting or defining the constitution of the company, and if the instrument is not written in the English language a certified translation thereof ; (2) a list of the directors—which includes any person occupying the position of director by whatever name called—of the company ; and (3) the names and addresses of some one or more persons resident in the United Kingdom authorised to accept on behalf of the company service of process and any notices required to be served on the company. In the event of any alteration being made in any such instrument, or in the directors, or in the names and addresses of any such persons as aforesaid, the company must within the prescribed time file with the registrar a notice of the alteration.

Filing of Balance-Sheet.—A foreign company established as above must in every calendar year make out a balance-sheet in such form and containing such particulars and including such documents as under the provisions of the Act it would, if it had been a company registered in this country, have been required to make out and lay before the company in general meeting, and deliver a copy of that balance-sheet to the registrar for registration. If the balance-sheet is not written in the English language there must be annexed to it a certified translation thereof.[4]

Issue of Prospectus.—Every prospectus of such foreign company inviting subscriptions for its shares or debentures in the United

[1] § 18.   [2] § 14.

[3] § 343.   [4] § 347.

Kingdom must state the name of the country in which the company is incorporated.

Name of Company.—Every such foreign company must conspicuously exhibit on every place where it carries on business in the United Kingdom the name of the company and the country in which the company is incorporated. Further, the name of the company and of the country in which it is incorporated must be mentioned in legible characters in all bill-heads and letter-paper, and in all notices, advertisements, and other official publications of the company.

Penalty on Infringement of Statutory Requirements.—If any such foreign company fails to comply with the statutory requirements, the company and every officer or agent of the company is liable to a fine not exceeding fifty pounds, or in the case of a continuing offence, five pounds for every day during which the default continues.

CHAPTER XV

THE LAW OF BANKRUPTCY

Meaning and Objects of Bankruptcy.—The term " Bankruptcy," as used in the law of Scotland, has no fixed technical meaning. It may be used to denote simple insolvency, *i.e.* the condition of inability of a debtor to meet his obligations, whether the inability be absolute in the sense that his liabilities are greater than his assets, or practical, owing to assets being immediately unrealisable. It is also and more correctly used to denote notour bankruptcy, *i.e.* a state of insolvency which has attained publicity, as evidenced by definite statutory indicia, and having definite statutory effects. Most commonly, however, it is used to denote the condition of a debtor's affairs under a public statutory bankruptcy process of sequestration, whereby he is divested of his estate for distribution among his creditors in payment of their claims. Insolvency is, of course, a common element in all conditions to which the term bankruptcy may be applied.

The law of bankruptcy has for its aim the systematic regulation of what is to be done when a man is insolvent, with the view to (1) the protection of the insolvent's estate against his actings to the prejudice of those to whom he is indebted ; (2) the securing in the interests of the insolvent's creditors as a whole that the estate shall be protected against the actions of particular creditors to their benefit and to the prejudice of the others ; (3) an equitable distribution of the estate among the creditors ; and (4) the setting of the bankrupt free from the claims of his creditors so that he may start afresh.

1. Insolvency.—Insolvency is present inability to meet present debts.[1] Thus, under the Sale of Goods Act, 1893, a person is deemed to be insolvent who either has ceased to pay his debts in the ordinary course of business, or cannot pay his debts as they become due, whether he has committed an act of bankruptcy or not, and whether

---

[1] Teenan's Tr. *v.* Teenan, 1886, 13 R. 833.

he has become a notour bankrupt or not.[1] Whenever the state of insolvency emerges the debtor must thereafter act as if he were a trustee or administrator of his estate for the benefit of his creditors, and is no longer free to dispose of it as he thinks best. If he does not so act his estate will be subjected to control by the law in various ways, which may be enumerated as the reduction of gratuitous alienations and fraudulent preferences, the equalisation of diligence and sequestration.

(1) Reduction of Gratuitous Alienations.—With a view to the protection of the insolvent's estate against his actings to the prejudice of his creditors, gratuitous alienations of his estate by the insolvent may be reduced either (a) at common law, or (b) under the Act 1621.

(a) **At Common Law.**—Any gratuitous alienation of his property by a debtor who was insolvent at or because of,[2] and subsequent to the date of making it, to any person, whether that person knew of the debtor's insolvency or not,[3] may be challenged by any onerous creditor, whether posterior or prior,[4] if the alienation was made to the prejudice of lawful creditors. The onus of proof of non-onerosity, and of insolvency, *i.e.* absolute insolvency both at the date of making the alienation and of the challenge, is on the person challenging. He does not require to prove fraudulent intent, for that is presumed from proof of the other circumstances. The kind of alienation struck at is, for example, the voluntary discharge of a debt owing to the insolvent,[5] or a conveyance by a third party direct to a conjunct person, the insolvent paying the price. The challenge would not be good, for example, if the alienation had been for value in money or money's worth,[6] or was in implement of a prior legal obligation,[7] or of an obligation undertaken as the counterpart of another, as in a marriage contract,[8] or of a natural obligation, such as that of a husband or parent to aliment wife or children.

(b) **Under the Act 1621.**—Any gratuitous alienation of his property to conjunct and confident persons by a debtor who was

---

[1] § 62 (3).   [2] Abram Steamship Co. *v.* Abram, 1925, S L.T. 243.
[3] M'Cowan *v.* Wright, 1852, 14 D. 901, 968.
[4] Edmund *v.* Grant, 1853, 15 D. 703 ; Wink *v.* Spiers, 1867, 6 M. 77, per L.J.-C.
[5] Laing *v.* Cheyne, 1832, 10 S. 200.
[6] Renton & Gray's Tr. *v.* Dickison, 1880, 7 R. 951.
[7] Taylor *v.* Jones, 1888, 15 R. 328.   [8] Bell's Comm., ii. 176.

insolvent at the date of granting it, and who is also bankrupt or insolvent at the date of the challenge, may be challenged by a prior onerous creditor or by a trustee in a sequestration whether he represents prior creditors or not,[1] if the deed was granted without true, just, and necessary cause. The challenger must prove that the receiver of the property was conjunct or confident, that the debtor was insolvent at the raising of the action, and that he (the creditor) was an onerous creditor prior to the alienation. Thereupon it is presumed that the alienation was granted without true, just, and necessary cause, i.e. that there was non-onerosity, and that the debtor was insolvent at the date of granting. The onus of rebutting these presumptions lies on the debtor. As under the common law, there is a presumption of fraud. The purpose of the Act 1621 was to facilitate the challenge of gratuitous alienations in prejudice of prior creditors of an insolvent by raising a presumption of insolvency at the date of the gift, and of non-onerosity, where the alienation was to a conjunct and confident person. Only practical insolvency is required. Conjunct persons are those nearly related to the debtor, such as parents, children, brothers, sisters, sons-in-law, uncles, stepsons, and the like. Confident persons are those standing in a confidential relation with the debtor, such as partners in business, servants, and the like.

(2) **Reduction of Fraudulent Preferences.**—With a view to securing that an insolvent's estate shall be protected against the actions of particular creditors to the prejudice of the creditors as a whole, fraudulent preferences acquired by particular creditors may be reduced either (a) at common law, or (b) under the Act 1696.

(a) **At Common Law.**—Every transaction voluntarily [2] entered into by a person in knowledge of his insolvency at the date of the transaction, and who was also insolvent at the date of challenge, whereby a preference was conferred on any creditors, whether in knowledge of the debtor's insolvency or not,[3] to the prejudice of others as being in satisfaction or further security of an existing debt, is reducible at the

---

[1] Galbraith v. British Linen Co., 1898, 36 S.L.R. 139.
[2] Stiven v. Scott, 1871, 9 M. 923, per L.P. Inglis at p. 933.
[3] M'Cowan v. Wright, *supra.*

instance of any other creditor. Fraudulent intent is presumed if it be proved the transaction was voluntary on the part of the debtor during insolvency and in the knowledge of his insolvency. Transactions so challengeable are, for example, the giving of a security to a creditor previously unsecured,[1] or the facilitating of proceedings by the creditor to obtain decree or execute diligence.[2] A trust deed for creditors is not, however, reducible at common law as a fraudulent preference.

The following classes of transactions are not reducible as fraudulent preferences except on proof of fraudulent contrivance between debtor and creditor [3] : (*a*) cash payments of debts actually due,[4] (*b*) *nova debita*,[5] (*c*) transactions in ordinary course of trade, and (*d*) transactions in implement of a prior obligation to grant a specific security.

(*b*) **Under the Act 1696.**—Fraudulent preferences are reducible also under the Act 1696. The statute facilitates a successful challenge by a prejudiced creditor. It provides for the declaring of an insolvent person notour bankrupt upon certain requisites concurring. The constitution of notour or public bankruptcy is now regulated by the Bankruptcy Act, 1913.[6] The differences between the Act of 1696 and the common law are that under the Act if notour bankruptcy be constituted at or before or within sixty days after the preference challenged, there is a presumption of insolvency at the date of the transaction sought to be reduced, and proof of insolvency at the date of the challenge is not required. The challenge under the Act, moreover, can only be at the instance of a prior creditor or trustee in sequestration, and a trust deed for creditors is reducible under the Act.[7]

As at common law, cash payments, *nova debita*, transactions in ordinary course of trade, or in implement of a prior obligation to grant security, are recognised as exceptions to the operation of the statute unless on proof of fraudulent contrivance between debtor and creditor. Thus

---

[1] Miller *v.* Philp & Son, 1883, 20 S.L.R. 862.
[2] Matthew's Tr. *v.* Matthew, 1867, 5 M., per L.P. Inglis at p. 963.
[3] Angus' Trs. *v.* Angus, 1901, 39 S.L.R. 119.
[4] M'Cowan *v.* Wright, 1852, *supra*, per L.J.-C. Hope.
[5] Miller's Tr. *v.* Shield, (1862) 24 D. 821.
[6] See *infra*, p. 291.   [7] Mackenzie *v.* Calder, 6 M. 833.

in the case of *nova debita* if there be security granted for a debt and completed at the date of the transaction, it cannot be reduced whether granted before, at, or after the date of notour bankruptcy. If the security is not so delivered or completed it is valid if its completion within the sixty days prior to notour bankruptcy does not depend upon some voluntary act of the debtor, but only upon some further action of the creditor.[1] The implement by an insolvent of an obligation to grant a specified security, instantly and unconditionally enforceable at date of taking the loan, is also valid.[2] On the other hand, an obligation to grant a specified security at some indeterminate time or on certain conditions,[3] or an obligation to grant an unspecified security,[4] cannot be implemented by the insolvent without risk of challenge under the Act.

(3) **Equalisation of Diligences.**—With a view to the equitable distribution of an insolvent's estate among his creditors the Act 1696 further provides for the reduction of preferences acquired by creditors by doing diligence against the insolvent estate. All diligences effected by creditors of an insolvent who is notour bankrupt, within sixty days prior to the constitution of notour bankruptcy, are in effect cut down and made to rank *pari passu* on the insolvent's estate. It is further provided by the Bankruptcy Act, 1913, that arrestments and poindings used within sixty days prior to notour bankruptcy, or within four months thereafter, rank *pari passu* on the subjects arrested or poinded. Those subsequent thereto rank only on the reversion.

(4) **Notour Bankruptcy.**—Notour bankruptcy commences when its several requisites concur, and continues until the debtor obtains his discharge and his insolvency ceases.[5] The constitution of notour bankruptcy is now regulated by the Bankruptcy Act, 1913.[6] It may be constituted (1) by sequestration, or by the issuing of an adjudication of bankruptcy, or the granting of a receiving order in England or Ireland ; (2) by insolvency concurring (*a*) with a duly executed charge for payment, where a charge is necessary, followed by the expiry of the days of charge without payment ; (*b*) where a charge is unnecessary, that is, where decree is granted against a debtor in a

---

[1] Caledonian Insurance Co. *v.* Beattie, 1898, 5 S.L.T. 349.
[2] Stiven *v.* Scott, 1871, 9 M. 923.   [3] Gourlay *v.* Mackie, 1887, 14 R. 403.
[4] Paterson's Trs. *v.* Paterson's Trs., 1891, 19 R. 91.
[5] Bankruptcy Act, 1913, § 7.   [6] *Ibid.*, § 5.

Small Debt Court when the debtor is personally present, with the lapse without payment of the days which must elapse before poinding or imprisonment can follow on a decree or warrant for payment of a sum of money ; (c) with a poinding or seizure of any of the debtor's moveables for non-payment of rates or taxes ; (d) with a decree of adjudication of any part of the bankrupt's heritable estate for payment or in security ; or (e) with sale of any effects belonging to the debtor under a sequestration for rent.

Notour bankruptcy of a company is constituted in any of the foregoing ways or by any of the partners being rendered notour bankrupt for a company debt. Corporations, public companies, and corporate bodies, whose members are not individually liable for the companies' obligations, can be rendered notour bankrupt in the mode prescribed by § 5 of the Act of 1913. Unincorporated associations cannot be made bankrupt at all, and recourse must be had against the individual members separately.

Apart from the annulling of preferences and the equalisation of diligence, the important effect of notour bankruptcy is that it enables creditors to take proceedings for the sequestration of the estates of a debtor. A debtor may himself take out sequestration although notour bankruptcy has not been constituted against him.

2. Sequestration.—(1) Definition.—Sequestration is a judicial process whereby the estates, of whatever kind and wheresoever situated, of a debtor, whether living or deceased, are transferred to and vested in a trustee for realisation and distribution among the creditors according to their just rights and preferences. The process is applicable to a firm or partnership, but not to a company incorporated by Royal Charter or Act of Parliament or under the Companies Acts. The statute at present regulating sequestration proceedings is the Bankruptcy (Scotland) Act, 1913.

(2) Requisites for Award of Sequestration.—In the Case of a Living Debtor.—The petition for sequestration may be at the instance of (a) the debtor himself, or (b) a duly qualified creditor or creditors. Where the petition is at the instance of the debtor, the only requisites are that the debtor should at the date of the presentation of the petition be subject to the jurisdiction of the Supreme Courts of Scotland and that the petition should be presented with the consent and concurrence of a duly qualified creditor or creditors. The debtor need not be notour bankrupt. The effect of the sequestration is to create notour bankruptcy. Where the petition is at the instance of a duly qualified creditor or creditors, the following are the requisites : (1) The debtor must be notour bankrupt ; (2) he must within a year before the date of the presentation of the petition have resided or had a dwelling-house or place of business in Scotland [1] ; (3) he must be subject to the jurisdiction of the Supreme Courts of Scotland ; (4) the petition is only competent within four months of the date of the debtor's notour bankruptcy.[2] Notour bankruptcy may, however, be constituted any number of times.

In the Case of a Deceased Debtor.—The deceased debtor must at the date of his death have been subject to the jurisdiction of the Supreme Courts of Scotland. The petition may be at the instance of a mandatary to whom he had granted a mandate to apply for sequestration, or on the petition of a duly qualified creditor or creditors. Where the petition is at the instance of a creditor, it may be presented at any time after the date of the debtor's death, but no sequestration can be awarded until the expiration of six months from the debtor's death unless he was at the time of his death notour bankrupt, or unless his successors concur in a petition or renounce the succession, in which several cases sequestration can be awarded forthwith. Where the petition is at the instance of a mandatary no concurrence of creditors is necessary, nor is notour bankruptcy requisite.

(3) Effect of Award of Sequestration.—The effect of the award is to vest in the trustee under the sequestration all estate whatever belonging to the bankrupt and attachable for debt, whether heritable or moveable, real or personal. As regards the heritable property, it is equivalent to a decree of adjudication, which means that the estate is vested in the trustee for behoof of the general body of creditors, subject only to such preferable rights as affect it.[3] As regards the moveable estate, the sequestration is equivalent to an arrestment in execution and decree of furthcoming and to an executed or completed poinding, which means that his whole moveable estate must be given over to the trustee to be disposed of by him subject to any legal preferences which may then attach to it.

The trustee is said to take a vested right in the estate of the bankrupt *tantum et tale*, *i.e.* such and of such a kind, exactly as the bankrupt had it. This will include estate situated in England or Ireland. Moreover, it will include *acquirenda*, *i.e.* all property acquired by the bankrupt prior to his discharge, non-vested contingent

---

[1] Bankruptcy (Scotland) Act, 1913, § 11.
[2] *Ibid.*, § 13.   [3] *Ibid.*, § 103.

rights of succession or interests in property, alimentary provisions in favour of the bankrupt in so far as in excess of an aliment suitable in his existing circumstances, and a portion of any salary, pension, or other emolument of which the bankrupt may be in enjoyment, and, generally, rights of action which the bankrupt has, *e.g.* actions of damages for personal injury. Further, the trustee has the right to adopt any contracts to which the bankrupt is a party, provided the element of *delectus personae* [1] is not present to prevent him. The trustee's title will not, however, suffice to vest in him property held by the bankrupt in trust,[2] nor property fraudulently in possession of the bankrupt. Necessary wearing apparel of the bankrupt, his wife, and family are also excepted, and working tools or implements of the bankrupt, necessary to enable him to earn a livelihood, do not vest in the trustee, these not being attachable for debt.

Concourse of Debit and Credit.—The concourse of debit and credit between the bankrupt and his creditors takes place as at the date of sequestration. The sequestration stops the running of interest on unsecured claims. Accordingly, where a creditor is entitled to interest either by contract or by law, *e.g.* in the case of a bill past due or other like obligation, he is entitled to interest at the agreed-on rate or, where no rate is fixed, at 5 per cent. from the due date of the payment of the obligation up to the date of sequestration. Where the payment is not due until after the sequestration, as, for instance, in the case of a bill current at the date of sequestration, the creditor must deduct from the amount of his claim interest at 5 per cent. from the date of sequestration to the due date of payment and rank for the balance. Where, however, the creditor holds a security for payment of his debt, he is entitled to hold that for payment of his full debt and interest up to the date of payment. Similarly, when the creditor holds the obligation of a third party for payment of his debt, he is entitled as against that third party to interest up to the date of payment.

(4) The Award.—*(a)* **Jurisdiction.**—Sequestration may be awarded by the Court of Session or by the Sheriff of the county in which the debtor, if alive, has resided or carried on business for the year preceding the date of the petition, and, if deceased, has resided or carried on business for the year preceding his death.[3] In all cases the pro-

---

[1] See Assignation of Contracts, *supra*, p. 46.

[2] M'Adam *v.* Martin's Tr., 11 M. 33 ; Heritable Reversionary Co. *v.* Millar, 1892, 19 R. (H.L.) 43.

[3] Bankruptcy (Scotland) Act, 1913, § 16.

ceedings begin by petition to the appropriate tribunal. If sequestration is awarded by the Court of Session the subsequent proceedings are in the Sheriff Court.

(b) **Qualification of Petitioning Creditors.**—Petitions for sequestration may be at the instance or with the concurrence of any one or more creditors whose debt or debts together amount to not less than fifty pounds, whether such debts are liquid or illiquid, provided they are not contingent.[1]

(c) **Interim Preservation of Estate.**—It is competent for the Court to which a petition for sequestration has been presented, whether sequestration can forthwith be awarded or not, to take immediate measures for the preservation of the estate.[2] This is usually done by the appointment of a judicial factor who holds office until the trustee is elected by the creditors.

(d) **First Meeting of Creditors.**—**Election of Trustee.**—In the deliverance awarding sequestration the Court appoints a meeting of the creditors to be held at a specified time and place for the election of a trustee, or trustees in succession. At this meeting the creditors or their mandataries make the election. The person who is elected must have a majority in value, even though a minority in number, of the creditors supporting him. The reason for this is that the control of the administration of the estate is given to the persons having the largest interest therein. In order to entitle a creditor to vote at this meeting it is necessary for him or a mandatary on his behalf to attend the meeting and produce an affidavit and claim duly sworn to before a Judge Ordinary, Magistrate, or Justice of the Peace as to the verity of the debt, and produce the vouchers instructing the claim. Where a creditor holds a security over any part of the debtor's estate, he must in his claim put a specified value on his security, deduct the same from his claim, and vote only in respect of the balance. To prevent the undervaluing of securities the trustee has power,[3] with the consent of the commissioners, within two months after the oath has been made use of in any meeting, or for the majority of creditors, excluding the creditor making the oath, assembled at any meeting and during such meeting, to require from the creditor a conveyance or assignation in favour of the trustee of such security on payment of the value specified by the creditor with 20 per centum in addition to such value, and the creditor is bound to grant such conveyance or assignation at the expense of the estate. To entitle a mandatary to vote he must

---

[1] Bankruptcy (Scotland) Act, 1913, § 12.   [2] Ibid., § 14.   [3] Ibid., § 58.

produce a duly signed mandate by the creditor authorising him to do so.[1] Before the trustee enters upon the duties of his office he must find caution for the due performance of the duties of his office, the amount of which is fixed by the creditors at the meeting for the election, and they also then decide on the sufficiency of the caution offered.

The Bankrupt's State of his Affairs.—The bankrupt is required at the meeting for the election of a trustee to deliver to the clerk of the meeting a state of his affairs specifying his whole property wherever situated, property in expectancy or to which he may have an eventual right, the names and designations of his creditors and debtors, the debts due by and to him, and a rental of his heritable property.[2] He is guilty of a punishable crime and offence if he does not fully and truly disclose the state of his affairs or does not deliver up to the trustee his property and documents [3] or otherwise fraudulently prevents his whole estate being made forthcoming for the purposes of the sequestration.

Election of Commissioners.—At the meeting for the election of the trustee, the creditors or their mandataries present elect three commissioners (if there be so many creditors who have claimed).[4] Commissioners do not require to find caution. The duties of the commissioners are : (1) to superintend the proceedings of the trustee, (2) to concur with him in submissions and transactions, (3) to give their advice and assistance relative to the management of the estate, (4) to decide as to paying or postponing payment of a dividend, (5) to assemble at any time to ascertain the situation of the bankrupt estate,[5] and (6) to fix the commission or fee payable to the trustee.[6] Any one of the commissioners may make such report as he thinks proper to a general meeting of creditors. While a creditor is entitled to purchase any part of the bankrupt estate which is publicly sold, a commissioner is precluded from doing so.

(5) Duties of the Trustee.—Confirmation of Appointment.—On being elected the trustee lodges with the Sheriff-Clerk a bond of caution for the due performance of his office, signed by him and a cautioner, for the amount of security fixed by the creditors at the first meeting. On this being done the Sheriff confirms the election, and the Sheriff-Clerk issues an Act and Warrant of Confirmation, which is the trustee's authority to act. A copy is immediately transmitted to the Accountant of Court, who makes an entry of the name and designation of the trustee in the Register of Sequestrations.

---

[1] Bankruptcy (Scotland) Act, 1913, § 59. [2] *Ibid.*, § 77.
[3] *Ibid.*, § 178. [4] *Ibid.*, § 72. [5] *Ibid.*, § 81. [6] *Ibid.*, § 121.

Taking Possession of the Estate.—As soon as may be after his appointment it is the duty of the trustee to take possession of the bankrupt's estate and effects and of his title-deeds, books, bills, vouchers, and other papers and documents.[1] The trustee is required to manage, realise, and recover the estate belonging to the bankrupt wherever situated, and convert the same into money according to the directions given by the creditors at any meeting, and if no such directions are given, he must do so with the advice of the commissioners.[2]

Deposit of Money in Bank.—It is the duty of the trustee to lodge all money received by him in bank,[2] and it must be so lodged in his official character. If the trustee keeps in his hands any sum exceeding £50 belonging to the estate for more than ten days, he must pay interest to the creditors at the rate of 20 per cent. per annum on the excess of such sum above £50 for such time as the same is in his hands beyond ten days. Unless the money has been so kept from innocent causes, the trustee may be dismissed from office upon petition to the Lord Ordinary or Sheriff by any creditor, will have no claim to remuneration, and will be liable in expenses.[3]

Examination of Bankrupt.—One of the first duties of a trustee is to present a petition to the Sheriff for the examination of the bankrupt. The petition must be presented within eight days after the date of the Act and Warrant confirming him. The bankrupt is bound to attend such examination. The object of the bankrupt's examination is to ascertain what his estate consists of, where it is, and what he has done with it or to affect it.[4] Questions directed to the investigation of the merits of a particular creditor's claims are incompetent. With the sanction of the Sheriff, any creditor or his mandatary may attend and put questions. The Sheriff may at any time on the application of the trustee order an examination of the bankrupt's wife and family, clerks, servants, factors, law agents, and others who can give information relative to his estate, on oath, and issue his warrant requiring such persons to appear.[5]

(6) Winding-up under Arrangement.—Instead of the trustee proceeding with the realisation of the debtor's estate, the creditors may arrange that the estate be wound up under a deed of arrangement, or they may accept a composition on their claims and reinstate the bankrupt in possession of his estate.

---

[1] Bankruptcy (Scotland) Act, 1913, § 76. [2] *Ibid.*, § 78.
[3] *Ibid.*, § 79. [4] Delvoitte & Co. *v.* Baillie's Trs., 1877, 5 R. 143.
[5] Bankruptcy (Scotland) Act, 1913, § 86.

Under Deed of Arrangement.—At the meeting for the election of the trustee, or at any subsequent meeting to be called for the purpose, a majority in number and three-fourths in value of the creditors present or represented at such meeting may resolve. that the estate be wound up under a deed of arrangement, and that an application should be made to the Lord Ordinary or the Sheriff to sist procedure in the sequestration for a period not exceeding two months. If such a resolution is carried, it is not necessary to elect a trustee.[1] The bankrupt or any person appointed by the meeting reports the resolution to the Lord Ordinary or the Sheriff within four days, and applies for a sist of the proceedings. The application is usually granted. If at any time within the period of sist the creditors produce to the Lord Ordinary or the Sheriff a deed of arrangement subscribed by or by authority of a majority in number and three-fourths in value of the creditors, the Lord Ordinary or the Sheriff, after such intimation as he thinks proper and hearing any parties having interest, may approve thereof and declare the sequestration at an end. The deed is thereafter as binding on all the creditors as if they had acceded to it. The sequestration receives full effect in so far as is necessary for the purpose of preventing, challenging, or setting aside preferences over the estate. The Act contains no provision as to the requisites or form of a deed of arrangement, the creditors and the bankrupt being left to arrange the terms of the deed as they choose.

Under Composition Contract.—At the meeting for the election of trustee, the bankrupt or his friends, or in the case of his decease his successors, and in case of a company, one or more of the partners thereof, may offer a composition to the creditors on the whole debts with security for the payment thereof. If a majority of the creditors in number and three-fourths in value present at such meeting resolve that the offer and security should be entertained for consideration, the trustee is forthwith required to advertise in the *Edinburgh Gazette* a notice that an offer has been so made and entertained, and that it will be decided upon at a meeting to be held after the examination of the bankrupt. The meeting requires to be intimated to all the creditors, and the notice must specify the offer and security proposed and give an abstract of the state of the affairs and of the valuation of the estate so far as the same can be done to enable the creditors to judge of such offer and security. If the offer is subsequently accepted by a majority in number and three-fourths in value of the

---

[1] Bankruptcy (Scotland) Act, 1913, § 34.

creditors assembled at the meeting, a bond of caution for payment of the composition must forthwith be lodged in the hands of the trustee. The resolution is then reported to the Lord Ordinary or the Sheriff (whichever may be selected by the trustee), and if he find that the offer with the security has been duly made and is reasonable, he pronounces a deliverance approving thereof. When the composition has been approved of, the bankrupt or, if deceased, his successors or other party offering the composition, must make a declaration that he has made a full and fair surrender of the estate and has not granted or promised any preference or security, or made or promised any payment, or entered into any secret or collusive agreement or transaction to obtain the concurrence of any creditor to such offer and security. The Lord Ordinary, or the Sheriff, as the case may be, on being satisfied with such oath or declaration, must pronounce a deliverance discharging the bankrupt of all debts and obligations contracted by him or for which he was liable at the date of sequestration, and must declare the sequestration to be at an end and the bankrupt reinvested in his estate, reserving always the claims of the creditors for the said composition against him and the cautioner. Before the deliverance is pronounced the commissioners must audit the accounts of the trustee, ascertain the balance due to or by him, and fix his remuneration. The expenses attending the sequestration and the remuneration must be paid or provided for to the satisfaction of the trustee and commissioners before the deliverance is pronounced. If the composition is not paid, the original claim of a creditor does not revive. He is thereafter only a creditor of the bankrupt and his cautioner for the amount of the agreed-on composition.

An offer of composition may also be made at any subsequent meeting after the bankrupt's examination, called for the purpose by the trustee with the consent of the commissioners.[1]

(7) Division of the Estate.—(*a*) **Payment of Dividends.**—The whole estate of a bankrupt when reduced into money, and after paying all necessary charges and a commission to the trustee, is divided among those who were creditors of the bankrupt at the date of the sequestration, ranked according to their several rights and interests.[2]

Time of Payment.—The first dividend should be paid, unless the same be accelerated, on the expiry of six months from the date of the deliverance actually awarding sequestration [3]; the second dividend on the expiry of ten months from the date of the deliverance actually

---

[1] Bankruptcy (Scotland) Act, 1913, § 136.   [2] *Ibid.*, § 117.   [3] *Ibid.*, § 126.

awarding sequestration [1] ; and subsequent dividends on expiration of every three months from the date of payment of the immediately preceding dividend until the whole funds are divided.[2] The trustee and commissioners, with the consent of the Accountant of Court, may accelerate the payment of any dividend if that is found expedient, provided that the date for payment of the first dividend is not earlier than four months from the date of the deliverance actually awarding sequestration.[3]

(*b*) **Ranking of Claims.**—All claims for ranking should be lodged within four months from the date of the deliverance actually awarding sequestration, if to participate in the first dividend. If a creditor does not produce his claim in time to be ranked for the first dividend, he may do so for a second or subsequent dividend, and is then entitled to an equalising dividend along with the new dividend. The claim of a creditor must be duly vouched. He must produce an affidavit and claim duly sworn to by him in like manner as a claim for voting,[4] and produce the necessary vouchers instructing his claim. He must specify what security he holds over the debtor's estates, and whether there are any persons bound to him with, or liable in relief to, the bankrupt. The creditor must value the security held by him, deduct such value from his claim, and rank only in respect of the balance.[5] The trustee, with the consent of the commissioners, is entitled to a conveyance or assignation of the security at the expense of the estate on payment of the value so specified without any addition or to reserve to such creditor the full benefit of his security. The security requiring to be deducted is only such security as but for the creditors' rights would go to increase the general estate available for distribution among the creditors. Consequently where the security subjects have been conveyed by a third person, while the security requires to be specified, the value thereof does not require to be deducted.[5]

Double Ranking of Claims.—It is a general principle of bankruptcy law that the same claim cannot be ranked for twice on a bankrupt estate. Accordingly if a creditor holds a guarantee for payment of his debt, both the creditor and the guarantor cannot rank for payment. If the guarantor pay the debt due to the creditor he is entitled to obtain an assignation from the creditor to the claim and to draw a dividend in respect of it.[6]

---

[1] Bankruptcy (Scotland) Act, 1913, § 128.

[2] *Ibid.*, § 129.　　　　　[3] *Ibid.*, § 130.　　　　　[4] See *supra*, p. 295.

[5] Bankruptcy (Scotland) Act, 1913, § 61.　　　　　[6] *Ibid.*, § 52.

Claims depending on Contingency.—When the claim of a creditor depends upon a contingency which is unascertained at the date of the lodging of his claim, he cannot vote or draw a dividend until it is valued. If the valuation requires to be made before the trustee is elected it is the Sheriff who makes the valuation. After the trustee is elected it is the trustee who does it.[1]

Valuation of Claim to an Annuity.—No creditor in respect of an annuity granted by the bankrupt is entitled to vote or draw a dividend until such annuity is valued. If the valuation requires to be made before the trustee is elected it is the Sheriff who does so, and after election it is the trustee.[2]

Claims against Firms and Partners.—Where a firm consisting of two or more partners is sequestrated, and the estates of the individual partners are also sequestrated, the ranking is as follows. The creditors on the estates of the firm are ranked upon the assets of the firm to the exclusion of the private creditors of the individual partners of the firm. The individual partners of the firm being liable for the whole debts of the firm, the trade creditors are entitled to be ranked on the private estates of the partners, after deduction from the amount of their claim of the estimated dividend to be received from the firm's estate, along with the private creditors of the partners on the individual estates.[3] Where a trader carries on business under a firm name and is the sole partner, no distinction is made between the trade and the private creditors. They all rank equally on the fund available for division.

Preferable Payments.—In the division of a bankrupt's estate the following are paid in priority to all other debts : (1) the remuneration of the trustees and the law agent's account ; (2) deathbed and funeral expenses in the case of a deceased debtor's estates, and thereafter the following : (*a*) all poor or other local rates due by the bankrupt at the date of his sequestration in the case of a living debtor, or the date of death of a deceased debtor, which became due and payable within twelve months before that date ; (*b*) all assessed taxes, land tax, property or income tax assessed on the bankrupt up to the 5th of April next before said date and not exceeding one year's assessment ; (*c*) wages or salary of any clerk or servants during the four months before the said date, not exceeding £50 to any one clerk or servant ; (*d*) wages of workmen or labourers, not exceeding £25 to any one workman or labourer ; (*e*) all sums, not exceeding in any one individual case £100, due in respect of compensation under the Workmen's

[1] Bankruptcy (Scotland) Act, 1913, § 49.   [2] *Ibid.*, § 50.   [3] *Ibid.*, § 62.

Compensation Act, 1906, the liability whereof accrued before the said date ; (ƒ) contributions under the National Insurance Act, 1911, payable by the bankrupt in respect of employed contributors or workmen in an insured trade during the four months before the said date. The foregoing debts rank equally and should be paid in full unless the assets are insufficient to meet them, in which case they abate in equal proportions.[1]

(c) **Application of Salary, etc., of Bankrupt for Benefit of Creditors.** —In certain circumstances specified in the Act the Lord Ordinary or the Sheriff may order a portion of the pay, half-pay, salary, emolument, or pension of the bankrupt to be paid to the trustee in order that the same may be applied in payment of the debts of the bankrupt until an order to the contrary effect is made.[2]

(8) **Undischarged Bankrupt.—Disclosure.**—Where an undischarged bankrupt obtains credit to the extent of ten pounds or upwards from any person without informing such person that he is an undischarged bankrupt, he is guilty of a crime and offence, and is liable on conviction to be imprisoned for certain periods specified.[3]

(9) **Discharge of Bankrupt.**—A bankrupt is not entitled at any time to be discharged of his debts unless it is proved to the Lord Ordinary or the Sheriff, to whom application must be made, that one of the following conditions has been fulfilled, namely, (a) that a dividend or composition of not less than five shillings in the pound has been paid out of the estate of the bankrupt, or that security for the payment thereof has been found to the satisfaction of the creditors, or (b) that failure to pay five shillings in the pound has arisen from circumstances for which the bankrupt cannot justly be held responsible.[4] The petition cannot be presented until the trustee has prepared a report, which must be produced along with the petition, with regard to the conduct of the bankrupt, stating how far he has complied with the provisions of the Act and in particular whether he has made a fair discovery and surrender of his estate, whether he has attended the diets of examinations, been guilty of any collusion, and whether his bankruptcy has arisen from innocent misfortune or losses in business or from culpable or undue conduct.

When Discharge Competent.—The bankrupt can apply for his discharge (a) at any time after the time appointed for the second meeting of creditors, provided every creditor who has produced his

---

[1] Bankruptcy (Scotland) Act, 1913, § 118.   [2] Ibid., § 148.
[3] Ibid., § 182.   [4] Ibid., § 146.

oath concurs in the petition ; (b) on the expiration of six months from the date of sequestration, provided a majority in number and four-fifths in value of the creditors who have produced oaths concur in the petition ; (c) on the expiration of twelve months, provided a majority in number and two-thirds in value of the creditors concur in the petition ; (d) on the expiration of eighteen months, provided a majority in number and value concur in the petition, and (e) on the expiration of two years without any consents of creditors. It is competent for any creditor to appear in the application proceedings and oppose the same.[1] Where the application is opposed either by the creditors or the trustee, the Lord Ordinary or the Sheriff judges of the objections and either finds the bankrupt entitled to his discharge, refuses the discharge, or defers consideration of the same for such period as he thinks proper, and may annex such conditions thereto as the justice of the case requires. Although the application may not be opposed, it is competent for the Lord Ordinary or the Sheriff to refuse the application if it appear from the report of the accountant or other sufficient evidence that the bankrupt has fraudulently concealed any part of his estate or effects or has wilfully failed to comply with any of the provisions of the Act.[2]

Effect of Discharge.—Although the bankrupt may be discharged, the sequestration may go on until the whole assets falling under the sequestration have been realised. The discharge does not reinvest the bankrupt in his estate,[3] but it operates as a complete discharge and acquittance to the bankrupt, and no claim can thereafter be made against him in respect of any debt that might have been ranked for in the sequestration. But it does not release him from any obligation incurred by him subsequent to the date of sequestration.

The discharge does not relieve the bankrupt of any debt due to His Majesty, nor any debt or penalty with which he stands charged at the suit of the Crown or any person for any offence committed against any Act or Acts relative to any branch of the public revenue, or at the suit of any Sheriff or other public officer upon any bail bond entered into for the appearance of any person prosecuted for any such offence unless the Treasury consent to such discharge.[4]

Penalties for the Granting or Receiving any Preference in Facilitating Discharge of the Bankrupt.—The Act contains very stringent

[1] Bankruptcy (Scotland) Act, 1913, § 143.
[2] *Ibid.*, § 149.
[3] Buchanan *v.* M'Culloch, 1865, 4 M. 135.
[4] Bankruptcy (Scotland) Act, 1913, § 147.

provisions against the giving or taking of any illegal preference or payment of whatever kind for facilitating or obtaining the bankrupt's discharge. The provisions were passed in the interests of commercial morality, and they are enforced without any attempt to mitigate their severity. When once the offence has been committed the Court has no power to remit or mitigate any portion of the penalty.[1] The offences struck at are all preferences, gratuities, securities, payments, or other consideration not sanctioned by the Act, granted, made, or promised, and all secret or collusive agreements and transactions for concurring in facilitating or obtaining the bankrupt's discharge either on or without an offer of composition and whether the offer be accepted or not or the discharge granted or not.[2] The penalties on the creditor are that he loses his dividend and must pay to the trustee double the amount of the preference given or promised, and the same is distributed among the other creditors in the sequestration. If the bankrupt has been concerned in or cognisant of the granting of the preference, he forfeits all benefits under the Act, and if his discharge have already been granted it may be annulled.

(10) Discharge of Trustee.—After a final division of the funds the trustee calls a meeting of the creditors by an advertisement in the *Edinburgh Gazette* and by letter posted to every creditor who has produced an oath in the sequestration to consider as to an application for his discharge. At this meeting he lays before the creditors the sederunt book and accounts with a list of unclaimed dividends. The creditors then declare their opinion of his conduct as trustee. The trustee may thereafter apply to the Lord Ordinary or the Sheriff, who may, after hearing any creditor who appears to object, pronounce or refuse decree of exoneration.

Unclaimed Dividends.—Before his discharge the trustee must deposit any unclaimed dividends and any unapplied balances in bank. The deposit receipt for the amount is transmitted to the Accountant of Court. After the discharge of the trustee it is competent to any person producing evidence of his right to apply to the Accountant of Court for authority to receive any such dividend which has been deposited as above within seven years immediately preceding the date of application. At the expiry of seven years from the date of deposit the deposit receipt is handed over to the King's and Lord Treasurer's Remembrancer, who obtains payment.[3]

---

[1] Carter (Pendreigh's Tr.) *v.* M'Laren & Co., 1871, 9 M. (H.L.) 49.
[2] Bankruptcy (Scotland) Act, 1913, § 150.   [3] *Ibid.*, § 153.

(11) Recall of Sequestration.—The deliverance awarding sequestration is not subject to appeal, but it is competent to present a petition to have it recalled.[1] A sequestration can be recalled prior to its natural termination on any ground which would have been an effectual ground for opposing the award or on grounds which have emerged since the awarding,[2] *e.g.* defects in the statutory requisites or in the statutory proceedings. The effect of a recall is to reinvest the bankrupt in his estate. Pending any petition for recall, and until sequestration be finally recalled, the proceedings in the sequestration go on as if no such petition had been presented.[3]

A petition for recall is competent (*a*) within forty days of the date of the deliverance awarding sequestration, at the instance of any debtor who has been sequestrated without his consent, or of the successors of a deceased debtor whose estate has been sequestrated without their consent unless on the application of a mandatary authorised by the deceased debtor, or by any creditor [4] ; (*b*) at any time if presented by nine-tenths in number and value of the creditors ranked on the estate [5] ; and (*c*) within three months after the date of any sequestration, on the ground that a majority of the creditors in number and value reside in England or in Ireland, and that from the situation of the property of the bankrupt, or other causes, his estate and effects ought to be distributed among the creditors under the bankrupt or insolvent laws of England or Ireland. In the last case the Court has a discretion whether or not to grant recall on that ground.

(12) Summary Sequestration.—The Act of 1913 abolished the old process of *cessio bonorum* and introduced a new process known as summary sequestration, applicable to estates where the debtor's assets of every description do not in the aggregate exceed £300 in value.[6] Subject to certain exceptions the whole provisions of the Act regulating ordinary sequestrations apply to Summary Sequestrations.[6] No provision is made for the winding up of the estates of a deceased debtor by summary sequestration.

Who may Apply.—The petition may be at the instance of (1) the debtor, without the concurrence of any creditor, or (2) of one creditor whose claim amounts to £10 or upwards, or two or more creditors whose claims in the aggregate amount to £10 or upwards, provided

---

[1] Bankruptcy (Scotland) Act, 1913, § 30.
[2] Campbell *v.* Myles, 1853, 15 D. 685 ; Muir *v.* Stevenson, 1850, 12 D. 512.
[3] Bankruptcy (Scotland) Act, 1913, § 32.   [4] *Ibid.*, § 30.
[5] *Ibid.*, § 31.   [6] *Ibid.*, § 174.

the debtor is notour bankrupt, within four months after the constitution of notour bankruptcy.

The Petition.—The petition must be presented to the Sheriff of the county within which the debtor has resided or carried on business during the year immediately preceding the date of the petition. There are two exceptions in which the petition may be presented to the Court of Session in the Bill Chamber, namely, (1) where the petition is at the instance of a creditor or creditors who do not know within which sheriffdom the debtor resided or carried on business during the year immediately preceding the date of the petition, and (2) if the debtor be furth of Scotland. Where the petition is at the instance of the debtor he must, along with the petition, lodge in the hands of the Sheriff-Clerk a state of his affairs subscribed by himself,[1] specifying his whole property wherever situated, property in expectancy or to which he may have an eventual right, the names and designations of his creditors and debtors, the debts due by and to him, and a rental of his heritable property.[2]

When the petition is presented at the instance of a creditor a warrant is granted to cite the debtor to appear in Court within a specified time, and ordaining him within six days after the service of the order to lodge a like state of his affairs as is required in a debtor's petition.

It is competent for the judge to whom a petition is presented to order the sequestration to proceed as a summary sequestration or not as he thinks expedient.

Procedure in Summary Sequestrations.—After sequestration has been awarded, the subsequent proceedings are similar to those in an ordinary sequestration up to the deliverance declaring the election of the trustee by the Sheriff, after which the proceedings are more summary. No petition requires to be presented for the examination of the bankrupt, but the trustee is required to apply orally to the Sheriff to fix a diet of examination. The debtor is ordered to attend the diet so fixed. Not less than seven days prior to the date fixed for the examination the trustee is required to give notice to the bankrupt to attend the diet. He must also give notice in the *Edinburgh Gazette*, and post to each creditor who has lodged a claim or who is mentioned in the bankrupt's state of affairs or is otherwise known to the trustee a circular intimating his appointment, the date fixed for the examination, and the period within which claims must be lodged,

---

[1] Bankruptcy (Scotland) Act, 1913, § 175.   [2] *Ibid.*, § 77.

and also specifying a date for holding the second meeting of creditors. Claims must be lodged not less than twenty-one days before the second meeting. If a dividend is to be paid, the trustee is required, not less than fourteen days prior to the second meeting, to adjudicate upon the claims of creditors, admitting or rejecting them. If a claim is rejected in whole or in part, this decision must be intimated to the creditor ten days before the second meeting. The bankrupt or any creditor may object to the deliverance of the trustee, and such objection is orally disposed of by the Sheriff.

Second Meeting of Creditors.—At this meeting the trustee and commissioners may fix a date for payment of a first or final dividend, or postpone payment of a dividend to a date not later than three months after the date of the meeting. Where there are no funds available for division the matter is reported orally to the Sheriff, who may thereupon in writing dispense with further procedure in the summary sequestration. If a dividend is to be paid the trustee's accounts are audited by the auditor of the Sheriff Court. Subsequent dividends are payable at dates to be fixed by the trustee and commissioners. If a creditor has failed to lodge his claim in time for the first dividend he may lodge a claim to participate in the second or subsequent dividends. In such a case he is entitled to an equalising dividend as well as to the new dividend upon the amount of his admitted claim.

Discharge of Trustee.—After a final division of the funds, or where the Sheriff has dispensed with further procedure, the trustee applies to the Accountant of Court for a certificate that he is entitled to his discharge. The trustee then reports the matter orally to the Sheriff, who fixes a diet for hearing any objections. The diet so fixed is intimated in the *Edinburgh Gazette*, and the bankrupt or any creditor may appear and oppose the application. If no objection is stated, or is stated and repelled, the Sheriff discharges the trustee.

Discharge of Bankrupt.—The provisions as to the discharge of a bankrupt in ordinary sequestrations apply to the discharge of a bankrupt in summary sequestrations, with the exception that where the Sheriff has in writing dispensed with further procedure in a summary sequestration the bankrupt may forthwith apply for his discharge.

3. Extra-judicial Settlements with Creditors.—Extra-judicial arrangements are usually in the form of either (1) a Trust Deed granted by the debtor, or (2) an offer of Composition by him.

(1) Trust Deed.—There is no statutory form of trust deed. The deed is one granted by the debtor in which he conveys to a named trustee his whole estate for realisation and division among his creditors, with a provision for restitution of any reversion to the debtor.[1] No creditor is, however, bound to accede to a trust deed, and one recalcitrant creditor may stultify the proposed arrangement. Such a deed is reducible under the Act 1696, c. 5, if granted after the constitution of notour bankruptcy or within sixty days prior thereto,[2] and also under the Act 1621, c. 18, if it defeats lawful diligence already begun.[3] Apart from these statutes a voluntary trust deed granted by a party insolvent but not bankrupt for behoof of all his creditors equally, and containing no extraordinary clauses, is irrevocable by the granter, and good and available to bind non-acceding as well as acceding creditors, if the estate be reduced into the possession of the trustee and the debtor is not rendered bankrupt within sixty days thereafter. A creditor's assent may be proved either by writing or by oath, or in some cases even by parole evidence. Where the creditor's assent is proved by writing or by oath he is bound by all the conditions of the deed. Where his consent is sought to be established from his actings the most explicit proof is required. The trust may at any time be superseded by sequestration at the instance of a non-acceding creditor, and upon this being done the estate is vested in the trustee under the sequestration.[4]

Ranking of Claims of Creditors.—It is now usually stipulated in the trust deed that the rankings of creditors are to be the same as under the Bankruptcy Act. This means that a secured creditor requires to value his security and rank only on the difference. If there is no such stipulation then a secured creditor would be entitled to rank for the full amount of his debt without deducting the value of his security.[5] The creditors may or may not be required to lodge sworn affidavits in support of their debts.

Position of Non-acceding Creditor.—A non-acceding creditor is not bound to accede to the terms of the trust deed as a condition of his drawing a dividend. He is entitled to his rateable share of the debtor's funds, and should he not be paid he has a direct action against the trustee for recovery thereof.[6]

---

[1] Bell's Comm., ii. 385.
[2] Mackenzie v. Calder, 6 M. 833.
[3] Mackenzie, *supra.*
[4] Kyd v. Waterston, 1880, 7 R. 884.
[5] Kirkcaldy v. Middleton, 1841, 4 D. 202.
[6] Ogilvie v. Taylor, 14 R. 399.

Audit of Trustee's Accounts.—It is now obligatory in the case of every trust deed where there is no provision made *in gremio* for the audit of the trustee's account and the fixing of his remuneration by a committee of the creditors, or where such committee is not appointed or does not act, for the trustee before making a final division of the estate among the creditors to submit his accounts to the Accountant of Court, who must audit the same and fix the amount of the trustee's remuneration. Any trustee who fails to observe these provisions forfeits all claim to commission or other remuneration in respect of his acting as trustee.[1]

(2) **Composition Contract.**—A composition contract is an agreement between a debtor and his creditors, whereby the latter agree to accept a portion of their debts in full discharge thereof. It may be carried out in a variety of ways. The most common is for a debtor to offer a composition of so much per pound with or without security. The debtor remains in possession of his estates and usually continues to carry on his business. Unless specially agreed to the contrary, a composition contract implies (1) that all the creditors will be treated with equality ; (2) that no undue preference is granted by the debtor to any of the creditors ; and (3) that they all concur in the arrangement. Unlike a composition under a sequestration, if the agreed-on composition be not paid at the time when it falls due the original debt revives,[2] and if such failure be at the second or any of the subsequent instalments, the creditor is entitled to proceed for his whole debt under deduction of the payments received, unless at the time of agreeing to the composition he has finally discharged the debtor, in which case he can only proceed for the amount of his composition. If the composition be not paid when due the creditor is not bound to accept it afterwards, but, where it has not been discharged, may proceed for payment of his full debt.

[1] Bankruptcy (Scotland) Act, 1913, § 185.
[2] Woods & Co. *v.* Ainslie, 1860, 22 D. 723

CHAPTER XVI

THE LAW OF INSURANCE

I. General Principles

Nature of the Contract.—The aim of all insurance is to make provision against the dangers which beset human life and dealings. Those who seek it endeavour to avert disaster from themselves by shifting possible loss on to the shoulders of others, who are willing, for pecuniary consideration, to take the risk thereof ; and in the case of life insurance they endeavour to assure to those dependent on them a certain provision in case of their death, or to provide a fund out of which creditors can be satisfied.[1]

Although risk is of the essence of the contract, insurance is not a gaming or wagering contract. In a pure wager the interest of the contracting parties in the event wagered on is created by the fact that they have contracted to pay each other certain sums in a certain event. In insurance the interest is in, and the risk is of loss of, something which exists already, and the owner pays, not merely risks, money in order to obtain security against the possible loss. As in a contract of suretyship the object is to shift the danger of loss, not to create an opportunity of gain.

The two leading principles of the law of insurance are the principle of indemnity and the principle that the contract is *uberrimae fidei*—*i.e.* one requiring the utmost good faith on both sides.

The Principle of Indemnity.—Indemnity is the controlling principle in insurance law.[2] Except in insurance on life [3] (and against accident) the insurer contracts to indemnify the assured for what he actually loses by the happening of the events upon which the

---

[1] Bell's Comm., 7th ed., p. 645.
[2] Castellain *v.* Preston, (1883) 11 Q.B. 380 at p. 386, per Brett L.J.
[3] See *infra*, p. 313.

insurer's liability is to arise, and under no circumstance is the assured in theory entitled to make a profit of his loss.[1] Were this not so the two parties to the contract would not have a common interest in the preservation of the thing insured, and the contract would create a desire on the part of the assured for the happening of the event insured against—temptation to crime, fraud, or such carelessness as to bring about the destruction of the thing insured being created.

The consequences of the principle of indemnity are as follows : (1) Limitation of the claim.—The amount which the assured can claim is limited, not only by the amount insured for, but also by the extent of the injury to the subject insured, and by the extent of the assured's interest in the subject. Only what has been actually lost need be made good, whether by payment or reinstatement of the thing damaged to its original condition, or construction of a new thing similar to it. If more than the amount of the loss is recovered the insurer can get the excess back again if he paid unawares. (2) The insurer's right of contribution.—As the assured cannot recover more than the amount of his loss, if there are two or more insurances covering the same interest in the same property, the aggregate amount insured being greater than the loss, the insurers contribute rateably to the loss in the proportions of the total sums insured by the different policies. The several contracts are taken together as parts of one contract of indemnity. This is known as double insurance. If, however, separate interests in the same property are separately insured—e.g. by a carrier of goods and by the owner—the insurers, as regards their liability *inter se*, stand in the place of the parties they have insured, so that if one of the parties is primarily liable for the loss in a question with the other, his insurer must make good the whole loss. Thus, if a carrier or warehouseman, primarily liable for the safety of goods in his custody, insures to cover the risk by a policy on goods for which he is responsible, and the owner also insures, there is no double insurance and no contribution.[2] (3) The assured's right of abandonment.—If the thing insured is not totally destroyed, but remains wholly or in part in a deteriorated or damaged condition, if the degree of damage is such that the identity of the property has been lost the assured may surrender it to the insurer and claim as

---

[1] Castellain v. Preston, *supra*.

[2] North British and Mercantile Co. v. London, Liverpool and Globe Securities Insurance Co., (1876) 5 Ch. D. 569 ; Scottish Amicable Heritable Insurance Association, Ltd. v. Northern Assurance Co., 1883, 11 R. 287.

for a total destruction of the thing insured.[1] This is known as the doctrine of abandonment. (4) The insurer's right of subrogation.— If the assured has any means open to him to repair his loss otherwise than at his own expense or at the cost of the insurer he must either exercise such means for the benefit of the insurer, or he must cede such means to the insurer on being paid the full amount of his loss. This is termed the insurer's right of subrogation. The assured cannot in such a case exonerate from liability to the detriment of the insurer third parties primarily responsible for the loss. The rule applies whether the liability of the third party rests upon contract or upon negligence or upon delict. The principle of subrogation would not apply in any case where the assured would be the third party in law responsible if the property damaged were not his own. For example, if an insured ship were damaged by collision with another ship also belonging to the owner of the insured ship, there would be no right of subrogation, because the assured could have no right of action against himself, and because the insurers take the risk of the assured's negligence, if not wilful, as part of the risk against which they insure.[2] On the other hand the liability of an insurer is a primary liability, not a secondary liability like a cautioner's, and, consequently, he is not entitled to require the assured who has suffered a loss covered by the contract to exhaust his remedies against third parties for the loss before making a claim against the insurer.[1] (5) Attachment of the risk is necessary.—The contract is contingent on the actual attaching of the risk. Unless the property insured is for a time subject to the risk insured against, the contract of insurance, even if made, never operates, and the premium, though paid, is recoverable. The assured is not obliged to run the risk because of the contract. It follows also that the contract no longer remains in force after the risk is determined one way or another, except in those special insurances where both parties, being equally ignorant of the position of the thing insured—*e.g.* a ship at sea—contract to insure it lost or not lost.

Insurance a Contract Uberrimae Fidei.—From the fact that insurance is a contract to shift risk flows also the principle that the contract is *uberrimae fidei*—*i.e.* one requiring the utmost good faith on both sides. This principle applies to every contract of insurance.

---

[1] Castellain *v.* Preston, (1883) 11 Q.B. 380.

[2] Trinder, Anderson & Co. *v.* Thames and Mersey Marine Insurance Co., [1898] 2 Q.B. 114.

The consequences are as follows : (1) There is a duty on the parties to make a complete disclosure to each other. The assured must disclose to the insurer every fact going to establish the character of the risk to be shifted by the contract which is within the knowledge of the assured, and which is not matter of common knowledge or speculation or mere opinion—that is, all material facts.[1] If the assured fails so to disclose, the contract is voidable,[2] and he will take nothing by the contract, although in the absence of fraud on his part, or contrary stipulation, he will be entitled to retain or be repaid the premium. So also if the insurer grants a policy of insurance knowing he will never run any risk thereunder, whether because facts invalidate it or the risk is already determined in his favour, he will be equally subject to the rule of good faith. The rule of full disclosure applies also during the running of the contract, and even after the risk has happened. (2) There is a duty on the assured to avert the happening of the risk. Hence if he accelerates the happening of the risk or, when it has happened, fails to do what he can to lessen the consequent damage, he imperils his chance of recovering under the contract—for example, if he prevents others from endeavouring to save goods which would otherwise be destroyed, or wilfully neglects without reasonable excuse to save insured property, provided that he so acts with the fraudulent intention and purpose to throw the loss on the insurers. On the other hand, he is not bound to save the subject-matter insured at his own cost. The insurers are liable for such costs.

II. The Contract of Life Insurance

1. Definition.—Life insurance is a contract by which the insurer, in consideration of a certain premium, either in a gross sum or by annual payments, undertakes to pay to the person for whose benefit the insurance is made a certain sum of money, or annuity, on the death of the person whose life is insured.[3] Where, as is common, the sum insured is payable on death or on the occurrence of a certain event, such as the attainment of a certain age, the principles applicable to the contract are the same.

2. Formation of the Contract.—A person desiring to insure against

---

[1] Carter v. Boehm, 3 Burr. 1905 at p. 1910.

[2] Bell's Prin., §§ 474, 522.

[3] Smith's Mercantile Law, 11th ed., p. 551 ; Dalby v. The India and London Life Co., 24 L.J. C.P. 2.

a contingency depending on the continuance of a life fills up a proposal
containing questions as to age, health, habits, and medical attendance
on the " life," and usually also signs a declaration that the answers are
true and are to be the basis of the contract. Information is also
usually obtained from friends of the " life," but as they are not regarded
as agents of the applicant, such information does not form the basis
of the contract. As a rule also an insuring company has the life
examined by its own medical officer. When an insuring company
accepts a proposal for life assurance, the contract is embodied in a
policy. The agreement to insure is not regarded as concluded until
tender of the premium,[1] and where a company accepts a proposal
the acceptance is usually subject to the condition that the insurance
shall not begin until the premium is paid.

Any completed contract for the payment of a sum depending on
a contingency connected with the duration of a life is a policy of life
insurance under the description in the Policies of Assurance Act,
1867, and for the purposes of stamp duty.[2] It is provided by the
Stamp Act, 1891,[3] that a policy must be made out and executed
within one month of the receipt of or taking credit for a premium or
consideration for any life insurance, under penalty.

3. Matters affecting the Validity of the Contract.—(a) **Void Policies.**
—**Insurable Interest.**—A policy of life insurance may be void if the
assured has not the necessary interest to insure. The Gambling Act,
1774, provides that no insurance should be made by any person
against the death of any person in whom he has not an interest, or
made by way of gaming or wagering. Such a policy is declared void,
but the insurance company may waive its defence on this ground.[4]
The Act also requires the insertion in every policy of the names of
the persons interested in the insurance.[5] Further, no person may
insure for more than the value of his interest.[6] Nevertheless, it has
been held that a contract of life insurance is not a contract of indemnity. Where a man insures his own life he cannot be indemnified
for the loss of it. It is usually a provision for relatives or creditors.
Nor, it has been held, where the insurance is over the life of another,
is it a contract of indemnity.[7] Such was not the earlier view, and

---

[1] Sickness and Accident Assurance Association v. General Accident Assurance
Corporation, Ltd., 1894, 19 R. 977.

[2] Stamp Act, 1891, § 98.   [3] Ibid., § 100.

[4] The Life Assurance Act, 1774, § 1.   [5] Ibid., § 2.   [6] Ibid., § 3.

[7] Dalby v. The India and London Life Co., 24 L.J. C.P. 2 ; Law v. London
Indisputable Co., 24 L.J. Ch. 196.

seems open to objection.[1] Accordingly, life insurance not being a contract of indemnity, where an insurance is effected by one person over the life of another—for example, by a creditor over the life of his debtor—the insurer must pay on the death, even though the debt be already discharged, and the same interest may be insured with several insurers and all be liable, without right of contribution. It also follows that a life policy may be validly assigned to a person who has no interest in the life insured. There must, however, exist an interest at the time the insurance was effected, otherwise the contract is void. The interest required is a pecuniary interest. The pecuniary interest required may arise either out of contract or of relationship. Where the interest arises out of contract, the contract must establish the relation between the assured and the person whose life is insured of debtor and creditor, or cautioner and principal debtor, or otherwise create a reasonable expectation of advantage from the continuance of the life. The debt need not, however, be of ascertainable amount, nor immediately exigible at the time the policy is made. Where not so ascertainable, the value put upon the policy by the parties, except in so far as it exceeds the actual extent of the assured's interest at any time, is held to be the value of the interest.[2] Thus a master may validly insure the life of his servant or agent whose services may be a source of profit, and *vice versa*.[3] But if the value of the interest is ascertainable at the time when the insurance is effected, the policy will be enforceable only for that amount.

Where the interest arises from relationship there is an insurable interest only where there is a legal obligation to support. Accordingly, while in England a parent has no insurable interest in the life of his child, having no direct claim for maintenance against it, in Scotland he probably has such a claim and insurable interest,[4] as have also husbands and wives in each other [5] and children in their parents.

(b) **Voidable Policies.**—A policy of life insurance may be voidable at the instance of the insurer if induced by concealment or misrepresentation on the part of the assured, or if the assured is in breach of

---

[1] Porter on Insurance, 6th ed., p. 11 *et seq.*

[2] Barnes *v.* The London, Edinburgh, and Glasgow Life Insurance Co., [1892] 1 Q.B. 864.

[3] Turnbull & Co. *v.* Scottish Provident Institution, 1896, 34 S.L.R. 146; Simcock *v.* Scottish Imperial Insurance Co., 1902, 10 S.L.T. 286.

[4] Hadden *v.* Bryden, 1899, 1 F. 710; Carmichael *v.* Carmichael's Exrx., per Lord Dundas and Lord Guthrie, 1919 S.C. 636; revd. 1920 S.C. (H.L.) 195.

[5] Wight *v.* Brown, 1849, 11 D. 459.

the conditions of the policy. In theory it is voidable also on these grounds at the instance of the assured, but any such question seldom, if ever, arises.

Disclosure and Representations.—The general rule applicable to mercantile contracts that they are voidable on the ground of non-disclosure or misrepresentation of any material fact applies in contracts of life insurance.[1] The concealment or misrepresentation need not be fraudulent. It is sufficient if the party misled would not have entered into the contract at all, or would not have agreed to its essential terms if he had known the true state of the facts.[2] These general rules are modified in the case of life assurance policies by the terms of the proposal and declaration, or of the policy. The policy itself declares that the proposal and declaration shall be the basis of the contract, or incorporates them. The effect is to make the answers in the proposal warranties or terms of the contract, and so to exclude the question whether they are material.

Conditions.—Breach of a condition expressed in the policy also makes voidable the policy at the instance of the insurer. Conditions in policies usually are as to occupation, place of residence, travel, and suicide. If suicide takes place during insanity the condition is not strictly enforced, and suicide is not allowed to affect the interests of third parties, such as lenders on the security of the policy, intimated to the insurance company before death.[3] Policies usually provide that in case of suicide the policy shall not be paid in full, but treated as surrendered, and the surrender value paid to the deceased's personal representatives or other beneficiaries named in the policy.

4. Construction of the Contract.—The language used in the policy being the language of the company insurer is, in the event of ambiguity, construed against the company and for the benefit of the assured.[4]

5. Assignation of the Policy.—The assignation of policies of life assurance is regulated by the Policies of Assurance Act, 1867. Assignees are given power to sue under the policy, and there is reserved to the insurance company any defence on equitable grounds which it would have had against the cedent, as in any other personal action.[5] The Act further provides for intimation of assignment being

---

[1] See Misrepresentation, *supra*, p. 22.

[2] London Assurance *v.* Mansel, (1879) 11 Ch. D. 363.

[3] Ellinger *v.* Mutual Life of New York, [1905] 1 K.B. 31.

[4] Life Association of Scotland *v.* Foster, 11 F. 351, 371.

[5] Policies of Assurance Act, 1867, §§ 1 and 2.

given to the company as a condition of a right of action by an assignee under a policy, for the specification in all policies of the company's place of business at which notices of assignment may be given, and for assignment being by endorsement on the policy or by separate assignment in accordance with a form given in the Act.

The right of an assignee to sue upon a policy depends on four conditions. The assignation must be in writing ; the assignee must have a right to grant a discharge to the insurance company ; the assignation must have been intimated to the company ; and the assignation must be properly stamped.

6. Married Women's Policies of Assurance Act, 1880.—A trust may be declared in a life policy by making it payable to a certain person as trustee for purposes set forth in the policy. Such a trust is not, at common law, effectual against creditors of the truster, unless the policy is delivered to the trustee [1] or intimated.[2] Special provision is, however, made with regard to such policies by the Married Women's Policies of Assurance (Scotland) Act, 1880, where the policy is effected by a married man over his own life for the benefit of his wife or children or both. Such policies vest in him and his legal representatives in trust for the purposes so expressed, but are not otherwise subject to his control, part of his estate, revocable as a donation, subject to the diligence of his creditors, or reducible on any ground of excess or insolvency. The Act dispenses with delivery or intimation. But if it be proved that the policy was effected and the premiums paid to defraud creditors, or if the assured be made bankrupt within two years from the date of the policy, the creditors may claim repayment out of the proceeds of the policy of the premiums so paid.

III. The Contract of Fire Insurance

1. Definition.—Fire insurance is a contract of indemnity, by which the insurer undertakes, upon the terms and conditions in the policy, to indemnify the assured for loss or damage by fire.

2. Formation of the Contract.—A contract of insurance against fire may be constituted by writing or by parole.[3] But in order to constitute a valid insurance the essential elements of the contract —namely, the subject insured, the risk and the premium—must be

---

[1] Jarvie's Tr. *v.* Jarvie's Trs., 1887, 14 R. 411.
[2] Carmichael *v.* Carmichael's Exrx., 1920 S.C. (H.L.) 195.
[3] Christie *v.* North British Insurance Co., 1825, 3 Sh. 519.

determined.[1] A policy is the usual and proper form in which a con
tract for fire insurance is expressed.[2]

Covering Notes.—Where an application is made for fire insurance
it is the practice of most companies to issue interim covering notes
by which the property is protected until the company have determined whether to accept or decline the risk. The period of endur-
ance of the covering note is usually limited to a month, and it is provided that on the termination of the insurance by the expiry of this
period, or by refusal notified to the assured, the part of the premium
unearned shall be returned. A covering note corresponds to a " slip "
in marine insurance, but may constitute a valid contract, whereas
a contract of marine insurance requires to be embodied in a marine
policy to be admissible in evidence.[3]

Agency.—An insurance entered into with an agent of a company
is only valid when it is proved that the agent was authorised to bind
the company.[4] The authority may be express or inferred from a
course of practice acquiesced in by the company. It is not the
practice of British companies to authorise their agents to issue policies
or conclude a final contract of insurance.[5] But in most cases local
agents have authority to conclude interim insurances by issuing
covering notes which will bind the company until repudiated by
either party.[6]

3. Matters affecting the Validity of the Contract.—(a) **Void Policies.**
—**Insurable Interest.**—Fire insurance being a contract of indemnity
against loss, there can be no loss and no indemnity unless the assured
has an interest in the property insured when the loss occurs, and
probably also when the insurance is effected. To constitute an
insurable interest there must be an expectation of benefit or advantage from the preservation of the property insured, and this
must be coupled with a legal right in the property. Accordingly,
an interest which is merely contingent, such as that of an heir, is
not insurable. On the other hand, an interest which exists, though
it be defeasible as being subject to a resolutive condition,[7] is insur-

---

[1] Christie, 1825, 3 Sh. 519.

[2] M'Elroy v. London Assurance Corporation, 1897, 24 R. 287, per Lord M'Laren
at p. 291.

[3] Marine Insurance Act, 1906, § 23 ; Thompson v. Adams, (1889) 23 Q.B.D. 361.

[4] M'Elroy v. London Assurance Corporation, 1897, 24 R. 287.

[5] Linford, (1864) 23 Beav. 291.

[6] Mackie, (1869) 21 L.T.S. 102.

[7] *Vide* Conditions, *supra*, p. 38.

able. And any right which is incidental to ownership, such as a right to the rents of the property, or a right in security over the subjects, is insurable. A creditor has no insurable interest over the property of his debtor.[1]

(*b*) **Voidable Policies.—Non-disclosure and Misrepresentation.— Materiality.**—A contract of fire insurance is made upon the implied condition that all material facts have been disclosed. If there has been any misrepresentation or concealment of material facts known to either of the parties, although without fraudulent intention, the policy is voidable at the instance of the other. The criterion of materiality of a fact is whether it is one which would usually be regarded in the business of insurance as material.[2] The following facts may be specially noted as having been held material facts, viz. those touching the terms upon which the insurers have undertaken the risk insured against, and over-valuation of the subject insured, if excessive. The question of the materiality of representations may be excluded by agreement of the parties. This is done by making the statements of the assured part of the contract, *i.e.* making them warranties.[3]

The duty of disclosure is subject to certain limitations. Thus the assured is not bound to disclose (1) what the insurer knows or ought to know as part of his business ; (2) what the insurer takes upon himself the knowledge of ; (3) what he has waived information of ; or (4) what is covered by warranty. Further, the assured need not generally state the nature of his interest or the fact that, prior to effecting the policy, he has contracted with third parties so as to deprive the insurer of a right of recourse in the event of a loss, unless, of course, the premium has been adjusted on the footing of a right of subrogation being kept open to the insurer.[4] If, since the policy was effected and before a loss, any material change of circumstances occurs, this must be communicated to the insurers.[5] The onus is on the insurers to prove a misrepresentation.

4. Construction of the Contract.—Where a proposal is accepted by a company upon the condition that the insurance shall not begin until the premium is paid, they are not bound to issue a policy or make

---

[1] Macaura *v.* Northern Assurance Co., [1925] A.C. 619.
[2] Ionides *v.* Pender, (1874) 9 Q.B. 531, per Blackburn J. at p. 537 ; Bhugwandass *v.* Netherlands Insurance Co., (1888) 14 App. Cas. 83.
[3] Dawson's, Ltd. *v.* Bonnin, 1922, S.L.T. 444.
[4] Tate *v.* Hyslop, (1885) 15 Q.B.D. 368.
[5] London Assurance *v.* Mansel, (1879) 11 Ch. D. 363.

good a loss, if, before the premium is tendered, the risk has terminated or has materially altered.[1]

The Policy.—The conditions upon which the policy is issued are set out in the body of the policy, and deal mainly with questions of misrepresentation, excepted risks, adjustment of loss, and contribution. The instrument being prepared by the company, if the conditions are ambiguous and admit of interpretation they are to be read in the sense most favourable to the assured. The policy is to be construed with reference to the principle of indemnity. Thus if two fires occur within the period of insurance, each causing a loss not exceeding the sum assured, but together exceeding it, the insurer is not liable beyond the amount assured.[2]

Policies are usually for a year, terminal days being included in the period. In some cases fifteen days of grace are allowed for payment of the premium, but this does not, unless expressly so provided, mean that the insurance subsists during that period. It gives an option to the assured to continue the insurance, if he pays.

The Risk Insured Against.—Proximate Cause.—The risk against which a fire policy provides is loss or damage by fire. There are usually exceptions to the general liability of the insurer expressed in the conditions of the policy. Usual exceptions are losses by lightning, explosion, incendiarism, riot, and by military or usurped power. In a question whether the loss or damage was caused by a peril insured against, the general rule is that where there are two or more causes forming a chain of events leading up to the loss, the cause nearest in point of time is to be regarded as the cause of the loss. Thus where a fire is caused by the negligence of the assured, or his servants, the proximate cause of damage being fire, the loss will be covered. And where loss results from a peril insured against, though not proximately the cause of it, yet as a material or necessary consequence of it, the loss is covered. Thus damages caused by water used to extinguish a fire or by the removal of goods will be covered. Where, on the other hand, the fire is a natural or reasonably to be expected result of an excepted risk—for example, lightning—the loss is not covered.

Reinstatement and Measurement of the Loss.—The amount required to reinstate the subjects injured is not necessarily the limit

[1] Sickness and Accident Assurance Association *v.* The General Accident Assurance Corporation, Ltd., 1892, 19 R. 977.

[2] Ferguson *v.* Aberdeen Parish Council, 1916 S.C. 715.

for which insurers are liable under a contract of indemnity.[1] That is not necessarily the measure of the loss. But the insuring company frequently makes it a condition of the policy that it may, if it think fit, reinstate or replace property damaged or destroyed, instead of paying the amount of the loss or damage. If the insurer elects to reinstate, the contract becomes a building contract, and the pecuniary measure of the insurer's obligation has no necessary relation to the amount for which he would have been liable as under a contract of indemnity.

Rights of the Insurer on Payment.—Subrogation.—Contribution.— The contract being one of indemnity, the insurer has a right of subrogation,[2] and the principle of contribution in double insurances applies.[3]

5. Assignation of the Policy.—It is a consequence of the contract being one of indemnity that an assignation to a person who has no insurable interest has no validity. A policy of fire insurance issued to a person named cannot be assigned upon a transfer of the property without the insurer's consent.[4]

IV. The Contract of Marine Insurance

1. History of the Law.—The law of marine insurance is contained in the Marine Insurance Act, 1906, a United Kingdom statute, which embodied and codified the law as developed and settled by the Courts during a long period of years. The practice of marine insurance is inseparably connected with the name of Lloyd's, and the development of the law with that of Lord Mansfield, when Lord Chief Justice of England in the latter half of the eighteenth century. Traceable originally to the Lombards, many of whom settled in England in the thirteenth century, the first statute relating thereto is in 1601, now repealed, and it well describes the objects which " such insurance " is designed to further. " And whereas it has been time out of minde an usage amongst merchantes, bothe of these realms and of foreign nations, when they make any great adventure (specially into remote parts), to give some consideration of money to other persons (which commonly are in no small number), to have from them assurance made of the goods, merchandises, ships, and things adventured, or

---

[1] Westminster Fire Office v. The Glasgow Provident Investment Society, (1888) 13 App. Cas. 699.

[2] Vide *supra*, p. 312.   [3] Vide *supra*, p. 311.

[4] Castellain v. Preston, (1883) 11 Q.B. 380.

some part thereof, at such rates and in such sort as the parties assurers and the parties assured can agree, which course of dealing is commonly termed a policy of assurance ; by means of which policy of assurance it cometh to pass that upon the loss or perishing of any ship there followeth not the undoing of any man, but the loss lighteth rather easily upon many than heavily upon few, and rather upon them that adventure not than those that do adventure, whereby all merchantes, especially the younger sort, are allured to venture more willingly and more freely." The business of marine insurance received its first great impetus with the advent of the coffee houses in London after the Great Fire of 1666. There met there the merchants and business men, and Lloyd's Coffee House in Lombard Street in time assumed prominence as the meeting-place of the leading merchants. The society so formed was responsible for fixing the terms of the printed form of policy known as Lloyd's S.G. Policy, which is the basis of all contracts of marine insurance.

2. Nature of the Contract of Marine Insurance.—A contract of marine insurance is a contract whereby the insurer undertakes to indemnify the assured, in manner and to the extent thereby agreed, against losses incident to marine adventure.[1] There is a marine adventure, in particular, (*a*) where any ship, goods, or other moveables are exposed to maritime perils ; (*b*) where the earning or acquisition of any freight, passage money, commission, profit, or other pecuniary benefit, or the security for any advances, loan, or disbursements, is endangered by the exposure of insurable property to maritime perils ; (*c*) where any liability to a third party may be incurred by the owner of or other person interested in or responsible for insurable property, by means of maritime perils. Maritime perils means perils of the seas, fire, war perils, pirates, rovers, thieves, captures, seizures, restraints, and detainment of princes and peoples, jettisons, barratry, and any other perils, either of the like kind, or which may be designated by the policy.[2] The contract may be extended, expressly or by usage of trade, to protect the assured against losses on inland waters or on any land risk incidental to a sea voyage,[3] and where a ship in the course of building or the launch of a ship is covered by a marine policy the Act applies.

3. Constitution of the Contract.—The terms of the contract are usually noted on a " slip " or memorandum, which is initialed by the underwriters. But a contract of marine insurance cannot be

[1] M.I.A., 1906, § 1.   [2] *Ibid.*, § 3.   [3] *Ibid.*, § 2 (1).

enforced in a Court of Law unless it is embodied in a stamped marine policy in accordance with the Marine Insurance Act.[1] That is to say, the policy must specify (1) the name of the assured or of some person who effects the insurance on his behalf, usually an insurance broker ; (2) the subject-matter insured, and that with reasonable certainty, and the risk insured against ; (3) the voyage or period of time, or both, as the case may be, covered by the insurance, and in the case of a time policy a period not exceeding twelve months, unless there be a continuation clause for a period up to thirty days in the event of the ship being at sea on a voyage when the policy expires [2] ; (4) the sum or sums insured ; and (5) the name or names of the insurers. The policy must be signed by or on behalf of the insurer, and in the case of a corporation may be sealed.[3] When the same policy is subscribed by two or more insurers, each subscription constitutes a distinct contract with the assured. The policy may be executed and issued either at the time when the contract was concluded or afterwards. The slip is useful evidence of the date at which the contract was concluded.

In specifying the subject-matter insured it is not essential to specify the nature and extent of the assured's interest,[4] unless perhaps where the interest is that of a lender on bottomry or respondentia. Nor is it essential that the value of the subject-matter insured be stated. Where it is stated, the policy is a " valued " policy ; where unstated, an " unvalued " policy. The value stated in the policy may exceed the actual value of the thing insured, and the stated value will be recoverable. The Act provides rules for ascertaining value in an unvalued policy in the case of ships, freight, and goods, and in the case of any other subject-matter states the value to be the amount at the risk of the assured when the policy attaches.[5] When cargo is insured, the name of the ship or ships in which it is to go need not be defined when the policy is signed, but may be so by subsequent declarations,[6] usually endorsed on the policy in the order of dispatch or shipment. This is called a " floating policy." In such policies, where a declaration of value is not made until after notice of loss or arrival, the goods in question are treated as unvalued. In every case the charges of the insurance are an item in the value. Nor is it necessary to specify in the policy the premium, which may be independently arranged.

---

[1] M.I.A., 1906, § 22.   [2] Stamp Act, 1891, § 93 ; Finance Act, 1901, § 11.
[3] M.I.A., 1906, § 24 (1).   [4] Ibid., § 26.
[5] Ibid., § 16.   [6] Ibid., § 29.

Unless otherwise agreed, however, the insurer need not complete the contract by delivering the policy except upon payment of the premium.

4. Matters affecting the Validity of the Contract.—(a) **Void Policies.**—**Insurable Interest.**—The contract being one of indemnity, the assured must at the time of the loss, but not necessarily at the time the contract is effected,[1] have an interest at risk. Accordingly a contract of marine insurance is void if the assured has not an insurable interest as defined by the Act,[2] and the contract was entered into with no expectation of acquiring such an interest. He cannot acquire an interest after he is aware of a loss.[3] So also are void contracts which bind the insurer " interest or no interest," or " without further proof of interest than the policy itself," or " without benefit of salvage to the insurer," unless there was no possibility of salvage.[4] Such policies are unenforceable as gaming or wagering contracts.[5] The taint of illegality is, however, not stretched to cover policies effected to insure interests which are merely defeasible or contingent.[6] In fact, such unenforceable policies are commonly entered into, the assured depending solely on the honour of the insurer. Such policies are known as " honour policies," and cover cases where there is doubt as to the assured having in law an interest. An exception to the rule that an interest must exist at the time the loss occurs is where the subject-matter is insured " lost or not lost." Such a contract is good even though the assured acquired his interest after the loss occurred, unless at the time of the insurance he was aware of the loss and the insurer was not. Such a contract is useful to cover the case of the insurance of a ship which is at sea.

Moreover, it is a criminal offence for a person to effect a marine insurance without having a *bona fide* interest or expectation of interest. So also is it a criminal offence for a person in the employment of the owner of a ship, other than a part owner, to effect an honour policy.[7] It is matter of public policy that life and property at sea be protected against the unscrupulous, who, without having an interest, effect insurances in order to obtain the insurance moneys by contriving the loss of the subject-matter.

(b) **Voidable Policies.**—**Disclosure and Representations.**—Like other

[1] M.I.A., 1906, § 6 (11).   [2] *Ibid.*, § 5.   [3] *Ibid.*, § 6 (2).
[4] See *In re* London County Re-insurance Co., [1922] 2 Ch. 67.
[5] See Illegal and Immoral Contracts, *supra*, p. 27.
[6] M.I.A., 1906, § 7 (1).
[7] Marine Insurance Gambling Policies Act, 1909, § 1 (1) (b).

contracts of insurance, marine insurance is a contract *uberrimae fidei*, requiring the utmost good faith as between the parties to it in negotiating the contract. If the utmost good faith be not observed by either party the contract may be avoided by the other party.[1] In negotiating, the assured must disclose everything he knows—and he is assumed to know everything which, in the ordinary course of business, ought to be known to him—which would influence the judgment of a prudent insurer in fixing the premium or determining whether he will take the risk.[2] The measure of disclosure required from an agent of the assured in making the contract is the same, unless it be of a circumstance which has come to the assured's knowledge too late to communicate to the agent.[3] An agent having knowledge material to be disclosed, though unknown to his principal, must disclose it.[4] In the absence of inquiry by the insurer the assured need not disclose any circumstance which diminishes the risk, or is known, or presumed to be known, to the insured, or as to which information is waived by the insurer.[5] Further, any material representation of fact which is made by the assured or his agent during negotiations must be true or substantially correct, and, if of belief, made in good faith. Non-disclosure and misrepresentation are to be tested when the contract is concluded, that is, when the proposal is accepted, whether the policy be then issued or not. A slip or covering note or other customary memorandum of the contract is usually made at the time the proposal is accepted, and is the usual evidence of acceptance.

5. Construction of the Contract.—(*a*) **Form of the Policy.**—The Marine Insurance Act gives a form of policy,[6] namely, that known as a Lloyd's S.G. Policy. It is in the following terms :—

LLOYD'S S.G. POLICY.—BE IT KNOWN THAT   as well in
      own name as for and in the name and names of all and every
other person or persons to whom the same doth, may, or shall appertain,
in part or in all doth make assurance and cause
and them, and every of them, to be insured lost or not lost, at and from

Upon any kind of goods and merchandises, and also upon the body,

---

[1] M.I.A., 1906, § 17.   [2] *Ibid.*, § 18 (2).   [3] *Ibid.*, § 19.
[4] Blackburn *v*. Vigors, (1887) 12 A.C. 531.
[5] M.I.A., 1906, § 18 (3).
[6] *Ibid.*, 1st Schedule.

tackle, apparel, ordnance, munition, artillery, boat, and other furniture, of and in the good ship or vessel called the

whereof is master under God, for this present voyage,
or whosoever else shall go for master in the said ship, or by whatsoever other name or names the said ship, or the master thereof, is or
shall be named or called ; beginning the adventure upon the said
goods and merchandises from the loading thereof aboard the said ship,

upon the said ship, &c.

and so shall continue and endure, during her abode there, upon the
said ship, &c.   And further, until the said ship, with all her ordnance,
tackle, apparel, &c., and goods and merchandises whatsoever shall
be arrived at

upon the said ship, &c., until she hath moored at anchor twenty-
four hours in good safety ; and upon the goods and merchandises,
until the same be there discharged and safely landed.   And it shall
be lawful for the said ship, &c., in this voyage, to proceed and sail to
and touch and stay at any ports or places whatsoever

without prejudice to this insurance.   The said ship, &c., goods, and
merchandises, &c., for so much as concerns the assured by agreement
between the assured and assurers in this policy, are and shall be
valued at

Touching the adventures and perils which we the assurers are
contented to bear and do take upon us in this voyage : they are of
the seas, men of war, fire, enemies, pirates, rovers, thieves, jettisons,
letters of mart and countermart, surprisals, takings at sea, arrests,
restraints, and detainments of all kings, princes, and people, of what
nation, condition, or quality soever, barratry of the master and
mariners, and of all other perils, losses, and misfortunes, that have
or shall come to the hurt, detriment, or damage of the said goods
and merchandises, and ship, &c., or any part thereof. [*Sue and
Labour Cause.*]—And in case of any loss or misfortune it shall be
lawful to the assured, their factors, servants and assigns, to sue,
labour, and travel for, in and about the defence, safeguards, and
recovery of the said goods and merchandises, and ship, &c., or any

part thereof, without prejudice to this insurance ; to the charges whereof we, the assurers, will contribute each one according to the rate and quantity of his sum herein assured. [*Waiver Clause*.]—And it is especially declared and agreed that no acts of the insurer or insured in recovering, saving, or preserving the property insured shall be considered as a waiver, or acceptance of abandonment. And it is agreed by us, the insurers, that this writing or policy of assurance shall be of as much force and effect as the surest writing or policy of assurance heretofore made in Lombard Street, or in the Royal Exchange, or elsewhere in London. And so we, the assurers, are contented, and do hereby promise and bind ourselves, each one for his own part, our heirs, executors, and goods to the assured, their executors, administrators, and assigns, for the true performance of the premises, confessing ourselves paid the consideration due unto us for this assurance by the assured, at and after the rate of

IN WITNESS whereof we, the assurers, have subscribed our names and sums assured in London.

N.B.—[*Memorandum*.]—Corn, fish, salt, fruit, flour, and seed are warranted free from average, unless general, or the ship be stranded—sugar, tobacco, hemp, flax, hides and skins are warranted free from average, under five pounds per cent., and all other goods, also the ship and freight, are warranted free from average, under three pounds per cent. unless general, or the ship be stranded.

(*b*) **Description of Subject-matter.**—The term " ship " includes the hull, materials and outfit, stores and provisions for officers and crew, the ordinary fittings requisite in a trader in a particular trade, and, in the case of a steamship, the machinery, boilers, and engine stores, if owned by the assured.[1] Freight does not include passage money.[2] Where the subject-matter insured is " goods," that means goods in the nature of merchandise, and does not include personal effects or provisions and stores for use on board, and in the absence of any usage to the contrary deck cargo and living animals must be insured specifically and not under the general denomination of goods.[3] If the subject-matter is sufficiently designated in general terms, and a question is raised what interest is covered, the interest intended by the assured will, in the absence of other indication, be held that insured against.[4]

[1] M.I.A., 1906, 1st Schedule, Rule 15. [2] *Ibid.*, Rule 16.
[3] *Ibid.*, Rule 17. [4] *Ibid.*, § 26.

(*c*) **Implied Warranties.**—A warranty is a term or condition of the contract. It may be an undertaking that some particular thing shall or shall not be done, or that some condition shall be fulfilled, or the affirmation or negativing of the existence of a particular state of facts.[1] It must be exactly complied with, whether material to the risk or not. If not so complied with, the insurer, unless otherwise agreed, is discharged from liability as from the date of the breach of warranty, although it does not relieve him of any liability incurred by him before the breach.[2] It is no defence for the assured to show that the breach has been remedied and the warranty complied with before loss.[3] Warranties may be express or implied. The Act lays down that certain warranties are implied in every contract of marine insurance. The implied warranties are :—

(1) Of seaworthiness of the ship ;

(2) Of legality of the adventure ; and

(3) Of neutrality.

(1) **Seaworthiness.**—Seaworthiness in a contract of marine insurance means seaworthy for the particular adventure insured.[4] A ship is deemed to be seaworthy when she is reasonably fit in all respects to encounter the ordinary perils of the seas of the adventure insured,[5] including, if the ship is in port when the policy attaches, the ordinary perils of the port.[6] Where the policy relates to a voyage which is performed in different stages during which the ship requires different kinds of or further preparation or equipment, there is an implied warranty that at the commencement of each stage the ship is seaworthy in respect of such preparation or equipment for the purposes of that stage. In a voyage policy on goods or other moveables there is a further implied warranty that the ship is reasonably fit to carry them to the destination contemplated by the policy,[7] but this warranty is rarely insisted on against the assured as the insurer in virtue of his right of subrogation [8] has a right to sue the shipowner. In a time policy there is no implied warranty that the ship shall be seaworthy at any stage of the adventure, but where, with the privity of the assured, the ship is sent to sea in an unseaworthy state, the

---

[1] M.I.A., 1906, § 33 (11).　　[2] *Ibid.*, § 33 (3).　　[3] *Ibid.*, § 34 (2).
[4] *Ibid.*, § 39 (1).　　　　　[5] *Ibid.*, § 39 (4).　　[6] *Ibid.*, § 39 (3).
[7] *Ibid.*, § 40.　　　　　　　[8] *Supra*, p. 312.

insurer is not liable for any loss attributable to unseaworthiness.[1]

(2) **Legality.**—There is an implied warranty that the adventure
insured is a lawful one, and that, so far as the assured can
control the matter, the adventure shall be carried out in a
lawful manner.[2]

(3) **Neutrality.**—Where insurable property, whether ship or goods,
is expressly warranted neutral, there is an implied condition
that the property shall have a neutral character at the
commencement of the risk, and that, so far as the assured
can control the matter, its neutral character shall be preserved during the risk, and in the case of a ship that she
shall carry the necessary papers to establish her neutrality.[3]

There is no implied warranty as to the nationality of a ship, or
that her nationality shall not be changed during the risk.[4]

(d) **The Risk Insured Against.**—The insurer remains liable under
the contract of insurance only in accordance with the risk undertaken. It is therefore important to define not only what is the
subject-matter insured and the perils insured against, but also when
the risk begins and when it ends.

Commencement of Risk.—In the case of a time policy the risk
commences at the date from which the policy runs. In the case of a
voyage policy it is indicated in the policy, and is introduced by such
words as " from," " at and from," " beginning the adventure on the
said goods," and " from the loading thereof." Where the subject-
matter is insured from a particular place the risk does not attach
until the ship starts on the voyage insured.[5] Where the ship or
chartered freight [6] is insured at and from a particular place the risk
attaches immediately the policy is concluded, or as soon thereafter
as she arrives, provided in both cases she is there in good safety.
In the case of other freight, as where the ship is a general ship,[7] the
risk attaches *pro rata*, as the goods and merchandise are shipped,
or, if the cargo is in readiness, as the ship is ready to receive the cargo.[8]
Where goods are insured " from the loading thereof " the risk does
not attach until the goods are actually on board.

Termination of the Risk.—The contract in the policy is against
the risk of loss until, in the case of the ship under a voyage policy, it

---

[1] M.I.A., 1906, § 39 (5).   [2] *Ibid.*, § 41.   [3] *Ibid.*, § 36.   [4] *Ibid.*, § 37.
[5] *Ibid.*, 1st Schedule, Rule 2.   [6] See Charter-party, *supra*, p. 124.
[7] See Bill of Lading, *supra*, p. 125.   [8] M.I.A., 1906, 1st Schedule, Rule 3.

has arrived at the port of destination and has moored at anchor twenty-four hours in good safety, and in the case of goods, they are discharged and safely landed in the customary manner and within a reasonable time after arrival at the port of discharge.[1] In the case of a time policy the natural termination of the risk undertaken is the expiry of the time. But the liability of the insurer in both cases may cease earlier. The underwriter only undertakes to indemnify the assured upon the implied condition that the risk shall remain precisely the same as it appears to be on the face of the policy as interpreted, it may be, by usage. Directly this risk is by the act of the assured or his agents in any degree varied, even though it be not increased, the underwriter's liability ceases by the breach of the condition on which alone he is engaged to be liable. The true proposition therefore is that every voluntary and unnecessitated departure from the prescribed course of the voyage, by which the risk is varied, is a deviation, whether the risk be thereby increased or not.[2] The real ground of the underwriter's discharge is change of risk. Any change of risk accordingly will be a good defence to an action by the assured if the underwriter can show it to have arisen from the fault or with the knowledge of the assured, but not otherwise. It is accordingly not every change of risk that releases the insurers.

The change of risk may take place at the very outset, so that the policy never attaches at all. That is so where the place of departure is specified by the policy, and the ship instead of sailing from that place sails from any other place.[3] Where the destination is specified, and the ship sails instead for any other place after the commencement of the risk, *i.e.* where there is a " change of voyage," the insurer is discharged from liability as from the time of change, that is, the time when the determination to change is manifested, whether the ship has or has not in fact left the course of voyage contemplated by the policy when the loss occurs.[3] Again, the change of risk may take place through the ship without lawful excuse deviating from the voyage contemplated by the policy, as from the time of deviation— that is, the departure from the course of voyage specifically contemplated by the policy, or the usual and customary course where not so designated. There must be a deviation in fact, and a mere intention to deviate is immaterial.[4] The ship is held to have deviated

[1] M.I.A., 1906, Rule 5.
[2] Per Lord Mansfield in Hartley *v.* Biggin, (1781) 3 Dougl. 39.
[3] M.I.A., 1906, § 43.   [4] *Ibid.*, § 46.

if, where several ports of discharge are specified in the policy, she does not go to them in the order designated by the policy, or in their geographical order if the policy is to ports of discharge not named but within a given area. A failure to prosecute the voyage with reasonable dispatch without lawful excuse likewise terminates the insurer's liability.[1]

Deviation or delay in prosecuting the voyage are excusable (1) where authorised by any special term of the policy ; (2) where caused by circumstances beyond the control of the master and his employer ; (3) when reasonably necessary in order to comply with an express or implied warranty ; (4) where reasonably necessary for the safety of the ship or subject-matter insured ; (5) for the purpose of saving human life, or aiding a ship in distress where human life may be in danger ; (6) where reasonably necessary for obtaining medical or surgical aid for any person on board the ship ; or (7) where caused by the barratrous conduct of the master or crew if barratry be one of the perils insured against. When, however, the cause excusing the deviation or delay ceases to operate, the ship must resume her course and prosecute her voyage with reasonable dispatch.[2]

Return of the Premium.[3]—If the risk has never attached, the general rule is the insurer must return the premium if it has been paid, and cannot recover it if not. The assured is, moreover, under no obligation to run the risk so as to let the insurer earn the premium. Thus if a ship insured from a port never sails, the premium must be returned. If, however, the ship starts, but immediately after deviates, there is no return. Where part of the subject-matter insured has not been put at risk, there is a proportionate return of premium. So also if the policy is voided, as by a breach of the implied warranty of seaworthiness, or void in respect that the insured has no insurable interest, there must be return. It does not prevent the assured claiming return that there has been concealment or misrepresentation. There will be no return where there has been either fraud or illegality on the part of the assured. In such cases the Courts decline to interfere.[4]

(e) **The Perils Insured Against.**—These depend on the will of the parties as expressed in the policy. Those referred to in the form of policy annexed to the Act are to be construed as set out in the Schedule to the Act.

[1] M.I.A., 1906, § 48.   [2] *Ibid.*, § 49.   [3] *Ibid.*, §§ 82-84.
[4] See Illegal and Immoral Contracts, *supra*, p. 27.

(1) *Perils of the Seas.*—This refers only to fortuitous accidents or casualties of the seas and does not include the ordinary action of the wind and waves,[1] nor scuttling nor barratry.[2] A collision with another ship is within the words, but not a claim against the insured ship of damage by collision due to the negligence of those in charge of her. This is usually covered by a clause called a Collision or Running Down Clause. The words cover risks which may, not those which must happen, as where a steamer insured by a time policy sailed with insufficient bunker coal and in consequence had to accept aid from another ship and to pay her salvage.[3] They cover sums which the assured have to pay for the salvage of the subject-matter insured from perils insured against [4]; but not claims for salvage in respect of life

(2) *Men-of-war, enemies, letters of mart and countermart, surprisals, takings at sea, arrests, restraints, and detainments of all kings, princes and peoples of what nation, condition, or quality soever.*—These are mainly war risks, *e.g.* capture. Insurers will not be liable for loss by perils insured where the assured at the time of the insurance are alien enemies or become so after the insurance is effected. On the outbreak of war the contract becomes void. By arrests, restraints, and detainments are meant generally not acts of an enemy of the assured's country, but in connection, it may be, with hostilities against another country, such as an embargo by which a government interdicts ships from sailing from a particular port. The words refer to political or executive acts, and do not include a loss caused by riot or by ordinary judicial process.[5]

Fire.—This does not cover a fire caused by the inherent vice of the subject-matter insured, nor damage caused by the explosion of machinery.[6] It includes fire voluntarily caused to avoid capture by an enemy.

---

[1] M.I.A., 1906, 1st Schedule, Rule 7.

[2] Samuel *v.* Dumas, [1924] A.C. 431.

[3] Ballantyne *v.* Mackinnon, [1896] 2 Q.B. 455 ; Park and Others *v.* Duncan & Sons, 1898, 35 S.L.R. 378.

[4] Aitchison *v.* Lohre, L.R., 4 A.C. 755.

[5] M.I.A., 1906, 1st Schedule, Rule 10 ; Nobels Explosives Co. *v.* Jenkins & Co., [1896] 2 Q.B. 326.

[6] Thames and Mersey Marine Insurance Co. *v.* Hamilton, (1887) 12 A.C. 484.

Pirates—Rovers.—Risks from pirates and rovers are covered by
" perils of the sea." Risk from pirates includes mutiny of passengers
and loss from rioters on shore,[1] but not loss due to the acts of persons
against the property of a State for a political end.[2]

Thieves.—The term thieves covers only losses caused by persons
not connected with the vessel who commit robbery with violence.
It does not cover clandestine theft or a theft committed by any one
of the ship's company, whether passengers or crew.

Jettison.—This is a peril of the sea.

Barratry of the Master and Mariners.—This includes every wrongful act wilfully committed by the master or crew to the prejudice of
the owner or charterer. If the master was also owner or did the
wrongful act with the privity of the owner to the loss of the charterer,
that would not be barratry.[3]

All other Perils.—These words cover, on the principle of *ejusdem
generis*,[4] only perils similar in kind to the perils specifically mentioned
in the policy [5] : for example, where dollars were thrown overboard
to avoid capture by the enemy,[6] this was held *ejusdem generis* of
jettison.

As already indicated, the parties may express the risks undertaken
in such terms as they please. Thus they may desire expressly to
cover the dangers and accidents incident to steam navigation, because
of the judgment in the *Inchmaree* case,[5] or expressly to exclude the
warranty of seaworthiness *quoad* latent defects, because of the judgment in the *Glenfruin* case,[7] or to cover risks to live stock where a
question might arise whether due to material causes or to perils
insured against,[8] or claims against a shipowner in respect of collision
between his ship and another (Collision Clause), or to exclude loss due
to capture or seizure, known as the F.C. and S. (free of capture and
seizure) Clause. Where a loss which would otherwise be covered is excluded the insurer has to prove the loss was due to the excluded risk,[9]
and the insurer's liability will then cease, *e.g.* on capture of the vessel.[10]

---

[1] M.I.A., 1906, 1st Schedule, Rule 8.
[2] Republic of Bolivia *v.* Indemnity Mutual Marine Assurance Co., Ltd., [1909]
1 K.B., C.A. 785.
[3] See Hobbs *v.* Hannam, 3 Camp. 93.
[4] See Interpretation of Contracts, *supra*, p. 40.
[5] See Thames and Mersey Marine Insurance Co. *v.* Hamilton, *supra*.
[6] Butler *v.* Wildman, 3 B. & Ald. 398.
[7] 10 P.D. 103.   [8] See Lawrence *v.* Aberdein, 5 B. & Ald. 107.
[9] Munro, Brice & Co. *v.* War Risks Association, [1918] 2 K.B. 78.
[10] Anderson *v.* Marten, [1908] A.C. 334.

(*f*) **Losses due to Perils Insured.**—Under this topic are considered the scope of the underwriter's liability, the rules applicable to total and partial losses, the meaning of the sue and labour clause, the rules as to successive losses and under-insurance, and the rights of the insurer on payment.

(1) Scope of the Underwriter's Liability.—Proximate Cause.—An insurer is not liable for any loss which is not proximately caused by a peril insured against.[1] The principle of proximate cause is more rigorously applied in marine insurance cases than in the case of other liabilities. The term " proximate " cause does not necessarily mean the cause latest in time. In marine insurance law, where there is a succession of causes which must have existed in order to produce the result, the last efficient or dominant cause only must be looked to and the others rejected, although the result would not have been produced without them.[2] To illustrate a question of proximate cause, the case of Montoya *v.* London Assurance Co.[3] may be referred to. A vessel loaded with hides and tobacco shipped a quantity of sea-water, which rotted the hides but did not come directly into contact with the tobacco. The tobacco was, however, spoiled by the reek of the putrid hides. It was held that perils of the seas was the proximate cause of the loss on both hides and tobacco. By this principle the underwriter's responsibility may be either limited or enlarged. Thus, where a voluntary act on the part of the assured to which the loss is more proximately due has intervened between the peril and the loss, as by abandonment with resulting loss of freight, the assured cannot recover.[4] On the other hand the insurer may be liable for losses proximately caused by a peril insured against, although remotely occasioned by the acts or negligence of the assured.[5] Loss attributable proximately to the wilful misconduct of the assured, to delay although the delay be caused by a peril insured against, to ordinary wear and tear, ordinary leakage and breakage, inherent vice or nature of the subject-matter insured, or caused by rats or vermin, and injury to machinery not proximately caused by maritime perils, are by the

---

[1] M.I.A., 1906, § 55 (11).

[2] Leyland Shipping Co. *v.* Norwich Union Fire Insurance Society, [1918] 1 A.C. 350 ; see also Britain S.S. Co. *v.* The King, [1921] A.C. 99.

[3] (1851), 6 Exch., 4 J. 1.

[4] M'Carthy *v.* Abel, (1804) 5 East 388 ; Scottish Marine Insurance Co. *v.* Turner, 1853, 1 Macq. (H.L.) 334 ; Samuel *v.* Dumas, [1924] A.C. 431.

[5] Busk *v.* Royal Exchange Assurance Co., (1818) 2 B. & Ald. 72 ; M.I.A., 1906, § 55 (2) ; Trinder, Anderson & Co., [1898] 2 Q.B. 114.

Act expressly excluded, unless the policy otherwise provides, from the scope of the underwriter's liability.[1]

(2) Total and Partial Losses.—The loss of the subject-matter insured owing to a peril insured against may be either (a) total, or (b) partial, with different effects in each case.

(a) **Total Loss.**—**Actual and Constructive Total Loss.**—A total loss may be either actual or constructive,[2] and an insurance against total loss includes a constructive total loss, unless otherwise provided in the policy. There is an actual total loss where the subject-matter insured is destroyed, or so damaged as to cease to be a thing of the kind insured, or where the insured is irretrievably deprived thereof. Where no news is received of a missing ship for a reasonable time a total loss is presumed.[3] There is a constructive total loss where the subject-matter insured is reasonably abandoned on account of its actual loss appearing to be unavoidable, or because it could not be preserved from actual total loss without an expenditure which would exceed its value,[4] so that a prudent uninsured owner would not prosecute the adventure to its termination. Where there is a constructive total loss the assured may either treat the loss as a partial loss, or abandon the subject-matter insured to the insurer and treat the loss as if it were an actual total loss.[5]

Abandonment.—The effect of a valid abandonment is that the insurer is entitled to take over the interest of the assured in whatever may remain of the subject-matter insured, and all proprietary rights incidental thereto.[6] Consequently where the assured elects to abandon to the insurer he must give notice of abandonment. If he fails to do so the loss can only be treated as a partial loss.[6] He need not, however, give notice where, at the time when he receives information of the loss, there would be no possibility of benefit to the insurer if notice were given him.[7] The notice, which may be in writing or by word of mouth, must indicate the intention of the assured to abandon his insured interest in the subject-matter insured unconditionally to the insurer, and should be given with reasonable diligence after receipt of reliable information of the loss.[8] Upon the

---

[1] M.I.A., 1906, § 55 (2).   [2] *Ibid.*, § 56 (2).   [3] *Ibid.*, § 58.   [4] *Ibid.*, § 60 (1).
[5] *Ibid.*, § 61.   [6] *Ibid.*, § 63 (1).   [7] *Ibid.*, § 62 (7).   [8] *Ibid.*, § 62 (3).

abandonment of a ship the insurer becomes entitled to any freight in course of being earned and which is earned by her subsequently to the casualty causing the loss.[1]

(β) **Partial Loss.—General and Particular Average.**—A partial loss may be either a general average or a particular average loss. A general average loss is a loss caused by or directly consequential on a general average act, and includes a general average expenditure as well as a general average sacrifice ; that is, where any extraordinary sacrifice or expenditure is voluntarily and reasonably made or incurred in time of peril for the purpose of preserving the property imperilled in the common adventure,[2] entitling the party on whom the loss falls to a rateable contribution from the other parties interested.[3] Every other loss is a particular average loss. A partial loss may be 100 per cent. of the sum insured or may even exceed it, although the insurer's liability is of course no more.[4] A sum payable for salvage proper, known as " salvage charges," is recoverable in the same way as a particular average loss.[5]

Particular Average.—The insurer may in the contract expressly limit his liability. An example is the Memorandum Clause at the end of the form of policy given above, whereby certain perishable goods are warranted free from particular average, certain other goods free from average under 5 per cent., and all other goods, also ship and freight, free from average under 3 per cent., unless general, or the ship be stranded. The term " average unless general " means a partial loss of the subject-matter insured other than a general average loss, and does not include particular charges.[6] Where the ship is stranded, the insurer is liable for the excepted losses, although these be not attributable to the stranding,[7] provided, of course, that the risk has attached, and the goods, if goods be insured, are on board.[8] A ship is stranded which takes the ground out of the ordinary course and remains fast, though only for a short time. It is usual to add to the Memorandum the words " sunk or

---

[1] M.I.A., 1906, § 63 (2).
[2] *Ibid.*, § 66 (2).
[3] See Average, *supra*, p. 149.
[4] Aitchison *v.* Lohre, L.R., 4 A.C. 755.
[5] M.I.A., 1906, § 65.
[6] *Ibid.*, 1st Schedule, Rule 13.
[7] The *Alsace Lorraine*, [1893] P. 209.
[8] M.I.A., 1906, Rule 14.

burnt [1] or in collision." The Memorandum is designed to relieve the insurer from liability for partial loss due to the action of ordinary sea-water on these particular goods.

Apart from the Memorandum, the insurer may confine his liability to such loss due to the risks insured against as amounts to a total loss. This is done by a clause called an F.P.A. (free of particular average) Clause which reads usually, " warranted free from particular average unless the vessel or craft be stranded, sunk or burnt, each craft or lighter being deemed a separate insurance. Underwriters, notwithstanding this warranty, to pay for any damage or loss caused by collision with any other ship or craft, and any special charges for warehouse rent, re-shipping or forwarding for which they would otherwise be liable. Also to pay the insured value of any package or packages which may be totally lost in transhipment. Grounding in the Suez Canal not to be deemed a strand, but underwriters to pay any damage or loss which may be proved to have directly resulted therefrom."

(3) Sue and Labour Clause.—It is the duty of the assured and his agents in all cases to take reasonable measures for the purpose of averting or minimising a loss, and they cannot recover for damage in so far as aggravated by want of care in these respects.[2] The sue and labour clause (contained in the Lloyd's S.G. Policy) is deemed to be supplementary to the contract of insurance. Under it the assured may recover any expenses properly incurred pursuant to the clause, notwithstanding that the insurer may have paid as for a total loss or that the insurance may be warranted free from particular average either wholly or under a certain percentage. General average losses and contributions and salvage charges are not recoverable under the clause.[3]

(4) Successive Losses.—The insurer is liable for successive losses, unless the policy otherwise provides, even though the total amount of such losses exceeds the sum insured. But if, under the same policy, a partial loss, which has not been repaired or otherwise made good, is followed by a total loss, the assured can only recover in respect

---

[1] See The *Glenlivet*, [1894] P. 48.

[2] M.I.A., 1906, § 78 (4) ; but see Gloag and Henderson's Introduction to the Law of Scotland, p. 317 ; Arnould on Marine Insurance, § 799 (*a*).

[3] See Kidston *v.* Empire Marine Insurance Co., L.R., 1 C.P. 535 ; 2 C.P. 357.

22

of the total loss.[1]   If, however, the partial loss is claimable under one
policy and the total loss under another, both can be recovered.[2]

(5) Under Insurance.—Where the assured is insured for an amount
less than the insurable value, or, in the case of a valued policy, for an
amount less than the policy valuation, he is deemed to be his own
insurer in respect of the uninsured balance.[3]

(6) Rights of Insurer on Payment.[4]—**Subrogation.**—Where one
person has agreed to indemnify another, he will, on making good the
indemnity, be entitled to succeed to all the ways and means by which
the person indemnified might have protected himself against, or reimbursed himself for the loss.[5]   Thus, where the assured abandons to
the insurer and claims as for a total loss, the property abandoned
becomes the property of the insurer.[6]   Likewise also, apart from a
transfer of the property, on the principle of subrogation, if the assured
has a right to recover from a third party, as in a case of loss by collision
through the fault of another ship, his rights and remedies pass to the
insurer as from the time of the casualty causing the loss, but only in
so far as the assured has been indemnified by such payment for the
loss.[7]   Thus in the case of loss of goods, where there is a claim under
the contract of carriage against the shipowner, the insurer can have
this claim enforced in his interest.   And the insurer of a mortgagee's
interest in, say, a ship is to the extent of any sum paid by him entitled
to be subrogated to the mortgagee's personal claim on the shipowner
for the debt secured on the ship.   But the insurers, as they stand in
the same position as the insured, may be met by any defence of and
against him.[8]

Contribution.—Where two or more policies are effected by or on
behalf of the assured on the same adventure and interest, if the several
insurances together make an over insurance the excess cannot be
recovered by him.   The assured can only recover what is sufficient
to indemnify him.   Accordingly if one of the insurers pays more than
his rateable proportion of the indemnity he is entitled to recover the
balance from the other insurers, or the assured if he has been overpaid.[9]

6. Assignation of the Policy.[10]—A marine policy is assignable by the
assured unless it contains terms expressly prohibiting assignation.

[1] M.I.A., 1906, § 77.   [2] Lidgett *v.* Secretan, L.R., 6 C.P. 616.
[3] M.I.A., 1906, § 81.   [4] *Ibid.*, § 79.
[5] Per L.C. Cairns in Simpson *v.* Thomson, (1877) 3 App. Cas. at p. 284.
[6] See *supra*, p. 312.   [7] M.I.A., 1906, § 79.
[8] See Société du Gaz *v.* Armateurs Français, 1925 S.C. 332.
[9] M.I.A., 1906, §§ 32, 80.   [10] *Ibid.*, §§ 50, 51.

It may be assigned either before or after loss. But where the assured has parted with or lost his interest in the subject-matter insured before he has expressly or impliedly agreed to assign the policy, any subsequent assignment is inoperative. Where the policy has been effectually assigned, the assignee may sue on the policy in his own name, and all defences open to the insurer under the contract against the original assured are open to the insurer against the assignee.

CHAPTER XVII

ARBITRATION

1. Definition.—Arbitration is the voluntary and contractual submission by parties of any matter in dispute between them to the amicable and final decision of a person or persons in whom they repose confidence. By referring a disputed matter to arbitration the parties exclude themselves from the ordinary jurisdiction of the Courts of law in regard to the merits of the dispute. There is practically no limitation to the nature or class of questions which may be referred, but questions of crime and questions of status cannot be made the subject-matter of an arbitration. The decision of the arbiter is termed the award or decree arbitral.

2. Capacity to Arbitrate.—The parties to all arbitrations must be capable of acting in regard to the questions to be arbitrated upon. Thus a minor cannot be a party to an arbitration, unless with the consent of his curator, except when engaged in trade and in regard to a trade question. A liquidator of a limited company in a compulsory liquidation can only enter into an arbitration with the sanction of the Court.[1] On the other hand trustees have by the Trusts (Scotland) Act, 1921,[2] unless otherwise provided in the trust deed, power to submit and refer all claims connected with the trust estate.

3. The Arbiter.—An arbiter should be unbiased and should not have an interest in the subject-matter of the reference. Hence he may be disqualified to act if before the submission he has committed himself and insisted on a particular view, or if unknown to one of the parties he has an interest in the matter in dispute at the time of submission or if he has acquired a substantial interest during the course of the procedure.[3] The arbiter has no right at common law to re-

---

[1] Drake's Patent Concrete Co. in Palmer's Company Precedents, 8th ed., pt. ii. 359. [2] § 4.

[3] Tennant v. MacDonald, 1836, 14 S. 976; but see Crawford Bros. v. Commissioners of Northern Lighthouses, 1925 S.C. (H.L.) 22.

muneration. He may stipulate for a fee, and is in practice recognised to be entitled to one where acting in a professional capacity, for example a lawyer in a dispute arising on the terms of a contract.[1]

Arbitrations may be classified as ordinary, ancillary, judicial references, and statutory.

4. Ordinary Arbitrations.—The submission in Scotland may be agreed upon verbally, by informal writing or by formal deed, the general rules as to the constitution and proof of a contract and proof of its extinction being applicable to the contract of submission and the award following upon it.[2]

(a) **Verbal Submissions.**—The verbal submission is common in mercantile affairs. Two business men having a difference may agree to accept the decision of a third, who may give his decision verbally. When the submission relates to a question of importance, if the fact of submission having been agreed on is disputed by one party the Court may not accept ordinary parole evidence, and may require proof by reference to the oath of the parties.[3] But verbal proof may be sufficient in such a case if followed by *rei interventus*.[4]

(b) **Informal Written Submissions.**—Informal written references are of common occurrence in the mercantile world. An informal reference is usually constituted by a joint letter to the arbiter requesting him to settle the points in dispute. Questions of law are frequently submitted to an advocate or solicitor in the form of a joint memorial. These are good references. A mere letter written by the arbiter's clerk and signed by himself has been held to be a valid and sufficient award under a mercantile reference.[5]

(c) **Formal Submissions.—Deed of Submission.**—A submission constituted by formal writing is usually in the form of a deed of submission. The deed states the question being referred and the arbiter to whom the question is referred.

The deed should, in addition to stating accurately the question referred and nominating an arbiter, provide for the following matters, viz. the arbiter's power to receive evidence, documentary, of witnesses or oath of parties ; a time within

---

[1] Macintyre Bros. *v.* Smith, 1913 S.C. 129.
[2] *Vide* Contract, p. 2 *et seq.*
[3] Ferrie *v.* Mitchell and Ors., 1824, 3 S. 75.
[4] Otto and Ors. *v.* Weir, 1871, 9 M. 660 ; see p. 11.
[5] Dykes *v.* Roy, 1869, 7 M. 357.

which the decree arbitral is to be pronounced ; a stipulated penalty on failure of either party to implement the award ; the continuing of the submission in force, after the death of either party, against his heirs and representatives ; the consent of parties to registration, for preservation and execution, of the deed itself and the decrees following upon it, so that they can be enforced against the parties by summary diligence, *i.e.* without the intervention of any Court. The deed may also provide for the appointment of a clerk to the arbitration, usually a solicitor, who guides the arbiter as to procedure and questions of law.

Sometimes each party nominates an arbiter. In such a case power is usually given to the arbiter to nominate an oversman, whose function it is to decide the question in the event of the arbiters differing in opinion. The oversman may, however, be nominated in the deed. By the Arbitration (Scotland) Act, 1894, the arbiters have power to name an oversman though not empowered in the deed to do so, and in the event of their failing to agree in a nomination the Court can make the nomination on the application of either party to the submission. The same Act provides that an agreement to refer to arbitration is not to be ineffectual by reason of the reference being to a person not named, or to be named by another person or to the holder of an office for the time being, and for the appointment of an arbiter by the Court failing an appointment by the parties.

It should be noted that an arbiter has, by implication, a power to award expenses,[1] that he has no power to award damages unless expressly so empowered,[2] that where no time is stated within which the decree arbitral is to be pronounced it is limited to a year and a day, and that the arbiter cannot prorogate the submission, *i.e.* extend the time, unless expressly empowered, or the parties consent.

The Decree Arbitral.—The finding of the arbiter, called the award or decree arbitral, narrates the submission and the procedure which has followed on it, including, if such is the

---

[1] Ferrier *v.* Alison, 1843, 5 D. 456; 1845, 5 Bell's App. 161; Pollich *v.* Heatley, 1910 S.C. 469.

[2] Mackay & Son *v.* Leven Police Commissioners, 1893, 20 R. 1093.

case, the difference of opinion between the arbiters and their devolution of the submission upon the oversman. Then the arbiter or oversman, as the case may be, states that being well and ripely advised, and having God and a good conscience before his eyes, he gives forth his final sentence and decree in the terms stated and finds and decerns accordingly.

The arbiter may, if he chooses, issue an interim award, but interim awards are inherently subject to alteration or recall by the final award. A final award should, advisedly, reaffirm any interim award. In common practice the arbiter, before issuing his award to the parties, submits the draft award or proposed findings to the parties, and allows them to lodge, and be heard on, representations regarding these. When the final award has been issued and delivered to the parties it is beyond recall, and is thereafter binding upon the parties, their heirs and successors.[1]

Reduction of Decree Arbitral.—By referring a disputed matter to arbitration the parties exclude themselves from the ordinary jurisdiction of the Courts of law in regard to the merits of the dispute. The arbiter's decision on the merits is final, and in that matter he is beyond the control of the Court. "He may believe what nobody else believes, and he may disbelieve what all the world believes. He may overlook or flagrantly misapply the most ordinary principles of law, and there is no appeal for those who have chosen to submit themselves to his despotic power."[2] But the jurisdiction of the Court is not wholly and to all effects ousted by a reference to arbitration. "It deprives the Court of jurisdiction to inquire into and decide the merits of the case, while it leaves the Court free to entertain the suit and to pronounce a decree in conformity with the award of the arbiter. Should the arbitration from any cause prove abortive the full jurisdiction of the Court will revive, to the effect of enabling it to hear and determine the action upon its merits. When a binding reference is (successfully) pleaded *in limine*, the proper course for the Court to take is either to refer the question in dispute to the arbiter

[1] Bell on Arbitration, p. 262.
[2] Lord Jeffrey in Mitchell *v.* Cable, 1848, 10 D. 1297.

named, or to stay procedure until it has been settled by
arbitration." [1]

There are, however, certain exceptions to the rule that
the arbiter's decision is final, even on the merits.

In 1695 there were passed, pursuant upon an Act of
Parliament, Articles of Regulation, which provided " that
for the cutting off of groundless and expensive pleas and
processes in time coming," the Court should not be entitled
to reduce the decree of an arbiter except upon the grounds of
" corruption, bribery, or falsehood to be alleged against the
Judges Arbitrators." [2]

Apart from the Regulations the Court will set aside an
arbiter's award if it be shown that he has gone *ultra fines
compromissi*,[3] *i.e.* beyond the scope of the submission, or
has violated any of the express conditions contained in the
submission, or the essential principles of justice and even-
handed dealing between the parties which the common law
holds to be implied in every submission.[4] In the last-
mentioned matter the arbiter as the judge chosen by the
parties is entitled to a very wide measure of discretion as
to the manner in which the proceedings are to be conducted,
for example, as to the extent and mode of proof. Thus
where the question in dispute is a purely practical one,
e.g. the valuation of farm stock, and the arbiter has been
chosen for his skill and knowledge of the matter in hand,
he may even decide the matter without proof at all, if he
takes proper means of informing his mind.[5] He may require
and obtain the assistance of a man of skill, *e.g.* an engineer,
or consult counsel. On the other hand a refusal to receive
proof where proof is necessary may amount to such misconduct of the case and want of fair dealing as will invalidate
the award, and it is impossible an award should stand where
the arbiter heard one party and refused to hear the other,[6]

[1] Lord Watson in Hamlyn & Co. *v.* Talisker Distillery, 1894, 21 R. (H.L.) 21 at
p. 25.   [2] Adams *v.* Great North of Scotland Railway Co., 1890, 18 R. (H.L.) 1.
[3] Traill *v.* Coghill, 1885, 22 S.L.R. 616 ; Miller & Son *v.* Oliver & Boyd, 1903,
6 F. 77.   [4] Lord Watson in Adams, *supra.*
[5] Paterson & Son, Ltd. *v.* Corporation of Glasgow, 1901, 3 F. (H.L.) 34 ; North
British Railway Co. *v.* Wilson, 1911 S.C. 730 ; Henderson *v.* M'Gown, 1915, 2 S.L.T.
316.
[6] Lord Chancellor Eldon in Sharpe *v.* Bickerdyke, (1815) 3 Dow 102 at p. 107 ;
Mitchell *v.* Cable, 1848, 10 D. 1297.

unless he decides wholly in favour of the latter.[1] Again, awards have been set aside where an arbiter refused to receive a claim tendered by one of the parties,[2] and where he had been misled by the improper and unfair proceedings of one of the parties.[3] And it has been held to amount to misconduct for an arbiter in a statutory arbitration, the opinion of the Court having been taken on a question of law, to refuse to apply the law as laid down.[4] On the other hand, in purely mercantile arbitrations, even though procedure may have been irregular, the Court will not set aside an award if it is substantially just, once the arbiter is agreed on.[5]

An award may competently be reduced in part with a view to correcting what was incompetently done if that part can be severed from what the arbiter has competently awarded. Otherwise, if not severable, the award as a whole must fall, for example, if the arbiter has to any extent proceeded *ultra fines compromissi*.[6]

Where there is a clause consenting to registration of the decree arbitral for execution, and summary diligence is done, any party having ground of objection to the award may state his objection by bringing a note of suspension. If there be no consent to registration for execution the party wishing to enforce the award must bring an action in Court for its implement, and in such case a party having ground of objection to the award can state and maintain all objections thereto by way of exception, *i.e.* in defence, without the necessity of bringing a reduction thereof unless the Court or Lord Ordinary shall consider that the matter can be more conveniently tried in a separate action of reduction.[7] If the action for implement is brought in an inferior Court, objection by way of exception is not open, and a substantive action of reduction in the Court of Session is necessary.

---

[1] Black *v.* John Williams & Co., 1924 S.C. (H.L.) 22.
[2] Drummond *v.* Martin & Ors., 1906, 14 S.L.T. 365.
[3] Calder *v.* Gordon, 1837, 15 S. 463.
[4] Mitchell-Gill *v.* Buchan, 1921, 1 S.L.T. 197.
[5] Hope *v.* Crookston Bros., 1890, 17 R. 868.
[6] Napier *v.* Wood, 1844, 7 D. 166.
[7] C.A.S., C, iv. 4.

5. Ancillary Arbitrations.—Ancillary arbitrations are those constituted by clauses of reference in deeds primarily regulating other matters. Thus in contracts of various sorts, *e.g.* contracts of copartnery or mercantile agreements, it is common to insert a clause referring to arbitration—frequently to the engineer, architect or other official of one of the contracting parties—the decision of claims or disputes arising in the execution of, or in connection with, the contract. The question frequently arises on the terms of such clauses whether they are confined to questions arising during the execution of the contract, or extend to questions arising out of it after its completion. The scope of the clause of reference is more strictly interpreted and defined by the Court in the case of executorial references.[1] Thus in an executorial reference as a general rule a claim of damages arising during the period of the contract's operation will not be covered by such a reference clause,[2] nor one arising after the completion of the contract.[3] On the other hand where liquidated damages were provided for in certain circumstances in the contract a reference as to the meaning of the contract entitled the arbiter, it was held, to dispose of a claim for liquidated damages.[4] Where there is doubt whether a dispute is covered by an ancillary reference it is usual to bring an action in Court, and if the clause of reference is pleaded in defence and the Court holds that the clause covers the dispute it will remit to the arbiter to decide the question in dispute, and to report to the Court, which will then apply his decision in its judgment. It may be noted that in English law the Court is not compelled to give effect to an arbitration clause in a contract.[5]

In references *in re mercatoria*, which are usually very briefly expressed, the Court will endeavour to give effect to them in so far as their terms will admit. The Court construes them liberally, but otherwise they are subject to the same rules as other ancillary submissions.[6]

6. Judicial References.—A judicial reference is one entered into between parties to an action proceeding in Court with regard to some

---

[1] Beattie *v.* Macgregor, 1883, 10 R. 1094; Mackay & Son *v.* Leven Police Commissioners, 1893, 20 R. 1093; and see R. & J. Scott *v.* Gerrard, 1916, 2 S.L.T. 42.

[2] Mackay & Son, *supra*.

[3] Aviemore Station Hotel Co., Ltd. *v.* Scott & Son, 1904, 12 S.L.T. 494.

[4] Levy & Co. *v.* Thomsons, 1883, 10 R. 1134.

[5] Municipal Council of Johannesburg *v.* D. Stewart & Co., 1909 S.C. (H.L.) 53; Hamlyn & Co. *v.* Talisker Distillery, 1894, 21 R. (H.L.) 21.

[6] Hope *v.* Crookston Bros., 1890, 17 R. 868.

matter in dispute between them arising in the action. It may be entered into at any stage of the proceedings. The submission is constituted by joint minute of the parties, to which the Court interpones authority. Once the Court has remitted to a judicial referee it cannot recall his appointment.[1] When the referee's award is issued it is lodged in process and the Court interpones authority to it.

The proceedings under a judicial reference are conducted in the same way as in an ordinary arbitration. Being a subscribed submission the referee is the final judge both in questions of fact and law relating to the matters referred to him, and the award is protected by the Articles of Regulation if the referee has exhausted the reference and the award is not *ultra fines compromissi*. The Court has, however, some control over the proceedings. Any of the parties may apply to the Court in regard to any alleged irregularities of procedure.[2] The Court may in certain cases order rehearing,[3] and if the award is ambiguous the Court may remit back to the referee for an explanation. The award is reducible only on the same grounds as in an ordinary arbitration.[4]

The judicial reference falls with the termination of the action under which it is made.[5] The referee and his clerk are entitled to remuneration and to decree for their fees against both parties to the reference jointly and severally,[6] and their fees are part of the judicial expenses of the action.[7]

7. Statutory Arbitrations.—A large number of Acts of Parliament provide for the settlement by arbiters of claims and disputes arising under their provisions. Perhaps the most important of these are the arbitrations conducted under the machinery of the Lands Clauses Consolidation (Scotland) Act, 1845, under which provision is made for the compulsory acquisition of land for public purposes and for the payment of compensation to the owners. The machinery of the Act is incorporated into many other Acts both public and private. In particular it is adopted by and embodied in the Railways Clauses (Scotland) Act, 1845, and is commonly incorporated in the various private Acts promoted by railway companies who require to take

---

[1] Walker v. Shaw Stewart, 1855, 2 Macq. 424.
[2] Welch v. Jackson, 1864, 3 M. 303.
[3] Baxter v. M'Arthur, 1836, 14 S. 549.
[4] Rogerson & Ors. v. Rogerson, 1885, 12 R. 583.
[5] Gillon v. Simpson, 1859, 21 D. 243.
[6] Beattie, 1873, 11 M. 954.
[7] Carphin v. Sturrock, 1913, 2 S.L.T. 288.

land compulsorily. The procedure is conducted in a very formal
manner, and the Act provides for speedy procedure. The arbiters
are confined to fixing the amount of compensation payable, and cannot
decide any question of title.[1] Another important class of statutory
arbitrations is those under the provisions of the Agricultural Holdings
(Scotland) Acts of 1908 and 1923, whereby compensation payable to
outgoing tenants for improvements made by them during the tenancy
and other questions arising out of the tenancy are determined.
The Act of 1908 provides that the arbiter may at any stage of the
proceedings, and shall if so directed by the Sheriff (which direction
may be given on the application of either party), state in the form
of a special case for the opinion of the Sheriff any question of law
arising in the course of the arbitration.[2] Appeal from the Sheriff
to the Court of Session is competent. The arbiter is bound to apply
the law as so laid down by the Court.[3] The Small Landholders Act,
1911, has similar provisions. Other important classes of statutory
arbitrations which may be singled out for mention are those under
the Workmen's Compensation Act, 1906, for assessing the compensation due to workmen for injuries arising out of and in the course of
their employment ; under the Finance Act, 1910, for the valuation
of lands for increment duty ; under the Acts regulating industrial
and provident societies and friendly and building societies ; and
under Acts empowering local authorities to acquire lands and buildings compulsorily, such as the Public Health Acts and the Housing
of the Working Classes Acts.

[1] Alexander *v.* Bridge of Allan Water Co., 1869, 7 M. 492.
[2] 1908, Schedule II. Rule 9.
[3] Mitchell-Gill *v.* Buchan, 1921, 1 S.L.T. 197.

INDEX

23

PRINTED IN GREAT BRITAIN BY NEILL AND CO., LTD., EDINBURGH.